Praise for Previous Editions of
Small Loans, Big Dreams

"This book will renew your belief in the American dream and show that there can be economic liberty and justice for all—here AND abroad!"—Mike Enzi (1944-2021), U.S. Senator, Wyoming

"Microfinance is the most effective and noble tool for combating poverty. It builds on the strengths rather than the perceived weaknesses of poor communities. In this memorable book, Alex Counts tells of working with Nobel Prize winner Muhammad Yunus, the pioneer of the movement, and he illustrates his analysis with fascinating and inspiring tales of how the process has worked."—Walter Isaacson, author of *Einstein, Steve Jobs,* and *The Code Breakers*

"Counts moves past facts and figures to show the human side—and human cost—of poverty. By focusing on the experiences of individual women, Counts demonstrates the power of microfinance to bring opportunity where it otherwise would not exist, and ultimately transform people's lives."—Pierre Omidyar, founder of eBay and co-founder and founding partner, Omidyar Network

"In *Small Loans, Big Dreams,* Alex Counts humanizes, through deft storytelling and solid analysis, the borrowers as well as the leaders of the microfinance movement. The 2006 Nobel Peace Prize broadened the awareness of microfinance and Grameen. This book deepens one's understanding of this emerging industry, and lets the reader see that it is about not just transactions, but transformations—of people and of entire economies."—Paul Maritz, chairman, Pivotal Software

"At a time when 'change' is the watchword, here is a story of the devotion and tenacity it takes to turn a powerful idea into a powerful reality."—Janet McKinley, founder and chairwoman, Advance Global Capital

Small Loans, Big Dreams

Also by Alex Counts

When in Doubt, Ask for More:
And 213 Other Life and Career Lessons for the Mission-Driven Leader

Changing the World Without Losing Your Mind:
Leadership Lessons from Three Decades of Social Entrepreneurship

Voices from the Field:
Interviews with Microcredit Practitioners for the Poor

Small Loans, Big Dreams

*Grameen Bank and the Microfinance Revolution
in Bangladesh, America, and Beyond*

2022 Edition

Alex Counts

Rivertowns
BOOKS

Printed in the United States of America • September 2022 • I

ISBN-13: 978-1-953943-19-4

LCCN Imprint Name: Rivertowns Books

Rivertowns Books are available from all bookshops, other stores that carry books, and online retailers. Orders and other correspondence may be addressed to:

Rivertowns Books
240 Locust Lane
Irvington NY 10533
Email: info@rivertownsbooks.com

For Norma Hakusa Counts

Contents

Foreword to the 2008 Edition by Muhammad Yunus   7

Introduction to the 2022 Edition   10

1. Muhammad Yunus—From Vanderbilt to Chittagong   31
2. The Birth of the Grameen Bank   56
3. Zianpur Bazaar   84
4. Les Papillons   115
5. Amena Begum's Dream   147
6. Omiyale DuPart   167
7. The Haldar Para   191
8. The Maxwell Street Market   216
9. Krishna Das Bala   240
10. The Hip Hop Shop   260
11. Dry Money in a Monsoon   282
12. The Black on Black Love Festival   299
13. The Sixteen Decisions   328
14. "We're Here for You"   354
Epilogue   371

Acknowledgments   380
Appendix: The Sixteen Decisions   384
Source Notes   386
Index   393
About the Author   404

Foreword to the 2008 Edition

Muhammad Yunus

FOR YEARS I HAVE BEEN ARGUING that credit should be recognized as a fundamental human right, and that the international community should work with urgency to place poverty in museums—the only place it belongs. More than ever before, we are making progress toward realizing these aspirations.

When it was held in 1997, the Microcredit Summit set a goal of reaching 100 million of the world's poorest families with microcredit by 2005. Some explained that goal by saying that it meant that to achieve it, the world would have the same microcredit market penetration by 2005 that Bangladesh had in 1995. It was an ambitious goal, but led by Asia and Bangladesh in particular (which continued to grow rapidly during the last decade), the overall outreach figure was reached, although one year late. This should be a cause for celebration worldwide. It has been an international effort that hundreds of thousands of people have played a role in achieving.

I cannot forget the people who said the original goal was too high, that it should be cut in half or more so that it was "do-able." It turns out that many people underestimate what is "do-able" when it comes to microcredit for the poor. Fundamentally, they underestimate the poor themselves. The microcredit movement recognizes the inherent strengths of the poor, and how their survival skills can be leveraged to create sustainable lending institutions.

We must remember that the purpose of microcredit is to eliminate poverty in the shortest possible time frame. High profits earned by microfinance institutions should be celebrated only if the borrowers are earning even greater profits and coming out of poverty rapidly. Otherwise, these lending institutions should aspire to earn a small profit to demonstrate their efficiency, and return anything beyond that to clients in the form of lower interest rates, rebates, or options to buy shares in the MFIs themselves, so they can become owners of the organizations that lend to them. The promotion of savings is also essential to building up the asset base of the poor and the MFIs that serve them. Regulations need to be amended to allow for this.

The Microcredit Summit Campaign set a goal for 2015 to reach 175 million poor families and to ensure that 100 million of them are free from poverty. This will require an all-out effort.　Impact measurement approaches such as Grameen Bank's 10 indicators of poverty, and Grameen Foundation's Progress Out of Poverty Index that was modeled on our 10 indicators, will be needed to ensure we reach both goals. One tool to aid in achievement of these goals, and the larger Millennium Development Goal of cutting extreme poverty in half by 2015, will be social businesses. These are for-profit institutions where the owners and management agree to maximize positive social impact while at least preserving the equity capital. Profits are plowed back into the work to create more impact. MFIs can be social businesses, and Social Businesses in other sectors can work synergistically with MFIs to bring people out of poverty faster. We have developed several Social Businesses in Bangladesh and are working to create more.

In his book *Small Loans, Big Dreams*, Alex Counts presents compelling stories of women benefiting from microcredit in rural Bangladesh and urban Chicago. He lived with these women for two years, traveling back and forth from the two "villages" he chose. The stories are well told and reflect the flexibility and adaptability of microfinance. They also are informed by Alex's 19 years of work in this movement, dating back from when he was a Fulbright scholar in Bangladesh in 1988–89. Beyond the stories of the women he followed, he profiles Grameen Bank, the Women's Self-Employment Project, the socioeconomic environments they operate in, and the microcredit movement. When I read it, I found it to be one of the most exciting treatments of microcredit. Many people who have read it have told me the same thing. I am told that at least two MFIs in India, including Grameen Koota, which is based in Bangalore, were inspired to start after reading the first edition of Alex's book.

The most important aspect of *Small Loans, Big Dreams* is that it lets the women speak for themselves. By listening to them, readers will gain confidence that poverty can be defeated if we create enabling environments for them. Poverty was not created by the poor, but by the institutions that place limitations on their problem-solving ability. MFIs and social businesses can unlock this potential. Alex convincingly shows, mostly through storytelling, that this can be done. His subsequent efforts as CEO of Grameen Foundation, based in Washington, D.C., have further advanced this movement and industry. Now what remains is for the international community, and each individual, to commit to drawing inspiration from the progress made so far and finish the job. Together, we can make it happen.

Muhammad Yunus
Dhaka
July 2007

Introduction to the 2022 Edition

ON OCTOBER 13, 2006, Professor Muhammad Yunus, the founder of the Grameen Bank, received a call from a Norwegian television station while sitting in his office in Dhaka, Bangladesh. The reporter said that there was a rumor that he would be declared the winner of the Nobel Peace Prize in a few minutes, in recognition of his three decades of anti-poverty efforts through a strategy that had come to be known as microfinance. He wanted to be the first to interview Yunus if that were the case, and so asked that the telephone line remain open. Yunus agreed, wondering if it was a prank of some kind. Within minutes, the announcement was made and a joyous, chaotic celebration began in his office, one that would quickly spread across the country and indeed, the world.

Mannan Talukdar, a midlevel Grameen field manager who started as a loan officer in 1980 and was one of more than 20,000 bank employees at the time (and one who will feature prominently in the pages to follow), immediately rented a bicycle rickshaw and loudspeaker, and began traveling up and down the streets of the southeastern town of Jessore, announcing the news of the Nobel Prize to the stunned citizens of this beleaguered nation. Within two hours, he raised a banner over the modest Grameen office there, celebrating the news of the first Bangladeshi to receive the world's most prestigious prize.

Pride welled up in Bangladeshis in Jessore and throughout the country. Celebrations spread to all corners of the world, especially to places where microfinance was practiced as a tool to promote self-help among the poor. While some questioned why a bank, however successful it may be in addressing poverty, should win a prize recognizing contributions to world peace, millions more intuitively understood the Nobel Committee's logic.

In the blink of an eye, a movement to address poverty through a businesslike strategy had gone from quietly making steady progress to the center of the world stage. One man's life's work, and the small, but very real, successes of millions of women who were touched by it, received the most significant affirmation possible.

Naturally, it changed everything instantly.

LIKE MOST DRAMATIC OCCURRENCES, the awarding of the peace prize to Grameen and Yunus was the result of years of effort. Over the preceding three decades, Yunus had doggedly worked to perfect his microfinance model while at the same time serving as a global ambassador for this bottom-up approach to poverty alleviation. While the modern microfinance movement is an expression of insights and techniques that go back centuries, what Yunus launched in 1976 was an historic breakthrough. It drew on the values and methods of both capitalism and social justice work—which, when combined with his effectiveness as a communicator, was a main reason for its broad appeal.

In 1985, a grainy video about Grameen produced by the International Fund for Agricultural Development, a U.N. agency based in Rome, caught the attention of anti-poverty activist Sam Daley-Harris. While hundreds of global development specialists and well-read citizens were aware of Yunus's work by this time, once he learned about it, Daley-Harris would emerge as one of its most powerful advocates. He led a global network of citizen activists called RESULTS, a group that had already won impressive victories for government funding of promising health programs around the world. In the mid-1980s, RESULTS was looking for something positive and practical that went to the economic roots of injustice and could have appeal across the ideological spectrum. Grameen microfinance model fit the bill perfectly.

At the time, I was the co-leader of the RESULTS chapter in Ithaca, New York. I quickly became obsessed with all things Grameen and Yunus. Shortly after graduating from Cornell University in 1988, I began a ten-month Fulbright fellowship in Bangladesh to strengthen the bonds between the Grameen Bank and RESULTS and to support a nascent international movement to apply Yunus's insights and techniques to all corners of the globe.

Two weeks into my fellowship, I traveled with Yunus to Tangail district in central Bangladesh to observe a series of massive rallies, marking the anniversaries of the establishment of a dozen of Grameen's earliest branch offices. Despite my wobbly command of Bengali at the time, the experience left a deep impression on my 22-year-old psyche.

These celebrations surpassed anything I had imagined I would see in Bangladesh—a country where the average income of $271 (as of 1988) was nearly 100 times less than in the United States. Reflecting my state of mind at the time, I wrote a letter to Daley-Harris on January 11, 1989. Despite its youthful exuberance, which I find somewhat embarrassing today, the letter was circulated to and pored over by hundreds of RESULTS activists. It ultimately led to an article in the *Christian Science Monitor* and an influential segment on *60 Minutes*, a popular television program in the United States. It included this breathless passage:

> Grameen Bank borrowers come out of the closet society puts them in. Seeing them come out is an awesome spectacle.
>
> Each year, Yunus comes to huge gatherings of centers, which is to say, groups of borrowers within the branch. One such celebration last week consisted of more than two thousand borrowers, hundreds of their children, and the local Grameen employees—people as far as the eye could see. Thousands more had gathered just to see what all the fuss was about.
>
> When Yunus arrived, we walked to an arch built of painted vases piled on top of each other, with a sign on top announcing the occasion in Bengali with appropriate exclamations. Two children walked forward, saluted Yunus, and handed him flowers. Bouquet in hand, he walked down a roped-off path while children on either side of him threw flower petals at his feet. At the end of the procession, two women borrowers saluted him, put garlands around his neck, and followed him to a small platform.
>
> At this point, the crowd stood and shouted slogans in Bengali—one translates as "Unity, hard work, and discipline, that is our creed"—and cheered. If you're wondering, three thousand landless Bengalis are LOUD.
>
> Then came Yunus's speech. He thundered, "And when our children finish primary school, they will not be finished with their education. We

will send them to high school. And when they graduate from high school, we still won't be finished—we'll send them to college. But we still won't be finished then. Only when they graduate from university will we be finished." The crowd roared in approval.

After the speech, Yunus walked among the borrowers for an hour, greeting everyone. Once, after such a celebration, I said to Yunus, "I was so moved seeing all those women in that crowd as we walked around. They seemed so proud of what they've accomplished." He looked at me and said slowly, "You know, one of them showed me something she'd made with a loan, and I asked her how much money she took out. She couldn't even answer, but spontaneously burst into tears." When he finished speaking, Yunus leaned back in his chair as we both sat silently.

I concluded the letter by relating a conversation I had with Yunus in between the celebrations, in which he put these gatherings in perspective: "Yunus describes these occasions as times when the poor can show off, be heard, be loud, make a stir. The slogans, the fanfare—it's all part of a process of overcoming the shame and isolation of poverty and expressing what he calls 'disciplined energy.' Society tells the poor: 'Stay in your cruddy houses; you are neither to be seen nor heard.' Grameen invites them: 'Come together, hold your head up high, be seen, be heard.' "

Yunus was teaching me some early lessons about how poverty can be a state of mind as much as a measure of income.

When Yunus was preparing to return to Dhaka five days after the trip began, I asked if I could spend a few weeks at a local branch office, preferably one that was situated in a remote area. He agreed. I told him I was determined to find out what all this celebrating was about, what had made so many thousands of people joyous in a nation that was among the most downtrodden in the world.

That field trip would be followed by many more over the next 30 years, both within Bangladesh—to see some of the hundreds of branches his team had set up—and later to organizations applying his model in Asia, Africa, Latin America and even the United States. In 1997, I would establish the Grameen Foundation in Washington, D.C., as a global hub for spreading Yunus's philosophy and methods, and I would lead it for 18 exhilarating and exhausting years.

But this is far from the end of Yunus's story and my partnership with him. Within five years of Yunus winning the Nobel Peace Prize, he was the subject of intense criticism and forced by his own government to resign from his position as managing director of Grameen Bank. More on that shocking development shortly.

AT ITS CORE, MICROFINANCE—the provision of loans, savings, and insurance to underserved populations—is pretty straightforward. But as with many things designed to be simple for the user—for instance, the iPhone— there are many layers of complexity and nuance below the surface. Indeed, Yunus became so disenchanted with the way some people were profiteering off of what they called microcredit—by charging excessive interest rates, levying hidden fees, and other practices that were antithetical to his values— he started calling his version "Grameencredit" so as to avoid confusion and reputational risk.

So what exactly is Grameen-style microfinance?

First and foremost, it is the rare anti-poverty approach based on the strengths of poor people rather than on their deficiencies. What strengths do poor people with little education possess? Some call them the "survival skills" that are honed in the process of eking out a living outside the mainstream economy in clever ways.

In developing countries, there aren't nearly enough jobs required to employ all those who want to work, and there is little or no social safety net. Most poor people face a stark choice—work for themselves, beg, or starve. The vast majority choose self-employment, regardless of how undercapitalized and modest their microbusiness may be, because of the unattractiveness of the alternative. Running those enterprises takes skill; I imagine that most readers of this book would fail in their first attempt to grind out a living under comparable circumstances if they were forced to give it a try. I am pretty sure I would.

Many of these small business owners in developing countries are forced to turn to loan sharks for their capital, and pay interest rates anywhere from 10 percent per month to 20 percent per day. These mostly home-based enterprises—ranging from raising livestock and running a tiny grocery shop or restaurant to processing food and weaving bamboo mats or other crafts— rarely provide enough income to allow the owner to get ahead, or even put three meals on the table each day. But they can keep slow starvation at bay most of the time. Schooling for children is often an unaffordable luxury, as there is no money for books and uniforms, and children are needed to help eke profits out of the family business. Girls are married off by the time they turn 15, so as to place the burden of feeding them on someone else.

Yunus discovered that being a reliable source of affordable loans to hard-working and in some sense highly skilled microentrepreneurs could break this vicious cycle for many and make the pain of poverty less intense for others. Grameen borrowers were so diligent and productive, so accustomed to paying high interest rates, and so grateful for the reliability and honesty of Grameen's staff, that they would go to great lengths to repay their loans on time and would willingly pay interest rates that might sound high to an economist but were far lower than those of most village moneylenders.

Yunus's insight was that people who had managed to survive poverty were often highly motivated entrepreneurs (even if many were "reluctant entrepreneurs" who might have preferred a traditional job in an ideal world). As such, they could be transformed from a group needing charity into an engine of national economic growth.

Leveraging this discovery, his Grameen Bank, which began as a pilot project in 1976 and transformed itself into the world's first bank for the poor in 1983, started a revolution in the banking and anti-poverty fields. While some organizations had tried providing business loans to poor people before, Yunus took the idea further than anyone had previously, proving the concept—at least its applicability in Bangladesh—for all time. Loans that might begin as little as $40 or $60 could grow over time to hundreds, and even thousands, of dollars. Many of the microbusinesses were profitable enough to allow for the owners to pay interest that would cover all of the costs of the microlending institution, which in turn enticed socially progressive bankers and businesspeople to learn about and support—and even invest in—the movement. In addition to starting or expanding a business, loans were also sometimes used to refinance high-interest loans taken out in the past or to support a promising child's education, which often represented productive uses of capital. By the time many microfinance institutions like Grameen reached even 10,000 clients, they could break even or possibly make a small profit.

One of the most important features of the Grameen Bank, which grew to serve 7 million families by the end of 2006 and in 2022 has 9.3 million, was that while borrowers received financing for their own microbusinesses (or whatever they chose to use the loans for), they were required to join a solidarity group of at least four other borrowers in order to get their loan. People who were known to be lazy or irresponsible were unable to find people to join their group until they changed their behavior. There were various incentives that were provided to clients only if all of the members of their group invested their loan as they had promised and repaid it on time. It became clear that women were better clients than men, mainly because they used their profits to reinvest in their businesses and ensure the health care, education, and nutrition of their children. For decades, more than 95 percent of Grameen Bank clients have been women, and many who have adapted it across the world lend *only* to women. This was initially revolutionary in a Muslim country, but over time, the counterculture that Grameen Bank represented became increasingly mainstream.

THIS BOOK ATTEMPTS TO BRING the microfinance story, one that has revolutionized global antipoverty efforts, down to a human level. For two years during the early 1990s, I immersed myself in the lives of a handful of women in rural Bangladesh, and another group in south Chicago, whose lives were being changed by microfinance. While the field has advanced in many ways, the basics of how microfinance impacts the lives of the poor remain much the same.

Since this book was first published in 1996 (under the title *Give Us Credit*), the collective outreach of the global microfinance sector has grown around 15-fold. Starting in the early 2000s, policy makers, philanthropists, and business leaders across the world began to realize that many of their programs and policies were based a vast underestimation of the capabilities of the world's poor women.

The late C.K. Prahalad helped popularize this insight with his influential book *The Fortune at the Bottom of the Pyramid*, but Yunus and other microfinance leaders drove a stake in the heart of the idea that most people living in poverty were unskilled, risk-averse, and shaped more by superstition than by ambitions for a better future. As Bill Drayton, the founder of Ashoka, once said to me at a low point in my career, "Yunus and his acolytes revealed to everyone the creditworthiness of the world's poor women. Nothing is ever putting that genie back in the bottle."

Yet old prejudices have a way of enduring. For that reason, I believe it is important to tell the stories of microfinance clients in detail, because they show both the power of this approach and also its limitations. The work of Grameen and its many imitators is no panacea, no silver bullet that absolves governments and businesses from the need to take into consideration the needs of the poor. In fact, I think that the existence of microfinance makes it *more* important that other sectors rethink the core tenets of their work. Furthermore, it suggests that the organized and growing network of microloan clients can be leveraged for other socially or financially profitable endeavors, such as enabling hundreds of thousands of them to purchase solar home systems on a commercial basis (as Yunus in fact successfully did).

I have observed that most people are told lies and half-truths about the causes of poverty and the capacities of poor people within their own societies. Breaking down those myths is necessary to understand how and why microfinance works as well as it does.

Each Grameen loan officer is required to conduct a detailed case history of a borrower often spanning more than 50 pages before they are certified to give out a single microloan. These minibiographies have been bound and cataloged in Grameen Bank's library. There are literally thousands of them, each representing the life journey of a poor woman from birth until the day she was interviewed by the trainee, spanning hardships and setbacks that most Americans can scarcely contemplate.

These testimonies also document the slow progress that borrowers achieved once they had access to amounts of capital that would barely pay for dinner for two in many U.S. cities. This book attempts to offer readers a window into this surprising world without having to travel to a developing country, learn the local language, and spend hours gaining the trust of poor women that is required to conduct an in-depth interview. That said, I encourage anyone who can take the time to experience this firsthand to do so.

THE CRISIS THAT LED to Yunus's ouster in 2011 was hardly Grameen's first. To take one example, the bank's original lending policies had failed to respond effectively to a series of natural disasters in the late 1990s. This led to a deterioration of Grameen's financial performance and a few negative articles, most notably one that appeared on the front page of the *Wall Street Journal*. But by the time this news broke, which brought with it an unfortunate burst of *schadenfreude* from some of Yunus's rivals and competitors, he was well on his way to securing the funds needed to shore up the Grameen's finances by issuing government-guaranteed bonds that the local banks quickly snapped up. Even more important, he modernized how Grameen provided services at the grassroots level to its millions of female clients—reforms that became known as Grameen II.

By April 2002, Grameen's revamped policies moved from a pilot effort to something used across the entire organization. As effective as the original Grameen model had been for more than two decades, Grameen II represented a quantum leap forward. It was much more responsive to the needs of the poor than its predecessor. Yunus designed into it the flexibility it needed to allow borrowers who were struggling to pay off a loan under the original timetable, often due to illness or a natural disaster, to reschedule it. This took the tension out of microfinancing, and eliminated the incentives for loan officers and fellow borrowers to be overly harsh with a woman who was unable to generate profits as planned, despite her best efforts.

One historical oversight that has troubled me over the years is that Grameen II was not widely recognized as the breakthrough it was, at least at first. Skeptics charged, more often in private than in public, that it was another effort to disguise or divert attention from Grameen's poor performance. Rumors circulated for years that Grameen was on the verge of financial collapse, partly because critics could not fathom how a bank that serves illiterate poor people could be on sound financial footing, let alone profitable.

This skepticism infuriated those like me who saw Grameen's success up close, though Yunus seemed content to let the strength of the approach become evident over time. It took a series of papers by Stuart Rutherford—an individual widely respected in microfinance circles—to get an emerging class of industry power-brokers (based in places like Washington, New York, London, Geneva, and Paris) to take Grameen II seriously.

It turned out that Bangladesh was not the only place where the delivery mechanisms for microfinance needed reinvention. As we'll see, in the United States, something astonishing happened in 2008 to the fledgling efforts to apply Yunus's model to combatting American poverty.

A 2011 REVIEW PUBLISHED on Amazon of an earlier edition of this book lodged several complaints. One was that it did not respond to the many criticisms of microfinance. What the reviewer failed to note or realize is that most of those criticisms had been lodged after the 2008 edition of this book was published.

A second review began with a compliment: "Perhaps the best part is the comparison of slum Chicago with Bangladesh. Chicago doesn't look that good in comparison." This reviewer picked up on the fact that despite my best efforts to put a positive face on one early effort to bring Grameen's approach to an urban American landscape, as of the early 1990s, when my field research was conducted, overall performance there paled in comparison to what was happening in Bangladesh, other developing countries, and even in a few places in Europe. Yet I saw glimpses of how Grameen-style microfinance could work as I immersed myself in the worlds of a half dozen African-American women touched by the work of the Full Circle Fund, which was based on Grameen.

After seeing how well microloans were received in Chicago, I was encouraged to try my own hand at U.S. microfinance after starting Grameen Foundation in 1997. I knew Yunus had a strong desire to prove the efficacy of his model in the United States, so I got myself appointed the chairman of a tiny start-up in New York City called Project Enterprise and we launched another microloan program in Dallas, Texas, known as the PLAN Fund.

Both programs ended up having some encouraging success stories. For example, Gina, a borrower in Dallas, went from being unemployed to having a thriving, home-based medical billing business. She would process claims for payment from Medicare and Medicaid for doctors, and received a percentage of the money that came in as a result. Gina had to learn a lot about the health care system and related technologies, which she was able to do despite little formal schooling. She initially borrowed $1,500 to get started, and later $3,000 and $6,000—and paid back each loan with 15 percent interest. Other clients launched or expanded tiny cosmetology, car detailing, home-based day care, floral, and catering businesses.

It became clear to me that there was no lack of entrepreneurial energy in American inner cities; what was missing was appropriate structures, policies, and organizations to support them. An additional insight that I had much later, courtesy of a dynamic social etrepreneur named Marq Mitchell, was that in many states, formerly incarcerated people are barred from many professions, making small business ownership one of the best options, and in some cases the only option, for them to earn an honest living.

However, both programs struggled on multiple fronts. My colleagues at Grameen Foundation argued for phasing out our support for these domestic programs, and after several years of resistance, I finally agreed. In the end, both organizations merged with more successful economic development nonprofits and continue within them to this day.

Yunus was initially patient with our slow progress. But he finally decided, in 2008, to send his own team into a low-income neighborhood in Queens to see what could be done. His choice of team leader was a wise one: Shah Newaz, a diligent and long-serving executive who had been deputized to work for Grameen Foundation for two years in the Dominican Republic, where he had picked up conversational Spanish.

Yunus assembled a board and hired Americans to work alongside Shah Newaz, who focused on field operations. Relations between the Bangladeshis and the Americans on the staff were initially a bit fraught, but ultimately everything came together when former Avon CEO Andrea Jung took over the organization and began a bold expansion effort as a capstone to her impressive career as a corporate leader.

When I paid a visit to Grameen America in 2014, it had 7,000 clients, which at the time was an astonishingly large number for an American microfinance program. Almost half of its clients were being served by its original branch in Queens that hosted me. It was a modest one-room space in a neighborhood where on a single block one could find store signboards with writing in English, Spanish, Hindi, Bengali, Arabic and Korean.

It was exciting, and a bit unnerving, to sit in the Grameen America branch office and see the six center managers counting imposing stacks of crumpled twenty-dollar bills on their desks that had been collected during borrower center meetings that same morning. By one p.m., the office was filling up with clients who were coming to receive their loans, which are renewed every six months if prior loans are paid on time (as almost all were).

The cash handling was a major security issue that needed to be dealt with. Technology was not Shah Newaz's strong suit, but he was a master at sizing up people and situations and making the right field-based decisions to allow the organization to thrive. Once she took over, Andrea did her part (and then some) by raising the funds needed to expand, streamlining and automating processes (including eliminating the handling of cash), figuring out how to work with banks and the government, dealing with regulatory hurdles, and bringing her star power, charisma, and work ethic to bear on making Grameen America a big success.

It turns out that most Grameen America centers, at least at the time of my visit, were populated by people from the same Latin American country. All except one woman in the center I visited were from Mexico (the lone exception was a woman from Ecuador). Others were dominated by Dominicans or Guatemalans, for example. (Over time, the number of African-American, Native American, and Caucasian clients has grown.) Most of the businesses were related to food (such as pushcart vending and catering), clothing, and other retail endeavors, like running a florist shop.

Much has happened in the years since then. As of March 2022, the organization has lent more than $2 billion to 142,000 clients. Grameen America passed the brutal test that the COVID-19 pandemic represented with flying colors by pivoting on a dime to use technology so effectively that it opened up new ways of serving rural populations. Perhaps most important of all, an 18-month long study tracked 1,492 women in 300 loan groups who applied to the Grameen America microlending program in Union City, New Jersey. This study, the first of its kind in the United States, showed impressive impact. Compared to a control group, clients enjoyed a reduction of material hardships by 15 percent, a 20-point improvement in credit scores, a $523 increase in monthly business revenue, and a $1,920 increase in nonretirement savings (63 percent more than those in the control group).

AS MENTIONED BRIEFLY ABOVE, my boldest attempt to advance Yunus's ideas and techniques was to start Grameen Foundation (GF) in 1997. I went on to lead it for its first 18 years, during which time we grew it from a tiny, nonprofit startup into a respected, mid-sized organization. Occasionally I mention some of the organization's milestones in the pages of this book, even though most of the field research it is based on took place in the mid-1990s, prior to GF getting going. Most of those updates cover the period through 2008, when a post-Nobel Prize edition of this book was published. Let me share a few GF updates since then.

GF has continued to take new ground in the battle to reduce and eliminate global poverty. In 2016, the year after I stepped down as CEO, GF joined forces with Freedom from Hunger, another global leader in the fight against injustice and hunger. I thought this was a great idea. Under the banner of Grameen Foundation, the union married Freedom from Hunger's focus on providing the world's poorest women with self-help tools and Grameen Foundation's expertise in digital innovation.

Applying the power of these combined skillsets, the organization has designed innovative solutions and partnered with high-quality local organizations to equip people living in poverty with tools and knowledge to leverage their own capacity. In its first cojoined year, programming included delivering nutrition programs to help tribal women in India improve their food security and teaching women in savings groups in Burkina Faso to use technology to enhance their financial security. In the Philippines and Ghana, GF-designed digital agriculture tools helped small-scale farmers improve crop yields and incomes and build resiliency.

In 2015, Grameen launched a Community Agent Network (CAN) pilot in the Philippines, which built on some promising GF programs during the prior decade as well as the networks of phone ladies and yogurt sellers that Yunus had set up so successfully in Bangladesh. The organization's CAN is composed of low-income, mostly female agents that GF trains and equips to deliver digital financial and agriculture solutions, as well as hygiene and health information, to neighbors in their remote communities. The network is now active in the Philippines, India, Uganda, and Ghana and has reached more than 3.3 million clients with essential information and services.

While GF is not a traditional relief organization, the sudden onset of COVID-19 compelled the organization—and many others—to pivot to help the vulnerable populations it serves survive. As the founder, I watched with pride as the organization took on these important responsibilities. For example, it quickly launched emergency relief programs to provide cash or grocery and pharmaceutical goods to more than 10,000 at-risk beneficiaries in India, Uganda, and the Philippines. In India, Grameen Community Agents, who were declared "essential workers," were able to ensure their neighbors could digitally access funds—many for the first time—when lockdowns prevented travel to distant banks.

As Grameen Foundation marks its 25th anniversary in 2022, there is much to celebrate. One fact tops that list: Since setting a goal in 2016 to impact 25 million people in poverty by 2025, Grameen Foundation has reached more than 16 million people with its three-prong focus on digital financial inclusion, digital farming, and women's empowerment. The GF team continues to make me, and more important, Professor Yunus, proud. I can't wait to see what they accomplish in their next 25 years!

YOU MAY BE WONDERING whether microfinance actually helps improve the lives of typical clients, which can't be confirmed simply by studying heart-warming anecdotes from hand-picked case studies. If so, you are not alone. Journalists, researchers, and students have been asking this question with varying degrees of rigor for the last 40 years. Let me try to summarize what the most serious evaluations have found, and how those findings have been used and, in some cases, abused.

The first major study of Grameen's impact was undertaken by the late Dr. Mahabub Hossain in the 1980s for the Bangladesh Institute for Development Studies. (It was later published by the prestigious International Food Policy Research Institute, and in fact became one of its all-time most popular reports.)[1] The findings were highly favorable. Grameen borrowers' incomes were 43 percent higher than comparable women in unserved villages, and extreme poverty had been cut from 75 percent to 48 percent in places where Grameen was operating.

In March 1993, another independent evaluation of Grameen was undertaken by Professor David Gibbons, who would later establish Cashpor, one of the most respected microlenders in India. Among women who had been borrowing from Grameen for eight or more years, Gibbons and his team found that 46 percent had crossed above the poverty line and had accumulated enough assets to be unlikely to fall back below it. Another 34 percent were close to coming out of poverty, while the remaining 20 percent remained mired in extreme poverty, mostly due to the chronic illness of one or more family members. When additional data were included, the measured impact was even greater. By contrast, among non-Grameen families, only four percent had come out of poverty over the same time period.

Yet when Yunus's work was extolled by many during the United Nations' International Year of Microcredit in 2005, critics claimed that there was no evidence that microfinance was an effective approach to reducing poverty. In response, I had Grameen Foundation commission Nathanael Goldberg, a rising star in the field of social science impact evaluation who would go on to work for Innovations for Poverty Action for the next 16 years, write a paper summarizing the findings of more than 90 studies by respected researchers on programs in dozens of countries. "Measuring the Impact of Microfinance: Taking Stock of What We Know" was published in December 2005 (and is available for free download from the Internet). This balanced paper—which I did not edit or change in any way—has helped ensure that discussions about poverty impact are grounded in empirical data. Follow-up reports in 2010 and 2015 by Professor Kathleen Odell of Dominican University took account of newer studies and were similarly encouraging, while pointing to unanswered questions and remaining gaps in the research literature.

The most widely cited and debated study was one published in 1998. Commissioned by the World Bank and undertaken by a research team led by Shahid Khandker, it found direct correlations between female borrowing and the likelihood of school enrollment among the borrowers' daughters, decreased malnutrition, and increased overall household expenditures on food and essential nonfood items. He also estimated that 5 percent of Grameen clients come out of poverty every year. Some of these findings were challenged by other academics, so Khandker recalculated them using a different approach and found that in a few cases, such as the increase in household consumption from incremental increases in borrowing, the impact was greater than his initial analysis had shown. He found that poverty rates among Grameen clients who had been borrowing since 1991–1992 had declined by more than 20 percent. Contrary to the conventional wisdom at the time, the impact he documented was *greater* on those in extreme poverty than on the moderately poor.

Two additional findings of serious studies on Grameen are possibly the most hopeful of all. Khandker found that Grameen had a sustained anti-poverty impact on women who *never joined but who lived in Grameen villages*. When this is included, he estimated that microfinance is responsible for 40 percent of the entire reduction of moderate poverty in Bangladesh in recent years. In addition, a 1996 study by Syed Hashemi, Sidney Schuler, and Ann Riley looked at the issue of women's empowerment, that is, their ability to make or influence major household decisions and engage with their community in meaningful ways (including advocating for more responsive local government). Grameen borrowers were 7.5 times more likely to be empowered than nonborrowers in non-Grameen villages. Perhaps more interesting, nonborrowers in Grameen villages were 2.4 times more likely to be empowered than nonborrowers in non-Grameen villages, strongly suggesting that the empowerment of women is "contagious," and that microfinance's impact is not limited to those who are directly served by microfinance institutions.

You might think that all this research would put to rest the question of whether microcredit and microfinance "worked" well enough to be pursued and further perfected. If so, you would be wrong.

Rather than focus their efforts on how this effective but imperfect approach that was in the process of being massively scaled up could be improved, many microfinance researchers turned their talents elsewhere. Sustained efforts were made to undermine the validity of past studies, especially the one by Khandker that had been published in peer-reviewed journals (and as a result was supposedly unimpeachable). After getting their critique rejected from at least one peer-reviewed journal, Jonathan Mordoch and David Roodman—two researchers I respect even though I don't always agree with them—finally had theirs published.

Other members of the academy chose a group of mostly second-rate microfinance organizations and applied a powerful but problematic research technique called randomized controlled trials (RCTs) to study them. RCTs had been popularized in the pharmaceutical industry to assess drug and vaccine safety and efficacy and were increasingly being used to study social development programs. These studies, which tried to take a second look at whether or not microcredit "worked," showed mixed results. But the authors and their public relations teams chose to emphasize the negative elements and downplay the positive findings, perhaps in order to gain visibility for themselves and their efforts. (Findings that confirm the conventional wisdom rarely get much attention.)

If you read these studies closely, as I have, you'll find a recurring theme. Whenever a positive finding is discussed, the writer somehow twists it into being a negative by saying that it wasn't positive *enough*—and therefore is evidence that microfinance failed to live up to its promise of transforming the lives of most of its beneficiaries over the short time periods that these studies typically covered.

In one memorable case, a press release put out by the group Innovations for Poverty Action came with this headline that overshadowed all the nuance of the findings (many of which were positive): "Microfinance does not live up to the promise of transforming the lives of the poor, six new studies show." When I confronted the founder of IPA about this, he lamely replied that he was not the person who wrote the headline. However, he did invite me to respond at a major conference, which I did in a speech that ridiculed the obvious bias in how the evaluations were being promoted and noted that microfinance also "failed" to cure the common cold while asking everyone whether these were relevant or appropriate standards.[3] Microfinance advocates and practitioners were energized by my speech, but the academic community predictably ignored the questions I'd been raising for many years.[1]

MANY RESEARCHERS' EMPHASIS on undermining the proof of microfinance efficacy (at the cost of identifying ways it could be further improved) combined with their obvious bias in favor of negative findings helped lay the groundwork for what in retrospect feels like the inevitable backlash against Yunus, Grameen, and the microfinance movement globally.

Beginning in late 2010—a scant four years after the Nobel Peace Prize was given to Yunus and Grameen and five years after the U.N. International Year of Microcredit—what had been rather isolated pockets of criticism, controversy, and government opposition to microfinance became much more widespread, and a story in itself.

In India, an October 2010 crisis in the state of Andhra Pradesh between local government and microfinance programs active there was inflamed shortly after the state's largest microfinance institution, SKS Microfinance, went public through an IPO, raising $350 million and making its foreign and local investors, including its Indian-American founder Vikram Akula, very wealthy. In the months after this windfall, Akula unwisely bragged in his rather immodest book, A Fistful of Rice, and in his public statements, about his talents, profitability, and virtual infallibility—which made an already tense situation much worse.

The local government alleged that pressure from microfinance institutions to repay loans was responsible for a series of "farmer suicides" and used these attacks to bring a halt to the entire microfinance industry in the state. In fact, the government officials were mostly motivated by embarrassment stemming from the reality that their own public sector microloan program was losing clients to more effective and efficient private organizations like SKS. Actually, farmer suicides in India have been tragically common since the mid-1990s, when pressures from globalization and changes in Indian agricultural policy caused widespread debt and despair. Careful studies showed that suicides in Andhra Pradesh did not increase in 2010 due to SKS or any other microfinance institution's acts, and were in fact lower across India than in 2009. But reasoned debate was notably absent from commentary on this crisis, which ended up impacting microfinance operators throughout the country.

In Nicaragua, beginning in 2008 and continuing into 2010, populist politicians urged microloan clients to not repay their loans, in what became known as the "No Pago" ("Do Not Pay") movement, leading a number of microfinance institutions to declare bankruptcy in that troubled nation.

Other countries, from Azerbaijan to Bolivia to Mozambique and beyond, had their own microfinance reckonings. But by far the most dramatic backlash occurred in Bangladesh, where it was focused mainly on vilifying a single individual. That individual was Muhammad Yunus.

In November 2010, a Danish documentary filmmaker named Tom Heinemann released *The Micro Debt*, which aired on Norwegian television. The documentary alleged that Grameen took advantage of its borrowers, engaged in aggressive collection practices, and misallocated aid funding from the Norwegian government. Yunus denied any wrongdoing, and the government of Norway would later clear him of any malpractice. In the end, nearly all of the accusations fell apart.

But in that moment, the film gave an opening to Grameen's critics and those who saw some advantage in vilifying him. Most notably, the criticism prompted the Prime Minister of Bangladesh, Sheikh Hasina, to make a highly critical statement aimed at Yunus and Grameen, calling them "bloodsuckers" of the poor. Later, Hasina claimed that she was the rightful recipient of the Nobel Peace Prize, among many other unhinged attacks. Many observers assumed that one of the factors motivating her was the fact that Yunus had publicly toyed with the idea of launching his own political party a few years earlier when Hasina was serving time in prison.

Her "bloodsucker" reference was based on the fact that Grameen charged interest to the poor. She failed to mention that Grameen's microcredit interest rates were in fact the lowest in Bangladesh, and among the lowest in the world. Within weeks, the nation's Finance Minister—who had previously been a strong ally of Grameen's since the early 1980s—relentlessly but unsuccessfully pressured Yunus to resign his position. In the meantime, there was a steady drumbeat of criticism, a major distraction for Yunus as he worked to defend Grameen's reputation.

Supporters of Yunus tried to parry the critiques and attacks, but the government and its allies in Parliament and the local press had much bigger megaphones. Ultimately, the government concocted a scheme to allege that Yunus, then 71, had been required by law to retire at age 60. Why a law that had not been deemed applicable to him for 11 years was suddenly grounds for his dismissal was never explained. Yunus appealed the case to the nation's Supreme Court. He lost the case, and subsequently resigned.

And yet the story doesn't end there. Yunus refocused his energy on promoting a generalized model of for-profit, socially motivated institutions he called "social businesses," of which Grameen was a prototype. Operating out of the Dhaka-based Yunus Centre and with the help of a network of organizations including Yunus Social Business, based in Germany, he built an ecosystem to support these nonprofit/for-profit hybrids, and made impressive progress. (For more on this work, I highly recommend his 2010 book *Building Social Business*.) He also became a strong ally of the movement to address climate change, which comes through in his book *A World of Three Zeroes*, published in 2017.

In the meantime, Grameen Bank recovered its footing due to the adroit operational management and sharp political skills of a series of Yunus proteges who have run the organization since 2011. While Nurjahan Begum stabilized the organization as the interim managing director in the immediate aftermath of Yunus's forced departure, I am proud to say that my close friend Rotun Kumar Nag did the heaviest lifting during his time in the role. He proved that even under the most trying conditions, Grameen was built to endure and to successfully navigate its founder transition.

The global microfinance movement has also recovered, in especially dramatic fashion in India. New products, operational efficiencies, alliances, and technological innovations kept most of the largest, socially-oriented, and dynamic organizations at the forefront of the battles to reduce poverty and build inclusive financial sectors in their countries. Indeed, one topic that researchers have failed to study is the strong correlation between the advent of the modern microfinance movement and the global reduction of extreme poverty by 75 percent over the last 30 years. The percentages of the poor and the extreme poor have dropped most dramatically in countries like India, Bangladesh, Indonesia, and Peru, where microfinance has been practiced intensively for years. (I am now working on a new book, due out in 2023, that will explore this and other underappreciated aspects of the microfinance movement.)

Yet, shockingly, most philanthropic leaders and members of the media have moved on from microfinance to other fads. This has been especially true in North America, where use of the term *microfinance* is often frowned on as antiquated and irrelevant. In Europe, where people seem to take a longer and more realistic view of history, the term is still in wide use. (This divergence may also be influenced by the fact that Europeans supported the movement mainly through social investments rather than grants, and because of that they understood that few other approaches had so many commercially viable and investible local institutions that delivered impact at scale.) The work on the ground continues to grow in reach and sophistication in most countries, which now include the United States.

The fact that fickle philanthropists and journalists have for the most part behaved as if microfinance disappeared from the face of the earth around 2015 has been rather mystifying, but not without its positive elements. On the one hand, if the philanthropy had not dried up, it could have helped cement and accelerate progress, as New York University researcher Tim Ogden persuasively argued in an important paper.[4] But being off the radar screen has allowed microfinance institutions to focus on delivering value to clients and keeping peace with local banking regulators and politicians outside the spotlight of the philanthropy/media industrial complex.

NO ONE CAN SERIOUSLY DOUBT that Muhammad Yunus could have become a multimillionaire or even a billionaire if he had gone into business and set his sights on amassing a personal fortune. He focused instead on creating institutions that allowed desperately poor people to work hard and become "multi-hundredaires" (and in the United States through Grameen America, "multi-thousandaires"). As a result, Grameen's clients have been given a fighting chance to ensure that their children become the first generation in their family to experience a life free from poverty.

What I have tried to do in this book is to trace the origins of Grameen and Yunus's socially-motivated entrepreneurship, and then to profile how they played out in one Bangladeshi village and one American neighborhood without airbrushing out all the messy human elements. Those stories, based on field research conducted in the early 1990s with some updates added in later editions (including this one), remain resonant, since the basic dynamic that gets set in motion when a woman decides to participate in a well-run microfinance program has not fundamentally changed.

We live in an age in which the overriding concerns include terrorism, climate change, inequality, the fragility of our public health systems, and perhaps above all, the lack of civility in our societies which causes leaders to eschew compromise and to deny the possibility of redemption. What results are brutal wars, whether they be cultural or traditional in nature.

These challenges are familiar ones to Yunus and to the organizations he created. In the early days of Grameen, it was operating principally in Tangail district, where Maoist terrorists were wreaking havoc on the local populace. Yunus's approach was to take simple precautions, but beyond that to ignore the terrorists and go about his work empowering poor women and men through microfinance. Later, he came to know that many of the insurgents quietly put down their arms and joined his staff, becoming some of the best workers in Grameen. Over time, the threat of terrorism in Tangail melted away. In fact, I lived there for many months during 1989 and 1993 without any fear whatsoever.

Based on a detailed study of long-time Grameen borrowers in Tangail conducted by Helen Todd, many borrowers had accumulated assets, educated their children, fought off malnutrition, and achieved enhanced status in their families and communities. Some leveled off at what one might call "stable subsistence," while others progressed to the middle class and beyond. Even those that never made it above the poverty line appear to have a decent chance of ensuring their children never fall below it as adults.

The humanistic values and endless tinkering that made Grameen and the global microfinance movement what they are today have many important lessons for our troubled world. I believe that to understand those insights, it is necessary to look under the hood and see how this approach powerfully but imperfectly unlocks new possibilities and also how large, locally owned and locally managed microfinance institutions like Grameen Bank can be built and sustained.

To those subjects, which are the lifeblood of this book, we now turn.

1. Muhammad Yunus—From Vanderbilt to Chittagong

IT BEGAN AS ONE stubborn man's desperate attempt to make sense of his life in a country racked by famine. In 1974, Bangladeshis were dying by the thousands for lack of even the meager nourishment to which they had grown accustomed. The skies blackened with vultures in search of another corpse to devour.

Three years removed from the glorious war of liberation, the country's dreams of freedom had been cruelly broken, transformed into a nightmare of hunger, wanton violence, and despair. U.S. Secretary of State Henry Kissinger famously called Bangladesh "the world's basket case."

On the streets of this poor nation, human beings walked around like zombies, waiting to die. Some had only a touch of life left in them, yet still they breathed, for at least one more day. On a village path, one starving man would eat for the first time in days, only to vomit what he consumed because it left his system in shock.

For one Bangladeshi, this was intolerable. He had to do *something*, even if it could only begin as a small gesture. Exactly what, he didn't have the faintest idea. Still, there was one thing he understood: The economic theories he had mastered at American universities while earning his Ph.D. would be of little use. Professor Muhammad Yunus would have to mix with the poor and see what he could think up after immersing himself in their reality. He hardly had grand illusions about what one man could do, working alone. But he had to act.

This is how it began.

AS HE EMERGED FROM his ground-floor apartment in the Grameen Bank living quarters, a small, red brick building behind the training institute, Muhammad Yunus strode forward with a purposeful gait. It was 8:05 on a hot summer morning in 1993. He was unencumbered by the stacks of files he had pored over the previous evening; a junior staff person had carried them to his office 15 minutes earlier.

Yunus turned a corner, following a narrow brick road that connects the back of the two-acre complex to the five-story main building, and passed a new structure under noisy, round-the-clock construction. The jarring sound of metal striking metal rang out in the air, muffled briefly by several loud thumps.

Three laborers spotted him as he passed the construction site. They immediately alerted each other, stood stiffly at attention, and saluted, military style. Yunus returned the salute in a casual, yet respectful, manner. Some of his junior colleagues, he knew, looked down on laborers in their longhis (simple skirts worn by men in South Asia) and tattered T-shirts, and either failed to salute them or performed the ritual perfunctorily. But it wasn't Yunus's style to upbraid his staff for acting that way; he simply tried to lead by example.

As he approached the front door of the complex's main office building, several more staff stiffened as they saluted the managing director. When he looked at them, he didn't smile—he knew it would most likely confuse them if he did—but he wanted to. This was the time of day when he was most relaxed and cheerful. Yet, when you run an organization with 11,000 employees, you have to keep up appearances by maintaining a professional demeanor. He sometimes yearned for the days when he knew the name of every person who worked for him.

It had been 19 years since famine had stalked the Bangladesh countryside, and Yunus was shepherding the organization he'd created to relieve hunger and poverty through a major turning point in its history. While for many years his venture had been known simply as a pilot project making tiny loans to destitute women, it was finally gaining recognition in Bangladeshi financial circles for its ability to disburse more than $1 million in loans each working day and earn a modest profit doing so. Later in 1993, the nation's finance minister, who had long been a critic of Yunus's work, would agree to lend his program millions of dollars. At the same time, Grameen Bank was becoming recognized as a model for poverty alleviation programs in Southeast Asia, Africa, North America, and beyond.

As Yunus climbed the stairs to his fourth-floor office, he reflected on the new era that was dawning for his organization. He sometimes thought it was approaching a critical mass that would allow Grameen to conquer problems that had previously stymied it. Yet he knew that getting big and famous held its own dangers. He often warned his staff about getting complacent and about "basking in their worldwide glory." The job, he told them, would not be finished until poverty had been eliminated from Bangladesh, once and for all, and the only place one could find destitution was in history books.

He entered his office at 8:11, before most of his 400 Dhaka-based employees had arrived. Three of his four personal staff, who had long since become used to the hours he kept, were there to greet him in the waiting room outside his office where they worked. He sat down behind his desk, and read the newspapers for a few minutes, looking for any signs that Bangladesh's emerging political crisis was ebbing. A few minutes later, he began receiving a steady stream of guests. They sat in front or at the side of his simple, sturdy wooden table. The desk had no drawers, symbolizing his commitment to conducting all business openly with nothing being hidden.

The first to come into his office were Khalid Shams and Muzammel Huq, his two senior deputies. The men shared tea, reviewed the previous day's developments, and looked ahead. All three had well-cultivated senses of humor and liked to laugh when they huddled together. This demeanor provided balance to the rest of their day, when uptight, often humorless junior personnel would meet with them. After the two men left, others in Yunus's inner circle, some of them students from the time when he was a university professor, began parading in and out of his office. A handful of foreign guests, including a journalist, were able to have a word with him. In between the meetings, he read letters, drafted responses, and made notes to himself in his diary.

Yunus owns a rounded, slightly pudgy face highlighted by expressive—some say magical—eyes and an eager smile. Visitors get the sense that their host is a jolly man, someone who takes his work considerably more seriously than he does himself. Quick with a witty remark in any of the several languages he speaks, Yunus has that rare ability to make nervous strangers feel like long-lost friends in a matter of minutes. Even when under stress himself, Yunus is known for giving guests his undivided attention. Akhtar Hossain, the managing director's unflappable personal secretary, often remarks that every visitor seems to emerge with an expression that says, "I must have been the most important person he met with today."

It had been a long and improbable road to building a Grameen network reaching into remote villages of Bangladesh, poverty-stricken islands in the Philippine archipelago, clusters of mud huts in Malawi, and decrepit slums in Chicago, Los Angeles, and Paris. Sometimes he paused between appointments to marvel at what he and his colleagues have accomplished and to wonder about what the years ahead have in store for his movement.

At 10 minutes before 6:00, after nearly everyone else had left, Yunus piled his files on his desk, tidied up the remaining papers, and checked his calendar for the following day. The sun was setting, and young boys were playing soccer on a grassy field adjacent to the complex, their screams and cheers drowned out by the relentless clanking and scraping at the construction site. As Muhammad Yunus left his office, his personal staff rose and saluted him, saying, "*As Salaam o Aleikum, sir*" in unison. He returned the traditional Muslim greeting that means "as peace be upon you" and headed toward the stairs. Several minutes later, a messenger carried the pending files to his residence and stacked them on the floor, near the telephone. After eating dinner, catching up with his wife Afrozi, a Bangladeshi physics professor he married in 1984, and playing with his seven-year-old daughter Dina, he began reading the files, making comments in red ink, followed by his initials. Often, he wrote *Tai houk* in Bengali script when a subordinate asked for his permission to move ahead on a project. The words mean, "Let it be." He believed in allowing people to make their own mistakes.

At 10:30, he retired for the evening, even as work continued apace at the construction site, located less than 50 yards from his bedroom.

IN 1961, MUHAMMAD YUNUS, the son of a relatively prosperous Muslim jeweler, was fresh from earning a master's degree at Dhaka University, which was Bangladesh's most prestigious seat of higher education. After graduation, he accepted a position as an economics instructor at Chittagong College. Yunus, just 21, was an impatient young man brimming with self-confidence, optimism, and ambition. With the first phase of his professional training complete, he felt it was time to launch one of the many projects he had toyed with during his student days.

While studying at Dhaka University, Yunus founded a nationally circulated literary magazine called *Uttaran* (Advancement). In the process of putting out the publication, he was surprised to learn that virtually all local packaging, up to and including the printing on cigarette packets, was being done in West Pakistan (today known as Pakistan). It occurred to him that opening a printing and packaging plant in East Pakistan (today known as Bangladesh) could be lucrative, and he promised himself to try to do so someday.

Soon after settling in Chittagong, Bangladesh's commercial capital and main port city, he began researching how he might follow through on this idea. With financial support from his father, Yunus made a fact-finding trip to West Pakistan and had the good fortune to meet a Bengali who was involved in a Swedish-Pakistani packaging venture. The man showed Yunus the ropes of the business and provided some tips on how to get started. By the time the next year rolled around, the long process of buying the necessary machinery—accomplished with the help of a half-million-taka ($12,500) loan from the Industrial Development Bank—and receiving government clearance was complete. In due course, the presses began to roll, providing gainful employment to 100 people and turning a small profit within two years. Yunus, responding to pressure from his father, repaid the loan to the Industrial Bank ahead of time. So rare was it that the bank had its loan repaid early and in full that it offered Yunus a 10-million-taka ($250,000) loan to finance the expansion of the operation.

After dividing his time between being a college instructor and running the factory, Yunus realized that his first love was teaching. To get on the academic fast track, though, required a Ph.D. from abroad. In 1964, he applied for and received a Fulbright scholarship to study in the United States. Having expressed a preference on his application form for studying "development economics," Yunus was rather improbably placed at Vanderbilt University in Nashville, Tennessee. He had never heard of Vanderbilt before, but when he located it on a globe he noticed that Tennessee had the distinction of being almost exactly halfway around the world from his home in East Pakistan.

Already an experienced traveler, Yunus relished the opportunity to expand his horizons again. His only anxiety came from what he read about the civil rights movement in the southern United States. Yunus was concerned that he'd be considered Black and be subjected to harassment. The fear, as it turned out, was unfounded: white classmates would inform him that only people they called "Negroes" were at risk; brown fellows like him, he was assured, had nothing to fear. Much to his disappointment, Vanderbilt's one-year master's program turned out to be something of a bore. Yunus applied for the university's Ph.D. program, and when he scored in the ninety-eighth percentile on the Graduate Record Exam, his acceptance was assured.

In his second year at Vanderbilt, Yunus enrolled in a statistics course taught by Professor Nicholas Georgescu-Roegen, a Romanian immigrant trained at the Sorbonne in France. Yunus found himself mesmerized by Georgescu's lectures. By the second week of classes, he realized that despite having taken three statistics courses previously, he barely understood anything about the subject. The elegance of Georgescu's two-and-a-half-hour orations touched something deep inside him; he and other admirers compared them to symphony orchestra performances. To Yunus, Georgescu's genius was in reducing statistics to its essence, breathing life into vapid concepts using storytelling and simple mathematics. Never had Yunus been in the presence of a master teacher, the kind who leads students down the long road to independent thought punctuated by "Aha!" realizations that are never forgotten. Now that he was under the wing of such a person, he couldn't get enough of it.

Georgescu's reputation as a difficult grader was, by all accounts, well earned. He was rumored to give no grade higher than a C. Most students, trained to memorize and regurgitate information, would do poorly on his exams, which tested understanding of the fundamentals of statistical theory. Yunus, determined to beat the odds, immersed himself in his mentor's approach and received an A-plus for his efforts. He would go on to take Georgescu's Economic Theory class and, later, become his graduate teaching assistant.

Georgescu's influence on the young Yunus was profound. Never was he to forget the distinction between a mere conveyor of information and a master teacher. As he saw it, the former informs while the latter empowers. Twenty years after first coming into contact with Georgescu, Yunus would write, "All human problems in their basic manifestation are quite simple. [It is merely our] arrogance [that] prompts us to put these problems in more and more complicated formulations."[5] On many occasions during the intervening two decades, he left learned audiences puzzled, unsure why they had been addressed in a manner a seventh-grade student could have understood.

With the exception of Georgescu and a computer center that, at the time, was state of the art, Vanderbilt had little of interest to offer Yunus as he pursued his Ph.D. By the time he completed his dissertation on "Intertemporal Allocation of Resources—A Dynamic Programming Model," he had already moved on and was teaching economics at Middle Tennessee State University in Murfreesboro.

Yunus happily passed his days in classrooms. By this time, he had married an American woman named Vera Forostenko. Then, suddenly, his nation called. In March 1971, the West Pakistani armed forces took control of Dhaka, the capital of East Pakistan, following public calls for regional autonomy and independence by Bengali political leaders. A full-scale civil war became a distinct possibility. On March 26, Major Zia Ur Rahman defiantly declared Bangladesh to be an independent nation, and the War of Liberation, in which more than three million Bengalis were to die, began. Yunus, hearing all of this over the radio in Nashville, immediately formed the Bangladesh Citizen's Committee with five other Bengalis who also lived in Tennessee. Together, they began to visit local radio and television stations and newspapers to explain the Bangladeshi cause.

On March 27, Yunus left for Washington, D.C., to attend a pro-Bangladeshi rally and seek out other Bengali patriots. There he met with Enayet Karim, a Bengali who at the time was the second-ranking official in the Pakistani embassy and who would later become the foreign secretary of an independent Bangladesh. Karim and other Bengalis in the embassy were working secretly with the Bengali-American community while they planned to form a separate Bangladesh embassy, with the support of the Indian government.

For the first three days after Yunus arrived in Washington, he and other activists lived with Karim. On one of those evenings, the Pakistani ambassador paid an unannounced visit to Karim's apartment, ostensibly to convey his sympathies for the loss of life in East Pakistan. Horrified at the prospect of his boss discovering Yunus and other activists living with him, Karim ordered his guests to grab the food they had been eating and flee into a room upstairs, where they had to remain completely still during the entire discussion. That was enough; Yunus moved into new living quarters the next day.

Yunus stayed in Washington to help run the Bangladesh Information Center. He relentlessly lobbied the U.S. Congress, particularly the Senate, and foreign embassies, hoping to win diplomatic recognition for the emerging nation. He organized an aggressive grassroots lobbying effort, principally by encouraging Bengali-Americans to educate their senators about the cause of liberation. Colleagues recall a young man who combined zeal and impressive organizational skills with the temperament of a diplomat.

The center's principal goal was to alter the Nixon administration's strong support of West Pakistan, to which it continued to send arms after the civil war began. Henry Kissinger was especially pro–West Pakistani. Yunus and his colleagues worked around the clock in an effort to counter Dr. Kissinger's exercise in realpolitik. But they failed to sway him, despite the support they received from a vocal minority in the State Department, including a small number of Dhaka-based diplomats who backed the Bengali cause.

When Bangladesh achieved its independence in December 1971, the young economist, swept up in the euphoria of victory and the prospect of helping to build a new nation, was eager to return to Bangladesh for good.

AS YUNUS PREPARED TO LEAVE the United States, a 14-year-old African-American girl named Connie Evans was living with her mother and siblings in Franklin, Tennessee (a town just outside of Nashville), and going to high school. She was being brought up to be an independent, self-assured, and achievement-oriented woman by a mother who supported the family as a self-employed caterer. While Connie understood what racism was, she knew little about conditions in Chicago, where she would move years later. She certainly didn't know much, if anything, about Bangladesh, and had never had occasion to meet Muhammad Yunus while he lived in Tennessee, though it is possible that they passed each other on the street, since Connie had traveled alone to school in Nashville from the age of six.

It would be nearly 20 years later that the two would be introduced. What Connie and Yunus would discuss in 1987 would be an approach to empowering the inner-city poor that few had ever heard of and fewer still believed would work. But that was later, much later.

YUNUS AND VERA ARRIVED IN DHAKA in June 1972. To his dismay, the only job he was offered at Dhaka University was a junior position in the Economics Department—an offer he declined. He was then recruited by Nurul Islam, a former teacher who was the chief of the new government's planning commission. When Yunus said he had no intentions of working for the post-liberation government, Islam refused to take no for an answer and pressed upon Yunus the contributions he could make to the process of nation building from inside the commission.

While he reconsidered the job offer, Yunus pondered the massive task of rebuilding the world's 139th independent nation. Despite the obstacles, he was far from discouraged. To the contrary, he felt that building the Bangladesh of his dreams, virtually from scratch, was the ultimate challenge. If Japan could become a powerhouse within a few decades of defeat in the Second World War, he reasoned that surely Bangladesh could reclaim its ancient glory and assume a dignified place among the nations of the world.

In the end, Yunus overcame his doubts and agreed to work for the government; his title was deputy chief of the General Economics Division of the Planning Commission, but his responsibilities were left unclear. Yunus was naturally anxious to get busy, but he waited for days, and then weeks, for someone to give him work to do. For reasons he never completely understood, nobody obliged. He collected a paycheck and spent his days reading newspapers. Disturbingly, his situation was far from unique. Throughout the government, officials sat about drinking tea and basking in their self-importance while millions of people tried desperately to put their lives back together in the wake of the war, with little or no outside assistance.

Yunus realized that before there could be any economic development as described in the computer models he had studied in Tennessee, a transformation in the mentality of thousands of bureaucrats, indeed the entire government, was necessary. A sense of urgency and responsibility had to be developed.

Even though he would later meet many dedicated civil servants, he came to believe that they were exceptions to a pervasive rule. In Yunus's view, bureaucrats seldom had any notion of serving the nation. Anyone who proposed new ideas was seen as someone likely to show up the boss. People learned to keep their mouth shut and to shower their superiors with compliments and gifts. Most of those who figured out how to manipulate the system would use their positions primarily for personal aggrandizement. In the meantime, Bangladesh languished while neighbors like South Korea, Malaysia, Sri Lanka, and India progressed.

Not surprisingly, in his brief time in the civil service, Yunus developed a lifelong mistrust of government. He saw that without firm political leadership, bureaucratic inertia was inevitable and expensive programs and schemes were rendered useless, mired in red tape. After two months of government work, Yunus left a note of resignation on his desk and departed for his home district in southeastern Bangladesh, where he took a job as an associate professor of economics at Chittagong University.

Professor Yunus was relieved to finally have some work to do: classes to teach, articles to write, and cultural events to organize and participate in. Based on his credentials as a Ph.D. from the United States with teaching experience, Yunus was named head of the Economics Department. He began talking to his colleagues about his interest in incorporating an aggressive program of "action-research" into the curriculum. His argument was that a more practical and interactive curriculum would help break down some of the hostility between the university and nearby communities while tapping into the experience of those villages for conducting original research. It would also give the students who were involved a grounding in real-life rural development that their peers at Dhaka University would only read about in books.

Most of his colleagues did not initially support his approach to experiential learning. Indeed, the idea that generated the most discussion was his proposition to vacate the large office reserved for the department head so that his 12 staff members, until then crammed into an office fit for one or two people, could have something approaching a dignified place to work. He constructed partitions for his staff with his own money and began to work in the office into which they had been squeezed. Nobody could quite understand why he was willing to forgo his privileges, and several junior faculty members who stood to benefit from his plan even tried to talk him out of it.

Faced with the unexpected reluctance of his staff to embrace his ideas, Yunus decided he needed an institutional base outside of the department to build the program he envisioned. In 1973, after he had tried to resuscitate the university's moribund Rural Development Program, he established his own Rural Studies Program (RSP). The RSP had no budget, no permission from the university to operate, and no staff. What it had, simply, was its founder's enthusiasm and some stationery he had printed up at his own expense.

As part of the curriculum offered by the RSP program, Yunus developed a course called "Issues in Rural Development" in which students would do original field research in the neighboring villages of Jobra and Fatehpur. His aim was to break the tradition in higher education, particularly prevalent in Bangladesh, of merely expecting people to read scholarly works and then repackage those views in their own papers. Rural development was happening right at the university's doorstep, so why should students rely only on books?

Initially, students responded slowly. Many were clumsy interviewers. After a few semesters, however, a small number started to catch on. Over time, the courses offered by the program became more popular, and by the late 1970s, enrollment was high. The Rural Economics Program (REP), as it was renamed, also began putting out research reports on issues such as agricultural development and community organization.

One of the program's earliest initiatives was to encourage farmers in Jobra to adopt high-yielding varieties of rice. (Traditional varieties yield less per acre, but do not need the constant attention that the high-yielding varieties do.) Students, together with Yunus and H. I. Latifee, one of the few departmental colleagues who had shared Yunus's enthusiasm for this kind of practical work, went into the fields to work directly with cultivators to grow rice using modern methods. The farmers were initially amused, but in a short time, Yunus and Latifee struck up warm friendships with many villagers. People were impressed at how the two men were developing an encyclopedic knowledge of Jobra, including the names of hundreds of farmers and their family members.

Unfortunately, most of the students dropped out of the program within weeks. Many were uneasy doing farmwork, feeling that the reason they were at university in the first place was to ensure that they never had to stand knee-deep in mud planting rice seedlings. A university publication put it bluntly: "the program was not a success. . . . Compared to the cost incurred, the achievement was negligible. Many students joined this program just as a fad to show off." The education of the professor had begun.[6]

Another program that Yunus inaugurated was the designation of plots of land on campus as student vegetable gardens. To spur some friendly competition, close attention was paid to whose plots were the most productive. The program, established in the famine year of 1974, initially set aside one-third of an acre to be cultivated by 30 first-year students. All but five of them, however, commuted from the city of Chittagong and were usually gone by noon (prompting Yunus to once write a report in which he criticized his employer for being a "part-time university"). Dipal Chandra Barua, a member of Bangladesh's tiny Buddhist minority who bicycled to class each day from his family's home in Jobra, was asked by his peers to look after their plots. When Yunus noticed that the vegetable garden was thriving under Dipal's meticulous care, he invited the young economics student to get involved in the REP. At the time, Dipal was something of a hippie—Bangladeshi-style: skinny with long hair and eager to try new things. He easily fit into the offbeat rhythms of the Rural Economics Program, and Yunus was quick to take him under his wing.

While he worked on the REP, Yunus kept abreast of the floundering efforts to jump-start the nation's economy. National politics, in particular, sapped his optimism. Yunus became increasingly frustrated by how little he was able to do that could bring tangible benefits to Bangladesh's poverty-stricken populace. Years later, he would say, "After a few years at the university, I felt the classroom was like a movie house, where professors have all the answers and the tale works out so neatly at the end of the day. But it's make-believe. When you turn on the lights and go outside, it's a completely different world, with problems about which professors have nothing much useful to say."

THE REGION THAT HAD BECOME Bangladesh has not always been the famine-ravaged shambles it had become by 1974. In the second century CE, the historian Pliny commented that dresses made from muslin fabrics imported from Bengal were in such demand among wealthy ladies in Rome that unthinkable amounts of precious metals were flowing from the coffers of the empire to Bengali traders and weavers.[7] In the sixteenth century, Bengal—made up of present-day Bangladesh and the Indian state of West Bengal—was an important part of the vast Mughal Empire and known for its booming textile trade and agriculture. Most historians agree that the average Bengali during this period was somewhat better nourished than their counterpart in Europe. Indeed, Bengal was known to be among the most prosperous regions in the world. A European visitor wrote, "Money is so plentiful in Dhaka that it is seldom counted, but always weighed. There is a profusion of food and other articles in the numerous bazaars of the city. The vastness of the wealth is stupefying."[8]

For centuries, economic activity in the rural areas was conducted principally at the level of the household, with complex supply networks based largely on the barter system linking cotton and silk cultivators with spinners, weavers, and traders. A British traveler touring Bengal during the Mughal period wrote, "When at some distance from the high road, or a principal town, it is difficult to find a village in which every man, woman, and child is not employed in making a piece of cloth. . . ."⁹

The eighteenth century marked the gradual dissolution of the Mughal Empire in India and the establishment of British rule, initially under the auspices of the East India Company. This enterprise, in search of quick profits, assumed control of Bengal's lucrative textile industry, which produced one-third of all the cotton textiles used in Europe at the time.[10] It appointed its own network of much-hated middlemen, the most important of whom were called *gomastas*, under the agency system of 1753. In the words of a former company employee, ". . . [the *gomasta*] makes [the weavers] sign a bond for the delivery of a certain quantity of goods, at a certain time and price, and pays them part of the money in advance. The assent of the poor weavers is in general not deemed necessary. . . ."[11] Rights to the production of individual weavers were freely traded among the *gomastas* as if their clients were slaves. Those who refused to participate in the system were flogged, and on occasion killed. The prices the weavers received were, by one estimate, 20 to 40 percent less than they could have gotten in the marketplace.[12]

This progressive impoverishment led directly to several famines during the next two decades, one of which killed one in three people living in Bengal. By the last quarter of the eighteenth century, many weavers who were faced with declining revenue that barely covered their costs had given up the trade and taken up day-laboring, fishing, or other work.[13]

While it was developing its own textile industry during the early nineteenth century, Britain began pricing Bengali textiles out of its domestic market through high tariffs, while at the same time making a handsome profit trading them with the rest of the world. By the 1820s, a series of technological innovations, including the spinning jenny, the power loom, and the use of chlorine for bleaching, had made the north of England the foremost producer of textiles in the world.

British yarn was soon being spun at less than half the cost of Indian yarn, and the drive to aggressively market British textile goods in Bengal and throughout India virtually finished off the indigenous industry. Between 1824 and 1837, the value of yarn imports from England increased 55-fold. Bengal's silk industry lasted somewhat longer, but by 1876 the value of silk exports had declined to less than 3 percent of what it was at the beginning of that century. It would take Mahatma Gandhi's campaign in the early twentieth century to shame people of the Indian subcontinent into wearing cloth spun at home to make any dent in this historic reversal.

By the second half of the nineteenth century, famines had become so common in Bengal that the British regime was pressed by growing unrest in the countryside into passing a series of reforms, including the creation of representative government at the village level and the promulgation of a famine code that was effective enough to prevent mass death from hunger for more than 50 years. But the province often teetered on the brink of starvation, and in 1943, with the British Empire focused on the Second World War and Japanese aggression in Asia, a famine killed three million people in eastern India.

When India gained independence from Britain in 1947, the colony became two separate sovereign nations—India and Pakistan. As part of the complex and improbable agreement negotiated among the British, Indian Hindus, and Indian Muslims, the regions where there was a Hindu majority became India and the remaining Muslim-dominated areas, with the exception of Kashmir, became Pakistan.

Of the many problems this compromise presented, the most obvious was that West Pakistan (known today simply as Pakistan) and East Pakistan (present-day Bangladesh) had no common border and were more than one thousand miles apart. It was as if California and Pennsylvania constituted one country and the rest of the United States a second, hostile nation. Furthermore, the two provinces of East and West Pakistan (or *wings*, as they were called), despite sharing a common dominant faith, had profound cultural and economic differences. Most fundamentally, East Pakistan was made up of Bengali speakers, while most West Pakistanis spoke Punjabi, Urdu, or Sindhi.

The Bengalis were initially pleased to be part of a Muslim-dominated Pakistan, their political leaders having been among the most vocal pro-Pakistan partisans during the negotiations with the British. But within a decade after partition, many Bengalis had come to feel betrayed. Their motherland, it seemed, had once again come under foreign domination, this time by the arrogant West Pakistanis.

Upon independence, East Pakistan was also separated from Calcutta, its former capital, whose jute mills were essential to the production of its primary cash crop. (Jute is the raw material from which gunnysacks are made.) It was this division that prompted Muhammad Ali Jinnah, the man whose efforts led to the creation of Pakistan, to complain that he had been given a "moth-eaten" state.[14] The sudden separation of Bengal's head from its body plunged East Pakistan's already precarious economic situation into dire straits. Sir Frederick Burrows, the last British governor in Bengal, assessed these conditions and predicted that East Pakistan would become "the greatest rural slum in history."[15]

After partition, East Pakistan slowly resumed exporting jute, though the money thus earned largely flowed to the coffers of West Pakistan. East Pakistan's "gold fiber" went a long way to financing West Pakistan's post-independence industrialization. Ultimately, East Pakistan became little more than a colony of West Pakistan.

Tensions mounted during the 1950s and 1960s over calls in the Bengali-speaking East for regional autonomy. Bengali anger was ignited by proposals to have Urdu, a common language in West Pakistan but virtually unknown in the East, adopted as the national language. Shortly before his death, Jinnah came to Dhaka for the only time in his life and, to the dismay of Bengalis, declared, "The state language of Pakistan is going to be Urdu and no other language. Anyone who tries to mislead you [on this issue] is really the enemy of Pakistan."[16]

The West Pakistanis feared that the Bengalis of East Pakistan would create a single political party and gain control of the Parliament. They worked to ensure that positions of influence were held by West Pakistanis, while largely ceremonial ones were occupied by Bengalis. During the 1950s and 1960s, the West Pakistani elite tried to institutionalize a civilian government that would be more responsive to Bengali aspirations while ensuring that West Pakistanis retained most of the power. Their efforts, however, were too little, too late. By 1971, negotiations between Sheikh Mujib, a charismatic Bengali political leader, and West Pakistani politicians had failed to produce a compromise on the issue of regional autonomy. Consequently, Mujib declared Bangladesh an independent nation. As a result, Mujib was arrested, the military took control of Dhaka, and what is known in Bangladesh as "The Independence War" began.

A campaign of genocide was unleashed by the Pakistani (almost entirely *West* Pakistani) armed forces, assisted by an influential minority of Bengalis who stayed loyal to the regime. In the spring of 1971, the Mukti Bahini (Bangladeshi Freedom Fighters) began filtering back into the country after receiving training and arms in India. Full-scale war was underway by June.

After the monsoon subsided, the pace of the battles picked up, with outgunned Mukti Bahini divisions often retreating into India when they were on the run. As Pakistani forces followed them, there were a series of escalating border clashes between Indian and Pakistani troops, culminated by a preemptive strike by the Pakistani air force in early December. Indian forces joined the conflict and helped the freedom fighters rout the Pakistani forces, leading to the signing of a peace treaty on December 16 in Dhaka and the birth of Bangladesh.

The new nation had its work cut out for itself. The communications and transportation networks, and hundreds of thousands of acres of standing crops, had been destroyed during the war; more than 20 percent of the nation's food had to be imported. A black market developed for weapons that had accumulated during the conflict, and violence raged. Real or imagined collaborators with the Pakistanis were slaughtered.

In January 1972, Mujib, who had been hours away from being executed when the cease-fire was declared, triumphantly returned to the new nation and became its first prime minister. Overwhelmed by the task in front of him, he lamented to a friend shortly after his return:

> [When I returned] I was brought face to face with the greatest manmade disaster in history. I could never imagine the magnitude of the catastrophe. They have killed more than three million of my people. They have raped our mothers and our sisters and have butchered our children. More than thirty percent of all houses have been destroyed. . . . What do you do about currency? Where do you get food? Industry is dead. Commerce is dead. How do you start them again? What do you do about defense? I have no administration. Where do I get one? Tell me, how do you start a country?[17]

Mujib was a better rhetorician than administrator, and had only limited success in dealing with these challenges. By 1973, frustrations with his inept leadership were being vented in public protests. Attempting to retain control of the fragile and violent nation, Mujib, the once-beloved *Bangabandhu* (Friend of the Bengalis), created the Jatiyo Rakhi Bahini, a shadowy paramilitary force responsible directly to him. Violence begat violence, with more than 2,000 politically motivated murders occurring in 1973 alone. Among the victims were several members of Parliament. In May of 1974, after the country's Supreme

Court reprimanded the Rakhi Bahini for having tortured and killed a seventeen-year-old boy, Mujib stripped the court of its powers to pass judgment over his personal terror force.

If 1973 was the year of violence, 1974 was the year of famine. As thousands of people died, the prime minister's party, the Awami League, disintegrated into warring factions. To impose order, Mujib declared a state of emergency in late December. His famine relief effort was poorly conceived and executed. Among the more odious aspects of the relief program was the herding of 50,000 Bangladeshi destitute people who had migrated to Dhaka into a camp bordered by a barbed wire fence and bereft of any medical or sanitation facilities. One unfortunate resident told a visiting journalist, perhaps mistaking him for an aid worker, "Either feed us or shoot us."

In June 1975, Mujib moved decisively toward a one-party state. He wanted to create a leftist government of national unity in which all power would be vested in a single authority— himself. As for an economic program, Mujib declared his intention to create compulsory rural cooperatives in every village. The system was to take effect on September 1.

Two weeks before his sweeping reforms were to come into force, Mujib and most of his family were assassinated in his home in Dhanmondi on the orders of a group of army officers. The plotters announced over Radio Bangladesh that Mujib was dead, martial law was in force, and Khondokar Mushtaq, one of Mujib's ministers, was to be sworn in as president. The senior commanders of the armed forces went along with the coup and initially recognized the legitimacy of Mushtaq, even attending his swearing-in ceremony.

The brief embers of democracy had been snuffed out; it would be 16 years before they would begin to glow again. During that time, great damage was done to the country and its people. Several remarkable success stories emerged, however, prompting people across the world to take notice of a country known in South Asia as "the land of poets and lovers."

As Muhammad Yunus contemplated the famine of 1974, he restlessly wondered what he should do. He recalled how aggressively U.S. intellectuals spoke out on controversial social, political, and economic matters. Yet, his colleagues at Chittagong University were unwilling to break the conspiracy of silence concerning Mujib's ineffective policies and his maddening unwillingness to even admit that there was a famine.

Yunus approached Abdul Fazal, the university vice chancellor, and suggested that he publish a formal statement to the press criticizing the government's role in creating and prolonging the crisis. Fazal was a well-known writer with a close personal relationship to Mujib. To the young professor's surprise, the vice chancellor agreed, provided that Yunus draft the statement and join him in signing it.

Within days, other faculty members signed, and the harshly worded antigovernment statement was sent off to the newspapers, where it was printed and widely commented on. In the following weeks, groups of academics at other leading universities followed suit and presented their own critiques. In subsequent years, as histories were written of Bangladesh in the mid-1970s, the statement was frequently mentioned as having stimulated an overdue public debate about the causes of the famine.

Yunus decided that another opportunity to speak out publicly would be the occasion of *Ekushey* (literally, "on the twenty-first")—the annual remembrance of the martyrs who had died on February 21, 1952, while protesting Pakistani government efforts to make Urdu the single national language. Each year, *Shaheed Dibosh* (Martyrs' Day, as it is also known) is observed in a diverse manner typical of Bengali culture. At dawn, wreaths are laid on *shaheed minars* (martyrs' monuments), citizens are expected to walk barefoot out of respect to the martyrs, festive book fairs are held, and pledges are made to ensure that "the Bengali language is used in all walks of life."

After the emergence of Bangladesh as an independent nation with Bengali as its national language, continuing to observe Martyrs' Day in the traditional manner seemed to Yunus somewhat like observing the Fourth of July in the United States by having people take a pledge to continue resisting British rule. With so many other challenges facing the country, Yunus thought that the martyrs should be remembered as people willing to die to ensure that Bangladesh actualized itself as a nation, rather than simply as supporters of the Bengali language. He submitted an article to a local newspaper proposing that *Shaheed Dibosh* be made more relevant to the contemporary reality. He proposed, for example, that Martyrs' Day be a time to honor the farmers coming in with sheaths of rice paddy and scientists improving agricultural yields.

His article was roundly criticized for being unfaithful to the legacy of the martyrs. Bangladeshi politicians, then, as now, felt safer fighting yesterday's battles than today's and dismissed the idea out of hand.

During his first few months on the Chittagong University faculty, Yunus had noticed that farmland adjacent to the university campus lay fallow during the dry season, and in response he joined his local member of Parliament in petitioning the government to sink an irrigation tube well—a driven well—in Jobra. Their lobbying was successful, and Yunus felt that this was one instance in which the government had been responsive and would make a difference in the lives of the rural people.

Yunus was surprised to find out that only 9 of 60 acres were irrigated during the first cropping season. Local farmers assured him that the well's use would improve once kinks in the management system were worked out. But the second season was hardly any better, with barely 10 acres receiving water. As the third year approached, Yunus was informed that there were no plans to operate the tube well at all.

Partly out of his frustration with the misuse of the tube well in Jobra, Yunus researched the state of irrigation nationwide. By the early 1970s, a significant number of irrigation pumps called deep tube wells (DTWs) had been sunk with foreign-aid funds to irrigate a dry-season rice crop using modern, high-yielding seeds developed in the Philippines. It was hoped that this would bring the nation's chronic food deficits under control.[18]

Unfortunately, it turned out to be far easier for the government to sink a tube well capable of irrigating 60 acres than to find an institutional mechanism ensuring that it actually irrigated five. The management structure for the tube wells was supposed to be a cooperative that local farmers would join to ensure fair and judicious use of the machinery. In practice, within a short time, most tube wells fell under the control of the wealthiest person within its command area. In most instances, the cooperatives existed only on paper. Huge bribes were often given to ensure that the DTW was sunk on a politically well-connected person's property. Worse still, slivers of poor people's land were often seized to build the canals that would carry the water to the wealthy farmers' fields. Over time, most of the pumps fell into disuse. Without maintenance of the machinery and the use of fertilizers in the paddy fields, irrigated agriculture is a risky venture.

On a fall day in 1975, Yunus asked his graduate student Dipal Chandra Barua to find out why the irrigation pump in his village was not going to be used during the upcoming season. Dipal reported that over the two and a half years since it was sunk, the farmers had been unable to afford the diesel fuel and the parts to keep it running. Those who had contributed toward the cost complained that because others refused to pay their share, the water had been shut off during critical periods. Rice harvests had been ruined, and participating farmers were sometimes worse off than if they had simply left their land lay fallow. On several occasions, unhappiness about mismanagement had boiled over into violence.

Yunus studied the problem, talking to farmers in the fields and at his home. He decided to convene a meeting of farmers whose land fell within the pump's command area. His aim was to persuade them to work together to ensure that there was a dry-season crop in the coming months. The gathering was held outdoors, in front of a tea stall in Jobra. As is customary in Bangladesh, most of the farmers who attended arrived late, and it was past midnight when Yunus interrupted the shouting matches that had broken out and presented a new model.

In his plan, Yunus and people he appointed to a management committee would run the tube well and supply all the seeds, fertilizer, and insecticide. In exchange, Yunus would receive one-third of all the crops harvested. The other two-thirds would be split equally between the owner and the cultivator of each parcel of land. Yunus would sell his share to recover the costs of running the program, and any surplus would be reinvested into the upkeep and improvement of the tube well. He liked the simplicity of his *tehbhaga* (three share) system—three parties shared the work, and the same three parties shared the fruits of the work. Each had incentives to make the initiative a success, and the farmers had the rare opportunity to cultivate under a scheme in which someone else bore most of the risk of crop failure.

When Yunus opened the meeting up for questions, there was a strong undercurrent of hostility. Old wounds and jealousies from earlier efforts to manage the tube well had been reopened. The larger farmers seemed particularly mistrustful. They were interested in increasing their yields, but resisted the idea of receiving only one-third of the harvest as opposed to the traditional one-half. They suggested that Yunus accept one-sixth of the crop instead. They also wanted no part of any loss the scheme might generate. If the government could sink the tube well without charging the villagers anything, why couldn't the university put together a management plan for free as well?

Yunus announced that he was willing to make up any loss with his own money, figuring it was the only way to gain everyone's agreement, but he stood firm on the issue of his share. He announced a cooling-off period of a week, during which several of Yunus's students aggressively talked up the program in the village. A procession of small farmers and sharecroppers called on Yunus at the university. Many of those who came had not even attended the original meeting but had got word of the proposal and were eager to get involved. The elites in the village, anxious to maintain their positions of influence, requested that they be given special status by being included on a largely symbolic advisory committee. Yunus agreed. When it was time to make a formal decision on whether to agree to the proposal, it was adopted nearly unanimously.

Yunus named the project the *Nabajub Tehbhaga Khamar* (New Era Three Share Cultivation Scheme), divided the participating farms into four blocks, and assigned a student to manage each. Assaduzzaman, a recent graduate of the Economics Department whom Yunus had hired to be the secretary of the Rural Economics Program, was named the project coordinator. Yunus and Assad (as Assaduzzaman is commonly known) began procuring the necessary seeds, fertilizer, diesel fuel, and insecticide with a 40,000-taka ($1,000) loan from a local branch of Janata Bank.

During the management and advisory committee meetings that were held soon after the water began flowing, farmers who had originally declined to participate asked to join in. Yunus resisted, fearing that if the command area were expanded too much, the pump might run dry toward the end of the season. Yet the farmers persisted. Finally, someone suggested that additional irrigation could be arranged by building an inexpensive cross dam in a nearby stream and digging a canal through which the water could flow to the rice fields. When objections were raised by farmers who lived seven miles downstream, it was agreed that Tehbhaga would divert water only two days during the week. To finance the expansion, Yunus took out an additional 25,000-taka loan from Janata Bank.

Everyone associated with the project was impressed by the degree of Yunus's personal involvement. The expectation was that he would have his students organize everything and simply come back after the harvest to inspect the results. Instead, he attended every committee meeting and spent considerable time in the fields talking to the farmers. His and Latifee's familiarity with every aspect of life in Jobra grew.

When the harvest was completed in early June 1976, the results were impressive. The land under cultivation ended up reaching 85 acres, and the yield exceeded 1.2 tons per acre, double the national average. Yet, the program posted a 13,405-taka ($335) loss after the bank loan was repaid because of an unexpected drop in the price of rice, the high cost of overseeing the program, storage problems, and some pilferage. Yunus, refusing to go back on his word, went ahead and covered the amount out of his own pocket. When word leaked to the village that the professor had absorbed the loss, many farmers were surprised and distraught. Some expressed a feeling of shame at having six months' worth of rice in their houses while the man who had organized the program was out thousands of taka.

When the 1976–1977 dry season began, the farmers begged Yunus to manage the program again. The professor refused, but he agreed to advise the farmers as they worked out their own management system and to provide the necessary introductions to the bankers and the wholesalers from whom he had bought the agricultural inputs. Yunus argued that he was a professor, not an irrigation specialist, and that his job was merely to demonstrate what was possible. It was now their job to institutionalize the program, or, if they so chose, to discontinue it.

In the second year, under the farmers' direction, overall production rose an additional nine tons. This time, however, the program recorded a profit of 8,522 taka, or about $210. By the fifth cropping season, the harvest reached 235 tons, more than double the inaugural year, and its profit exceeded 39,000 taka. Yunus never considered asking to be repaid the money that he lost during the first year from the surplus generated later on.

In 1977, while Yunus was out of the country, a senior civil servant asked Dipal to draft a nomination that he would submit so that Yunus could receive the President's Award for his involvement with Tehbhaga. Not only did Yunus receive the award, but a nationwide government initiative called the Package Inputs Program (PIP), designed on the Tehbhaga experience, began to be planned. (Sadly, it was imposed from above, without the active involvement of the farmers it was supposed to benefit, and as a result, it failed.)

By the late 1970s, Yunus kept himself apprised of the developments of Tehbhaga and PIP, but he was by then deeply involved in another demonstration project from which it was proving much harder to extricate himself.

THE INTERRELATED PROBLEMS of poverty and misuse of resources were not unique to Jobra. If anything, conditions there were somewhat better than those in far-flung villages in the western half of the country. For the most part, however, as control of the central government changed hands during the second half of the twentieth century, the situation in the rural areas worsened as the politicians squabbled. On more than one occasion, Yunus said he believed Dhaka to be virtually a foreign country. He told people that he would never agree to be based in the capital because he felt that people who lived and worked there got hopelessly out of touch with their countrymen.

As the years passed, the conditions outside the urban centers were becoming progressively more desperate. Periodic famines, chronic ill health, and uncertain food prices that punished marginal farmers and rewarded speculators combined to ensure that the number of landless poor families steadily increased. In the process, small farmers became sharecroppers and sharecroppers became day laborers. As the pool of day laborers grew, their wages were forced lower. Even such traditional work as raising livestock and manufacturing handicrafts was done on an exploitative basis, in which middlemen reaped the lion's share on the benefits produced by someone else's labor.

By 1983, despite nearly 10 years of an "assault on poverty" declared in the wake of the 1974 famine, real wages were 2.3 percent lower than in the last year of Pakistani rule, and a day's work in the fields bought a laborer three kilograms of rice instead of the four it had fetched in 1970. At the same time, the nation had three million new mouths to feed every 12 months. By the mid-1980s, per capita consumption reached an all-time low of 1,943 calories and 48.9 grams of protein.[19] (According to the Food and Agriculture Organization, the minimum daily requirement to sustain sedentary life is 2,150 calories and 65 grams of protein.)

Under the stress of this impoverishment, the Bangladeshi family unit began to disintegrate. Deprivation drove fathers to abandon their wives and children in previously unheard-of numbers. It was no longer routine for sons and daughters to take care of their parents when they became old and infirm. In a society historically characterized by strong ties between the generations, it became increasingly common for parents to spend their final days in a state of semi-starvation, with their children refusing to deplete what little cushion they had against destitution. Fathers were often bullied into handing over their inheritance to their grown children as early as possible. After doing so, assistance they had been promised by their offspring was sometimes cut off.

The glory of independence wore thin, and many tea stall conversations in the rural areas centered on the strengths of the British and Pakistani regimes, perceived deficiencies of the Bengali race, and people's dreams of sending their sons to the United States, Europe, or the Middle East. A growing cottage industry of agents claiming to be able to place young men in jobs abroad came to cheat thousands of poor families out of millions of taka.

As people searched for answers to these vexing problems, Islamic fundamentalism gained ground. Although the Bengali people were known throughout Asia for their tolerance and their commitment to secularism, relations between the Muslim majority and the nation's Hindus, Buddhists, Christians, and animists slowly deteriorated. Politicians fanned ethnic and religious hatred and used student-front organizations as pawns in their quest for power. Violence, politically inspired or otherwise, became commonplace, and thievery a popular profession. Prostitution and abuse of drugs and alcohol were on the rise, while gambling, an old problem, was reaching epidemic proportions.

The plight of women in rural Bangladesh became increasingly severe. Even in good times, women prepare the feasts but are only permitted to eat the leftovers after the men are finished, to wash their husband's new clothes while wearing tattered saris, and to hope, often in vain, that the money their guardians earn is being saved or productively invested rather than being frittered away. In bad times, women go the hungriest, work the hardest, and have to stand by helplessly while their children cry out for food. All year round, in good times and bad, women suffer many other humiliations. They are unable to initiate a legal divorce, though their husbands need only say "I divorce you" three times to end their marriage. They cannot travel outside their immediate home after puberty without becoming the subject of lurid rumors. They are the victims of frequent beatings and verbal abuse by husbands and in-laws, and against all reason are blamed for floods, droughts, and disappointing harvests.

Life for a Bangladeshi woman is, more than anything else, one of isolation. In certain parts of the country, it is common to find women who have not strayed from an area smaller than a few hundred square yards for decades at a time; who have never held currency in their hand or seen a market; who have no friends; who have never played any meaningful role in the politics of their family, their village, or their country.

With an annual per capita income of around $200 in the early 1990s, and a population of roughly 115 million people packed into 68,000 villages in a country the size of the state of Wisconsin, the fundamental problems in the political and economic management of Bangladesh are manifest. Blame can be liberally spread among the government, the private sector, and the foreign aid agencies. But to understand the depth of the sorrow this nation has suffered, one need not open a single history book or read a fancy economic printout. One need only stand in a village for a few hours and look around at all the frail women with sunken, toothless faces hunching over earthen stoves or carrying water on one hip and a child in their arms as they walk barefoot down muddy village paths strewn with animal and human feces.

Particularly striking will be the moment a woman in rural Bangladesh realizes you're looking at her; reflexively, she will pull her sari over her face in shame. A brief conversation with any of these women is almost too much for those unaccustomed to life in rural Bangladesh—a lesson of what life is like when it is nasty, brutish, and short, and when the only legacy you can leave any of your offspring who survive childhood is a life of poverty deeper than what you inherited at birth.

2. The Birth of the Grameen Bank

AT THE TIME, SURPRISINGLY FEW PEOPLE mourned the violent passing of Sheikh Mujib in 1975. For many, in fact, the founding father's death came as something of a relief. Mujib's successor, Khondokar Mushtaq, chose Mahabub Alam Chashee, a colleague and acquaintance of Yunus's, as his principal secretary (a post roughly equivalent to White House chief of staff). One of Mushtaq's first acts was to call a conference whose purpose was to rally around the idea of *Swanirvar Bangladesh* (self-reliant Bangladesh). People were concerned about becoming overly dependent on other nations, often citing the example of how the United States government had cut off aid to Bangladesh after it exported some jute to Cuba in 1973. Many claimed that this action by the United States was a contributing factor to the 1974 famine. Later research, however, revealed that despite the sanctions there was plenty of food in the country; the famine actually came on the heels of a record harvest. The real villain was an inadequate distribution system.

The mood of the conference, held in September 1975, was tense, as it was the first major gathering since Mujib's assassination. The army generals were conspicuous by their presence from beginning to end, and no one mentioned Sheikh Mujib for fear of their reaction.

Muhammad Yunus delivered a paper at the conference. Chashee had chosen him to speak because he admired Yunus's ability to weave diverse concepts, objectives, and strategies into coherent theoretical frameworks. Now, he wanted to hear what the Ph.D. from the United States had to say about self-reliance.

In his presentation, Yunus defined the concept of self-reliance as a state in which a nation or region is not involved in any dependent relationship. This did not, he emphasized, preclude the possibility of mutually beneficial trade. To be self-reliant as a country, he argued, Bangladesh must first and foremost have self-reliant families. Building up independence was not something to be done from the top down, but rather from the bottom up.

To illustrate his point, Yunus provided the example. A farmer will likely feel helpless if he hears a government proclamation stating that there is a national rice shortfall of several million tons. The farmer, or for that matter, any individual, feels that he is powerless to solve such a huge problem. He is left believing that the remedy can only come from the government. But, if the farmer is instead told that there is a shortfall of fifty tons in only *his own* village, the problem immediately becomes easy to grasp and, more important, solvable.

Goals and strategies, Yunus went on to assert, must be broken down to the family and village level, and then solved from there, with supplementary assistance from the central government. He believed that the entire exercise in planning should be turned upside down so that the national plan is mainly the sum of thousands of smaller plans developed at the village level.

As he saw it, the challenge facing the nation was to tap into the idealism and willingness to sacrifice that had characterized the liberation struggle, and to channel these attitudes toward the awesome task of economic and social development. The framework that would stimulate this vision, he told his audience, would be *gram sorkar* (village government).

"Sheikh Mujib was right in that the village must have its own institutions," Yunus said. "But he called for *compulsory* village cooperatives. This was his mistake—cooperation cannot be mandatory." *Gram sorkar*, a system in which the bulk of the nation's political decisions would devolve to the villages, was a pragmatic way to fulfill the martyred leader's vision. For perhaps the first but certainly not the last time in his public career, Yunus then relinquished the podium and listened as his idea was dismissed by most of the people present at the meeting.

Yet a change in government soon gave *gram sorkar* a friend in a high place. General Zia Ur Rahman, the army chief of staff, seized power in a bloodless coup in late 1975, ending the fiction that Mushtaq represented a civilian government. After taking over, Zia discussed the matter with Yunus and indicated that he, with the help of Mahabub Alam Chashee, intended to implement *gram sorkar* nationwide. Many Bangladeshi intellectuals were outraged that the proposal was being taken seriously, perhaps because on some level it valued the knowledge of semiliterate villagers more than theirs.

In March 1976, Yunus was invited to elaborate on his idea of *gram sorkar* at the national convention of the Bangladesh Economic Association (BEA), a group dominated by utopian intellectuals. After presenting his paper titled "Institutional Framework for Swanirvar Bangladesh," there was an immediate and fierce attack. The assembled economists and politicians were contemptuous of the idea of organizations in which the poor, and women, would have a central role in national affairs. (In Yunus's revised proposal, the poor, who constituted the majority in nearly every village, would be assured a strong voice in the running of *gram sorkar* through a system of proportional representation based on social classes.) The election of *gram montri* (village ministers) was criticized as being insulting to the national ministers. One prominent participant commented, "You cannot have an organization made up of poor people. Look at the history of poor people's organizations—they never amount to anything. Remember, if you add zero to zero to zero to zero, no matter how many times you do it, you still end up with zero."

Yunus responded to this criticism and skepticism by making two comparisons. He first asserted that if you had a national minister and a village minister, and asked them both about the socioeconomic conditions under their jurisdiction, he bet that the village minister would give the more accurate answer every time. To try to rule entirely from the center of power, he suggested, is like groping in the dark. Second, he countered the argument that poor people's value equaled zero. He said that this number may be *close* to the truth, but is not the precise truth. In fact, every poor person represents a very small positive number *near* zero. By using that slightly different approximation, if millions of very small numbers are added together, they will amount to a very large number.

Finally, addressing his most vociferous critics, he added, "Let's be honest. I have not organized a poor man's organization, and neither have you. We're talking without experience. Let us go back to our campuses and actually organize poor people's organizations, and report back next year on what we found. That way, we can have a real discussion."

Yunus was working on the Tehbhaga tube well project at the time, and was thinking about what he could learn from its successes and shortcomings as he planned to establish a poor people's organization. One lesson was that government solutions, such as the sinking of the tube well, rarely worked by themselves. By donating expensive machinery, such as the irrigation pump, outright without asking for anything from the community in return, the government was sowing the seeds of underuse, mismanagement, and graft. Local problems needed to be solved by local people and by organizations in which they actively participated. Government, he felt, could play a supportive role and even be a catalyst, but it had to be recognized that the responsibility for success or failure ultimately rested solely with the local people. Any program failing to recognize this was doomed to end in disappointment.

Yunus and his university colleagues analyzed the success of the irrigation scheme and tried to apply these ideals about local participation. They concluded that while poor sharecroppers had, relatively speaking, gained the least from the program, it was their willingness to try something new that had turned the tide of opinion that had been running against the initial proposal. It was decided that future efforts spearheaded by the Rural Economics Program would try to take advantage of the unexpected eagerness of the poor to participate in community reform by ensuring that the bulk of the benefits accrued directly to them.

Yunus recalled a conversation with a woman in Jobra who complained that the recently completed Tehbhaga program had not helped her very much. In response, Yunus had asked whether she had got additional work. "Yes," the woman replied, "but only for two weeks." After the postharvest processing was complete, the farmers had half a year's worth of rice while the landless women had only gained a few days of backbreaking work at low wages. Yunus recalled how the laborers threshed the rice in the traditional manner, brushing the stalks with their feet until the individual grains came loose. The image of women fighting each morning for a shady place where they could perform this hard labor, for which they would receive only one kilogram of rice per day, was seared into his memory—a reminder that his program had brought disproportionate benefits to relatively prosperous farmers while creating grueling, low-wage work for the poor. Yunus was determined not to make the same mistake again.

Still, Yunus and his colleagues in the REP felt that Tehbhaga was an early success about which they could feel proud; indeed, many professors would take such an achievement and spend the next 10 years lecturing and writing about it. But Yunus wasn't that type of person. Instead, he began walking through Jobra and the nearby village of Fatehpur in search of the issue around which he could organize his next project. From the beginning, he felt he should try to again involve the bank that had underwritten the tube well. Otherwise, he had few concrete ideas of how it should look.

Progress in developing a new project was slow. On occasions when he wanted to talk with poor women in the Muslim *paras* (neighborhoods), he often had to conduct the dialogue with a bamboo wall separating him and the women to whom he was talking. The Muslim concept of *purdah* (literally, curtain or veil), the practice of keeping married women in a state of virtual seclusion from the outside world, was strictly observed in Chittagong at the time. When Yunus's or the women's voices could not carry through the fence, a female intermediary (usually a student in the Economics Department or a local schoolgirl) would run back and forth with messages.

After several weeks of talking with poor men and women, Yunus asked two students from the REP to conduct a survey in which families would be classified into five categories—those producing enough food for the entire year; for nine months; for six months; for one month; and finally, those living hand-to-mouth. Yunus then began a series of in-depth interviews with those who fell into the final group.

Yunus became intrigued when he saw many of the women in the poorest families making *mora* (finely woven bamboo stools). Because they lacked money, the women were forced to deal with *paikars* (middlemen) who sold them raw materials on credit and bought the stools for a pittance. The women's effective daily wage was 8 anna, or half a taka ($0.02). Yunus had several of his students find out how many people in the village were working under this type of arrangement. It turned out that there were 42 people who worked for roughly 2 pennies a day because they collectively lacked capital amounting to 856 taka ($27). Some needed only 10 or 20 taka, and the greatest amount any one person needed was 65 taka.

Yunus was flabbergasted. Years later, he would say that he "felt ashamed to be part of a society which could not make $27 available to 42 hard working, skilled human beings so that they could make a decent living." This lack of investment capital, he came to believe, was one of the root causes of the poverty that blighted rural Bangladesh.

In an effort to remedy this ghastly exploitation, Yunus quickly gave the stool-makers loans from his own pocket. Meanwhile, he approached the local bank manager and asked whether the bank could make loans to poor craftspeople. The professor explained how he had done so in Jobra, and argued that if a bank would agree to do it, it would represent a permanent solution to the problem of exploitation by village moneylenders.

Yunus was politely received, but his proposal was firmly rejected. He was told that if the poor wanted to borrow, they had to provide collateral. Moreover, the manager explained that the kinds of loans Yunus was talking about were so small they were hardly worth the paper on which the proposals would be written. The manager also asked who would write the proposals, since the people Yunus was talking about were illiterate.

Yunus tried his luck next with R. A. Howlader, a regional manager for Janata Bank who was based in the city of Chittagong. Howlader responded warmly to Yunus's proposal, but he saw obstacles to actually implementing it. Howlader told Yunus he could sanction the loans if every borrower could identify a wealthy person in the village to serve as a guarantor. Yunus knew that was unworkable—potential guarantors would exact a high price from the poor for helping them—but the proposal gave him an idea. Yunus suggested that *he* be the guarantor of *all* the loans. Howlader couldn't find a valid reason to reject the proposal and accepted it, provided that total loans advanced under this program would be initially limited to 10,000 taka, or around $300.

Yunus agreed, but added that if the people defaulted, Janata Bank would have to take him to court to get its money back. He said he'd be willing to accept any consequences the court imposed on him, including jail. Howlader laughed at that one. What bank, he asked Yunus, would want the negative public relations of bringing to court a professor who didn't take any money for himself, but gave it all to the poor? At meeting's end, Howlader simply wished Yunus success in his endeavor.

It took four months to work out the formalities with Janata Bank. The first loans were released in early January 1977, and as the borrowers received their precious taka, others began to come forward with their own ideas and proposals. Both men and women were eager to borrow. The project, at long last, had been launched.

AS THE FIRST LOANS WERE DISBURSED in Jobra, Vera was in her seventh month of pregnancy. In March, she gave birth to a girl. Yunus and Vera named their daughter Monica, one of the few names that was common for girls in both the United States and Bangladesh. But almost immediately after Monica's birth, the family became engulfed in a crisis.

Vera had been growing progressively unhappy after moving to Bangladesh. She felt isolated and bored, as the house the university provided Yunus was in a remote area surrounded by hills on all sides. She became a voracious reader, and tried to get out when she could, but her husband was first and foremost obsessed with his work. Immediately after Monica's birth, Vera insisted that they return to the United States. Bangladesh, she felt, was the wrong place to raise their child. To his dismay, Yunus discovered that his wife no longer shared his optimism for the country.

In July 1976, at Dhaka's old international airport, Vera and Monica boarded a flight bound for the United States. Yunus would never emigrate as his wife had hoped he would. Ultimately, they divorced. Yunus was able to see his daughter only sporadically over the next 20 years, always in the United States.

As destiny would have it, Monica Yunus and Grameen Bank were born within three months of each other. One would have only intermittent contact with Muhammad Yunus over the next two decades, while the other would receive his constant attention. In his quiet moments, Yunus longed to be able to nurture both of his creations. He had to wait a long time in order to realize that vision, as it was only in the 1990s that he began to develop a strong bond with Monica, who was by then an adult.

AS THE DATE FOR HIS FIRST loan disbursement came and went, Yunus decided that the safest way to ensure timely repayment of the loans was to mandate repayment on a daily basis. For the first months of 1977, loans were made individually and installments were collected by a shopkeeper who sold *paan* (spiced nuts wrapped in betel leaf) at a central point in the village. After a time, it was decided that weekly repayments were more practical for borrowers whose businesses did not yield daily income. Continuing to rely on one shopkeeper to collect payments proved unworkable and Yunus decided that there would be regular, weekly meetings during which installments would be collected.

Over time, all the daily installments were converted into weekly repayments, and everyone was required to come to the meetings. Yet there was little continuity and discipline at these gatherings. One borrower would come to the meeting place, drop off their installment, and rush off before the next person came.

Later in 1977, Yunus decided to organize groups of borrowers according to the purposes for which they took out their loans. Consequently, there were "cow groups," "rickshaw groups," "puffed rice groups," and so on. These so-called activity groups began meeting separately, on particular days, to make their payments. But groups made up of people taking loans for the most popular activities started becoming unwieldy as their numbers grew, while others remained stuck at two and three members. Moreover, there was no force bonding these groups together; rickshaw owners, for example, competed fiercely on the streets, and this sometimes spilled over into tension at the meetings. Yunus finally decided that groups would be limited to between 5 and 10 members who selected one another based on their affinity for and trust in each other.

As he moved from an individual- to a group-based lending strategy, Yunus felt that he had an opportunity to demonstrate how a cooperative organization could be successfully run. Since his return from the United States, he had been a leading critic of Bangladesh's cooperative movement, and particularly of cooperatives run by the government. He believed that one of the principal reasons for their failure was that they were too large. Yunus's 5- to 10-member groups were far more manageable than cooperatives that might have dozens or even hundreds of members. The larger the number of members, he believed, the less likely it was that the poor would participate in any meaningful way and that the money would be handled with integrity. In such village organizations, domination by the elites was virtually inevitable.

Some cooperatives required members to save money that could be mobilized for investment. Yunus liked this idea in principle and wanted to adopt it in his new program in some form, but he feared that if the savings requirement was too large, poorer borrowers would be unable to participate. Ultimately, each group was asked to identify the person for whom weekly savings would be the biggest hardship. Whatever that person was able to save would be the amount everyone in the center would contribute into their respective group's fund. In most cases, the amount was set at one taka, though in a few cases it was 25 or 50 poysha (100 poysha is equal to 1 taka.) Later on, Yunus became frustrated with the slow growth in savings and wanted to link it to the size of the loans people were receiving. With that in mind, a group tax of 5 percent of the loan amount was charged at the time of disbursement. This was also deposited in the group fund, from which loans could be taken by individual members of the group, provided that all members agreed.

In explaining to borrowers the rationale for the group tax, Yunus likened it to the traditional practice of *mushti chaal* (literally, "a handful of rice"), in which a mother puts aside a small amount of rice every night to build up stock for a rainy day. By her putting it away a little at a time, the rice is not missed, but as it accumulates it provides a cushion against future food shortages and famines.

In the months following the first disbursement of loans, the repayment rate was perfect, and the male rickshaw pullers who plied the roads from the university gate to the classrooms became the proud standard-bearers of the new project. In time, they began putting signs on the rear of their rickshaws that identified them as part of the project and had the words *maleek-chalok* (owner-driver) prominently displayed. Many of the borrowers had spent years renting the rickshaws they peddled in exchange for a daily fee. Even though the total amount a puller would pay the owner over the years could easily surpass the value of 10 rickshaws, the puller could barely dream of ever owning a single rickshaw for lack of the investment capital to purchase one. Loans from the project changed all that.

As 1977 progressed, meetings were held regularly and were well attended, and new loan proposals were coming in at an accelerating rate. Unfortunately, it turned out that Janata Bank, whose local staff members were far from enthusiastic about administering the project, became a significant bottleneck. Each proposal, no matter how small, had to be sent to Dhaka for approval, where it had to compete for the attention of bank officials who were also dealing with loans that were thousands of times larger. During all of 1977, only 65 people were able to access credit, and hundreds of others to whom Yunus had promised loans were becoming restless. He needed to find a more flexible sponsor.

In April 1977, Yunus paid a courtesy call to A. M. Anisuzzaman, a senior civil servant and the managing director of Bangladesh Krishi (Agriculture) Bank, in his office in Dhaka. The professor had planned on briefing his host about the progress of his project, but instead found himself on the receiving end of a long monologue about how useless academics were because they never had ideas that were of any practical value. Yunus countered that he *did* have a practical proposal.

Yunus argued that the entire concept of a Krishi Bank was wrong, since many of the people in rural areas, particularly the landless, were not involved in agriculture, or at least not the whole year round. Krishi Bank should strive to be a rural bank or village bank (in Bengali, *grameen* bank) that would make loans for *all* of the productive activities in which villagers were involved, not just for agriculture.

Yunus spelled out his plan. Krishi Bank would put an entire branch at his disposal, a branch where he would make the rules, deciding who borrows and on what terms. If he demonstrated that lending to the poor was viable, Krishi Bank could replicate the program in other areas, and ultimately rename itself as Grameen Bank. To test out this idea on a practical level, Yunus's branch would be called the *Poreekkhamulok Grameen Shakha* (Experimental Rural Branch) of Bangladesh Krishi Bank. Despite the boldness of Yunus's idea, the managing director was receptive and told Yunus that when he returned home, he would tell his top man in Chittagong to meet Yunus to work out the details.

And indeed, the regional manager appeared at Yunus's office the next day. The two drafted a proposal and sent it to Dhaka, where Anisuzzaman was having problems selling the idea of an experimental branch under the direction of an outsider to his colleagues and to the government-appointed directors of the bank. He began looking for some way that would allow him to follow through on his commitment to Yunus. It was finally decided that Yunus would be given an office that would technically be a minibranch, or outpost, formally under control of the Krishi Bank branch in the city of Chittagong, but in practice enjoying a high degree of independence.

As these negotiations proceeded, operations continued, albeit at a snail's pace, with Janata Bank. Frustration set in among prospective borrowers and the people who administered the project—mostly young villagers with a little bit of education who received a small stipend from Yunus, and a few university students. Yunus was not allowed to delegate anything or stray from many of the bureaucratic rules that governed Janata's operations. When, for instance, Yunus spent three months at the end of 1977 in the United States as part of the Bangladesh delegation to the United Nations General Assembly, he was forced to make arrangements for individual loan proposals to be sent to him in New York, where he would sign them in his hotel room and hurriedly send them back to Chittagong by airmail.

In April 1978, the minibranch office under Krishi Bank was opened. Yunus received an appointment letter as project director, and Assad, the project coordinator of the Tehbhaga initiative, was named to that position again. Nurjahan Begum and Jannat-i-Quanine, two unemployed female students who had recently completed their master's degrees, were given jobs as bank workers. Within two months, more loans were made under this format than had been made during 15 months with Janata Bank. By September 1978, credit had been extended to 398 people, amounting to almost half a million taka (equivalent to $12,500).

As the project grew, Yunus was forced to formalize its regulations and set up a staff training program. He and his team quickly drew up a *bidhimala* (constitution) that finally laid down a set of uniform written rules, which included several of the innovations that had emerged in the project's second year. The most important idea was that the groups should federate into centers. These centers, in turn, should select a "center chief" from among the group chairpersons. Then, the centers would federate into a village association of the landless. If the other social groupings, such as the landowners, youth, and so on, could be organized into their own village associations, the foundation for Yunus's *gram sorkar* would be laid. Since the major argument against *gram sorkar* was related to the difficulties his colleagues had seen in forming an organization of the poor, Yunus theorized that if he could scale that hurdle through his lending program, the case for *gram sorkar* would be considerably stronger. It turned out that the idea of a village association of the poor was unwieldy, and it was later dropped.

The *bidhimala* also incorporated a rigorous definition of who was poor and thus eligible to join a group. On several occasions, Yunus had met borrowers who had been allowed to join a group despite being fairly prosperous. The professor soon recognized that a villager might seem to one staff member to be poor or landless, while clearly being outside that group in the eyes of someone else associated with the program. In a few cases, families that were clearly poor had been excluded because they owned a few hundredths of an acre of land; in others, a wealthy merchant who had given up farming was included when he claimed to be landless.

In an effort to rectify this inequity, a more flexible formula was agreed upon and included in the *bidhimala*. To join a group, a person's household had to be "functionally landless," which was defined as cultivating less than one *kani* of land. One *kani*, a common measure in Chittagong, amounted to four-tenths of an acre. If someone owned a plot but had leased it out, or was sharecropping some land, it was not counted in the total. Conversely, if someone had leased and was cultivating land owned by another household, it was counted in the total. Also, to be eligible, the value of a household's total assets (including its farmland) could not exceed the value of one acre of medium-quality land. This definition of who was landless poor remains essentially intact to this day.

By the end of 1978, Yunus felt confident that his mechanism for ensuring the recovery of his loans was working. Peer support and peer pressure had replaced traditional collateral requirements. In his mind, the poor had demonstrated that they were creditworthy and also that reducing hard-core poverty was feasible. Still, there were problems. Recruiting women, who formed their own women's associations after some initial experiments with mixing men and women in the same groups and centers, proved difficult. Yunus's original goal was to keep the number of female borrowers at least equal to that of male borrowers. Yet women constituted barely one-quarter of the project's membership by September 1978. During the third year, some problems with repayment and with borrowers dropping out of the program began to surface.

Yet visitors from Dhaka rarely got deeply enough into the project to see its weaknesses. In a country conditioned to failure, they latched on to the dramatic effect the loans were having on many borrowers. Jowshan ara Rahman of the United Nations Children's Fund visited in 1979 and wrote about her experience in UNICEF's national journal *Shishu Diganta* (Children's Horizons). She described the plight of Zorina Begum, a beggar woman thrice deserted by husbands:

> [Zorina] came to know about the bank loan. Initially, she was afraid to even think about taking a loan. . . . [Overcoming her fears, Zorina] took a loan of 250 taka [$6]. She invested the money in trading grocery goods in the neighborhood. She paid off the entire loan in weekly installments. She did not have any problem. As soon as the first loan was repaid, she took a second loan. This time she was bold. She borrowed 1,000 taka [$25]. Now she is an independent businesswoman. . . .
>
> Zorina now finds no problem feeding all the mouths [in her family]. She has repaired the roof of her hut. She is dreaming of a new life for herself, her children, and her grandchildren. . . .[20]

In 1978, as the project neared the completion of its second year, Bangladesh Bank, the nation's central bank, held a seminar on "Financing the Rural Poor" that was funded and dominated by bureaucrats, academics, and consultants connected with the Agency for International Development (AID), the semi-autonomous arm of the U.S. State Department responsible for disbursing American foreign aid. Anticipating a hostile reaction to a presentation about his pilot project, Yunus decided to write and deliver a two-page paper about the Experimental Grameen Branch, to be followed by nearly 15 pages of tables and charts detailing how much money had been taken out and paid back, who had taken it out, and for what purposes. He ended his presentation by asking those in attendance to "tell me what our experience means."

The audience was skeptical. Several people expressed the belief that the project's impressive-looking statistics were the result of a onetime miracle that was dependent on the charisma of a well-respected local university professor. The obvious implication was that it could not be repeated anywhere else. Other participants argued on more technical grounds. Some felt that the project should be run as a business, and for it to be profitable, Yunus would have to charge a higher interest rate than 13 percent. The consensus was that 36 percent—the rate being charged by the AID-funded Experimental Rural Finance Project—would be the right amount. Such a high rate, it was argued, would cover the greater risks that were thought to be associated with lending to the landless. It would force poor people, who were assumed to be reckless, to think twice before proposing to take out a loan. And it would be near the market rate—that is, the rate that would generate income sufficient to cover the costs of administering the project.

In reply, Yunus said he believed that his program could cover its costs while charging the same interest rate levied by the government banks when lending to established businesses, which at the time was 13 percent. The main thing, Yunus argued, was the *recovery* rate, not the *interest* rate. The corruption-plagued government banks were known to have repayment rates in the range of 40 to 60 percent. The Industrial Bank, serving the nation's elite, had a *default* rate in excess of 85 percent. If a program charged negative 5 percent interest, and actually got *repaid* 95 taka for every 100 taka it lent, it would be doing far better than any real or hypothetical bank that charged 36 percent interest but failed to get back even half the principal of its loans.

At the end of the day, Yunus was challenged by a banker to demonstrate that his methodology could work over an entire district—a challenge that he accepted on the spot. Yet there was the question of who would provide him with the resources necessary to do the work.

As luck would have it, one person who listened sympathetically to the debate was in a position to let Yunus try his hand at transforming his small project into a much more serious enterprise. Toward the end of the seminar, Yunus was invited to meet with A. K. M. Gangopadaya, the deputy governor of Bangladesh Bank and a widely admired figure in financial circles.

Gangopadaya was impressed with Yunus and promised to bring up the subject of expanding his project at an upcoming meeting with the managing directors of the so-called nationalized commercial banks. When that meeting was held, Yunus argued that he had demonstrated that the poor could borrow, invest, and repay better than the wealthy, and hoped that the banks would take it from there, freeing him to return to teaching full-time.

The bankers were skeptical. One participant said he would support the expansion of the project if Yunus resigned from the university and if it were carried out in a district other than Chittagong. Yunus countered that he would be willing to take leave from the university for two years, as long as the bankers agreed that if the project succeeded, he could return to teaching and the Bangladesh Bank would then expand the program elsewhere. He readily agreed to conduct this two-year experiment in any district they chose. The meeting ended inconclusively, but Gangopadaya was slowly softening his people up.

When the issue was discussed at a Bangladesh Bank board meeting, Mafazul Huq, a former minister of the central government of Pakistan, spoke up in support of the idea and suggested that the board members take a field trip to Jobra to visit the project. Huq was something of an anomaly in government circles; long a champion of cooperatives and agricultural development programs, he always came to Bangladesh Bank meetings dressed in a traditional *longhi*. (This would be a bit like the U.S. secretary of agriculture coming to cabinet meetings in overalls.) He claimed to be an authentic rural Bangladeshi farmer, and looked forward to the excursion to Jobra as an opportunity to entertain his colleagues at his ancestral home in Mirsharai district, north of Chittagong. With Huq's support, the trip was arranged for December 1978.

Several board members, joined by the managing directors of Janata, Krishi, and Sonali banks, made the trip to Jobra. During a discussion held at Yunus's residence after a tour of the villages, the managing director of Sonali Bank suggested Yunus open an experimental branch in a nearby subdistrict. The managing director of Janata Bank, feeling that his bank had started the project but was now out of the picture, expressed interest in getting involved again. And Anisuzzaman said that Krishi Bank was keen on expanding its existing collaborative operation with Yunus's program.

But the Bangladesh Bank took the lead and Gangopadaya began formalizing the role it would play in the project's expansion. He approved a budget of 1.3 million taka for expanding the project, just a quarter of what Yunus asked for. But it was enough to get started. The site of the project was identified—the troubled district of Tangail, some 70 miles north of Dhaka. On June 8, 1979, Yunus, Assad, and Dipal officially began work for Bangladesh Bank.

After completing some formalities in Dhaka, the three men moved to Tangail. Yunus found office space and began discussing with local officials how many project offices there would be and where they would be located. It was finally agreed that there would be 19. Negotiations often got bogged down, since so many institutions were involved in the project. Bangladesh Bank provided the funds for the head office, while six banks, including Janata, Krishi, and Sonali, each agreed to host three project offices, and another bank agreed to house one. Later, a United Nations agency got involved and further complicated matters. Something as trivial as the way the head office's signboard was written—"Grameen Bank Prakalpa: A Project of Bangladesh Bank" or "Bangladesh Bank: Grameen Bank Prakalpa"—stirred people up.

It was decided that Yunus's star pupils would be project officers responsible for overseeing the day-to-day operations of the project; Dipal was responsible for nine offices, Assad the remaining 10. Yunus asked Sheikh Abdud Daiyan, a young statistician, to come on board as a research officer. To give Daiyan some field experience, he was given the additional responsibility of supervising one of Assad's project offices. Nurjahan, later to become Assad's wife, and Jannat turned over their responsibilities in Jobra and joined the group in Tangail. Yunus assigned them responsibilities for designing a series of social development workshops for female borrowers, and their salaries were paid by UNICEF rather than by Bangladesh Bank.

Before the project could get going, several issues needed to be resolved. The first issue was to recruit and train staff for the 19 project offices. In Bangladesh, the process of hiring is usually done to ensure that the power, stature, and financial position of the recruiter is enhanced. Jobs often go to relatives of the ultimate decision maker, sometimes in exchange for some sort of social obligation, such as marrying someone's daughter or sister. In other instances, the job goes to the person who pays the largest bribe. The suitability of someone for a particular post is, at best, a secondary consideration. It is even rarer for a person, once hired, to be expected to do much work. Practical training is provided only in exceptional cases. Yunus, however, was committed to selecting employees on the basis of their qualifications. The recruitment process was designed to be simple and free of bribes.

By the beginning of October, Yunus began hiring the young men and women who would be his first field managers and bank workers. To be selected, applicants, who usually responded to advertisements in newspapers, needed to have scored reasonably well on their high school level exams. In addition to these qualifications, prospective field managers needed to have a university degree and not raise any red flags during a brief interview and written examination. Salaries were set at 500 taka ($12.50) per month for bank workers and 1,200 taka ($30) for field managers.

Several staff members were recruited in unusual ways. Abdul Mannan Talukdar, who years later would raise a banner over his local Grameen office shortly after the surprise announcement of Grameen Bank's Nobel Peace Prize, was a frequent companion of Yunus's in a tea stall near his office in Tangail. The project director would occasionally hear this robust young man with long, curly black hair spinning stories of how he helped win the country's liberation as a freedom fighter. Yunus asked Mannan one day what he was doing with himself during the rare moments when he was not in the tea stall. It turned out that he was managing a sawmill owned by some of his relatives and earning 150 taka per month for his efforts. Yunus suggested that he apply for work with the Grameen Bank Project, where he could earn 500 taka per month. Within a few weeks, Mannan applied for the position of bank worker and was appointed to a GBP office in the Narandia bazaar. Among Mannan's colleagues, there was a high school graduate who until recently had been plying a rickshaw on the streets of Tangail.

In another instance, dozens of interviews had been scheduled on a day that a transport strike had been called. Sitting in his office on that quiet day, Yunus was stunned to meet a young woman named Asma Siddika, who had walked 21 miles in the scorching heat to make sure she arrived at her appointed time. Yunus told her no interview was necessary; she was given a job on the spot.

The new staff members were given some instruction on a slightly revised *bidhimala*—the numbers of borrowers in each group was, for example, set at five rather than allowed to vary between 5 and 10—and were told to come to Tangail once a week for a free-flowing training seminar at which the project director would preside. During these sessions, the staff were sometimes comfortable enough to ask the most sensitive questions, such as—Why didn't I have to give a bribe to get this job? Am I really expected to work hard? Why are the local bank staff members with whom I am supposed to work so hostile? Since this work is temporary, should I keep looking for a permanent job? By March 1980, 49 staff members had been hired and 15 of the 19 planned project offices had been opened.

Another issue facing Yunus was the intransigence of the local bureaucrats. When Yunus arrived, there was immediate confusion over his rank. Bangladesh Bank referred to him as the project director, which was not very helpful. Nobody could find mention in government manuals of where a *project director* fit into the rigid hierarchy of the Bangladeshi civil service.

In Bangladesh, before people want to know anything about a new colleague's assignment or ability, they usually want to know his rank. For Bengali bureaucrats, talking to someone without knowing whether he is junior or senior to you can be a disorienting experience. No one was sure whether Yunus should have to call on the local bank and government officials or whether they should go to him. Yunus decided to break the tension by paying courtesy calls on all the relevant officials. When he described what the GBP was trying to do, and failed to even attempt to pull rank on them, all that registered in their minds was how they could use the program to expand their influence. Within weeks, requests began coming from various local bureaucrats, by way of their PAs (their personal assistants, or male secretaries), asking Yunus to sit on this or that committee or to set up a branch in a particular village. Yunus, busy with his work, rejected most of the invitations as soon as he realized that the bureaucrats' sole purpose in extending them was to show off that the new project director was at their beck and call. As a result, Yunus was frequently interrupted by hostile phone calls from the PAs of bureaucrats throughout Tangail throughout the early months of the project.

In one case, Abur Rahman, one of President Zia's ministers whose home district happened to be Tangail, stormed into the GBP office with a considerable entourage and began shouting at Yunus for not having hired a boy he had recommended for employment in the project. The project director kept his cool, politely asking his enraged guest to have a seat and join him for tea. Surprised by the reaction, Rahman stormed out as quickly as he had come in, saying, "I have not come here to talk with you. I have come here to find out who it is that is willing to defy me!"

Recruiting staff and dealing with people like Abur Rahman were time-consuming and often tedious. But figuring out what to do about the campaign of terror being carried out by the violent left-wing group called the *Gonobahini* (People's Army) was probably Yunus's most pressing concern.

By the time of Yunus's arrival in Tangail, most wealthy families with large tracts of land in the rural areas had fled to the city for fear of their lives. Rarely did a day pass when the professor and his students were not confronted by dead bodies strung from trees or lying in the gutter, the latest victims of the People's Army terror campaign. For a brief period, Yunus considered calling off the entire project for fear for his staff's safety.

Frantically, Yunus tried to make contacts with people reported to have ties with the *Gonobahini;* his intermediaries were usually recently graduated students who had been involved with radical politics at the university level. On a few occasions, they assured Yunus that he and his staff were not at risk. But Yunus had no way of knowing how close these young men were to the terrorists or whether they were telling him the truth. He nonetheless forged ahead and recommended that everyone be cautious and keep a low profile.

By the time the project entered its second year in Tangail, Yunus had learned that several members of the *Gonobahini* had actually joined the project as staff members. On a few occasions, Yunus was startled to see his employees toting machine guns under their shawls when he paid unannounced visits to project offices. In one instance, he confronted an armed bank worker and ordered him to put his weapon away. The young man resisted, saying defiantly that he was a *mukti judda* (freedom fighter). Yunus responded firmly, saying that the War of Liberation was over, and that now it was time for the liberators to work for a living and build up their country.

At one branch, this volatile mix of politics, action-research, and guns boiled over. The local Krishi Bank manager, like many of his colleagues, was annoyed at having to take on additional responsibilities related to serving the GBP without an increase in salary or bribes. As a result, he continually tried to humiliate Yunus's local staff. One evening, as the manager was returning home, he was ambushed by the local field manager and a bank worker. They pinned him to the ground, nearly suffocating him as one gun was pressed against his throat and the barrel of another pointed at his chest. Before they let

him go, the bank manager was forced to promise that he would treat the GBP
staff with more respect.

Despite Yunus's ministrations, the manager, fearing another encounter
with the GBP staff, left his branch. Yunus quickly fired the bank worker and
demoted the field manager, who subsequently quit. But the damage had been
done. Rumors circulated among the government staff in Tangail about GBP
workers being terrorists. Relations with Krishi Bank, historically the most
cooperative of the banks with which GBP worked, took many months to
recover.

AMID ALL THE COMMOTION, the work of forming groups and disbursing
loans was progressing well. Yunus spent most of his days moving from branch
to branch, sitting in on center meetings and group training sessions or simply
talking to borrowers in their homes. When his staff learned of his personal
sacrifices—eating in a communal kitchen, living alone in a dingy apartment,
forgoing a pay increase—many became even more motivated to put in the long
hours needed to ensure that the project worked.

The diversity of skills that the poor could capitalize with loans from GBP
impressed Yunus and his staff. There were the weavers of Deojan Delduar, the
confectionery makers of Rokkhitbelta, the puffed rice fryers of Narandia, and
the mustard oil crushers of Ghatail. More than ever, he was becoming
confident that the approach worked. The effects on people's lives were often
dramatic. One memorable example was the *dakat* ("bandit") who was known to
have killed several people and who had escaped death by evading angry mobs
on several occasions. Unexpectedly, he began petitioning his local branch
manager, Dulal Chandra Kor, to allow him to form a GBP group so that he
could borrow. "What am I supposed to do?" Dulal asked Yunus. "If I don't let
him in, he may kill me; if I let him in he will certainly default, as no bank worker
will have the courage to demand payment from him. And then people will
think Grameen Bank is a bunch of *dakats*." Dulal, a hulking young man with
curly hair and an infectious smile, had spent his first night at his branch
sleeping on a primitive bed he had retrieved out of a pond. Yunus considered
him among the more promising new managers, and had entrusted him with
training many new managerial recruits. With Yunus's help, he had

transformed the local political boss from an enemy into an ally. But in the case of the *dakat*, Dulal thought he had met his match.

Against the advice of his staff, Yunus suggested allowing the *dakat* to form a center, agreeing to take full responsibility if he defaulted. Dulal agreed to go along. The *dakat* quickly formed a group and a center and became a strong center chief, and for many years was among the most successful borrowers in his area. By the time Dulal was transferred, the *dakat* had become very religious, wearing a beard and Muslim dress everywhere he went. There was talk of the village pooling its resources to allow him to perform hajj by making a pilgrimage to Mecca during the festival of Eid-ul-Azha.

Years later, the *dakat*'s past caught up with him, and he was imprisoned for crimes committed before his conversion. But he repaid his Grameen Bank loan in full, sending his final installments from his jail cell.

Despite the project's successes, there were concerns about how much it was costing to run. Sonali Bank started claiming in 1981 that its new Sonali Bank—Krishi Shakha (SBSK)—was accomplishing the same objectives as the Grameen Bank Project at considerably lower cost. This was at a time that Yunus was petitioning the bankers to allow him to expand to three new districts so he could prove that the program could thrive without his close supervision. Field trips to Ghatail, where Grameen Bank and Sonali Bank were operating side by side, were arranged for senior people in the banking community. The trip was a success for Sonali Bank; the senior banking officials who visited were suitably impressed. The GBP branch there was under instructions to not match the elaborate tour that was arranged by its rival.

Yunus was concerned. The statistics provided by Sonali Bank, if true, made a strong case for the expansion of the competing program instead of his own. He soon discovered, however, that someone in the SBKS branch in Ghatail was cooking the books. The manager was transferred, but Sonali Bank argued that other branches were performing well. After this embarrassment, however, people no longer made the argument that SBKS was superior to GBP. This helped pave the way for the expansion of the project in 1982 to the districts of Dhaka, Rangpur, and Patuakhali.

While he was working to establish his ideas at the local level, Yunus continued to be involved with national political figures. He had a warmer and more complex relationship with President Zia Ur Rahman than he'd had with Sheikh Mujib. The two had first come into contact in 1977 when Yunus received the President's Award on behalf of the Tehbhaga Khamar project. On several occasions, Zia called on Yunus as a representative of the younger generation of academics to speak out on subjects ranging from the wisdom of conducting state planning on two-year cycles (rather than the traditional five) to the proposal for beginning to transmit television signals in color instead of black and white. Yunus usually argued the minority view while the other side carried the day, but important people in government circles noticed his ability as a debater.

By 1978, Zia was trying to institutionalize his regime by creating the Bangladesh Nationalist Party (BNP). In April 1978, soon after Krishi Bank had opened the experimental Grameen branch run by Yunus, a close political adviser to Zia called the professor to Dhaka to meet with the president. The discussions were supposed to be about *gram sorkar*, which at the time was the subject of vigorous debate. But the conversation soon turned to politics. Yunus was invited to continue his development work, but instead of doing it while based at Chittagong University, he would become a salaried employee of the BNP. It was implied that were he to join the party, he would be made a minister in due time. Yunus resisted the offer, but when the president asked Yunus to join him on an upcoming field trip to the drought-ravaged district of Pabna, he agreed to go.

Zia will be remembered, if for nothing else, as being one of the most energetic leaders of modern times. When he went on his frequent visits to the rural areas, he would insist on traveling by foot, marking his path through the villages on maps provided by the military. He wanted to be close to his countrymen. In addition, he refused to accept any fancy meals. Plain rice, simple *dal* (lentils), and a modest portion of either fish or chicken (but never both) were the most he or anyone in his party would accept.

On that hot Friday in April, Yunus followed Zia and his entourage for seven miles. On two occasions, he listened to the president's speeches, and both times Zia made sure that Yunus was sitting next to him when he delivered his remarks. After the second speech, Zia and the people traveling with him stopped for lunch. After he finished eating, he began his daily half hour afternoon rest that his doctor insisted on. Soon after Yunus left Zia so that he could unwind, presidential assistants came running in search of him. He was told that the president wanted to speak to him. When Yunus, still drenched with sweat from the walking, entered the room where Zia was resting, he was ushered into a chair by the president's bedside. Zia looked up at his guest and said, "So, what did you think?"

Taken aback, Yunus innocently asked, "About what?"

"About my speech."

Measuring his words carefully, Yunus said: "Well, I think people were very inspired to hear from you." He paused, and then continued:

> But there is one thing I would have changed. You see, people are talking about how bad this drought is, but I saw a lot of water in the river we passed over in the helicopter. If some of that water was diverted to the fields by canals or even lifted by hand, then we would be seeing some green fields instead of brown ones. And that's something people can do right now.
>
> What I'm trying to say, Mr. President, is that in your speech you kept telling people what you are going to do for them. I think it would be much more useful if you talked about what they could do for themselves.

BY 1983, YUNUS'S MAIN PREOCCUPATION was addressing concerns from his staff that were forcing some to leave. The issues included low pay, lack of job security, and the abuse they continued to suffer at the hands of the government bank employees with whom they were forced to work. It was time to find a permanent solution that would address these problems while at the same time allowing for expansion.

Yunus asked Gangopadaya and the managing directors of the banks participating in the project to consider a proposal that would transform Grameen Bank into an independent financial institution specializing in bringing banking services to the poor. This new institution, he boldly proposed, would be *owned* by the poor people who borrowed from it. As Yunus would recall years later, "The assembled bankers spoke in one voice against the absurdity of the idea." Yunus looked for allies and began discussing various organizational structures for his proposed Grameen Bank.

Yunus's investigations were interrupted by another change of government in Dhaka. General Hossain Muhammad Ershad, the army chief of staff, staged a coup d'etat and declared martial law. Ershad named M. A. Muhith, a participant in the bank's reorganization discussions, as finance minister. Yunus knew Muhith from his days running the Bangladesh Information Center in Washington in 1971, when he had been one of the most openly pro-Bengali Pakistani embassy officials. When Yunus pressed his case to Muhith, he found the new minister receptive but unable to build any support in the banking community for the proposal to create an independent Grameen Bank. Muhith decided to directly approach Ershad, who threw his support behind the idea and ordered Muhith to draft an ordinance that would establish Grameen as an independent bank. Kamal Hossain, a onetime Awami League presidential candidate and a leading legal scholar, recommended that Yunus and Muhith propose that the government own a 40 percent share in Grameen Bank. Such an institution, Hossain argued, would be more palatable than one completely owned by the borrowers. Hossain and Yunus finalized the text of the proposed ordinance.

The ordinance was issued by Ershad on September 30, 1983, and became effective on October 2. To Yunus's surprise, however, the ownership provisions had been reversed in the final document. The government's share was set at 60 percent instead of 40. Yunus was furious at first, but when he calmed down, he asked Muhith whether, at some later date, the borrowers would be allowed to buy up the government's shares. Muhith said he thought it would be possible. (This did, in fact, occur—that is, over the next decade, the government's share was gradually diluted to less than 10 percent.) The disagreement did not prevent a joyous celebration at the formal launching of the Grameen Bank as an independent financial institution at Jamurki branch in Tangail, at which both Yunus and Muhith spoke.[21]

Upon achieving independence, some Grameen Bank Project employees were faced with the choice of staying with the participating government bank that they officially worked for or joining the fledgling Grameen Bank. For many, this was a difficult decision, as there were still fears that a change in government or substantial loan losses could lead to the dissolution of this new entity. Others were attracted by the bribes and other benefits (such as pensions) that government bank employees received. In the end, most threw in their lot with Yunus, though one notable exception was Assad, the original Jobra project coordinator. One day, Assad came into the director's office and handed him a letter stating that he was not going to join Grameen Bank. Although surprised and taken aback, Yunus accepted the letter, without any discussion. In later years, some of his colleagues would blame the managing director for failing to talk such a gifted leader as Assad out of leaving. But that wasn't his style. Had Assad come to talk, his mentor would have been more than willing; but Assad's coming to him with a letter in hand signaled to Yunus that he had already made his decision.

By the end of 1983, the long process of transferring all the accounts and loan ledgers over to the new Grameen Bank was nearing an end. The ranks of the borrowers had swelled to nearly 100,000 across five districts, and the number of staff members was nearing 1,000. In a small country that was at that time home to 80 million poor people, ruled by a military dictator, and repeatedly thrashed by tornadoes, floods, and droughts, this was a modest beginning. Still, there was no denying that Yunus, based in the Dhaka suburb of Shyamoli by this time, had already beaten long odds.

Update: Since the 1990s

YUNUS'S EARLY EXPERIENCE IN AGRICULTURE through Tehbhaha opened doors later on. During the first half of the 1990s, some enlightened Bangladeshi bureaucrats decided to divest the government of hundreds of irrigation tube wells and fish ponds in the northern part of the country. Seeing the idealism, work ethic, and incorruptibility of Yunus and his team, they decided to transfer these potentially productive assets to Grameen. This led to the establishment of two nonprofit companies—Grameen Krishi (Agriculture) Foundation (GKF) and Grameen Motscho (Fisheries) Foundation (GMF).

After some early successes, GKF suffered a series of setbacks because of mismanagement, while GMF did reasonably well. In both cases, Grameen applied its development philosophy, trained workforce, nationwide reputation, and infrastructure to turn an underused resource into something that could benefit the poor and the nation. These early efforts pointed to the potential of a Yunus-initiated family of for-profit and nonprofit companies carrying the Grameen brand that continued to grow through the 2000s.

Perhaps the best-known member of the family, besides Grameen Bank itself, is GrameenPhone. In March 1997, GrameenPhone and its nonprofit sister organization, Grameen Telecom, were launched in Bangladesh. A bold alliance with the Norwegian company Telenor, GrameenPhone sought to be a profitable mobile phone company in one of the poorest countries in the world—one where, as of 1997, there were only 400,000 landline phones, of which perhaps 300,000 were working on any given day. It was to be a telecom with a twist—an estimated 50,000 Grameen Bank borrowers would be set up with mobile pay phones, financed by a Grameen loan.

The entire initiative was met by skepticism and faced major uncertainties, and it was hobbled when the Bangladesh government blocked interconnection with its fixed line network and put up other roadblocks to success. A never-before-tried approach was adopted as a last-ditch effort to save the company from collapse—potential subscribers were offered an attractive rate to buy phones that would reach only other mobile phones. This strategy worked brilliantly, and today GrameenPhone is the largest and most profitable company of any kind in Bangladesh and is the country's biggest taxpayer. By the mid-2000s, it had more than 10 million subscribers. It remains highly successful and profitable as of 2022.

The village phone strategy, whereby Grameen Bank staff identified borrowers who could be the first to buy a mobile phone with a Grameen loan and set up a pay phone for people in their villages, exceeded all expectations. In fact, it became a model for microentrepreneurial empowerment strategies worldwide, confirming the thesis of C. K. Prahalad that there was a fortune to be made at the bottom of the economic pyramid if business models could be rethought. Ultimately, more than 300,000 Grameen members (more than six times the number originally projected) set up profitable pay phone businesses. At one point, these women had 4 percent of the company's phones but used 17 percent of the airtime—demonstrating the power of so-called shared-use approaches to bringing technology to the world's poor. Borrowers allowed local people who could not afford a phone of their own access for a few minutes a day to check market prices or otherwise advance their business, or to deal with personal or family situations. Grameen Telecom bought airtime in bulk at a wholesale rate from GrameenPhone, marked it up slightly, and then sold it to the village phone operators at a price well below the going rate in Bangladesh. The women pay phone operators earned profits of $2 to $3 per day, and in some cases many times more than that. Over time, many of their customers got their own phones, but in the meantime, the operators had a thriving business that gave them a surplus to invest in other income-generating ventures.

A few years later, Grameen Foundation, in alliance with MTN (Africa's largest telecom), Nokia, and Qualcomm, and with the support of Grameen Telecom, brought this strategy to Uganda, Rwanda, Cameroon, the Philippines, Indonesia, and Haiti. GF's technology program was launched with a grant from the Craig and Susan McCaw Foundation and has been supported by Yunus, who attended a news conference that formally launched it. The program was ably led for its first decade by Peter Bladin, a retired Microsoft executive who did a tremendous job attracting staff and volunteers from among those who made fortunes in the technology sector in the 1990s and wanted to start second careers focused on solving the problem of poverty. Later, the center was fully integrated into Grameen Foundation, which focused largely on using mobile technology to empower the poor from 2010 onwards.

A key element of the success of GrameenPhone is that it leveraged the Grameen brand, which was widely known and respected in Bangladesh long before the Nobel Peace Prize was awarded to it. Grameen Telecom's success was likewise based on its leveraging the extensive infrastructure of Grameen Bank. The bank had thousands of staff throughout the country that had earned the trust of the poor over years, even decades. They had enough credibility to explain this high-potential business opportunity to people who had never made or received a phone call in their lives. Furthermore, a Grameen loan officer could finance the phones and allow the borrowers to pay their monthly bills (based on the airtime rate, which was discounted since the minutes were purchased in bulk) in the center meetings where clients already gathered on a weekly basis. An independent infrastructure would have taken years and millions of dollars to set up, and most likely would never have been built. In that case, Bangladesh's poor, like those of almost all other nations throughout history, would have been the last, rather than the first, to adopt a new technology and profit from it.

This piggy-backing approach, where "businesses in a box" (some call them *microfranchises*) could be delivered to the poor efficiently and effectively through microfinance institutions, has begun to draw the attention of antipoverty experts. By the early 2000s, Grameen had already established a network of 23 companies—of which GrameenPhone and Grameen Telecom were just two—that were attacking various dimensions of poverty, often in active collaboration with Grameen Bank field offices. (The number of companies continued to grow and ultimately exceeded 50 in total.) Other social entrepreneurs around the world were exploring how microfinance could be a means to bringing breakthrough business and social service models to the poor in highly cost-effective and profitable ways. Again, Yunus was a leader and innovator throughout this exploration.

Seeing that borrowers' health crises were the leading cause of default, he set up a nonprofit organization called Grameen Kalyan (Welfare), to be led by one of his original students, Sheikh Abdud Daiyan. This company developed a network of 35 health clinics that were attached to Grameen branch offices. Since 2005, they have been recovering more than 90 percent of their costs through an innovative health insurance program that would have been impossible to implement if the clients had not also been Grameen Bank members. Such a high level of cost recovery in health care for the poor is virtually unheard of. In another effort, Grameen Shakti (Energy) went from being a tiny organization to one of the three most successful renewable energy programs in the developing world. By June 2007, it had installed more than 100,000 solar home systems, and by 2022 an astonishing 18 million. Just as important, it has been profitable for years while being a beacon of hope in the fight against global warming. In addition, several approaches to ensuring high educational attainment by the children of Grameen clients were successfully launched, both within Grameen Bank and through Grameen Shikkha (Education), an organization run for many years by Nurjahan Begum.

People began to speak of microfinance not as a suite of financial products but as a platform for development. In this way of thinking, a microfinance institution like Grameen's key asset was not its loan portfolio but rather its high-quality relationships with millions of poor entrepreneurs. Some people, especially bankers, saw this type of thinking as a step backward— microfinance regressing from its increasingly commercial orientation to its origins in social work. But in reality, the Grameen paradigm was truly forward-looking with a long-term commercial orientation. It was based on the kinds of strategic alliances that characterize leading businesses today, alliances that—in the microfinance context—can create real value for poor (and formerly poor) clients. These initiatives can also strengthen the capacity of the poor to take larger loans, invest them properly, overcome family crises that might preclude success, and repay the loans on time with interest.

I was overjoyed when Marge Magner, soon after her retirement from Citigroup where she had run the consumer bank and arguably become the most successful female banker in world history, immediately grasped the power of this paradigm and agreed to write a paper about it. Grameen Foundation released "Microfinance: A Platform for Social Change" in May 2007. This paper immediately sparked vigorous debate among microfinance professionals and international development experts around the world. For those who felt that microfinance's core business was reducing poverty, not simply providing banking services, it was a welcome and timely endorsement.

AROUND THE TIME THE FIRST EDITION of this book was published in the mid-1990s, Yunus began to spend more time with his daughter Monica during his trips to the United States. Their relationship flourished during Monica's twenties, a time when she was becoming a highly regarded opera singer. She is a remarkable woman whose performance at the Nobel Peace Prize concert in Oslo brought down the house and ended with her walking offstage hand-in-hand with her father. Soon thereafter, she pledged to hold a concert to raise money for a fund established by Grameen Foundation to support educational scholarships for the children of Grameen Bank borrowers in Bangladesh. It was my first time working with Monica on a project, and it was a pleasure. My colleague Tania Ashraf, the talented daughter of a senior Bangladeshi diplomat, was the champion of the effort alongside Monica. With only a few months to plan to event, we raised more than $200,000.

It was heartwarming to see Yunus and Monica reconcile and develop a strong father-daughter bond. I was delighted to attend Monica's wedding a few years back, where I was even able to have a dance with her mother, Vera. It was a magical day.

Monica and her husband, Brandon, have lived happily ever after—she as an opera singer, and he as a management consultant. Sadly, Monica and everyone connected with her family mourned the loss of her mother a few years back.

3. Zianpur Bazaar

AS AN INCOMING PLANE APPROACHES Zia International Airport in Dhaka, a passenger can see rice fields and tiny thatch huts dotting a vast, marshy swampland that extends for miles in all directions during the monsoon season.[22]

By the early 1990s, Dhaka had become a crowded, ugly city, but it wasn't always that way. Many of its streets and alleys reek of urine and feces, its roads are pockmarked with gaping potholes, and the major intersections are congested with all manner of motorized vehicles and the odd cow that might roam into the traffic. Apart from a few neighborhoods populated by diplomats, foreign aid workers, and the small but growing class of superrich Bangladeshis, Dhaka is an overpopulated, dirty, slum-ridden city of eight million people whose rapid horizontal and vertical expansion shows few signs of proceeding according to any plan. Cows, bullock carts, bicycle and motorized rickshaws, cars, and buses so overcrowded that they are on the verge of tipping over compete for narrow lanes on streets dotted with stoplights that few pay attention to.

Families for whom serfdom in the countryside had become unbearable live virtually on top of one another in wretched squatter settlements. Many of the children living in these slums do not receive any form of schooling.

Dhaka is not, however, without redeeming features. It is arguably cleaner and more spacious than Calcutta or Katmandu. While many police officers extort small bribes, they are rarely menacing, particularly to foreigners, to whom they are almost always helpful. One can usually stay out of the way of armed gangs, unless one intends to purchase land or a building. Common people, despite conventional wisdom to the contrary, are remarkably honest. More likely than not, a shopkeeper or bus conductor will return money if a customer overpays. And above all, there is work, either in construction, rickshaw-pulling, garment-making, or, for hundreds of others, in various crafts; artisans make and sell their wares out in the open, so that customers can watch the products they buy being made.

From the Gabtoli bus station in Dhaka's northwestern edge, a region that less than a generation earlier was farmland, buses leave every few minutes for Aricha, a small port city on the edge of the huge Jamuna River, known to many simply as "the Dancing River." (Together with the Meghna and Ganges, the Jamuna makes this tiny nation home to three of the world's ten largest rivers.) Passengers wearing shirts and pants pay the full fare and pass their bags to those on top, who are clad in tank-top T-shirts and longhis and pay half price. A bus will lurch forward and then stop, and prospective passengers who have waited to see which bus will leave first will jump aboard. An animated conductor will chant his final destination—"*Man-eek-ganj, Man-eek-ganj, Man-eek-gaaanj*"—to the beat of the engine, often grabbing people with luggage and refusing to release his grip until they have heard a pitch for his particular carrier.

In the early 1990s, 25 taka was enough to get a ticket to Aricha, though for most, this town is simply where their bus boards a ferry headed for western Bangladesh, whence travelers can continue their journeys to the northwestern cities of Rangpur, Pabna, Rajshahi, and Dinajpur. The sheer volume of vehicles going to and from the port made for deadly games of chicken on the narrow Dhaka-Aricha highway, which resulted in hundreds of fatalities each year.

Roughly 10 miles north of Aricha lies the Zianpur bazaar, which consisted in 1993 of two tea stalls, three tailors, two general stores (each about the size of a small bedroom), a fertilizer retailer, and the union *porishod* (council) building, the only concrete structure in the marketplace. (A union is an administrative unit composed of roughly 10 to 20 villages. It selects its leaders, one chairman and several members, by direct election. Zianpur is the name of both the union and one of its constituent villages.) Travel between Zianpur and Aricha is primarily by bicycle and rickshaw along a single jagged road composed of dirt and sand that at times runs along a cliff on the edge of a tributary of the Jamuna and at others crisscrosses fields sown with peanuts, rice, and jute. Bamboo jungles in which villagers have erected tiny thatch huts line both sides of the road for much of the way.

Travel to and from Zianpur—or Shaymganj, as it is also called—used to be by boat, but on an angry night in the summer of 1991, the Jamuna burst through a dike in the village of Bagutia and a new tributary began slicing its way through a landmass that had contained five hamlets. Four of the villages survived in truncated form, while one was completely swallowed up, and the destruction the river wrought left hundreds of families homeless. With the sudden creation of this new tributary, the competing river that had flowed by the western edge of the Zianpur bazaar, and was thought to threaten its very existence, began to wither, and within three months it dried up entirely.

Bordering the bazaar to the east is the Zianpur high school and the field on which its students take recess. The school is composed of three rectangular tin sheds filled with weathered wooden benches behind long tables on which the students work. The only concrete structure in the school complex is the science laboratory. For lack of supplies, the lab is hardly ever used, and starting in 1988 the school rented out half of the building to Zianpur's newest organization—the Grameen Bank. For the right to use half the building, Grameen paid a monthly rent of 500 taka ($12).

For the 30,000 inhabitants of the two dozen villages that fall within a five-kilometer radius of Zianpur, the bazaar is the principal market and meeting place. It lacks running water, modern medical facilities, electricity, a public latrine, and a restaurant. If any of the people in the area get seriously ill, their likely fate is to die on the two-to-three-hour rickshaw ride to understaffed hospitals located in Aricha, Daulatpur, or Ghior. Complicated pregnancies, rarely detected until the mother is about to go into labor, often result in the death of the infant and mother. Common and serious illnesses alike are usually treated by traditional healers or with medicine purchased from one of two pharmacies located in the bazaar. Neither the healers nor the pharmacists have any training in modern medicine.

Thursdays and Sundays mark the *haat* (twice-weekly market), during which vendors roll out tattered bedsheets and sell their wares from 4:00 in the afternoon until 7:30 in the evening. Hundreds of men (and virtually no women) jam the market on these days, making their weekly purchases, exchanging gossip, and trying to line up work for the coming week. The unemployed and the simply curious wander among the stalls, inquiring about the prices of essential goods.

A rusting signboard with a gaping hole in the lower righthand corner is propped precariously on a ledge outside the western wall of the science lab building, identifying it as the local Grameen Bank office. The name of the branch, Shaymganj Daulatpur, is written in Bengali alongside the code number, 393-0188, signifying that this was the 393rd branch opened by the bank and that the first loan disbursement was made in January 1988. The signboard is an island in a sea of political graffiti that covers the building from top to bottom.

On a hot summer day, the 800-square-foot office is dark and musty. Most of the windows are closed to keep the dust and sand in the air from settling on the tables and in the employees' eyes and lungs. The manager, Muhammad Jobbar Ali, sits at his table with the door to his immediate right and the bazaar visible through the window behind him. He is in a commanding position, overlooking smartly dressed bank assistants sitting behind tables to his left and in the rear, and bony female borrowers wearing colorful saris sitting on benches that are placed against the southern wall.

The bank's three steel cabinets and safe are in advanced stages of rust and decay. Neatly arranged piles of loan ledgers line the walls behind the chairs where the assistants sit and do their paperwork each afternoon. Moldy ledgers that have been closed are bundled together and stacked on top of the cabinets. The only decorations are a few sayings of Grameen's managing director, written on plain white paper with marking pens imported from China. One, faded to the point of being virtually unreadable, says in Bengali, "Credit is a fundamental human right."

WHEN MUHAMMAD ABDUL ROHIM opened his eyes one morning in April 1993, they fixed briefly on the top of his mosquito net, and then on his black digital watch. Even after all these years, it still amazed him that his biological clock woke him at precisely 6:00 in the morning most days. Rohim put both hands over his face, rubbed hard, and released. As he sat up, he swiveled his torso so that his muscular legs dangled off the side of the bed, just above the floor, where they could feel around for his rubber sandals.

Rohim was one of seven men, all in their early thirties, who were housed in a small shed composed of four walls and a sloping roof made of lightweight corrugated tin. On both the northern and southern ends of the shed, two *choukis* (simple bedsteads) were jammed together. A six-inch gap separated those beds from a third that ran north-south along the shed's western wall, giving the living quarters six beds in all. A small open space, in which the men took their meals in shifts sitting on mats woven from thin strips of bamboo, was left in between the two sleeping areas. Above the beds and the mosquito nets, thin ropes on which each man's wardrobe hung crisscrossed the shed. A set of chess pieces, a deck of ragged playing cards and two tiny radios (the men's entertainment) were carefully stored away in well-worn cardboard boxes.

Rohim slid out from his bed, grabbed an extra *longhi*, his *gamchha* (a thin towel), and a bar of soap, and stepped outside the shed into the early morning sun. He paused for a moment, took a deep breath, and looked back to see if any of his colleagues would join him. When he saw that they were only beginning to stir, he started walking toward a nearby pond.

On his way, he walked past Aklima, the group's cook, who was squatting in a straw hut that functioned as a kitchen; she had begun boiling the morning rice and cooking the vegetable gruel for which Rohim had long since lost his taste. In exchange for preparing three meals a day, Aklima, abandoned two years ago by her husband, was paid 15 taka (37 cents), with which she tried to feed herself, her two children, and her mother. Rohim grunted as he passed her and continued down a gentle, grassy slope that led to the pond.

In rural Bangladesh, most bathing is done outdoors, requiring strenuous efforts to preserve the local concept of modesty. Public bathing is a ritual performed fully or partially clothed, and it requires the simultaneous use of the arms, legs, and mouth to hold clothing in place so that one does not become exposed.

When Rohim returned from the murky pond, he hung his wet *longhi* on the main clothesline just outside the shed's entrance, where it would stay until Aklima folded it and put it on his bed before lunch. Then he unrolled a mat, crouched down on it, scooped some rice onto an aluminum plate, and poured one ladle of vegetable curry on top of it. Rohim ate with his right hand, rolling the rice and curry into balls and pushing them from his palm into his mouth with his thumb in the traditional South Asian style.

After finishing his meal, he brushed his teeth and put on a white dress shirt and gray slacks. At 6:40 he left for the branch office, just 70 yards away from the living quarters (or communal *mess*, one of many English words in use in modern spoken Bengali) on the other side of the bazaar, where he collected two piles of paper, stuffed them into a small bag, and strapped the bag onto a storage rack on the rear of his bicycle. The first bunch of blue and white papers had a huge "2" written on it in Bengali, while the second wad was labeled "42."

Before departing, Rohim double-checked his bag to make sure he had his calculator and two pens, one filled with black ink, the other with red. His bag had become disorderly since his transfer to Shaymganj, and as he rustled through its contents, he decided that he would clean it out that night. At 6:50 he departed for the village of Kholshi.

Becoming a Grameen Bank employee in 1987 had been an improbable blessing for Muhammad Abdul Rohim. The year before, he had completed his intermediate (high school) degree—the first person in his family ever to do so—with dreams of pursuing higher education by going to college. But his father became ill and the medical treatment absorbed a large chunk of the family's savings. Suddenly, it became a priority for Rohim to get a job. After several months of frustration, Rohim responded to a Grameen newspaper advertisement and sent an application to Dhaka. A month later, he received a letter assigning him a time and date to appear at Grameen's head office.

Rohim's trip to Dhaka was the first visit there for anybody in his family, and he had no idea of what to expect. The magnitude of the capital overwhelmed him, but not as much as what he saw when he arrived at Grameen—nearly 600 other applicants who had formed long lines to sign in and await their interviews. Rohim felt sure that he had no chance at being selected from such a large pool, but after he had his five-minute session that included Yunus and his deputy Muzammel Huq, he felt more confident. After the interview, he headed home. Three weeks later, he received a letter informing him that he was being offered a job—setting off several days of celebrations in his family's small compound.

Rohim performed well during his six-month training period and his first few years as a bank worker. He received two quick promotions, outperforming virtually all of his peers. He worked hard and lived frugally, enabling him to send as much as half of his monthly salary of 2,100 taka ($52) to his parents. But in 1991, things began to go awry. He asked for a transfer to a branch that was closer to home, but when he arrived his new manager was abusive and prone to giving poor evaluations to the half dozen bank workers he supervised, causing him to fall behind his peers at other branches.

Rohim greeted his transfer to Shaymganj in 1993 with relief; he knew he would enjoy a good relationship with his manager, since he had worked with him previously. Krishna Das Bala, a colleague who would take over some of Rohim's responsibilities in Kholshi some months later, had the opposite reaction to being posted there—it annoyed him. Bank workers often wanted access to a bustling market, electricity, running water, and a main road served by buses. Shaymganj was the kind of place that many Grameen employees would consider a "punishment branch," meaning an inhospitable place an employee gets sent to as a result of their poor performance. But he resolved to make the best of it.

In many respects, Rohim and Krishna, a Muslim and a Hindu respectively, both hailing from southwestern Bangladesh, are typical of the 8,000 men and women who travel to center meetings every morning to conduct business with the bank's clients in accordance with its policies and rituals. They share the first trip to Dhaka, the shock at getting work without paying a bribe, the unfamiliarity with Grameen when they applied (though this has become less common over time), and the financial hardship that prevented them from pursuing higher education. Most employees sign up not out of idealism but because they have few other choices. Typically, only after joining and seeing the impact that can be made are their commitment to the poor and their willingness to work long hours internalized.

April is among the cruelest months in rural Bangladesh. It marks the end of winter and the beginning of a brief summer that is soon overtaken by the annual monsoon rains. Temperatures, even in the shade, are routinely scorching; the heat causes dirt roads to become so parched that they become covered in several inches of dirt and sand. Tornadoes wreak havoc throughout the country during the summer, killing hundreds and flattening entire villages. Even the wind provides little relief, as it tends to whip up sandstorms that make it impossible to see farther than six feet in any direction. The inhaling of sand and dust leads to widespread respiratory problems that, along with fevers and stomach ailments, cause many Bangladeshis to be ill for long stretches of the summer.

April is also a month of hunger, as families agonize over whether their irrigated rice harvest, still four to six weeks away, will be large enough to meet the needs of their aching stomachs during the coming monsoon. With each passing day from mid-March until mid-May, thousands of rural Bangladeshi families consume the last of their household stock of food from the previous harvest and join the millions of others who must buy their rice. Each new entrant into the market nudges the prices up a little more, pushing millions from two meals a day to one, from 90 percent of the minimal caloric intake that nutritionists claim is needed to sustain life to 70 percent.

The chronic malnutrition leads not just to death but to widespread stunting. Bangladesh is the only country on earth where each successive generation is getting smaller and lighter than the one before it—meanwhile, the rest of humankind gets heavier and taller. It is no wonder, then, that as of the mid-1990s, one out of ten severely underweight children in the world is a citizen of this tiny, luckless nation—though malnutrition has thankfully improved somewhat since then.

As Rohim weaved his way between trees, around potholes, and through sand traps, he was often forced to grimace, and briefly close his eyes, as the wind whipped up a foul combination of dirt and sand that only a few months back had been submerged in inches of rainwater. The gravelly dirt road on which he pedaled his bicycle was raised six to eight feet above the rice fields on either side of it, having been built so as to ensure that even during floods, communications with the larger townships of Zianpur, Ghior, and Daulatpur would not be completely severed and that there would be some place for families whose homes were inundated to take refuge. Beads of dusty sweat began to form on Rohim's face as he entered the home stretch of his three-mile journey.

Roughly 100 feet before reaching the Kholshi bazaar, Rohim steered his bicycle down a steep slope onto a thin strip of land raised six inches above two rice fields on either side of it, serving as a pathway connecting the road to a Hindu *para*. When he reached the first of the homesteads, he dismounted and walked his bike up the slope, put down the kickstand, locked the back wheel (so as to avoid theft), and dislodged his bag. Rohim ducked as he walked into a small hut with a tin roof, a bamboo frame, and no walls. Inside, 35 women sat in rows of five on bamboo mats, perched in those awkward-looking deep crouches that people of the Indian subcontinent apparently find so comfortable.

Each had her eyes fixed on Rohim, and as he moved toward a weathered chair placed in front of the first row of women, Amodini Rani Haldar called out the Bengali word for one, *Aek*. Upon uttering this command, the air was pierced by the sound of dozens of knee joints cracking as the women instantaneously stood up in unison. Then Amodini shouted *Dui* (two), precipitating a coordinated military salute, the making of which required some agility, since perhaps one in three of the women had a baby in her arms. Rohim stood at attention in front of the first row of five women, surveying the group without looking at anyone in particular. He finally nodded his head slightly, which Amodini took as a cue to call out *Teen* (three) and *Char* (four). Hearing those orders, the women first put their arms at their sides and then reassumed their crouches.

This was Rohim's first day servicing this center, and the look on his face suggested that he was already impressed. "You are the center chief?" he asked Amodini.

"Yes, sir," she replied firmly. Rohim was slightly startled by the way Amodini looked him directly in the eye when she spoke, and he self-consciously averted his gaze before reaching into his bag for his collection sheet, pens, and calculator.

Amodini, dressed in a patterned pink sari with a red blouse underneath, has piercing eyes, a skinny face highlighted by slightly raised cheekbones, and a facial expression that wanders between anger and hilarity. Her jet-black hair, parted in the middle and pulled back tightly, glistened as the sunlight reflected off the thin layer of coconut oil she had applied earlier in the morning. As she spoke, her hands often gestured wildly, pointing at real and imaginary figures, slicing through the air with high intention and, on occasion, fury. On this day, at least, Amodini was in charge.

Rohim laid his supplies on his lap and put his bag on the ground so that it leaned on one of the legs of the chair. He looked up and counted the number of rows of women, noting that although there were only six groups on his collection sheet, there were seven in the hut. Good, he thought, all five women in the new group have come. I'll need to talk to them after all the loan installments are collected.

When he'd arrived at the branch two weeks earlier, Rohim had presented himself and his transfer order to Jobbar Ali, the manager, and arranged to be briefed on each of the nine centers he would service. Reports about center number two, the Kholshi landless women's association, were mixed but generally positive. This center, he had been told, was like precolonial Bangladesh—Hindus and Muslims coexisting peacefully, with the former being in the minority but nonetheless exercising power disproportionate to their numbers.

Rohim unfolded the large wad of papers marked "2," revealing a large grid with Bengali-language headings in black type identifying the columns and the names of each member in the row. He made a few initial markings on the sheet, looked at Amodini, and said, *"Pash boi den"* (Give the passbooks). The center chief lifted up the edge of the mat with her right hand, clenched the booklets, and thrust them in front of Rohim.

Inside each passbook was detailed information about a loan taken out by one of the five members of Amodini's group. Shandha Rani Haldar, Amodini's predecessor as center chief, who sat immediately to her left in the first row, had taken out a 6,000-taka general loan for weaving fishing nets. This week, she gave back 120 taka, her thirty-ninth of 50 installments.

Four of the five women in Amodini's group had used their loan capital to buy the expensive thread needed for weaving high-quality fishing nets. Before joining the bank, they were forced to weave nets on a contract basis for others, arrangements under which they earned next to nothing for their efforts. Rasheda Begum, the only Muslim in the group, invested her 5,000 taka ($125) in a small grocery store she ran from her home. When her group had been formed six years earlier, the four other original members wanted no part of Rasheda, until the manager who founded their branch told them sternly, "Grameen Bank was created for people like Rasheda, the dirt poor. If you do not take her, there will be no group here."

Many of the women were making payments on two or three different types of loans, each with its own skinny passbook in which repayments and a running balance were recorded by hand weekly. Brown passbooks were used for general loans (given for enterprises such as livestock-raising, trading, and net-weaving) and newer seasonal loans (sanctioned for borrowers whose families were involved in agriculture, usually on a sharecropping basis). General loans were normally in the range of 5,000 to 6,000 taka ($125 to $150) for fifth- and sixth-time borrowers. Seasonal loans tended to be half that amount.

Much-coveted pink books signified housing loans, which were given to borrowers able to demonstrate a strong need for a new house and a dependable income source capable of paying a loan back in weekly installments of at least 40 taka. Blue and yellow passbooks were for recording savings in accounts that were managed by the entire center or individual groups. Each borrower in the center deposited three taka of savings per week: one into the special savings fund, one into the children's welfare fund, and one into their group's fund.

It took 45 minutes for Rohim to mark up all the passbooks. In each case, he took the booklets from the group chairperson, who sat on the extreme right-hand side of her row. Rohim first counted the money from each group, making sure it matched the total amount due, which he had calculated the day before.

Then he deducted the installment from the previous week's balance in the passbook and made a corresponding mark on his collection sheet. After all that was complete, he handed a ragged wad of bills to Shandha, who placed them in piles according to their denominations. Ten-taka notes were the most common, though there were quite a few hundreds, fifties, and twenties.

As Rohim went through his paperwork, he occasionally looked up, trying to get a sense of how the women interacted with one another. He noticed a lot of touching, giggling, gossiping. Some seemed to talk primarily with members of their row, while others were more ambitious, carrying on animated dialogues with women from several different groups at once. A few were preoccupied with their children, who lay asleep in their laps; Khulsum Begum, a member of the fourth group, spent the entire meeting breastfeeding her young son. Those who expended more energy in their conversations were, by the end of the meeting, drenched in sweat. The quieter ones were able to keep dry by occasionally wiping their faces with their saris.

Rohim noticed the one piece that was out of place in this sweaty mosaic of weathered faces, skinny arms, and colorful saris—Devi Rani Haldar, a proficient fishnet weaver and influential borrower in the fourth group. She sat outside the center hut on a bamboo mat. Rohim wondered why, but decided not to ask. Several weeks later he heard Devi's story. Three years before, a traditional healer in the village had given Devi some advice on how to overcome infertility. She was told she would be more likely to conceive if she kept a greater distance from groups of people; this would give the baby space to be created and grow inside her womb. After following this advice for 18 months, Devi became pregnant and in due course delivered a healthy baby girl. She continued sitting outside in hopes of getting pregnant a second time.

When all the preliminary computing was complete, Rohim began a series of cross-checks to make sure the figures and the cash he had collected added up. (Were he to fall short once he arrived back at the office, he would be held accountable by his manager or auditors.) Finally, he counted all the stacks of bills, and when that sum came out to exactly 6,400 taka, the accounting was finished.

Rohim turned his attention to the five women sitting in the seventh row. Throughout the meeting they had remained quiet, and had not forwarded any passbooks or money; this last group was still in its training period.

Diverting his gaze to the center chief, he asked, "Amodini, you know that today is the day for the group *shikriti* [recognition]?"

"Yes, sir."

The five women were now staring directly at him, each looking like a deer caught in a set of oncoming headlights.

"Group number seven, stand up," Rohim barked. The women briefly looked at one another before rising in unison. "I'll be coming here at four-thirty this afternoon. With me will be the manager and a senior manager from the area office in Tepra. He will test you on all that you have learned in your group training." Rohim paused, studying the women as they began, one by one, to divert their eyes from his. "Are you ready?" Three of the women adjusted their saris, covering more than half their faces in the process.

Nobirun Begum volunteered a feeble "Yes, sir" in a barely audible whisper. She was the group chairman (another of the many English words used in modern colloquial Bengali). Rohim lifted his eyebrows and looked at Amodini, who immediately stood up and shouted, "Speak up!" As she spoke, her long bony arms pointed threateningly toward the women six rows behind her. Several drops of perspiration dripped from her forehead onto Bedana, one of her group members, who was crouching below.

"Yes, sir," the women repeated in unison.

"Are they going to pass?" Rohim asked Amodini.

"Yes, sir," she said firmly. "We've worked hard training them. They'll be ready."

"Make sure to get them here by four o'clock."

Rohim bundled together the wad of bills with four rubber bands, sticking them and the collection sheet in his bag. Looking at Amodini, and then at his watch, he said, "End the meeting."

"*Kendro . . . Aram . . . Kendro . . . Aram . . . Kendro.*" With each instruction, the women changed the position of their arms, stretching them forward with their elbows touching their knees on the first command and folding them across their knees on the second.

"May I have permission to end the meeting, sir?" Amodini asked in a firm but respectful voice.

"End it."

When she called out *Aek,* the women stood up, again causing another chorus of cracking knee joints and a few poorly suppressed sighs. On *Dui,* the women resumed their crouch. After repeating the standing and crouching once more, they were called to their feet and ordered to prepare to give the salute meant to symbolize the Muslim farewell greeting of *Salaam*, short for *As Salaam o Aleikum*, meaning "May peace be upon you" in Arabic.

On the count of *Aek*, the women saluted Rohim and he returned the gesture. On the count of *Dui* they put their arms at their sides, and on *Teen*, they resumed their crouch and so concluded the meeting rituals that were performed, to varying degrees, across the country by Grameen borrowers in thousands of villages in an effort to create and demonstrate a cohesive and disciplined culture.

With the meeting over, Rohim exchanged a few words with Amodini, and then rushed off to center number 42. After he left, many of the women lingered for a while, savoring a brief respite from their work and the opportunity it presented for camaraderie and gossip. The five women in group number seven huddled with Shandha and Amodini, discussing how to make sure that they all arrived at the center house on time for their test. When that was settled, each of the trainees grabbed a stick from a pile of firewood Shandha had collected, knelt down, and began carving her signature in the dirt. Shandha and Amodini stood over the women, holding hands as they inspected the prospective borrowers' work.

Nonibala Ghosh, the perennial chair of group number two, had long since hurried back to her home. She and her family had a massive job ahead of them that day—procuring more than 70 gallons of milk, turning it into *chhana* (cottage cheese), and delivering it by dusk to a confectionery shop in Dhaka more than 60 miles away. To accomplish this, all they had at their disposal was a few thousand taka in working capital, an industrial-size tin pan, a clay oven, and two rickety bicycles. Nonibala would have liked to catch up with people and help train the new group, but the clock was ticking. She had no time to lose.

Except on national holidays, every weekday in Bangladesh witnesses a unique ritual. (When the first edition of this book was published, the Bangladeshi workweek was Saturday through Wednesday, with a half day on Thursday, which in the Grameen Bank was reserved for clearing the weekly accounts. Later it was changed to Sunday through Thursday, with Friday and Saturday constituting a two-day weekend.) Each workday, thousands of Grameen Bank employees set off by foot, bicycle, or boat to take part in meetings attended by hundreds of thousands of poor women living in tiny hamlets scattered across Bangladesh. By noon, the bank workers travel a combined distance exceeding several times the circumference of the globe and collect, count, and deposit millions of taka in small bills—all without turning on a single car, motorcycle, or computer. (In the years to follow, however, motorcycles and computers were increasingly used by bank workers.)

The women and men they meet with in cramped bamboo houses are taking part in one of the world's most daring experiments in rural development; they are both the borrowers *and the owners* of Grameen Bank. Loans they receive are invested in more than 500 income-generating enterprises as diverse as cow-fattening, rice-husking, trading, tailoring, light manufacturing, and landloom weaving.

When Rohim returned to the branch office from his two meetings, he parked his bicycle outside with the others and took his seat behind a wooden table that he shared with Abdul Mustafiz, another bank employee. As he began the long process of entering all the installments into their respective ledgers by hand, a task that would take nearly two hours, Rohim was startled by a scream. Abdul Ahlim, a fellow bank worker, had been hit by a small chunk of concrete that had fallen from the office's crumbling ceiling as he was walking to his desk. Seven women sitting on a long bench who were waiting for loans they would receive later that day looked on in dismay. Several inspected the ceiling above where they were sitting, apparently trying to anticipate any additional debris that might fall on them. As the office boy began sweeping up, Ahlim, apparently unhurt, brushed himself off, and Rohim and the others returned to their paperwork.

A smell of dried sweat filled the air, and dust that the hot summer wind was whipping up had begun to enter from the two windows facing east. Rohim took his handkerchief, wiped his face, and scanned the room. Never before had he been posted at such a remote and backward branch office. On days like this one, he sometimes wondered what had prompted him to take this job. Without pausing to ponder this question, Rohim dipped his right forefinger into a small damp sponge in a plastic tray given to all Grameen Bank employees as a work aid, flipped the page in the loan ledger, and began entering another loan payment he had collected from center number two.

FOUNDING THE BRANCH IN ZIANPUR, several years before Rohim was transferred there, had not been an easy task. In 1987, Shah Alam was the zonal manager in charge of some 100 branches within roughly 60 miles of the capital. He is a brusque man—most who work for him simply call him "the big sir."

Founding a branch in Zianpur was his personal project, a bold statement that he had the nerve to open an office in a place so poor and remote that most of his colleagues would avoid it. The area included *chars* (large silt sandbars that shift every few years) to the west where people were forced to move periodically to stay a step ahead of the river. (Grameen employees are often told in their training period to avoid recruiting *osthayee*—transitory—people as members, as they are the most likely to take a loan and disappear before repaying it.) The people there lived in grinding poverty reinforced by superstition, lawlessness, and a near-complete lack of government services. Some thought that these areas were too backward even for Grameen.

After one candidate fled at the sight of the place, Shah Alam chose Abdul Mannan Talukdar for the job. Mannan was one of the first Grameen employees to rise from the position of bank worker to become a branch manager. Shah Alam knew that Mannan came from Sirajganj, where there were similar problems of migration from shifting rivers, and figured that he would be less intimidated than most of his peers in such an environment. When Shah Alam picked him up in a far-flung area of southern Sylhet and dropped him near Zianpur, the local managers didn't think he had a chance.

Mannan's first night in the Zianpur bazaar was spent in an abandoned room of the union *porishod* building, with only a thin mattress and bedsheet he had brought with him separating his body from the cement floor. Some biscuits he had bought from the only tea stall in the bazaar served as dinner. This style of entering the village humbly dated to Grameen's birth, when Yunus would mix freely with the villagers near his university and do nothing to flaunt his education, wealth, and status.

The next morning Mannan began a series of more than 100 community meetings in 15 villages where he would introduce himself and Grameen's approach. People doubted what he said about the Grameen Bank program he was going to bring to the area. Loans to women? Loans to the poor? One rumor suggested that this bank was a front for an organization that would kidnap women and send them to the Chittagong Hill Tracts, a jungle that the government was trying to colonize with ethnic Bengalis. Another asserted that Grameen Bank was a Christian missionary organization.

Mannan's one request at the end of his meetings was that anyone who had even the slightest bit of interest come to an upcoming open-air meeting on the field in front of the Zianpur high school. He tried to encourage the villagers, saying that in some nearby districts Grameen Bank had been established and poor people were prospering; if the meeting in Zianpur was well attended, they could have a branch too. He mentioned that a high-ranking bank official would come that day to explain the rules of the bank, and if the crowd was too small, he might call off the preparations. Mannan remained confident in public, but he was actually very anxious.

On the morning of December 5, the appointed day of the meeting, Mannan rolled out of bed after a restless night's sleep. The meeting was to begin at 10:00; when the field lay empty at 8:30, Mannan began to worry. At 9:30, a few people started to trickle in. By this time, he was in a panic. Would Shah Alam arrive to see a small, uninterested crowd? If he did, would Mannan ever receive another promotion? Little did Mannan know that huge processions of men and women of all ages were, at that very moment, converging on the bazaar from all four corners.

Thirty minutes earlier, Nonibala Ghosh had emerged from her house with the intention of going to the meeting. She was scared, as this was the first time in her life, at age 37, that she would be going to the Zianpur bazaar. She was relieved to see so many other people heading in the same direction, and set off on the three-mile trek with Zomella, a Muslim neighbor with whom she was friendly.

Back on the field, the zonal manager's car arrived, pushing its way through the crowds that had suddenly descended on the sleepy bazaar. Wave after wave arrived, forcing those who had come earlier into an ever-smaller space. Later, shopkeepers claimed it was the largest crowd ever to gather in the area—one more piece of evidence that poor people in backward places can sometimes show keen interest in new opportunities if the process of introducing them is done sensitively.

Suddenly, Shah Alam became worried that the crowd was too large. At the time, the country was under martial law, which prohibited meetings of more than five people, and here were at least 5,000 people waiting to hear him speak. He took the microphone and begged the latest arrivals to turn around and go home. Students who had agreed to help Mannan were instructed to form human barricades at all entrances to the field.

Desperate to get the crowd to disperse, he gave only a perfunctory description of the bank and promised that a branch would be created. Slowly, and after considerable exhortation, the crowd began to break up.

Years later, Nonibala Ghosh still vividly recalled the walk home. Some were still convinced that the bank would never sanction a single taka to lend to any poor person in the area. Others took Mannan and the zonal manager at their word. Still others continued to circulate the rumors about Grameen being a Christian missionary organization.

Nonibala paid attention to the discussions swirling around her as she walked. Yet her main preoccupation centered on a single question: How could she get into a Grameen Bank group as soon as possible?

BACK IN KHOLSHI, RUKIA BEGUM, a member of the seventh group-in-formation of center number two, stuck her head out of her tiny, rotting thatch hut, squinted, and looked at the sun. From its position in the sky, she figured it was time to leave for her group recognition test, an oral exam given to prospective Grameen Bank members after their training period. Fixing her sari, she contemplated the nausea she felt and the volume of material she and the other members of her group had memorized. For a moment, she thought she was going to vomit.

The oral exam requires all prospective members to demonstrate that they understand the rules of the bank, making it difficult for an unscrupulous bank employee to take advantage of them. It also makes it easier for them to recruit new members once they begin borrowing, should they want to do so. The idea is that this is *their* bank and they must assume their roles as clients and owners with eyes wide open, understanding each and every rule.

An integral part of the training is learning Gramen's social constitution known as the Sixteen Decisions, which was drawn up by a meeting of center chiefs in 1984. Requiring new borrowers to memorize it was part of the bank's attempt to respond to the social dimensions of poverty; it was a series of principles and goals to ease the workings of the bank and help borrowers focus on getting themselves out of poverty. They included limiting the size of one's family, educating children, not accepting or giving dowry (since doing so devalues girls and women), planting vegetable gardens and fruit-bearing trees, and building sanitary latrines. Other decisions were more philosophical; for instance, members pledged to help one another and not let anyone do injustice to them. Borrowers were required to memorize these commitments as part of their group training. Furthermore, the staff was urged to motivate members to implement them, and a special programs division that received funding from UNICEF for many years organized workshops and delivered supplies (such as iodized salt and packets of vegetable seeds) in hopes of speeding their realization.

Perhaps the most important purpose of the recognition test is to allow the area manager or his deputy to observe how new members respond to a demanding male authority figure. Can a woman speak loudly and clearly while looking an area manager in the eye? When pushed, does it seem that she will agree to *anything*, or can she stand up for herself? In short, the bank wants to know whether a lifetime of oppression by men has left a prospective member so compliant that she would turn over money she had received from the bank to her husband without raising a fuss. The bank leaders want to have some confidence that in such a case, the woman would alert her group members and center chief and ask them to intervene. With the exception of ill health, the most frequent cause of missed installments and default among Grameen Bank members is male relatives forcing borrowers to disinvest in their business venture and hand over the money.

With her daughter hoisted on her hip, Rukia looked briefly at her niece's son, closed her eyes, and said a prayer. "I'll be back soon," she said softly. It was not clear anyone was listening.

Rukia began walking on a narrow village path, which after an eighth of a mile joined up with the raised dirt road that cut through the heart of Kholshi. She quickened her pace, not wanting to be the last to arrive at the center house. As it turned out, she was the fourth to show up, with Nobirun being the last.

At 4:25, Rohim walked briskly into the center house, which was on Shandha's small homestead plot. Three chairs had already been arranged in the front end of the hut, one for Rohim, one for Jobbar Ali, the manager, and one for the area manager, Sirajul Islam Bhuyian. Before Rohim could lose his temper about Nobirun being late, she arrived and assumed her position on the end of her row. Outside the house, Shandha and Amodini crouched down, their knees barely touching as they watched.

In February 1988, the first two groups of Shandha's center had been recognized, and they had immediately begun meeting every Tuesday morning at 8:00. During the next 12 months, another four groups were added. Now, in April 1993, a seventh group was finally being prepared for group recognition. Rohim's job was to ensure that this group was trained the right way and that it made progress out of poverty in the coming year. It was a challenge he had met elsewhere, but it still thrilled and frightened him.

Rohim turned his attention to the chairs. Which one would he sit on? Which one would the area manager sit on? Suddenly, the sound of a motorcycle engine was audible, and in a moment the vehicle was visible. Some 50 children from all over the village chased the motorcycle as it approached Shandha's home by carefully negotiating the narrow pathway through a field of shimmering rice paddy.

In an act of bravado, Siraj drove up the slope leading to Shandha's courtyard, almost losing his balance. As he turned off the engine, put down the kickstand, and removed his helmet, he looked behind him at the advancing army of children for whom this was possibly the closest they had ever gotten to motorized transport. Jobbar Ali, who had been sitting behind the area manager, nervously ran his fingers through his hair and scanned the scene, checking to see that all the pieces were in place.

Rohim saluted the area manager, who returned the greeting casually as he entered the center house. As Siraj took a step toward the chair reserved for him, Amodini poked another member of the group, Korimun, in the ribs with her finger, prompting Nobirun to call out, "*Aek.*" The five women stood up together, their eyes trained on the man they had never seen before.

Siraj sat down in the chair, his puffy face trying to restrain a trademark smile. "Sit down," he said to the women. Everyone in the hut, including Jobbar and Rohim, took their seats. Rukia began looking at the ground, her lips moving slowly as she repeated something to herself.

"Begin the meeting," Siraj said.

Nothing happened. Korimun Begum, sitting next to Nobirun, grabbed her chairman's foot with her right hand and squeezed. Nobirun, startled, jumped to her feet.

"Are you feeling sleepy? Perhaps we should come back another time?" Siraj had decided that the time for good humor was past.

"*Kendro . . . Aram . . . Kendro . . . Aram . . . Kendro . . .*" At each command, the women repeated the ritual movements of their arms that had been performed at the center meeting that morning.

"May we begin this special meeting, sir?" Nobirun asked.

"Begin the meeting."

"*Aek.*" The four women stood up. On "*Dui,*" they reassumed their crouches. "*Aek . . . Dui . . . Aek . . . Dui . . . Aram.*" The women assumed a relaxed crouch, and several looked at the children observing the scene, many of whom were giggling. Amodini, with a wild look in her eyes, stood up and began shooing away the youngsters. Many would flee, then return minutes later.

"May I sit down, sir?"

Siraj frowned as he studied Nobirun and then the other four women, all crouching five feet in front of him. "Sit down," he said flatly after a long pause.

He began by introducing himself to the women as the local area manager who supervised their branch and eight others like it, and then called Nobirun to her feet and asked her to tell him her name and that of the center and group she was hoping to become a member of. Then he asked her to recite the responsibilities of being a group chairman. Slowly, with her eyes trained on the roof of the hut, she told him what he already knew: that a group chairman was elected each year during *Choitro*, the month of the Bengali calendar that corresponds to the period from mid-March to mid-April. The chairman was responsible for every aspect of the group's performance—use of the loan for the stated purpose, attendance at weekly meetings (including signing the attendance register), and, of course, timely payment of installments.

"What is the eleventh decision?" he asked finally.

Nobirun began covering her sad-looking, weathered face with her sari, then resisted the urge and let it drop. "Decision number eleven . . . We shall neither take nor receive dowry in our children's weddings. We shall eliminate the curse of dowry from our center. We shall also not engage in child marriage."

Siraj crossed his legs, sighed, and asked Nobirun to sit down. After asking Korimun, Zorina, and Alow a few questions, he turned to Rukia. As she stood, her child woke up and began to cry. Before Siraj could say anything, Amodini grabbed the little boy and put him in her lap as she reassumed a crouch outside the hut. Looking Rukia in the eye, the area manager asked, "In what different ways is money deposited in the group fund?"

Rukia opened her mouth slightly, but nothing came out. Thirty seconds passed, then a minute. Terror spread among the squatting women as Rukia's eyes glazed over.

"Don't you understand the question?" Siraj tried. Silence. "Well, tell me decision number six."

Zorina covered her mouth and began reciting the answer softly, so that Rukia would hear and be reminded. "We shall keep our families small, we shall . . ."

Jobbar Ali's face flushed as he said to Zorina, "The question was for *her*, not *you!*"

Another minute passed, and Rukia began crying softly. Her legs became unsteady, and without warning, she resumed her crouch.

By then, it was over. They had failed the group recognition test.

WORD SPREAD QUICKLY THROUGH THE VILLAGE that Nobirun's group had fallen short, and within a few days, three of the women—Korimun, Zorina, and the unfortunate Rukia—were wavering on whether they wanted to go through with it a second time. Apparently, they felt that they had been humiliated enough already. Eager to have their center rebound from such a setback, older members began spreading the word that there were openings for as many as three new members in the seventh group.

Amena Begum heard the news from a Hindu neighbor, Oloka Ghosh, a borrower who had joined Nonibala Ghosh's group in 1990. Oloka had used her loans to build up a business making sweets (the livelihood often pursued by those in her caste), trading milk, and raising cows. Three years and thousands of taka later, she wanted to encourage Amena to get involved. Oloka knew that Amena's son had recently been ill, and that the family had been forced to disinvest from its business to pay for medical treatment. She had also heard the rumors that Amena's husband beat her.

Amena Begum, a relatively tall Muslim woman with a slight build and a nervous smile, had arrived in Kholshi three years earlier. She had taken refuge at her grandfather's homestead land after the place she had been staying with her husband and in-laws was swallowed up by the Ganges River. The journey to Kholshi, almost 10 years after her marriage, had been a difficult one.

Just under her chin, but plainly visible, is a scar that is nearly an inch long; it is a reminder of the time her husband beat her with a bicycle chain until she lost consciousness. That incident, and many others, had motivated her to take refuge with her grandfather; she hoped that her husband would go easy on her if she was surrounded by her relatives. (Her in-laws seemed to encourage the abuse.) And indeed, the beatings had abated somewhat.

Amena, her husband, and their four children were squatters on her grandfather's land; on the day they arrived, they began clearing a small patch in an overgrown jungle where they were told they could build a house. After selling virtually everything they owned, they were able to build a small hut for

8,000 taka ($200). They had no furniture, and slept side by side on a blanket and some straw they laid on the ground. Her husband then began selling aluminum cookware door to door. It was not a lucrative enterprise, but it was the best they could do.

Amena had once looked in on a center meeting being held near Shandha's hut. She had heard about Grameen, and was curious to see what it was. She thought *that* was the bank—a single hut, with one man and 30 women sitting inside it. She had no idea there were other centers and employees, not to mention a concrete building in Zianpur. As the meeting broke up, Amena had hurried away, hoping that no one would see her. But Oloka Ghosh, her neighbor, caught a glimpse of her, and now, more than a year later, brought her the news of the opening in group number seven.

Within days, Amena met Nobirun and Alow, who were determined to pass this second time, and two other new trainees—Fulzan Begum and Firoza Khatoon. They studied quickly, learning all the information from both Rohim and older members like Amodini and Shandha. Amena was forced to miss a few training sessions because of illness (she was pregnant with her fifth child), but everyone was relieved when they heard that Oloka was giving her supplementary training in her home. Having studied as far as third grade, Amena had an easier time learning the material than the other women, who had not gotten that far in school.

On the appointed day, the women were told to come to another center in Kholshi; they were one of six groups being tested at the branch that day. Amodini and Shandha went with the fivesome, and when the area manager came to them, he recognized Nobirun and quickly scanned the other faces. He was behind on his work that day—he had more group recognitions to perform at another branch—and decided to take a shortcut. He picked out the new member who looked the most timid and decided to ask her one question and one question only. If she got it right, they passed.

He pointed to Fulzan, and when she was able to recite decision number nine—"We shall build and use pit latrines"—the women were astonished to hear that they had received their recognition, pending the area manager's inspection of their homes (done to make sure new borrowers are in fact poor enough to be eligible to join). That was easy; none of the five women were in danger of being outside of Grameen Bank's target group—the "functionally landless" as defined by Yunus since the bank's earliest days.

When a new group becomes eligible for loans, two women, normally the poorest in the group, submit loan proposals, which will in most cases receive formal approval by the bank in a few days. The first line of defense against bad business decisions is not the bank or its employees, but rather the other women in the group. If the first two borrowers to receive loans have any difficulty repaying, the remaining three will have their proposals delayed, reduced in amount, or, in extreme cases, denied altogether. Each member therefore has strong incentives to scrutinize her fellow borrowers' loan proposals and to apply a delicate combination of pressure and support to ensure that the money is invested properly and that their income-generating activity succeeds. In practice, this means that poor families that would normally have no contact, or perhaps have an antagonistic relationship born of religious or caste differences or a generations-old feud, are almost forced to help one another. A group member might tip off a fellow borrower to the fact that she is about to buy a cow that is suffering from a disease likely to kill it—even if the seller is a relative of the one giving the tip. Another might help steer business, including her own, to a woman in her group. The impersonal forces of supply and demand are thus softened by a network of friends who want you to succeed for a combination of financial incentives and human empathy.

For a woman to get into such a network, husbands and village elders may need to be defied, and rules and regulations will need to be memorized, trust built up, and finally, the group recognition test passed. For women like Amena and Fulzan, isolated from their society by illiteracy, poverty, and custom, these are considerable obstacles. A weeding-out process inevitably occurs; the loss of three women from group number seven after their humiliating failure to pass the test was not unusual. Sometimes, when dropouts occur, village elders complain about Grameen's policy of not forming men's centers. But by the mid-1990s, Grameen's senior management had concluded that women repaid their loans—and attended meetings—more regularly than men did; furthermore, there was growing evidence to suggest that lending to a family's husband helped the husband, whereas lending to the wife helped the entire family. As a result, the percentage of women borrowers in Grameen had been steadily increasing, from less than 50 percent in the early 1980s to more than 90 percent a decade later.

On a hot early summer day in 1993, about two weeks after being recognized, all the members of group number seven and center chief Amodini headed off for the Zianpur bazaar. Fulzan and Alow were to receive their loans that day, having been notified at the meeting the previous Tuesday that their loan proposals had been approved. All the women got into their best saris, which in the case of these new borrowers were old and rather plain. Amodini wore a fresh-looking green sari with red trim, and when the clouds dispersed, she opened up a black umbrella she had bought used for 70 taka. As the center chief, she had to accompany any borrower who was going for a loan. As she walked down the dirt road that connects Kholshi to Zianpur with these first-time borrowers—women who had never been to the area's central bazaar in their lives—Amodini recalled her own entry into the bank six years earlier.

Her group had included three other net weavers like herself and Rasheda. They, together with Nonibala's group, were trained by Ruhul Amin, a bank worker they remember as a strict disciplinarian. And then there was Aduree, poor Aduree. Everyone had been opposed to her joining the center. Hers was perhaps the poorest family in the entire village. One measure of her destitution was that of her 34 siblings (including many half sisters and brothers), only eight had lived past the age of five; 26 had succumbed to hunger and disease. When Aduree wanted to join one of the first two groups, everyone said no. "What if she dies, or her husband dies?" people asked. "She will default, and we will have to repay—those are the rules of the bank."

In desperation, Aduree, a Muslim, approached Nonibala, who had appeared to oppose her entry with less conviction than any of the others. Every day she came by to beg her Hindu neighbor to stand up for her and let her into a group. Finally, Nonibala relented and told the other women that she alone would bear the risk of Aduree's default. That opened that door wide enough for this formerly luckless woman to jump in. When Ruhul Amin and the manager suggested a 500-taka ($13) loan for Aduree, Nonibala supported her new friend in arguing for one three times as large. Again, they prevailed.

Now years later, the six women approached the northern tip of the Zianpur bazaar and Amodini smiled. She reminded herself that Aduree had not only never missed a payment in six years but had become something of a disciplinarian in the center, admonishing women who arrived even a few minutes late to their weekly meeting. Maybe these newly recognized borrowers would transform themselves as Adree had, she thought to herself.

When the bazaar came into sight, Amodini noticed that the women's eyes had bulged as they stared at things they had never seen before—so many tin sheds so close together, the crush of people, and dozens of men sitting in tea shops, many staring at them as they walked by. Amodini pointed to the

Grameen Bank office. Again, she noticed the women stare with wonder at something they had never seen before—a concrete building.

As they entered the branch, Amodini motioned the women to a bench against the wall while she walked up to Rohim's desk and informed him that they had arrived. He looked up from his paperwork and smiled at his center chief. "Is the group chairman here?"

"Yes, sir," Amodini answered.

"I'll call for you when the papers are ready."

Amodini walked over to where the women had huddled. Many of the people around them spoke in an animated and excited manner, but her new members were silent.

As Fulzan looked around the office, she studied each of the eight men who were sitting behind wooden tables arranged to form an inverted U. Five men sat facing the wall against which the women sat, and two were to their right, looking straight ahead at the desk where the manager sat alone on the other end of the office. They seemed so purposeful to her; she'd had no idea that there were so many bank employees like Rohim.

As she sat there, the enormity of what she was involving herself in overwhelmed her. Did they all know that she was a ditchdigger, one of a handful of women for whom poverty had become so extreme that she had been forced to compete for jobs that were normally reserved for men? Did they know that at that very moment her sister, who lived in a dilapidated thatch hut next to hers, was going around in the village begging? Had some mistake been made?

"Fulzan Begum, come here," Rohim barked without looking up, interrupting her thoughts. "Alow Khatoon, you also come here." The two women, accompanied by their center chief, approached the table. Following Amodini's lead, they stopped just short of the desk and stood at attention. The two women's faces reflected the tension of the moment.

"The manager," Rohim began as he looked up from his papers, "will ask you some questions about the rules of the bank and your loan, as at a group recognition. Will you be ready?"

"Yes, sir," Amodini answered.

"You had better make sure they are prepared." Looking at Fulzan, he said, "Okay, you sign this," pointing as he spoke, "here and here." He made the same request of Alow, and after they had signed, he asked them to sit down and wait until the manager called for them.

Fulzan began watching as the manager started handing out bunches of bills to groups of women who were gathered around his table. At his side stood a man who was dressed similarly to Rohim; he must be another bank worker, she guessed. It was at this moment that she realized she had never in her life touched any bill larger than a 10-taka note. She was often paid in wheat for her work as a ditchdigger, but on rare occasions she was paid in cash—three taka for a full day's work when she started working 12 years ago, and more recently 26 taka (65 cents)—that would come in 10-taka, 5-taka, and 1-taka notes. Fulzan leaned over to Alow and asked, "Have you ever touched a twenty-taka note before?" With a blank look on her face, Alow replied, "I've never touched *any* taka before."

Rohim looked toward the benches, and his eyes met Amodini's. Not a word was spoken. They both knew it was time. The Hindu fishnet weaver tapped Fulzan on the leg and stood up. The other women followed her to the manager's table.

These were to be the twenty-fourth and twenty-fifth loans that Jobbar Ali would give out today, though the first to new borrowers. He studied the group, his eyes fixing on each one briefly. All but Amodini averted their gaze when he looked at them. "Fulzan Begum?"

"Yes, sir," she replied in a whisper.

"What is the group fund?"

"It is . . . it is . . ." Beneath the table, Amodini gently grabbed Fulzan's left hand and squeezed. "It is an account," she finally blurted out.

"Who owns the group fund?"

"The group of five."

"Are you sure?"

"Yes, sir."

"How much did you ask for in your loan proposal?"

"Fifteen hundred taka, sir." She looked at a small pile of blue and white currency notes near the manager's right hand. Her heart raced, and she squeezed Amodini's hand harder.

"Your loan proposal passed. How much will you receive in your hands today?"

"Thirteen hundred seventy-five taka." Amodini had prepared her for that question, and she was proud to answer it in a loud voice that was beginning to suggest confidence.

"Where will other taka be deposited?"

"In the group fund."

"And what will you use your loan for?"

"I will buy a cow and sell the milk."

Jobbar Ali looked down, counted the bills, handed them to Rohim for a recount, and then placed them and a few slips of paper into a crisp brown passbook. As he held it over his desk with his right hand, Fulzan slowly reached forward. Her hand was shaking, and her lips began to tremble. Slowly, she wrapped her fingers around the passbook and, as the manager released his grip, brought it towards her. She stared at it at her side, but didn't open it at first.

"In the name of the Almighty Allah," Jobbar Ali offered, "use it well." Rohim looked on approvingly, and a broad smile broke out on Amodini's face. As attention turned to her new friend Alow, Fulzan finally let go of her center chief's hand and opened the passbook. There she saw notes larger than any she had ever seen before, such as 100-taka bills. After staring at them for a brief moment, she closed her eyes and took a long, deep breath.

Update: Since the 1990s

FLOODS ALWAYS DO THE MOST DAMAGE to places like Zianpur, which are close to the country's largest rivers. My visit there in 2004 showed a breathtaking change in the area's topography. Two entire villages, and parts of several others, had fallen into the ever-shifting Jamuna River. As a result, some of the branch's borrowers were transferred to other, mostly nearby branches closer to where they ended up taking refuge. The Grameen II methodology mentioned in this edition's introduction proved up to the task of helping the staff respond to this chaotic situation in a humane yet disciplined manner.

The limitations of Grameen I might have made getting the borrowers impacted by the disappearance of the villages back on their feet a difficult if not impossible task. Its inflexibilty gave critics of the bank an opening to make a variety of accusations about how it could sometimes put its clients in a bind and ultimately lead to defaults that were being covered up to buy time. In fact, a preview of the attacks that would be leveled against Grameen starting in late 2010 came in the form of a critical article that appeared on the front page of the *Wall Street Journal* in 2001. The authors of this deeply flawed piece failed to grasp what microfinance was trying to accomplish. Their thesis was that Grameen was on shaky financial ground and was somehow hiding information about its problems. Their argument was built around a single erroneous statistic in Grameen's English-language web site that had not been updated for a couple of years to account for the loan losses and slow repayments in the years after the 1998 floods. (Grameen conducts all of its business in Bengali and had put up the English-language site as something of an afterthought to respond to the many requests for information from abroad.)

Refuting the article's conclusions was not difficult, but damage was nonetheless done to Grameen's reputation as this article was circulated around the world. This fleeting setback, however, was overshadowed by a much larger tragedy when Danny Pearl, one of the authors of the article, was kidnapped and killed by terrorists the following year in Pakistan.

The more interesting story that the reporters unfortunately missed was that Grameen Bank was well on its way to reinventing itself in 2001 by creating Grameen II, which is worth probing into a bit more here. A key element of this strategy was vastly increased flexibility in loan products, where loan amounts and repayment schedules (among many other things) could be customized to the needs of an individual borrower's business. The peer pressure element to ensure on-time repayment, which was described in this chapter, was abolished in favor of allowing borrowers to simply reschedule loans when they faced difficulties. When describing Grameen II, Yunus often spoke of his center managers being transformed from "mechanics to artists."

Another aspect of the system was its greater emphasis on savings, especially individual savings (group savings remained but was deemphasized). The success of their efforts to attract deposits enabled Grameen to mobilize several hundred million dollars' worth of capital, which in a few short years exceeded the demand for loans by more than $50 million. One-third of the savings was from nonclients, mostly businesspeople in the rural areas attracted by the highly competitive rates, ranging from 8.5 percent to as much as 12 percent on long-term certificates of deposit.

Another Grameen II enhancement was an elegant and easy-to-use 10-point checklist that enabled field officers and external parties to track how quickly Grameen families were emerging from poverty. This concrete list brought a clarity of focus and an unprecedented degree of transparency to Grameen's core poverty reduction mandate and its progress in meeting it.

Finally, Grameen II contained a new incentive structure that was developed for branches and their staff. In classic Grameen style, this configuration was based on a mix of indicators that covered both financial performance and social impact, and was marketed internally by awarding each branch up to five stars, based on their achievements. This entire system was described in rich detail in the important book *The Poor Always Pay Back* by Asif Dowla and Dipal Barua, which was published a few weeks after the 2006 Nobel Peace Prize was announced and was later translated into French with support from Grameen Foundation during my time as its president.

ONE OF THE ENDURING MYSTERIES of Grameen and the wider microfinance movement that I was reminded of while rereading this chapter is why unarmed loan officers who, for many years, carried significant amounts of cash every day on predictable routes were so rarely mugged. After spending many months living in rural Bangladesh and talking with people who were steeped in the local culture, I have come up with a hypothesis as to why the staff were almost always unmolested.

While there is often initial opposition to microfinance groups like Grameen when they enter a community, owing to the fact that they exclude the well-off, prioritize women clients, and run afoul of various cultural norms and vested interests, most critics develop some grudging admiration for them over time. People see that the staff members deliver affordable and reliable financial services to clients (and increasingly, attractive savings products to the public), are almost always incorruptible, provide both loans and jobs without favoritism, nepotism, or bribes, and perform their jobs conscientiously year-in and year-out.

I believe people's respect for these qualities is the main reason why Grameen Bank loan officers were so rarely attacked, even during the eras when they handled large amounts of cash. I also have come to sense that their manner of doing business is gradually raising societal expectations of how all institutions, private and public, should behave. Tim Ogden, a microfinance expert based at New York University's Financial Access Initiative, once mentioned to me that this may ultimately be one of microfinance's greatest contributions. I wish the research community would ease off on trying to disprove that microfinance "works" and focus instead on questions like the extent to which Ogden's hypothesis is valid and also on determining which techniques employed by microlenders work best in particular contexts.

I also wish that more organizations claiming to provide microfinance did so in the Grameen spirit, which would have blunted some of the attacks in the early 2010s and probably motivated more clients to demonstrate publicly against regressive, anti-microfinance policies. It was striking that, after the first few months of the confrontation between Grameen and the government of Bangladesh, the criticisms were almost entirely focused on Yunus as an individual rather than on Grameen Bank itself. The wider microfinance community in Bangladesh, the most robust in the world on a per-capita basis, was almost entirely spared government harassment after the Prime Minister's opening volley accusing Yunus and Grameen of being "bloodsuckers."

I will be revisiting these larger issues of what microfinance accomplished, failed at, and what that track record means for other social movements in a new book that is due out in 2023.

DHAKA TODAY IS A MORE INVITING and livable city than it was in the 1990s, and the country as a whole is in some ways unrecognizable to someone who lasted visited it during that era. I remember when Dr. Yunus, reading a draft of the first edition of this book in 1995, asked me to say something nice about Bangladesh's capital city. I struggled to come up with anything. Today, it is not nearly as difficult. The airport is modern in most respects. The Jamuna Multipurpose Bridge, completed in 1998, has allowed for much quicker and easier travel between the eastern and western regions of the country, making the Aricha port near Zianpur much less important to the country's transport infrastructure. The worst-polluting vehicles are off the streets, and many cars that continue to ply the city's thoroughfares run on compressed natural gas, which is much cleaner than diesel or even unleaded gasoline. The cheap plastic bags that clogged up the sewage system have been outlawed and are nowhere to be found. Skyscrapers are going up everywhere, and foreign businesspeople can be seen in significant numbers at the airports and in the growing number of five-star hotels. Minding stoplights has become more common.

The national economy has been growing steadily, though not quite as quickly as India's. Just as important, Bangladesh's poor people are apparently benefiting more from their nation's economic growth than are those of India. A U.N. report in the mid-2000s stated that if India's child mortality rate had been declining during the last decade as quickly as Bangladesh's had been, some 140,000 children would have been saved from premature death annually.

The causes of Bangladesh's overall improvement are obviously complex and the subject of impassioned debate. Microfinance has clearly played a significant role. Columbia University professor Jeffrey Sachs, in his influential book *The End of Poverty*, distinguished countries that are on the "development ladder" and can expect steady (if sometimes slow) upward progress to ones that cannot reach the ladder and are effectively unable to develop into modern, prosperous societies. He cites Bangladesh as a case study of a country that went from unable to reach the bottom rung of the ladder to one that is now slowly ascending. He cites two principal causes—first, the proliferation of sweatshop labor (mostly related to making ready-made garments), which has created jobs and raised exports. The second major cause he identified was microfinance.

4. Les Papillons

STARTING IN 1976, THE FORD FOUNDATION'S OFFICE in Bangladesh supported Yunus's work with small grants, first to Chittigong University's Rural Economics Program and later to the Grameen Bank Project in Tangail. After Grameen became an independent bank in 1983, Yunus approached Ford with a request for funding to expand in the Dhaka, Patuakhali, Chittagong, and Rangpur districts. He worked out how much money he would need on his calculator, wrote a proposal in longhand, and presented it to Ford program officer Steve Biggs, who wanted to have some people with experience in banking take a look at Grameen before he approved the grant.

After Biggs consulted with foundation officials in New York, it was decided that Mary Houghton and Ron Grzywinski of the South Shore Bank in Chicago should come. Yunus agreed because their résumés suggested that they were asking the same sorts of questions about poverty, institution building, and community development that he was. As Houghton recalls, "We were chosen because we were the bankers who looked the least like bankers."

Years earlier, Houghton and Grzywinski had joined with two friends and raised the capital to buy the South Shore Bank, located in a struggling South Chicago neighborhood, which had been on the verge of failure. Under their leadership, South Shore Bank restored the community's confidence in it, won its depositors back, and began lending to people and businesses that other banks would have avoided. They came to Bangladesh twice in 1983, and were intrigued by Yunus and what he was doing. After analyzing his five-year growth plan for Grameen, they recommended that Ford support it, and went beyond their brief by suggesting that the Foundation pay for Yunus to come to

Chicago to explore the possibility of replicating his program in the United States. Houghton, in particular, had been concerned about the plight of inner-city women and had been informally researching strategies that could address their problems. She was honest enough to admit to herself that her bank, for all its success, did not have products that were relevant to microentrepreneurs, even though South Shore had developed loan packages for small and medium-sized businesses, as well as pathbreaking savings and home-loan programs that were oriented toward wage-earners. She knew that some disadvantaged people were benefiting from being employed by neighborhood businesses that were able to expand after receiving much-needed financing from South Shore. She sensed, however, that South Shore Bank was not meeting the pent-up demand of the poor people in Chicago who wanted to start or expand their microbusinesses, but couldn't because the loans they needed were far smaller than the ones her bank typically approved. Grameen's group-based format struck her as a potential way to meet this demand.

Yunus came to Chicago in 1985, and a series of meetings was arranged with the staff of South Shore Bank and local nonprofit organizations. People were skeptical about the idea of the Grameen model working in inner-city Chicago, but Yunus won over several of his critics. One University of Chicago scholar, for example, had some disillusioning experiences working in India and was convinced Houghton had been bamboozled by Yunus. He felt certain that no program of any size on the Indian subcontinent could be free from corruption. But when he met Yunus in person, the sociologist became a convert.

Much of their discussion centered on Yunus's description of Grameen Bank's target group—"the poorest of the poor." In the United States, he was told, the poorest people need social services, not investment capital. But Yunus held firm, saying that his program was designed to work with the poorest and that he had little interest in working with people if they didn't share his commitment. He recounted similar arguments that Bengali academics had confronted him with when he was getting started in Jobra, and reiterated his philosophy that every human being had the capacity to use credit to get out of poverty. Recalling those conversations, Houghton said, "While for most of us it was a leap of faith to believe what Yunus was saying, we *wanted* to believe it was true." So they kept listening.

At one meeting, Yunus asked a participant what he thought a poor person would need to start or expand a small business in the United States. He was shocked by the answer—$50,000. Yunus went on to say that if there weren't people who were willing to take loans under $5,000, and capable of making a go of it with that amount, then there were no poor people in Chicago that a Grameen-style program could help.

Over the next few years, it would take several more trips between Dhaka and Chicago for Houghton and several colleagues to establish the Women's Self-Employment Project (WSEP), one of the earliest attempts to adapt the Grameen methodology in the United States.

On his second Ford-sponsored trip to the United States in February 1986, Yunus met Bill and Hillary Clinton in a restaurant in Washington, and both expressed enthusiasm about starting a Grameen spin-off in Arkansas, where Bill Clinton was governor at the time. Hillary Clinton, Yunus remembers, was especially gung ho. "She wanted to start right away!" he recalls. Yunus had just returned from his first visit to Arkansas, where he had been driven through rural areas to meet with "the poor" so he could judge the feasibility of adapting the Grameen approach there. Based on his observations, he told the Clintons that he thought the program had a good chance of success in Arkansas.

That trip, however, had got off on the wrong foot. His hosts—senior officials of the state government, South Shore Bank, and the Rockefeller Foundation—thought Yunus appeared less and less interested in meeting with the local people at each successive stop. Yunus would later complain that he didn't think that any of the small business owners he was supposed to meet were poor. Didn't they understand that Grameen was for truly poor people? Yunus remembers thinking that his time was being wasted. On the second day, Yunus persuaded the man from the foundation to bring him to meet some unemployed people and welfare recipients. It was at this point that Yunus began showing interest in the discussions.

Years later, Yunus recalled:

> I asked the welfare recipients and unemployed people, "Suppose that your bank lends you money to do something—what kind of thing would you decide to do?" Almost everybody said that a bank would not give them money, so why bother to talk about it. I said, "Suppose they *would* lend you money." I got more blank stares. "Look, I run a bank in Bangladesh that lends money to the poor people there. I just had a meeting with Governor Clinton and he asked me to bring my bank to your community. I am thinking of starting a bank right here. Now I am trying

to find out if somebody is interested in borrowing money from me. Because if there is no business, why should I come here?" I mentioned that my bank does not need any collateral, nothing.

A woman who had listened very carefully said, "Oh, I would like to borrow some money from your bank!" I said, "Okay, now we are in business. How much money would you like?"

She said, "I would like three hundred seventy-five dollars." I was surprised, because normally, people don't say "Three hundred seventy-five dollars"; they make it a round figure, so I asked her what she wants to do with this sum. She said that she was a beautician, and that her business was limited because she did not have all the right supplies. If she could get a box of supplies costing three hundred seventy-five dollars, she was sure she could pay me back with the extra income. She also said she did not want to take a penny more than what the box actually costs.

Another woman, unemployed after the textile factory she'd been working at closed and moved its business to Taiwan, needed a few hundred dollars for a sewing machine. Still another woman wanted $600 to buy a pushcart from which to sell her hot tamales, which she informed the Bangladeshi professor were "famous" in her neighborhood. These interviews tickled Yunus, and he regretted that the trip was nearing its end.

One of the final interviews held during the trip was with a successful Black Arkansas rice farmer.

Yunus asked the farmer, "How many acres do you plant?"

"Oh, about two thousand."

"Do you have any problem marketing it?"

"No."

"Do you sell it locally?"

"No."

"Oh, you must export it to countries like my home country of Bangladesh, where there are food deficits."

"No."

"Then where *do* you sell it?"

"You see, there are three churches in New York City, and they feed the hungry and those without homes. We call them the homeless here in America. They are a good business for me. Always reliable buyers. The demand gets stronger every year. I just send it to these churches at such and such address, and they have plenty of use for it."

About a week later, Yunus was in New York addressing the board of directors of CARE, one of the largest private relief organizations in the world. They had asked him talk about his work and to advise them on the issue of whether CARE should consider beginning operations in the United States. In his presentation, Yunus talked about Grameen's work in Bangladesh and his experience in Arkansas. One board member raised the issue of whether someone on welfare was actually poor, if you defined the poor as people who went hungry. In response, Yunus said that while he didn't know whether CARE should open a domestic program, he thought there *were* hungry people in the United States. He told the story of meeting the rice farmer in Arkansas, and how he supplied tons of rice to churches that were just a couple of miles north of CARE's office. "If you're not sure where these shelters are exactly, I can give you the phone number of this farmer, and he can tell you the addresses of all his customers up here. Then you can go see for yourselves if there is a hunger problem here in America or not."

EFFORTS TO ADAPT GRAMEEN'S SUCCESS in other countries had gotten under way in the mid-1980s. Yunus helped a pilot project in Malaysia in 1986. The Malaysians discovered that the more they strayed from the Grameen system, the more problems their project experienced. Conversely, the more closely they copied what they had seen in Bangladesh, the more success they had. A 1989 delegation recounted their experiences to Yunus and expressed their belief that the Grameen approach had near-universal applicability.

While the Malaysian experiment was progressing, Yunus was coming to the same conclusion on his own: cultures differ, but people are fundamentally the same. To Yunus, the culture of poverty transcended differences in language, climate, race, and custom. Pilot projects modeled after Grameen were springing up on five continents, and many were achieving success on a small scale. Yunus was coming to believe that many of the 200 million families living in absolute poverty in the world might be a $50 or $100 loan away from making real progress.

The arguments he heard against the possibility of adapting Grameen in the United States had a familiar ring, since he had heard versions of them in Bangladesh—that the poor can't invest, that they can't save, that they need training and social services before they can start a business, and so on. But the relative sophistication or general wealth of a society was and is irrelevant to Yunus. The fundamental point was always the same: The worst-off in any country are denied affordable and reliable credit, the access to which, under the right conditions, can enable them to stabilize and improve their situations.

In August 1990, Yunus was sitting in his office in Dhaka, trying to write a speech that he would deliver several weeks later in Miami, Florida. He jotted down some notes concerning the ways banks don't recognize the intrinsic worth and capacity of human beings but instead look at the condition of their clothes and especially their ability (or inability) to provide collateral. His bank didn't take any of these things into account, and he was searching for a way to illustrate the feasibility of his approach to an American audience.

While taking a break from writing his speech, Yunus opened up his mail, as he always did. On that August day, he received a letter from a Tennessee woman named Tami White, who had read about Grameen and somehow located its address. "When I was a child trying to open up a simple savings account," she wrote, "I was put off by the bank's demand that I produce two pieces of photo identification. What would a child be doing with photo ID in the first place?"[23]

White's experiences with banks since becoming an adult had not noticeably improved. She continued:

> My mother recently received a $500 money order refund from the U.S. government to pay her back for a money order the post office had lost. She took it to the bank we were using, the day we went to close our accounts, and they refused to cash it for her because, as they said, "You no longer have an account here." She had to take it to one of the check-cashing companies that have sprung up in the United States in recent years, and we were shocked when they took 20 percent ($100) as a fee for cashing it.
>
> I started checking into these places and found that many people are forced to use them, mainly elderly people who live on Social Security checks and the working poor who cannot establish bank accounts because they cannot keep minimum balances, afford the per check charges or service charges, or show the bank they already have good credit. Some people have trouble providing ID to open accounts.

White went on to say that even cashing a paycheck can be difficult. "I always took my paycheck to the very bank it was drawn on and always to one of the same tellers. Every week they insisted on seeing my driver's license, and as if having a state-issued driver's license with my photograph was not enough, they demanded to see a credit card, too—presumably if I am in debt, I must be honest!"

She added, "So to discover you, with your faith in people and your willingness to make money work for people in need, has delighted me to the very core of my being."

Yunus read this letter aloud near the end of his speech in Miami and concluded his remarks by saying, "The system we have built refuses to recognize people. Only credit cards are recognized. Driver's licenses are recognized. But not people. People haven't any use for faces anymore, it seems. They are busy looking at your credit card, your driver's license, your Social Security number. If a driver's license is more reliable than the face I wear, then why have a face? A voice? A smell? A touch?"

The title he gave to his speech was "Anything Wrong?"

By the time he delivered the speech, Grameen replication efforts were underway in Chicago, among impoverished rural people in Arkansas, and on an Indian reservation in South Dakota. The grand experiment—to discover whether a revolutionary idea hatched in a developing country like Bangladesh could work in fighting America's poverty problem—had been launched.

ON A HOT SUMMER AFTERNOON IN 1993, Gwen Burns sat at her desk, stared briefly at the bulletin board nestled in the deep recesses of her cubicle, and sighed. Looking at her watch, she saw that it was 5:30 and time to go. She delayed a few more minutes, tidying up a little and collecting what she needed for the meeting—a pad of receipts, pens, a sign-in sheet, and her appointment book. Placing them in her small briefcase, she stood up and walked out of her room, past the workstations of her colleagues Colete, Durga, and Jackie, and into a dark hallway. Before closing the outside door, she turned off the hall lights and flipped the knob that locked up their office.

She walked east on Washington Street in downtown Chicago. As she stood waiting for the southbound Clark Street bus, Gwen looked at City Hall and the Daley Center, two imposing monuments to the city's storied political establishment. Gwen Burns was on her way to meet with nearly 30 women whose lives were far removed from the downtown scene. She pondered the fact that three of them had recently fallen behind on their loan payments. She was troubled—not so much because they were having problems in their businesses, which she understood, but rather because two of the women were becoming resigned to defaulting. Worse still, their "circle sisters" had barely lifted a finger to pressure them to make an effort to repay or to support them. Gwen had initiated a fund-raising campaign, to be organized by the members, to cover the missed payments. She wondered whether her prompting had been enough or too much. There was a fine line between encouraging the women to come together and show unity and bullying them into it. If she stepped over the line, she knew the campaign would likely come to nothing.

Gwen caught her bus. As it passed under the train tracks over Van Buren Street, she clutched her bag, trying to recall whether she had brought her book of receipts. When she felt them, it reminded her that she would be leaving the meeting tonight with several hundred dollars in an unpredictable combination of cash, personal checks, and money orders. The morning after meetings with borrowers, Gwen always felt nervous as she walked downtown to deposit the money. She had never been robbed with her repayments in hand, but in a city with so much senseless crime, one could never be too careful.

When the bus stopped at Cermak Avenue, Gwen stepped down and began trudging toward her car. Earlier that morning, she had parked it in a huge lot used by many South Siders who work downtown but can't afford to keep their cars in one of the pricey garages near their offices.

There was a pronounced lack of a spring in Gwen's step that Monday evening. The last three years had taken a toll on her. The long hours, the promotion she felt she deserved and didn't get, the fact that her leadership wasn't always recognized, and the rivalry with a young, white, college-educated colleague all weighed her down. Yet as she said a prayer, started her car, and began driving toward the Dan Ryan Expressway, she believed more than ever that the project's goals were righteous and its strategy sound. After all, a soft-spoken man from Bangladesh had told her so.

OF ALL THE MANY PROGRAMS run by the Women's Self-Employment Project, the one that was the most difficult to launch, and has generated the most interest and controversy, is the Full Circle Fund (FCF). It has the distinction of being an effort to solve poverty in the industrialized world by using a strategy designed in a developing country. It encourages economic development in depressed communities by giving women access to investment capital of $300 to $1,500 if they agree to join a group of five peers and are able to persuade them of the soundness of their business proposal. Prospective borrowers' credit ratings and their ability to pledge collateral are not considered as part of the process of approving loans.

WSEP was started in 1986 by Mary Houghton, Elsbeth Revere, and Gail Christopher, with initial funding arranged by Sheila Leahy of the Joyce Foundation. It began by offering a training course for low-income entrepreneurs and setting up a loan fund for those who completed the course and wanted to start or expand a business. The FCF formally began operations in August 1988. The training programs were easier to secure funding for, and Connie Evans, WSEP's founding executive director, was eager to hit the ground running. After meeting Yunus, Connie committed herself to adapting the Grameen Bank approach as part of the organization's empowerment strategy. Her board debated the pros and cons of such an approach, with Mary Houghton giving the most vocal support while admitting that South Shore Bank had experienced problems lending to low-income entrepreneurs. Connie and Mary plotted to raise the funds to begin a pilot project modeled on Grameen. The first step would be to send two WSEP staff members to Bangladesh.

When the funding was secured, Connie decided to bring Susan Matteucci, a recently hired MIT graduate, along with her. They wanted some practical experience before they went to Dhaka, so they used a Grameen handbook to set up two groups and dispense four loans to borrowers before leaving for Bangladesh in November 1988—one month before I arrived there for the first time.

The two women had profoundly moving experiences in Bangladesh that provided the basis of a strong friendship. They met women like Amodini and Shandha, who, with initial loans in amounts as small as $50, had gradually improved their lives. They spent long sessions with Grameen field staff, a zonal manager named Shamim Anwar, and Yunus. Susan continually had to explain that Connie was the boss, as nearly everyone assumed that the white woman was in charge. By the end of the trip, they jokingly called themselves "Grameen groupies" and vowed to make the program work in Chicago.

THOUSANDS OF PEOPLE COMING to do business in Chicago arrive each day at O'Hare International, one of the busiest airports in the world. Most who visit the city for business or pleasure never leave the downtown commercial district, known as the Loop (so named because it is circled by elevated trains) and the prosperous areas north of the Loop and in the suburbs. The Chicago they see is a world-class city with stores, restaurants, museums, and all the amenities of modern life. But another Chicago also exists, one considerably less inviting to most visitors.

Midway Airport, located in the far reaches of southwest Chicago, is closer to this other Chicago. It borders on some of the more depressed communities on the South Side and the West Side. In January 1994, a new elevated train line was opened, linking Midway Airport to the Loop, sparing tourists who had come on inexpensive flights the trauma of traversing this section of Chicago by bus or rental car.

Among the most violent and economically depressed neighborhoods on the South Side is Englewood, where the average family income was about $15,000 in the mid-1990s, half the city average.[24] Gang-related violence was epidemic. Drive-by shootings had become so commonplace that many residents are too frightened to sit on their porch during hot summer afternoons. Shards of glass and garbage littered Englewood's streets, which were also full of abandoned cars. Men and women too high on drugs to move lay on its sidewalks, and conversations among its residents often centered on the latest teenager to be shot or arrested.

Englewood began in the 1850s as a small settlement known as Junction Grove, and grew up around a railroad station along the Southern and Northern Indiana line.[25] Two decades later, one settler suggested that the village's name be changed because the dense oak forests that surrounded the local cottages reminded him of Englewood, New Jersey. The largely Irish, Scottish, and German residents had ideas of developing their village into a prestigious community. In 1889, Englewood was annexed by Chicago, and transportation links with the city's downtown were soon improved.

By 1920, the neighborhood's population had surpassed 85,000 and the corner of Halsted Avenue and 63rd Street was the largest shopping district in the country that was not in a downtown area. East of Halsted were upper-class families holding steady white-collar jobs, while west of the thoroughfare were working-class neighborhoods with more modest dwellings. As late as 1940, only 2 percent of Englewood's population was Black —nearly all of them living along the western boundary of Racine Avenue and along Stewart Street to the east.

By 1950, Chicago's "Black Belt" had expanded toward Englewood's boundaries, and 10 years later 69 percent of Englewood's residents were African-American. By 1968, the *Chicago Daily News* was moved to write, "The Englewood area, an urban badlands, has become the city's latest battleground for teen-age gangs. More than ten thousand youths there belong to fifty-nine gangs with descriptive names ranging from the Maniac Disciples to the Junior Loafers."[26] Block by block, real estate speculators bilked homeowners and home buyers for tens of thousands of dollars as the complexion of Englewood changed. By 1970, 98 percent of all residents were Black and 35 percent were living below the poverty level. By 1990, Englewood's non-Black population fell to 1 percent, its unemployment rate was more than double the city average, and half of its families were living below the poverty line—grim statistics that remained essentially unchanged 15 years later.

The mutually reinforcing processes of so-called white flight (when white residents of a neighborhood flee en masse because they fear that Blacks are becoming too numerous) and capital flight had turned Englewood from a diverse working-class area into a depressed inner-city neighborhood. The same thing had occurred in many communities in the southern and western parts of Chicago. One rule of thumb was that once the Black population in an area exceeded 8 percent, there would be a sudden drop in real estate prices, followed by panic selling. Few distinctions were made by whites about the specific Black people who moved in. To some white Americans, a Black white-collar worker and a Black dope pusher were, at the end of the day, simply two people who both pushed down property values.

A walk through Englewood in the mid-1990s brought the visitor face to face with boarded-up factories where Germans and Irish people once worked, crumbling and often charred houses, and overgrown vacant lots. Groups of young Black men and boys paraded aimlessly through the streets, while frightened schoolchildren waited for public transit to take them home before they fell victim to the dangers that lurk outdoors. Residents believe that teens who regularly venture out of the house after dark are often in prison by age 17 and dead by 24.

Most people who had the opportunity to get out of Englewood have done so. The population declined for decades, reaching 60,000 in the 1990 census and bottoming out at 30,000 in 2010. Many who remain are numbed to the violence, often holding out the faint hope that at least one of their children will avoid the temptations of gangs and, in the case of girls, early pregnancy.

Nineteen-ninety-two was a record-breaking year for murders in Chicago, and Englewood's homicide rate was the third-highest among nearly 80 communities in the so-called Second City. The final slaying occurred on December 29th on 75th Street, a short distance from the eastern border of Englewood. When paramedics came to the aid of the 647th victim of gun violence, they found the bullet-riddled body of a Black high school student surrounded by some 50 young men in the street. One paramedic recalled the scene, saying, "All hell broke loose. There was shooting; the cops were outnumbered. Fifteen years on the job, and this was the worst scene that I have ever come across."[27]

THE MEETING BEGAN LATE, but not without ceremony and some fun. Within the sterile confines of a recreation room in the Lindblom Park Field House on 61st Street and South Damen Avenue in Englewood, Omiyale DuPart stood up and brought silence to the room with a wave of her hand. Omiyale— named Veronica Wilma Ramsey at birth; her adopted African name means "great, overflowing river"—then began the meeting.

"I would like to invite Ms. Pack to lead us in prayer." Twenty-six women, their skins different shades of brown but all of African descent, stood up and bowed their heads as Leverta Pack, an older woman wearing the kind of kinte cloth hat then fashionable in South Chicago, delivered an inspirational prayer for the next 10 minutes. She praised the Lord and gave thanks for the Full Circle Fund, family members, and much else. African-Americans have a vibrant oral tradition, and many, like Leverta Pack, are able to extemporize with power and passion at a moment's notice.

Gwen then took over. "We've been adding some women to the center," Gwen began. "Since we start our meetings with some kind of game, tonight we'll start with the name game.

"Each lady in the circle will say her first name and a word which begins with the first letter of her name and that describes her tonight." A low murmur ran through the room; there was a lot of shifting in chairs and at least one audible groan. "Then," Gwen continued, "the person to your left will repeat the name of each person who went before her and make up her own name."

After some general confusion, one woman volunteered, "Joanne, joy." All eyes moved to the woman to her left. "Leverta, loving," Ms. Pack blurted out with a laugh.

"But you need to say the name of the person who went before you," Gwen said quickly.

"Oh. Joanne, uh, joy; Leverta, loving." In quick succession there was an alert Andree and a likable Lynn. (Andree was the nine-year-old son of a woman sitting in the circle.) The game quickly got hard. Some women fumbled more than others. Two at first refused to play at all, saying they couldn't possibly remember so much; with gentle encouragement from Gwen, and poorly suppressed laughter from their peers, each did a respectable job. Finally, the game came to Glenda Harris, a heavyset woman sitting at the end of the circle. She recited all 26 names without a single error. The room erupted in applause.

When the commotion died down, Glenda said, "You know what this goes to show you? Yeah, you *can't* say *you can't*." A few women reflexively said "Uh-huh." "I looked at where I was sitting and I said, I can't remember all those names. It's im-*possible*," Glenda continued, with a chorus of "That's right"s and "Uh-huh"s echoing in the background. "But when you concentrate your attention on something, and give it your best effort, nothing is impossible—nothing. You just *can't* say you *can't*."

Omiyale stood up and brought the meeting back to order. The first item on the agenda was announcements. Several women stood up and talked about recent and upcoming sales events. The Black Expo, held two weeks earlier, had been a disappointment to some of them. The Ghana Fest, an outdoor festival celebrating African and African-American culture that was scheduled for the following weekend, aroused strong interest. One woman described a seminar to be held for Full Circle Fund borrowers on the subject of repairing bad credit histories. "It costs five dollars to participate in the class, which isn't a bad deal if it ends up allowing you to get a credit card and mortgage for a home," she said. From the number of nodding heads in the circle, it was clear that there was more than one person in the room with a spotty credit history.

Then came the subject of the three women who were behind on their loan payments. Omiyale reported that a decision had been made to hold a raffle to help them catch up, and urged everyone to help sell tickets. Lynn Hardy, one of the women who was having difficulty paying off her loan, reported that the first prize would be a television set and that raffle tickets would be available at the next meeting. From the looks on people's faces, the subject of impending loan default had been a matter of some controversy. An awkward silence fell on the group.

Gwen surveyed the room, let the tension build for a few more seconds, and broke in, "You all know the good name that the Full Circle Fund has, and that Englewood is a model for the program. This center was formed with great enthusiasm, but I feel the spirit is dying out. Women are saying, 'I'm paying my loan, why do I have to worry about the *other* ladies?' Rest assured, y'all"— her voice became just a little sassy here—"just as easily as the Full Circle Fund came to Englewood, it can pack up and leave. So let's get this taken care of." The women immediately broke into applause. Gwen, with a beautiful light brown face and hair braided in a checkerboard pattern, was clearly in command.

In short order, the center broke up into its constituent groups. Each circle had its own name, and the ones in the Lindblom center included "Kids First," "LIFE," and "Divine Principles." Chairs were rearranged so that groups of five women could meet in relative privacy to conduct their business. In one corner of the room, five women gathered; they had named their circle *Les Papillons* ("the Butterflies" in French).

The first point of business in the group meetings is for borrowers to pay their biweekly installments to the chairperson. Queenesta Harris, a slender young woman with oversized glasses, opened her purse, pulled out a checkbook, and wrote a check for $27. As she passed it to Omiyale, their eyes met briefly, and both smiled.

Another member named Thelma Dean Ali handed her check to Omiyale. It was the largest payment made that night: $100. The loan, Thelma's third, was for $3,500. She had used each of her loans to buy inexpensive merchandise that she sold at street fairs and bazaars in the Chicago area. The relative success of her business had made her something of a leader in her circle and center, but her strong opinions sometimes isolated her. Among the women in the center, Thelma was one of the least race-conscious. She was, for example, a vocal opponent of a proposal that the center join a protest against Arab and Korean merchants on 63rd Street. On occasion, she would clash with fellow Muslims in her community who belonged to the Nation of Islam. Their combination of racial separatism and Islam disturbed her; she couldn't understand why they would refuse to let a white Muslim into their mosque to worship (a courtesy commonly extended at hers). Sometimes relations would become so strained that Nation followers would fail to return Thelma's traditional Muslim greeting of *"As Salaam o Aleikum."*

As her center meeting drew to a close, Queenesta looked at her watch; it was almost nine o'clock. How long will Shayna hold out, she wondered to herself, looking at her daughter as she explored the bulletin board in the back of the room. So many of Queenesta's hopes and fears were tied up in Shayna, who at the tender age of four seemed to have inherited her mother's intelligence and father's oversized body.

Omiyale got up from her chair and brought the checks to the table, where Gwen was collecting installments and issuing receipts. When she returned, Omiyale said, "How are we doing this week? Who's going to the Ghana Fest?"

"I'm *definitely* going there, sister. There's gonna be some heavy traffic at the Ghana Fest, I'll tell you that. There's gonna be some money to be made there, honey," Thelma answered quickly.

"Geri, how are you doing this week?" Omiyale asked a frail woman, perhaps 50 years old, who was sitting quietly in the group.

"Well . . . okay, I suppose. . . ." Her voice trailed off. She looked up and gulped. Her glasses fell down her nose a bit, drawing attention to her pronounced cheekbones, slightly sunken cheeks, and freckled, light brown skin.

"What's the matter, Geri? You're among friends. If you can't bring it here, where *can* you bring it?" Omiyale said softly.

"It's just . . . I have this business selling, you know, aprons and gift baskets, but . . . but . . . it's hard. I feel so angry sometimes, having lost my job after seventeen years. It's hard . . . getting going in the morning, making my aprons—who's going to buy them, anyway?" Her eyes began to moisten, and she suddenly buried her face in her hands.

"I hear you, Geri. I was laid off too, and sometimes I felt *so* angry," Queenesta said. "I felt worthless, another recipient of unemployment aid. Now I feel, I'm going to *show* the guy who laid me off by making my business succeed. That's how you can take out your anger, Geri. But as my friend Victor says, self-employment has got to be your dream—it can't just be your hobby anymore."

"Listen, Geri, you have *got to* put the past in the past," Glenda added forcefully. "You've got to. . . ."

"There's no problem with your merchandise, girl," Thelma interrupted. "You just gotta get into the habit of *selling* it." Thelma drew out the word *selling*, and punctuated it with a right-handed karate chop into her outstretched left palm. "You know what happened to Glenda here. She said, "No way can I sell." Then we got her out selling her jewelry one day, and before she could say a word, she made eight hundred dollars on her first time out."

"You make beautiful aprons, Geri," Omiyale added softly.

Thelma elicited a promise from Geri to complete two aprons per day, no matter how down she felt. In return, she and the others would work with her to find more buyers. "We're gonna be *calling* you," Thelma added, with a touch of humor in her voice.

The meeting broke up at 10:30. As the women slowly filed out of the room, halfway around the world 35 women would soon be gathering outside Shandha's hut in Kholshi. It was 8:30 a.m. in Bangladesh. By the time their repayment meeting there was over, Queenesta, Thelma, and Omiyale were in their beds, fast asleep.

QUEENESTA LIVED ON THE WESTERN EDGE of Englewood. Like most of her neighbors, she feared the roving gangs of teenage boys who wrought violence upon one another and the Englewood community. Sometimes it just seemed like too much for her—raising a precocious young girl, living in a struggling neighborhood, relying on sporadic child support from her daughter's father, and meeting living expenses from the proceeds of a fledgling business subject to seasonal fluctuations.

It was nearly a year since Queenesta had first met Omiyale and Thelma, the charter members of Les Papillons. All three had been vendors at an annual sidewalk sale in South Shore, a predominantly Black neighborhood somewhat more stable than Englewood. At the time, Queenesta had just begun selling Black-oriented children's books to supplement unemployment insurance checks, which was due to expire. Her daughter, Shayna, then three, had come with her to the event and was, like Queenesta herself, drawn to these two women from the moment they met.

The three talked about many topics over the South Shore festival's four days: upcoming summer festivals, a rumored teachers' strike in the fall, violence on the streets, and marketing strategies. At one point, Thelma talked about her participation in the Full Circle Fund. As the event wore on, Queenesta was impressed by the business skills that these two women demonstrated, and when the opportunity arose, she asked whether it would be possible for her to join the program. The FCF appealed to Queenesta because she considered any aid from the state—even unemployment insurance—to be a crutch, and to be avoided whenever possible. She attended a meeting 10 days later, but, at the time, the only space for a new borrower was in a circle whose members grated on her.

"That girl looked extremely uncomfortable the first night she came to our center meeting," Omiyale recalled months later, "but after seeing her work, her business, I thought she had a lot of promise." Queenesta had what Omiyale knew was most needed in a vendor—a willingness to actively engage potential customers and the ability to entice them, without seeming pushy, to take a look at your table. Success at outdoor events takes a kind of street charisma that not everyone is willing to cultivate in themselves. Omiyale knows; her children sometimes cringe when they see her hawking jewelry and African artifacts on the street. One day, she hopes they all—there are seven—will know the pleasures of owning their own business. It pains her to see succeeding generations of Black people single-mindedly pursuing what seems like an ever-shrinking number of jobs provided by white-led companies, while thousands of immigrant families slowly build lives for themselves by running stores that serve Black consumers.

When a spot opened up two weeks later in Omiyale and Thelma's circle, Queenesta was the first person they called. She immediately agreed to begin training for the recognition test, which she passed in January 1993. A short time later, she received a loan for $1,000, promptly investing it in cassette tapes and compact discs that she was selling from a small counter that she rented in a West Side bookstore.

Queenesta was an unlikely person to be selling music to teenagers, but joining the Full Circle Fund gave her access to needed investment capital. She figured she knew less about the rap, hop-hop, and house recordings that sell so well on the West Side than any other Black person in Chicago. She didn't even own a radio, much less a stereo. And when she listened to the lyrics of the songs, she didn't like much of what she heard. But financial necessity gave Queenesta enough motivation to gain a working understanding of the market within three months. By July, she knew most of the popular artists and their bodies of work. A remaining challenge was to persuade her North Side wholesaler to reserve at least a few of the most popular cassettes for her.

At about the same time that she began selling music, she had taken to bringing Afrocentric children's books to schools and day care centers that primarily serve Black youngsters. Popular titles included Afro-Bets's *First Book About Africa: An Introduction to Young Readers* and versions of fairy tales such as *Cinderella* and *Beauty and the Beast* with Black characters. As she sold more, she read more, and slowly she became convinced that Black children like Shayna needed to be exposed to stories with Black heroes from a young age. She would read some of the books to her daughter, carefully preserving each one so that she could sell it later on.

When the music and children's book businesses were slow, she would often sell general books, merchandise imported from Africa, and dollar earrings at street fairs or bazaars, and on college campuses. During Black History Month, she sold these goods in the staff cafeteria of Allstate Insurance, which had laid her off in 1991. During her first year of operation, her businesses were shaky but growing, and little of her success, she believes, would have been possible without credit from the Full Circle Fund and the guidance of her circle members. "Being a single mother is very stressful. Sometimes you stop believing in yourself. But not these ladies," Queenesta once confided in her diary.

STANDING BEHIND HER SMALL GLASS CASE of compact discs and cassettes in West Side Books, Queenesta Harris greeted her customers with a smile on a hot Wednesday in early August 1993. Shayna sat on the floor beneath her, drawing on a piece of construction paper with crayons.

Business was slow. In the early afternoon, two Black teenagers came in the door and said in loud voices, "Hey, Queen." They wore baggy jeans and turned-up baseball caps worn backwards, and they had a mission.

"Queen, you got the Briny mix yet?"

"Naw, but I should be getting it next week."

The two teenagers looked at each other, and then briefly toward the back of the store. There they saw African clothing and head-wear, and racks of books about Black liberation, including Carter Woodson's classic *The Miseducation of the Negro*, the Koran, a sympathetic treatment of the Nation of Islam, and *Black Economics: Solutions for Economic and Community Empowerment* and *Countering the Conspiracy to Destroy Black Boys*. The two young men had never read those books and, in all likelihood, never would. Queenesta often thought that the intensity and seriousness of Victor McClain, who was the owner, and of the store itself made the boys who bought her music uncomfortable.

After whispering something in his companion's ear, the larger of the two boys volunteered, "Catch you later, Queen." Both quickly headed out the door.

On days like this, Queenesta often questioned whether having her own business would be enough to support herself. Several bills were already weeks overdue. When her doubts overwhelmed her, as they often did that summer of 1993, she pondered her past, wondering how she got into this vulnerable and uncertain position.

Despite living in the heart of South Chicago and attending Full Circle Fund meetings there, Queenesta Harris considered herself a West Sider. She grew up there, commuting to predominantly Jewish public grammar and high schools in northwest Chicago. While her education was first-class, and is reflected today in her speaking and writing skills, she never felt at ease with her white classmates, with whom she had little in common.

Queenesta's brother Delbert was killed in 1970 in a racially motivated highway attack by a white teenager who drove his pickup truck into Delbert's motorbike. Whatever stability had existed in the family before that began to crumble. Her sister June fell into a depression from which she has never fully recovered; two of Delbert's brothers got themselves into trouble; and her father left the family for good. With only one meager income to rely on, the family sometimes skimped on meals. Queenesta was outwardly stoic about it all, but the turmoil took its toll.

After graduating from high school, Queenesta took a job as a secretary with a large printing company that, at the time, had contracts with *Playboy*, *Jet*, and *Ebony* magazines. It was 1982, and her salary was $13,000 a year. When a Black colleague urged her to get further education to improve herself, she pursued and earned an associate degree in industrial engineering. But by the time she completed the degree, her company had lost the *Playboy* account. Anticipating her employer's failure, Queenesta took a job with the Allstate Insurance Company in 1986 as a claims associate.

At Allstate, Gary Williams, an African-American colleague, became Queenesta's mentor. He urged her to save and invest her salary rather than engage in the conspicuous consumption that he said was the curse of their race. A former professional football player, Gary showed Queenesta and other African-American staff at Allstate his books—not literary, but financial: he had a quarter of a million dollars in the bank. When Queenesta became pregnant in 1988, Gary rebuked her for being on the verge of becoming another single Black mother with an uncertain future. But he also urged her to start investing so that when the money was added to some modest savings she already had, she would have $15,000 stashed away before her child reached her first birthday. Queenesta took up the challenge, and began sending $500 each month—about half of her take-home pay—to an investment adviser Gary had introduced her to.

Shayna was born in September 1988. Queenesta secured $200 per month in child support from Shayna's father and somehow managed to meet the goal of saving $15,000. She was able to live off the interest from her savings and the sporadic child support payments she received while taking a year off to be with her daughter, again following Gary's advice. To reduce expenses, she moved in with her mother.

In January 1991, Shayna's father said he was a changed man. He urged Queenesta to move into her own apartment in the suburbs, and when she agreed, he paid for the move. At his urging, Queenesta adopted a different lifestyle—snappy clothes bought in the right downtown shops, nails and hair done just so, and a new car that came with hefty monthly payments and insurance. He arranged it so that the car was in his name and Queenesta made the payments. Gary Williams looked on all these developments disapprovingly.

In early June, Shayna's father moved into Queenesta's Oak Park apartment, and promises of marriage were in the air. But before that month was over, her life was unexpectedly turned upside down. Queenesta was involved in an accident that left her car in the shop needing $4,000 worth of repairs. By the end of the month, the arguments she and Shayna's father were having were heated enough to prompt Queenesta to abandon most of her belongings and move in with her childhood friend Doreen. Two days after moving out, Queenesta returned one final time to salvage what she could of her possessions—her's and Shayna's clothes, some keepsakes, and a sleeper sofa.

At the time, Queenesta was on medical leave from Allstate because of the car crash, and her supervisor was growing impatient. Just as she was due to return to work, Queenesta was forced to take some additional sick days when Shayna fell ill. Even after returning to work, she was often late (owing to a two-hour commute and having to bring Shayna to day care). On one occasion when traffic had delayed her for nearly an hour more than usual, she drove into the parking garage and left Shayna sleeping in the car until she could show her face and do enough work so that she could sneak away to drop her daughter off at day care.

When Shayna fell ill again in early November and Queenesta was forced to take another few days off, her exasperated boss made her the victim of corporate retrenchment that would culminate a year later in Allstate's closing down most of its Chicago-area operations. She applied for and received unemployment insurance benefits that amounted to $233 per week for an initial period of six months. Suddenly, the reality of poverty and vulnerability hit home at a new level.

Queenesta's friend Doreen was a single mother on welfare, a prospect that, at the time, seemed an increasingly likely fate for Queenesta herself. The two resolved to turn their lives around together. Doreen began going to college at night and doing secretarial work during the day. As she saw her friend struggle with her assignments, Queenesta realized that Doreen had never properly learned to read, write, or do simple arithmetic, and she decided to take it upon herself to tutor her.

As for Queenesta, the thought of getting another job was not an attractive one. As she had seen, the demands of taking care of Shayna, now three years old, were not always consistent with those of a nine-to-five job. Yet the prospect of relying on public assistance was even less appealing.

During her final days at Allstate, Queenesta had gotten into the habit of spending her lunch hours at Victor McClain's store, a ten-minute drive from her office. Surrounded by condemned storefronts, fast-food take-out joints, and a thrift store, West Side Books is an unlikely place to be a center of cultural and social ferment. Queenesta met Victor there one day when she was browsing among his bookshelves—he usually had only one copy of each book, and perhaps three hundred titles in stock. On repeated visits, she shared her troubles with him; in turn, he suggested that she read about Black empowerment and get into business for herself.

"The Koreans, the Caucasians—they recirculate money and capital within their communities close to ten times before it leaves," he once told her. "In the Black community, we hardly recirculate it twice. We spend our money with white businesses, and we have a lower rate of entrepreneurship than virtually any ethnic group in America." One of the first books that Victor gave Queenesta—*Black Economics* by Jawanza Kunjufu—notes that the rate of business ownership in the white community is seven times greater than among African-Americans.[28] Besides discussing the obstacle of lack of access to capital, Kunjufu argues that status-conscious African-Americans prefer the stability of working for white-owned firms in downtown Chicago. As consumers, he admonishes, they incur spiraling debts amassed while buying fashionable clothes and cars manufactured and sold by other ethnic groups, rather than using their incomes to open businesses in the Black Belt that could serve their own race. He argues that entrepreneurs from other ethnic groups fill the gap. As a result, according to his calculations 93 percent of the $200 billion to $300 billion African-Americans spend annually goes to firms owned by other ethnic groups.

African-American scholars and activists such as Kunjufu contend that lack of racial solidarity opens the door for immigrants from Korea, South Asia, and the Caribbean—the so-called model minorities—to start successful businesses in the inner city.[29] Yet, there is more at work here than meets the eye. Work ethics (or lack thereof) are only one of many factors at play in business ownership and success. Many of America's immigrants in recent decades were highly educated, well-off people in their own country. They are therefore often able to use their own money as investment capital to start a small business here, or are able to tap into the support network of people who migrated here before them for advice and capital—or both. Korean-Americans, in particular, borrow from informal rotating credit and savings associations and can often obtain merchandise manufactured in Asia at preferential rates.

While other immigrants came to America at a time and in a manner that *they* chose, and can access support networks both here and at home, African-Americans were denied these opportunities. Even after slavery was abolished, its legacy left Blacks economically disadvantaged.

While Black people like Victor understand the historical reasons for their race's troubles, they try not to dwell on it. They work instead to motivate other African-Americans to achieve new levels of racial solidarity and economic self-reliance.

One day, Queenesta was hurrying out the door of Victor's store to get back to work on time when she stopped to read a poster on the wall. It read, "Black Man, why do you spend 100 percent of your money with white society [and] then turn around and blame them for 98 percent of your problems? Let us exchange our millions with ourselves. Let us establish an economic system among ourselves. We could change our conditions in 24 hours or less."

Queenesta mulled over her future and wondered if she would have the wherewithal to start her own business. At the moment, it seemed like an adventure in personal and communal uplift in which she was unlikely to ever take part. Little did she know that within several months, it would be her only realistic alternative to living off of public aid.

FOR THELMA, QUEENESTA, OMIYALE, and the other women in Englewood who borrow from the Full Circle Fund, the coming of spring and summer means dozens of festivals and street fairs and opportunities for making fast money. Small-scale vendors without a fixed storefront depend on people being out and about and in a mood to spend.

The biggest event at the beginning of the summer of 1993, the Black Expo held at McCormick Place, Chicago's preeminent convention center, was disappointing for those FCF borrowers who were able to scrouge together enough money to pay the discounted, but still substantial, booth fee. Queenesta, however, did quite well. She had taken a $2,500 short-term loan from the Full Circle Fund to buy forty dozen T-shirts to sell there. Victor McClain, by then her mentor and landlord, bought another forty dozen, and as a result they received a substantial volume discount, paying only $3.25 per shirt. They grossed $3,500, which retired Queenesta's debt and the cost of renting their booth. The plan was that as they sold the rest of the T-shirts, Victor would get back his investment of $2,500, and then the profit on the remaining 400 T-shirts would either be split by Queenesta and Victor or plowed back into the venture to buy more inventory.

In July, to her surprise, Queenesta closed a deal in which she sold $1,900 worth of Afrocentric books to a local high school. It was her largest deal ever, on which she earned a profit of $800.

One afternoon in August 1993, Queenesta was pleasantly surprised when Omiyale stopped by Victor's store, the first time that any of her circle members had made the long trip from Englewood to the far West Side. Omiyale chatted with Queenesta for a while, dropped off some earrings she made that Queenesta had agreed to display and try to sell from her case, and talked business with a seamstress who worked in a room in the back of the store. Before long, Omiyale was off for her next appointment.

As her chairperson left, Queenesta radiated a quiet pride. Having space in a store let her do something for Omiyale—display her merchandise every day in a good location. She would get a small percentage of the proceeds if the jewelry sold, but that didn't matter as much as Omiyale's recognition of the progress she was making. It was also comforting to see a friendly face and perky personality at a time when tensions were rising in the store between Victor and some of his tenants who were behind on their rent.

Towards the end of August, reports of public budget shortfalls that threatened to shut down the entire Chicago school system began to worry Queenesta. (Only twice during the prior 20 years had August been without the prospect of such a crisis.) She was counting on selling a lot of books to schools in neighborhoods with predominantly Black populations. A shutdown or strike would throw a wrench into her plans for a big breakthrough in book sales. And then there was her daughter to consider. If the schools closed, she would have to take Shayna with her as she did her business.

As the fall got going, Queenesta had a lot on her mind.

IN THE HEART OF DOWNTOWN CHICAGO, on the seventh floor of a building on Washington Street, are the offices of the Women's Self-Employment Project (WSEP) and its founding director, Connie Evans. Some 25 women, two-thirds of whom are African-American, work there in close quarters. The enterprise agents, who collect the loan payments and form the borrowing groups, along with support staff, interns, and volunteers, work side by side in small cubicles with little privacy, while the professional staff members each have their own, albeit modest, offices. Connie's is the only office that has space for more than one guest.

Connie was one of four children raised by a mother who ran her own catering business in rural Tennessee. At the age of 36, Connie was running an organization with an annual budget exceeding $1 million. As a chief executive, she appreciates and rewards hard work, and like Yunus, sets high standards for herself and her colleagues.

When alone with her friends and close confidantes, among them some of the most talented people working on social justice in Chicago, she enjoys the opportunity to open up about the challenge of running a growing organization that is often scrutinized by foundations, the media, and academics. More than anything, Connie likes to laugh. It reminds her of when she was younger and wasn't responsible for running an organization as large and complex as WSEP. The laughs had been less frequent in the last few years. She sometimes felt like leaving the organization she had founded, but—despite a series of lucrative offers—she could never quite make the break. Still, when times were tough, as they were in the summer of 1993, she certainly toyed with the idea. The prospect of working overseas appealed to her, and any number of international organizations would gladly have offered a senior position to someone of her caliber.

During the summer of 1993, Connie was troubled by a spate of resignations within WSEP and the prospect of several more in the fall. She was also bothered by divisions within her inner circle. She suggested hiring a chief operating officer, someone who would manage the staff and sweat the details. This new hire would also leave her free to do what she does best—communicating her vision of WSEP so that foundations, media, and policy makers took notice. But not all of her colleagues and trusted advisers agreed.

Connie was also dealing with the issue of WSEP's possible nationwide expansion, which Subway sandwich tycoon Fred DeLuca had expressed interest in supporting. Connie presented the expansion idea to her board of directors in the fall. Their first question was whether she was committed to staying on as WSEP's director to see the process through. Connie said she could not guarantee that she would stay indefinitely; in fact, she went so far as to say that she might resign the following year. The board agreed to study the feasibility of the idea.

Meanwhile, Connie knew that she had some soul-searching to do. She decided to seek out the advice of a mentor. She finally got the opportunity that spring to speak to Yunus and asked whether he thought she should leave WSEP and turn the job over to someone else. Connie, drained by all the long hours and stress that the work demanded, was hoping he would give her the green light. Yunus, however, told her in no uncertain terms that she shouldn't leave. He recognized how special Connie was, perhaps seeing some of himself in her. Losing her, he feared, would cripple WSEP's finances and more important, its heart; for Connie, despite her relative youth, was unusually gifted in program design, identifying talent, fundraising, and leadership. "Look at all the organizations that lost their leaders and within five years were in chaos," he said. It was not the answer Connie had been looking for.

WITH MUCH OF HER HEAD WRAPPED TIGHTLY in a scarf despite the torrid heat, Thelma Dean Ali stood in front of a card table that long ago had begun sagging in the middle, hoping to make a few dollars selling her merchandise: socks, berets, earrings, Indian scarves and purses, African oils, and spices. Her table, just west of Halsted Avenue, was in a prime location in the Maxwell Street Market, which at the time was the largest and best-known open-air market in a major North American city. Her place of business was less permanent and attractive-looking than Queenesta's, but it was often more profitable.

Around noon, a beat-up white Cadillac cruised by slowly, and the driver, a haggard-looking Black man in a white undershirt, leaned out the window and pointed at a pack of tube socks. "How much?" he asked with a frown.

"Five bucks. Six in a packet. Most people charge six."

Deal.

Another man, apparently intoxicated, greeted Thelma a short time later and asked for a body oil imported from Tunisia. When he realized he had only 50 cents, Thelma measured out half of her smallest vial, perhaps a few milliliters of fragrance.

Every weekday and Saturday, Thelma arrives at Maxwell Street by bus before 11 a.m., having spent the morning saying her prayers toward the holy city of Mecca at 5:30, preparing her children for school, and then doing some shopping in downtown Chicago. While shopping, she eagerly searches for bargains (going-out-of-business sales are the best) so that she can snatch up merchandise to resell in a few hours at a profit, while also checking out the competition at five-and-dime stores. (Because she has so little overhead, Thelma can normally undersell even the chain stores.) A few wholesalers, her friend Harry Zimmerman, and auctions also supply her with goods that move well here. By 11 a.m., she sets up her table, and she usually stays open until dusk.

Sunday is special at Maxwell Street.[30] Thelma leaves her house at 5:00 a.m., arriving at the market by bus before 6:30, with the sun barely peeking through the gaps in between the skyscrapers that line Lake Michigan. If she were to arrive in "Jewtown"—as the market is commonly called among many Black Chicagoans as an expression of their admiration for Jewish industriousness—any later than that, she would risk not having a 4-by-10-foot slot from which to sell. Some vendors are known to come as early as Saturday afternoon and to sleep in their cars overnight, even in the dead of winter, to ensure a choice spot for the Sunday bazaar. Fights are known to flare up when one seller begins to encroach on another's space by even a few inches.

Vendors and customers who come to Maxwell Street are looking for bargains, and, as one Full Circle Fund borrower put it, *real people*—that is, other folks of humble origins who had not lost touch with their roots. Literally in the shadow of downtown Chicago, this is one place where Blacks, Puerto Ricans, and Mexicans can let it all hang out. Geographically, the dominant Anglo-European culture is only a few blocks away; but for one day each week, it is thousands of miles away in spirit.

By 7:00, the market is jammed with merchants and customers. There is hardly anything that you can't buy at a bargain—toys, spices, fresh produce, air conditioners, bicycles, adult magazines and videos, sports equipment, coffeepots, computers, books, shirts and sweaters, doorknobs, hardware, tires, diamonds, barber's chairs, vacuum cleaners, crutches, office supplies, bunk beds, pancake syrup, eight-track cassette tapes, jumper cables, perfume, sweatshirts, automobile and motorboat engines, typewriters, carpets. Many items are available in one of three conditions—new, used, and very used.

Cars edge through the market with drivers and passengers looking in every direction for a good deal. They often haggle over a price and make a purchase without ever leaving their vehicle; they are, as they say, "cruising." Near accidents between cars and other cars, cars and customers, and cars and vendors occur every few minutes.

Dense crowds—some 20,000 bargain-hunters come on a typical Sunday—push from one stall to the next. The sweet aromas of exotic cuisines mingle in the open air with the acrid smell of two-week-old garbage. Live blues is pumped out by two or more bands, as it has been for decades. (Some claim that Chicago-style blues was born on Maxwell Street.) In these ways—and others that are less easily discerned at first glance—the Sunday market is strongly reminiscent of Bangladesh.

It's been that way for some time. In the late nineteenth century, the Maxwell Street area was an overpopulated, immigrant (mostly Jewish) slum with a bustling, Old World–style bazaar. Over time, the market became known as the Ellis Island of the Midwest, a place where an immigrant could get a toehold in an economy and culture they barely understood. Even today, one can hear more than a dozen languages being spoken by vendors and customers.

Many well-known personalities have roots here. Joseph Goldberg, father of the late Supreme Court justice Arthur Goldberg, was a fruit peddler on Maxwell Street. Ira Berkow, the *New York Times* columnist, sold nylon stockings. Samuel Paley, the father of William Paley, who founded the Columbia Broadcasting System, was a cigar vendor.

Despite the market's history and its role as a primary source of self-employment for low-income Chicagoans, there was serious talk of redeveloping the area in 1994 to make way for the expansion of the University of Illinois's Chicago campus. In the waning months of 1993 and early 1994, a pitched battle for the very existence of the bazaar was being fought. It was a struggle between history and modernity, and between the economic needs of struggling entrepreneurs and the establishment's thirst for expansion. (Indeed, where the university's campus stood then was once a tight-knit, lower-class Italian neighborhood that succumbed to Mayor Daley's pursuit of a new center of higher learning within the city limits.)

By the late afternoon of that hot July day, Thelma had $436 in her pocket and judged it a fair day, considering the heat. As she began to pack up her table, a Black youth ran across Halsted Avenue with a hamburger in his hand and an old man in close pursuit, waving a spatula. Thelma chuckled at the scene, yet it reminded her of the challenges of raising Black boys in this sometimes-cruel city, a job made even more difficult when you are raising them to be Muslims.

ON AUGUST 5, THELMA, OMIYALE, and a woman from another group set off for Milwaukee's annual Afro-World Festival in Omiyale's van, a vehicle she recently inherited from her father. Three days later Thelma, selling T-shirts, sequined hats, hair accessories, and toys, had made $1,500, while Omiyale had grossed close to $2,000. Thelma, whose theory is that you only make consistent money on things that retail for between $1 and $3, was impressed at her chairlady's ability to talk people into buying merchandise that she sold for $80 to $100.

The festival ended at 11 p.m. on Sunday, August 8, and the three women began their journey home at 1 a.m. and talked about their center meeting on Monday. The main item on the agenda that evening was how to get the women who'd lost money at the Black Expo to catch up on their loan payments. Thelma suggested that the newly constituted loan committee of herself, Omiyale, and Leverta Pack should take a more active role in scrutinizing future loan proposals and working with WSEP staff to negotiate solutions for cases of default. "This here center is about sisterhood, about us helping each other," Thelma said with her head tilted to the right and her arms gesturing wildly. "But let's have it be about *sisterhood* and not about *stupidhood*."

Above all, she wanted to prevent future problems with loan utilization. As it was, the entire center had to hold fund-raisers for the three women who were in trouble—one whose airbrushing business had slowed down, another whose merchandise was mysteriously stolen after being delivered by the United Parcel Service, and a third who took the money and promptly used it to pay her son's tuition after telling her fellow borrowers she was buying a computer for a vaguely described business venture she had only described vaguely.

Omiyale led the discussion, but she felt uneasy about doing so, having fallen a few payments behind on her own short-term loan. After taking $3,000 from the Full Circle Fund to purchase inventory for the Black Expo, which was to be repaid by the beginning of October, Omiyale had grossed a mere $1,300. She had taken more than half of those earnings to make a first installment on her loan, and used the remainder to catch up on business and personal bills that had been piling up. Thelma, Geri, Glenda, and Queenesta had no idea that Omiyale was courting disaster by carrying a debt of more than $2,000 without any credible plan to repay it on time. In the classic Grameen system that WSEP followed, the credit line of *each* circle member is dependent on timely repayments by *all* of them. With the number of days of warm weather dwindling, Omiyale was playing with fire.

Throughout August, Thelma was hard at work selling her oils, hair accessories, and toys (plastic water guns were especially popular). August 14th was the traditional Bud Biliken Parade, for which no fee was required to vend. She exceeded her goal of $1 in sales every minute, bringing home $364 after five hot, sweaty hours.

August 15th was a rainy Sunday at Maxwell Street, so she grossed only $50. Since she usually pays about 40 to 50 percent of the retail price for her merchandise, that meant a $20 profit after paying for carfare. On a hunch, she arrived early on Monday, anticipating that some of the rained-out Sunday shoppers would come by. She was right, and made $115. The next day she met the organizer of an event called the Cocofest and reserved a booth for $11. On Friday, August 20, she went to the Cocofest and made $120.

At a center meeting in the second half of August, two aldermen were guest speakers. When several of the women asked about the possibility of taking over one of the buildings the city had recently seized so that they could start a "cooperative manufacturing venture," one alderman said, "I'll turn the deed over to you today for free. But then you'll have to find about one million dollars to get it up to fire and safety codes." When she heard that, Thelma, who began participating in the Full Circle Fund by taking a $300 loan, leaned over to Queenesta and said, "Why don't these women stop their million-dollar dreams and just work their businesses a little harder?" She was, above all, an entrepreneur with both feet firmly planted in reality.

BY THE END OF AUGUST, strange things were happening that would ultimately change WSEP and impact the women who met in the Lindblom Field House every fortnight in significant ways. Gwen told Omiyale that she would be announcing her resignation from WSEP soon, which would be effective at the end of September. Omiyale, the first person to hear the news, was crestfallen, but tried to be supportive. She told Gwen that she would organize a going-away party worthy of her service to the center—a center whose viability Omiyale doubted without the tenacity of the only enterprise agent she had ever known.

Around the same time, Queenesta was talking to Thelma about the Afro-World Festival in Milwaukee and mentioned her disappointment that Victor hadn't been able to sell more than $1,200 worth of the T-shirts they had bought together for the Black Expo. When she said that, there was a brief silence on the other end of the phone. After the pause, Thelma said, "Girl, Victor was selling them T-shirts so fast that Thelma Perkins and me had to leave our booths to help him. He sold more than twelve hundred dollars on the first day alone. We could hardly keep up with the demand."

As Queenesta put down the phone, she contemplated her mentor's possible deception and began mentally preparing herself for a decision that would profoundly affect her business, and his.

Update: Since the 1990s

DURING THE TIME WHEN THIS FIELD RESEARCH for this book was carried out, Chicago—like many major cities across America—was experiencing a crime wave that seemed to have no end in sight. It was a subject that the media and the people I talked to were constantly discussing. Black teens were seen as the most common perpetrators and victims of the violence. Few people thought this trend could be reversed; at best it could be managed. Fewer still talked about the systemic racism and structural factors that contributed to this sorry state of affairs.

And then, unexpectedly and delightfully, violent crime across the country dropped significantly over a period of two decades, beginning in the late 1990s. Chicago was one of the prime beneficiaries of this trend. While people had been quick to blame African-American families and their teenagers for the early 1990s crime wave, few gave them credit for the reversal. In fact, experts never figured out the factors driving what in many metro areas was a reduction in crime of 80 percent or more from its high-water mark.

However, when the trend reversed itself and ticked up a bit in the late 2010s and early 2020s, Chicago was again at the forefront, and politicians went back to playing the blame game with strong racial overtones. Still, the situation was far better than it had been two decades earlier. At least this time, there was some recognition that racial injustice, police brutality, educational disparities, and rising inequality played a part in the struggles of African-Americans and other people of color.

As I reread this chapter and those to follow about the women in Chicago in preparation for publishing this edition, I have mixed feelings about them. Occasionally my observations and even the language I used have a dated quality and seem to reinforce negative stereotypes. However, when I wrote those chapters decades ago, I tried to honestly portray the situations and mindsets of those women as I observed and perceived them. The emphasis of people like Victor, Gary, and Thelma on Black self-help as opposed to blaming their struggles on racism was as much a part of that era as investigations of mass incarceration and police brutality are in the early 2020s.

What comes through most powerfully to me as I read this chapter 30 years later is the way so many African-Americans find time amidst their struggles to help and counsel one another, even as they raise children and manage the realities of modern life as best they can without the benefit of generations of accumulated wealth and privilege. These underappreciated elements of African-American culture are clearly contributing factors to the success of Grameen America, which is a more-than-worthy successor to the pioneering microlending efforts of the Full Circle Fund.

5. Amena Begum's Dream

SQUATTING IN A SMALL THATCH HUT, Amena splashed some water onto the aluminum plate from which her husband had just taken his morning rice and began swishing around the contents with her index finger.[31] As she did so, Amena snuck a glance at her husband, Absar Ali, as he retied a *longhi* around his skinny waist and spat out some phlegm from his mouth. Amena always kept an eye on her husband when he was around the house, though she tried to do it inconspicuously, peeking up from her cooking or cleaning. Experience had taught her that when she had a few seconds to prepare herself for a beating, she was able to protect herself.

Absar Ali pulled a *biri* (an inexpensive, undersized cigarette popular on the Indian subcontinent) from behind his ear, lit it, and settled into a deep crouch. As he drew the smoke into his lungs, he looked absentmindedly into the cloudy horizon. His wife could see beads of sweat forming on his back. The heat and humidity of the monsoon season were upon them; within a few weeks traveling from village to village would become much more difficult. He knew it was critical to make as much money as he could now that the canals were dry and his inventory had been replenished. With one final puff, Amena's husband stood up, strode into their hut, crouched down, and maneuvered a four-foot-long piece of bamboo so that its midpoint rested on his right shoulder. Baskets full of aluminum pots and pans hung from rope tied to each end of the bamboo.

For the last two generations, the men in Absar Ali's family have made their living selling clay and, more recently, aluminum cookware door to door. They buy the pots in bulk at wholesale prices in Dhaka, mark them up about 25

147

percent, and spend their days as barefoot traveling salesmen. For many years, Absar, his older brother, and their father ran the business with little more than $100 in working capital. Family illness, unwise selling to customers on credit, and other setbacks could deplete their inventory, but with three people working the business together, it was rare that all would run into difficulty simultaneously. When they did, there was always the village loan shark as a lender of last resort, but that carried a high price—interest of 10 percent per month, or more.

It was understood that when sacrifices had to be made to pay off debts, it was the women and children who usually made them. While nobody liked to see them go hungry, it was simply common sense that the men of the house needed their energy to go out and make the money necessary to pay off high-interest loans.

Absar Ali adjusted the bamboo slightly, retied his *longhi* a second time, and began walking down a gentle slope towards a narrow path dividing an acre of maturing rice paddies. After snaking his way through the field, he lumbered up a slope leading to a dirt road that brought him into the heart of Kholshi. He neither said good-bye to his family nor looked back once he was on his way.

As she watched her husband, Amena splashed more water on the pots and plates and swished it around until everything began to look clean. Just then, a small flock of ducklings, perhaps a dozen in all, appeared from behind the tiny thatch hut where Amena cooked, waddling behind their mother. They were a noisy bunch, and they wanted to be fed. It was not quite far enough into the monsoon that Amena could trust that her ducks would find enough to eat in the shallow puddles that would become knee-deep swamps soon enough. She threw a handful of rice husks, and as the ducklings crowded around it, she deftly trapped them under an inverted bamboo basket. She stood and looked at them briefly; her eyes and fingers gave the impression that she was counting her brood.

Barely four weeks earlier, Amena had given birth to her fifth child. While she still felt weak, Amena had no intention of spending 40 days in bed, as is customary in Bangladesh. She was a busy woman now.

Two weeks after accompanying Fulzan and Alow to the Grameen Bank office to receive their loans, Amena had been due to receive hers along with Firoza. She had been determined to complete the transaction before she gave birth, though with each passing day, it had seemed less likely that she would have time. Without the money actually in her hands, she feared there might be some plan to eliminate her from the group at the last moment.

Already she'd overcome the doubts of her group and some of the older members, such as Shandha, and persuaded the Grameen staff to conduct the group training sessions in her home, as she was too weak in the last weeks of her pregnancy to go elsewhere. The worst obstacle had been having her character questioned by other borrowers. In their eyes, she was a *nodi bhanga lok* (roughly translated as "a person of the broken river," meaning someone who repeatedly migrates because of changes in the course of the river).

Nodi bhanga lok are thought to lack the civilized qualities that come from living in one place all one's life. For membership in the Grameen Bank, these people must overcome the suspicion that they are eternal migrants who will pick up and flee with their loans at the first sign of trouble. Even the poorest people in the area looked down on the disheveled refugees who were forced to set up a shantytown near the Zianpur bazaar after the river changed course in the aftermath of the 1988 flood. "Nobody has *ever* lived there before," one could hear people saying from the market as they pointed at the makeshift huts with barely suppressed contempt. Amena had a leg up on those people, as she was able to take refuge on her grandfather's land. Yet, when she and her husband were clearing a small patch of land from a jungle on the edge of the house plot, Amena could feel the eyes of the entire village staring at them.

If it hadn't been for the determined support she received from her Hindu neighbor Oloka Ghosh and a Muslim woman named Zorina, she would never have been able to join Nobirun's group after the original quintet failed their recognition test. Once she came in, however, her leadership skills and relatively high educational attainment (she started, but did not complete, third grade) made her a natural selection as group secretary.

The evening before Amena was due to receive her loan, she went into labor. She called a cousin who was living with her grandfather to come and assist with the process.

At 3:30 a.m., Amena gave birth to a baby boy, whom she and her husband would name Shahjahan. It was a difficult birth, but not the most painful she had experienced. Still, after it was over, she was unable to go to the bank, and the torrents of rain that had been thrashing the village since the previous evening showed no signs of letting up. As Amena lay on a thin blanket draped across the dirt floor of her hut that morning, she hoped that Nobirun and

Firoza would walk the half mile to see her, but feared that instead they would go to the bank and get her in trouble for not showing up.

As it turned out, the women waited an hour for Amena before heading to the Zianpur bazaar with only leaves from a banana tree shielding them from the rain. When they told Rohim that Amena was late and might not arrive, he flew into a rage and tore up her loan documents. No one considered that she might have gone into labor; Rohim and the women guessed that she had been unwilling to walk the three miles to the bazaar during a rainstorm—a poor excuse, as far as the bank was concerned.

When word about the birth of Amena's son reached Rohim the following day, it was suggested that a new date for disbursement be set two weeks in the future, but Amena let people know that she would be ready in three days. All five women walked to the bank on the appointed day, and Amena received her 3,000-taka loan.

She promptly turned over 1,900 taka to her husband, with which he was to recapitalize his cookware business. She told him that she had taken a 2,000-taka loan, of which 100 taka had been taken out for the "group tax" and he was getting was the remainder. The next day, Absar Ali went to Dhaka and bought aluminum cookware. It was the first time since his and Amena's arrival in Kholshi that his merchandise had not been bought with a loan from a moneylender. There was a noticeable bounce in his step once he got working again, and longer intervals between what had once been nearly daily beatings he administered to his wife.

While her husband was in Dhaka, Amena was secretly negotiating the purchase of ducks, ducklings, and chickens with the 950 taka that she had kept back. Her plan was to build up a small livestock business without her husband's knowledge. Amena figured that part of the profits she earned would be saved, while the rest would go toward her children's education and food. She wanted to save to ensure herself against the thing she, and virtually all women in rural Bangladesh, fear most—abandonment by their husbands, either by divorce or death.

Until receiving the loan, Amena had felt powerless in the face of her husband's laziness—he would work for a few days and then rest until the money he earned had run out. She also had to contend with his fits of rage when he beat her and the children, and his occasional expressions of interest in taking a second wife, as his brothers and father had done. She had tried for years to raise ducks and chickens on the side, stashing away what little she could save so she could purchase little gifts for her children—something their father would never think to do. She would sneak them a boiled egg to go with their vegetable curry, especially during the dry season. But without a source of working capital, her activities were extremely limited. If two chicks died, it might close her business for a year or more.

Now, with nearly 1,000 taka in hand, she had a chance to build up some assets. A week after getting her loan, Amena was visited by Oloka Ghosh, who had heard her neighbor's cries during the frequent abuse of the last three years. Oloka told Amena to tell her husband that there was a Grameen Bank rule stating that if a borrower was regularly beaten by her husband, she would be unable to get future loans, including much-coveted housing loans. She followed the advice, and the frequency of the beatings went from every other day to once a month, and within a few months stopped altogether. Oloka then recommended that Amena tell her husband that borrowers whose husbands remarried were also at risk of being forced to resign from their group. For Amena, such trickery dredged up bitter memories of her fighting with her husband when he wanted to marry another woman during the time when they lived in Rajshahi. It was during that conflict that she received the most frequent and severe beatings, including the time she was hit repeatedly with a bicycle chain.

"Aaki, come here," Amena called out to her eldest daughter as she wiped her face with the end of her sari. "It's time for school."

Aaki hurried out of the hut, poured some water in her hand from a clay pot, splashed it on her face, and, still avoiding her mother's gaze, said, "I'm going, Mom." She broke into a run as she crisscrossed a rice field on her way to the dirt road that her father had mounted a short time before.

Four months earlier, Amena had enrolled Aaki in a private school run by a nongovernmental organization called the Bangladesh Rural Advancement Committee (and now known simply as BRAC). It didn't cost anything except her and her daughter's time, and it was better run than any of the other schools around. The BRAC schools are something like privately run Head Start programs that aim to give poor children who have dropped out of the school system a way back in and those who are at risk of dropping out a boost in confidence. Yet in Kholshi, as in thousands of other villages in Bangladesh, local religious leaders were making threats against the BRAC school, saying it was set up to convert its students and their parents to Christianity. Many pointed to the fact that BRAC's female supervisor, who came each week from

Ghior, rode a bicycle, an act of defiance against cultural tradition that hardly any female Grameen Bank staff dared to replicate. There was talk that Islamic fundamentalists were plotting to burn down the school and perhaps the houses of some of the students, as had already happened in a few places in Bangladesh.

Amena was frightened of being ostracized by the community—a recurring theme in her life—but she also had a dream that she dared not tell anyone else yet: that her daughter would pass her matriculation examination and get a job, perhaps with the government or a private group like BRAC. At a parent-teacher meeting held soon after Amena was recognized as a Grameen Bank member, the BRAC instructor took Amena aside and congratulated her on joining. Taken aback, Amena asked the woman how she knew. "I am a borrower in another center in the southern part of the village," she said with a smile, "and I encouraged Nonibala to stick up for your right to join her center. With the help from the Almighty Allah, we will all come through this all right."

As Amena watched her daughter disappear into the horizon, she turned her gaze briefly to a small plot of land in front of her hut that she planned to turn into a vegetable garden. For years she had helped tend her mother-in-law's vegetables, though she hardly ever got to taste the fruits of her work. Now she planned to have a garden of her own, and if she could find a way to buy a hand-pumped tube well, she could tend it year-round, even in the dry season. It would also give her ready access to clean drinking water. Buying and setting up a hand pump would require close to 2,000 taka, but now that she was a member of Grameen Bank, even that seemed within reach.

In the distance, Amena heard her chickens squawking. In one motion, she lifted the bamboo basket from over her ducklings and began calling her chickens—"*Ah-woo, ah-woo.*" As the ducklings and their mother began scuttling away, the chickens appeared from the underbrush in front of the house and scampered to Amena's feet. After they were fed, the secretary of group number seven began preparing lunch for her family. With the temperature approaching 95 degrees, and the humidity already quite oppressive, she had a long day ahead.

MUHAMMAD YUNUS TENDS TO EXUDE an uncommon degree of confidence, warmth, and, when necessary, firmness. He pushes his colleagues hard, but usually knows when to stop. He has a legendary memory that allows him, at any given time, to keep track of hundreds of projects carried out by thousands of people. To most, he appears at peace with himself and his work. But appearances are sometimes deceiving. In the spring of 1993, in a meeting with Grameen borrowers in Manikganj district, Yunus passed out from internal bleeding from a previously undiagnosed ulcer. It turned out that he had a lot on his mind at the time.

Few things anger Grameen's founder more than politicians who abuse their public trust—which sadly characterizes most elected leaders in his native land. On several occasions, he was offered his choice of government ministries to run under President Ershad, and each time he refused without considering it seriously. "Ministers, even the president," he was known to say when people asked him why he turned down such prestigious and lucrative offers, "are hostages of the party they belong to. Theirs are largely ceremonial positions, with little scope to effect change."

When democracy returned to Bangladesh in 1991, Yunus and his colleagues were initially inspired by the discipline and restraint shown by the nation's 115 million citizens during parliamentary elections that were universally hailed as free and fair. But the optimism was short-lived. Newly elected parliamentarians spent most of their first session discussing their own privileges rather than the nation's problems. A famine in the northern region of Rangpur, for instance, went ignored.

Two years after the elections, Yunus made a brief appearance on the nation's political scene. In August 1993, Dr. Kamal Hossain, one of the leaders of the center-left Awami League, announced that he was forming a breakaway party called the Gano (Democratic) Forum. Hossain had discussed the idea with Yunus before he made his move, and Yunus had reluctantly argued in favor of forming a new party. He admired Hossain's integrity and hoped that a new party would be free of the political hacks that filled the ranks of both major parties. "If you form a party," Yunus said, "don't let anyone join who has been part of any other party." Yunus's vision was a political force for those who felt alienated from politics.

Hossain scheduled the Gano Forum's inaugural convention for August 27 and asked Yunus to speak at it. Yunus initially had no interest in getting involved. Grameen already faced enough groups—Islamic fundamentalists, leftist academics, and moneylenders, to name just three—who wished the bank would go away. Being seen as favoring one political party over the rest would only make things worse. Yunus searched for a way to say no to this friend, who had gone to such lengths for him in the past.

Yunus declined at first, but Hossain kept working on him. He sent M. A. Muhith, the onetime finance minister who had successfully pushed for the issuing of the Grameen Bank ordinance in 1983, to urge Yunus to accept the invitation to speak. Muhith had recently left a job at the United Nations and was working with Hossain to launch the Gano Forum. The meeting came and went, and still Yunus did not commit. Yet the phone calls, from Hossain and others, kept coming. Finally backed into a corner, Yunus agreed to give a speech, but only if he was part of a panel of speakers.

When Yunus arrived at the conference, he was struck by how many quotes from his earlier writings had been blown up and put on the walls. With more than 1,000 activists assembled, Yunus delivered a speech that sent shock waves throughout Grameen Bank and the country's political circles. The title of his speech was "Some Political Thoughts from a Nonpolitical Citizen." The subtitle, in parentheses, was "If I Offend Anyone, Please Forgive Me."

Yunus fleshed out the problems plaguing the political scene in Bangladesh in stark terms. Heavily armed student wings of the nation's major political parties were making instruction at the universities all but impossible. The major economic issues facing the country, including an increasingly exploitative relationship with India, were being ignored. Senseless work stoppages called by the opposition groups, mudslinging and character assassination, and outright violence had replaced rational dialogue as the principal means of political discourse. Characteristically, Yunus resisted the temptation to merely criticize; he offered his own version of a political party, and generically called it *Amar Dol* (My Party).

Amar Dol would be managed from the bottom up rather than from the top down. Village-level party committees, traditionally the lowest position on the totem pole, would have real power. They would be promoted to higher levels by virtue of tangible successes in their villages—improving education, raising agricultural output, bringing better health services. The local party leaders would be development workers first, political workers second. There would be no student front of his party, and any person who perpetrated violence in the name of Amar Dol would be punished, not promoted.

When in opposition, Yunus's party would cooperate with and, when appropriate, commend the government. All criticisms would be constructive, and no *hartals* (general strikes) would be called under any circumstances.

While in power, his party would ensure that opposition parties have access to the media. An environment conducive to domestic and foreign investment would be created. Those who flouted the laws would be punished, no matter how influential they might be, and poor people who tried to help themselves would have more places to turn for support, though fewer places to turn for handouts.

The speech was a stinging, if indirect, indictment of both the ruling and opposition parties of that era. Even though Yunus stopped well short of joining Gano Forum, with his speech he put himself on the political map. With a network of thousands of employees and millions of families who claimed membership in Grameen Bank, many knew that he had a potentially formidable political machine.

The media response was mixed. *Jai Jai Din*, a popular weekly magazine, reprinted the speech in full, along with a positive editorial. Bodruddin Umar, a Marxist academic, wrote one of the first major responses in a daily newspaper. After castigating *Jai Jai Din* and others for being uncritical of Yunus's proposals, he accused Grameen's founder of being naïve and hiding his true intentions behind "foggy" ideas. But then came the clincher: Professor Yunus, who was widely known to have met Bill Clinton when he was governor of Arkansas, was an agent for U.S. imperialism who was about to launch his own party. The entire country, he warned, was in danger.

For weeks afterward, dozens of articles commenting on Yunus's speech from across the political spectrum appeared in national periodicals. The managing director observed the fallout with bemused detachment, and never considered writing to correct some of the outlandish things his critics said about him.

Six weeks after the Gano Forum event, Yunus's name was back in the news for a different reason. The *Doinik Janakantha*, the paper that published Bodruddin Umar's article, ran a story that began, "Yesterday, Professor Yunus met with President Clinton in the Oval Office of the White House." Suspicion of Yunus grew.

"WHAT DO YOU MEAN, you left it over there? That is *my* rice—taken from *my* land. You must bring it here," Fulzan Begum shouted at her husband, gesturing wildly with both arms as she spoke. Her undersized, 10-month-old daughter, sitting naked on the ground, started crying as her parents continued an argument that had begun earlier that morning.

Harun, Fulzan's husband, looked at the ground and said meekly, "I was going there after I cut the rice in the field. I just . . ." His voice trailed off, and for a moment he seemed lost in thought.

Fulzan picked up a shovel and took a threatening step towards her husband. "Go, now, and tell her you are bringing the rice here!"

"Okay, I'm going. I'll be back in a little while." He started walking down into the muddy culvert that separated Fulzan's tiny plot of land from those around it.

It was three and a half months since Fulzan had received her loan from Grameen Bank, and during that time she had taken the first steps down the bumpy road from destitution to stable subsistence.

Four years earlier, Fulzan and her two older sisters had suffered the last in a long series of abandonments. Their father, Hazrat Ali, a widower since his wife's death one month after Fulzan was born, succumbed to a mysterious disease. By then, Hazrat Ali had long since lost his ability to care his daughters, and for the 10 years before his death he had survived by begging. Besides losing their parents, Fulzan and her sister Shundari had been abandoned by their husbands and were forced to spend many months on their own, a dangerous position for women in rural Bangladesh. Only their sister Golapi, who lived with her husband, had enjoyed any protection.

The three sisters had never been to school. At the age of 10, Fulzan joined her sister as a ditchdigger, a job of last resort for landless men and destitute women in rural Bangladesh. In exchange for a day's work, the girls received a small bag of wheat or three taka. (Grown men received nearly 10 times that amount.) Between what they earned and what their father could manage, they missed only occasional meals, though eating fish and meat were out of the question except during the Muslim festivals. Over the years, Fulzan gained a reputation as the best female ditchdigger in Kholshi. By the time she was an adult, her skills were recognized in an unprecedented way—she was paid nearly as much as men were.

During each dry season, thousands of rural Bangladeshis are employed to "move the earth." With a virtually inexhaustible supply of rich topsoil, fishing ponds can be excavated, roads built, rice fields lowered, and housing plots raised with only shovels and muscle. Proper preparation for the coming monsoon can mean the difference between a dry homestead full of rain-fed rice that is connected to the bazaar by a dirt road, and a flooded, isolated hut whose owner's rice crop perishes in the swamp. Thus, the dry season means consistent demand for ditchdiggers like Fulzan, who can often find employment four or five days a week and earn 30 taka (75 cents) or a few pounds of wheat.

Whatever amount she could save was always spent during the rainy season, when work was slow. When it came time for Fulzan to be married, there was no money for a dowry, so the best that could be arranged was a union with a young man from Faridpur district whose family was so poor that it was agreed that he would come to Kholshi to live with Fulzan and her father. (Normally, the new wife moves in with her husband's family.) It was only a matter of time before Fulzan joined the growing numbers of Bangladeshi women who are abandoned by their husbands.

In 1992, two years after Fulzan's father died, she began being visited by a man she had met while working. He was married to a woman in the village and lived with his wife's family, but he was unhappy with her, primarily because she had been unable to bear him any sons. Harun said he wanted to take Fulzan as his second wife, but his mother-in-law told him she would never agree to such a union. To her, Fulzan was far beneath them on the social ladder—an earth-cutter, for God's sake! But Harun's wife told him that it was okay with her if he took a second wife, and shortly thereafter a small ceremony was held.

In the days immediately following the wedding, Fulzan lived with her *shoteen* (the word that describes the relation of one wife to another in a polygamous Bangladeshi household). While the two wives got along, Harun's mother-in-law made Fulzan's life miserable. As the household's "little" (meaning second) wife, Fulzan was expected to do the lion's share of the housework, while getting little to eat. When Harun was out working, Fulzan was forced to listen to repeated insults, delivered in vulgar language. After a month, Fulzan left. When Harun came to bring her back—she lived only a quarter mile away—Fulzan said that while she hoped he would spend time with her from time to time, she was going to stay put on her father's land. She believed that if she stayed with Harun's mother-in-law, she would become too weak to work and would slowly starve to death.

Settled back at home, Fulzan heard about an opening in the Kholshi center from Oloka and began taking steps to become a Grameen Bank member. When her group was recognized and she was allowed to make a loan proposal, Fulzan said she wanted to buy a calf. Up until then, she'd been able to raise livestock only on a sharecropping basis, under which the owner would receive half of the increase in value of the animal. When the second recognition exam came and went successfully, she dreamed of finally being a cow owner. But as the day of the loan proposal drew closer, her husband began arguing for a different investment—leasing one-third of an acre of land with their $50-dollar loan. Just as Fulzan raised livestock on a sharecropping basis for lack of the investment capital needed to buy a calf or a goat, the little land Harun farmed was also cultivated on that basis. With half of the harvest going to the owner of the land, there was little reason for Harun to hope that he would ever realize the aspiration of most Bengali peasants—to eat rice grown on their own land all year round.

The couple argued for many days about what to do with the loan. Harun, in an effort to soften Fulzan up, began spending more of his time, including nights, in his second wife's rotting thatch hut. Harun's mother-in-law was, naturally, not very amused. But even though the tin roof his first wife lived under shielded him from the elements, she could not provide that which would transform Harun from a sharecropper into a farmer—a Grameen Bank loan.

It was ultimately agreed that Fulzan would give Harun the money to lease the land, but she had to be present when he finalized the deal with the landowner. The two would share the burden of paying the 40-taka ($1) weekly installment, and Fulzan would receive all of the crops when they were harvested. (Harun, as always, would be welcome to come and eat at her house after the harvest.) That way, Fulzan would be able, for the first time, to eat rice from her own land rather than to buy it in the market—which felt to her like a major step up the social ladder. Furthermore, she would get to keep the rice husks, which she could use as feed for her livestock. It was also agreed that if and when she became eligible for a seasonal loan for buying fertilizer and insecticide, Fulzan would consider applying for the loan to improve the yield. Finally, Harun was made to agree that if they were able to repay the first general loan, Fulzan would be able to buy a cow with the second general loan.

Two days earlier, Harun had brought in the first rice crop harvested from the land. It was a good yield that would, after threshing, leave about two *maunds* (or 164 pounds) of unhusked rice. Yet Harun had brought the fruits of his labor (and his wife's investment) to his mother-in-law's home—and that had provoked Fulzan's wrath. Her angry words had their desired effect. Later that afternoon, Harun delivered the paddy he had cut the day before. As Fulzan watched it arriving, she tried to appear calm and relaxed, as though she had expected it all along. Nothing could have been further from the truth—as the conflict subsided, Fulzan Begum picked through her harvest meticulously, her heart racing the entire time.

BEFORE INDEPENDENCE FROM GREAT BRITAIN, Kholshi was primarily a Hindu village. Perhaps one in five households was Muslim, and nearly all of the Muslims were day laborers who worked in the homes and fields of the more prosperous Hindus. Relations between the two groups were generally distant but peaceful.

Older people in Kholshi remember the famine of 1943 as the event that undermined this tranquility. Several dozen people, mostly women and children, succumbed to starvation. It was during this time that widespread thievery, petty as it may have been, began. The social discipline that had reigned for so long in Kholshi was shattered.

Upon independence in 1947, Kholshi became part of East Pakistan. At the time, there was no fear of Muslim dominance over the Hindu majority. Only the wealthy Hindu landlords fled to India, their ornate estates left to crumble in the open air, their land in many cases confiscated by opportunistic and well-connected local farmers, with the rest reverting to government ownership.

One significant improvement in the early years of Pakistani rule was that education became much more accessible, at least in theory, to low-caste Hindus and to Muslims. A government school was built in Kholshi, and even though most of the teachers were high-caste Hindus—nobody else knew how to read or write—for the first time, students included boys from all walks of life. While few children actually studied more than one or two years, it was nothing short of a social revolution that the son of a Muslim day laborer could be sitting next to the son of a Brahmin in the area's primary school.

For centuries, the economy of Kholshi had been based on rainfed rice cultivation and fishing. As the Pakistani period progressed, irrigated agriculture was introduced. Low-lying land that had been virtually useless for monsoon agriculture (because it was submerged in as much as six feet of water) became prime soil for rice cultivation during the dry seasons, with the use of high-yielding seeds that required fertilizer, irrigation, and constant weeding but that produced yields almost three times greater than those of traditional varieties sown during the rainy season.

Kholshi was virtually untouched by the independence war in 1971, although terrified families from other villages sought refuge there from the fierce fighting nearby between the Mukti Bahini and the Pakistani army. Refugees would often arrive with bamboo, thatch, and livestock in hand, ready, if necessary, to rebuild their huts on a generous stranger's homestead plot until it felt safe to return home.

In December 1971, when independence was at hand, people of all social classes, castes, and religions looked forward to peacetime. Many thought that the future would bring about a society with all the social harmony and low crime of the British period, the widespread access to education and stable prices inaugurated under Pakistani rule, and the pride of living under a government run by ethnic Bengalis. Bangladesh would finally have its own industries, its own jute mills, and its own government. But those hopes crashed headlong into reality. Prices of essential goods skyrocketed, the law-and-order situation deteriorated precipitously, and the wheels of government ground to a halt. For the first time, virtually nothing happened without a bribe, and it often didn't happen even then. The only improvement people experienced was that for the first time, girls joined boys in primary school classrooms.

The 1974 famine hit Kholshi hard. Prices of staples such as rice, salt, and cooking oil went through the roof. Those who had access to land, money, and productive assets made out well buying and leasing land from poor families at rock-bottom prices. Moneylending thrived. During the years immediately following the famine, things returned to normal, except that the social landscape was littered with scores of families who were now deeply indebted to wealthy families without any hope of getting out.

Beginning in the early 1980s, the Muslim community slowly became more assertive, but communal peace in Kholshi reigned until the destruction of the Babri mosque in India in December 1992, when young ruffians, emboldened by those among their elders who stood to gain from a Hindu exodus, went on a rampage that left all four major Hindu temples in Kholshi little more than rubble. In the months that followed, "Hindu flight," much like the "white flight" in South Chicago, took on the character of an inevitable and ever-accelerating process.

The early 1990s were a time of turmoil in Kholshi, not only among the two religious groups but also among the sexes and the generations. The Grameen

Bank, which by 1993 had more than a hundred members there, was well positioned to help shape that change, in subtle but profound ways.

Update: Since the 1990s

GRAMEEN BANK, AND MICROFINANCE IN GENERAL, have been targets of criticism since long before the crises of 2010-2011. Leftists scoffed at their acceptance and even embrace of capitalism, while conservatives accused them of subverting family values. Muslims were suspicious of charging interest, which some Islamic scholars say is *haram* ("forbidden"). (A more liberal Islamic interpretation is that only the charging of excessive or usurious interest rates is *haram*, in which case affordable microlenders like Grameen Bank might be considered pro-Islamic, since they represent an alternative to loan sharks and moneylenders.) Meanwhile, some Christians seemed to regret the loss of supposedly ennobling opportunities to provide charity when the poor are instead supported in helping themselves.

But beneath these common critiques lie others that are more sophisticated and, in some ways, more insidious. One is that microfinance is based on the false assumption that all or most of the world's poor want to be entrepreneurs and have the potential to succeed as business owners. Another is that women don't use the loan money they receive to build businesses, but simply hand it over to their husbands, giving the lie to the idea that microfinance empowers women. A third is that microlenders like Grameen don't help their beneficiaries rise above the poverty line, a claim that is supported by some research but contradicted by others (especially when data is collected over longer time periods and covers well-run microfinance institutions).

Spending many months in Grameen villages in 1989, 1993, and 1994, as I did, and then following up a few times in the later years, gave me an opportunity to evaluate these charges on the basis of clients' lived experience viewed up close over dozens of encounters. While I suppose it is true that many Grameen borrowers would have like to have a job with good pay and benefits as an alternative to running a tiny business (or more commonly, several tiny businesses that rotate seasonally), the reality is that these options are not commonly available to uneducated rural people. Life, especially for those without the privileges enjoyed by critics in academia or politics, is not about "following your dream." It's about choosing between actual alternatives that are far from ideal.

It is likewise true that not all microfinance clients are equally adept at running businesses. Some, like Nonibala and Shandha, are natural entrepreneurs, while others struggle. But no one is forcing these women to borrow and invest in income-generating ventures, and in fact most of them are already involved in such ventures before they take their first microloan. Organizations like Grameen simply allow them to pursue business ownership with more capital as well as with the support of fellow borrowers and staff who are incentivized to help them if they get into trouble. Some experts define these tiny businesses as "income-generating activities" as a way of conveying their informal nature and small scale, and the fact that several might be activated and later go into hiatus over the course of a year or even a few months. This alternative term in English is, in my view, a better way of describing the majority of Grameen's clients' pursuits than the term "businesses."

Finally, even in cases where female borrowers turn over all or part of their loan money to their husbands—as Fulzan and Amena did—their leverage and power within the family and their economic independence may still be noticeably enhanced. I wonder whether researchers commissioned by MIT, had they studied this center in the early 1990s, would have realized that Amena was holding back a portion of her loan for her own use even as she gave some of it to her husband. I didn't discover that myself until I'd been wandering around the village and gaining people's trust for more than six months.

More broadly, I often worry about what is lost when methodologies like randomized controlled trials—that were designed to test the efficacy of a precise dosage of medicine in the closed system represented by the human body—are deemed the "gold standard" of social science research. When such trials are used to test whether microfinance works, few consider that the inputs (loans, peer support, staff assistance, savings options, and more) are much more varied and the environments considerably more heterogeneous than is the case in the laboratory or in a medical trial. Based on my experience doing extensive field research and later engaging in some heated policy debates with researchers, I fear that quite a bit is lost along the way—not just in terms of understanding how well-designed microfinance services open up new options for people, but also in terms of how specific social innovations can and should fit into the global effort to end poverty.

THE NOBEL PEACE PRIZE RAISED Yunus's profile internationally as well as in his home country. But well before that, he had been recognized within Bangladesh as an incorruptible leader with a commitment to poverty reduction, secularism, and modern, forward-thinking domestic and foreign policies. It was those elements of his reputation that made his speech at the Gano Forum in 1993 such a newsworthy event. In the ensuing years, his accomplishments became increasingly well known, even though some of the country's political and economic elite tried to minimize his work and diminish his stature. Jealousy remains a powerful force in human relations in every society.

Bangladesh fell into a political crisis in 1996 because of the inability of the two major political parties to agree on a formula for fair elections. Just as all seemed lost, a compromise was reached. For the three months leading up to the election, an interim government headed by a retired Supreme Court justice would run the country and oversee the election. The ministers would be respected, nonpolitical figures. Inevitably, Yunus was asked to serve as a minister in the interim government for three months. Surprising many of his colleagues, he accepted, and played an influential role in ensuring that the election was fair and resulted in a peaceful transfer of power.

At the time, my wife and I were living next door to the husband of the leader of the opposition party. I can remember the day when the media came to their house to interview Sheikh Hasina about her victory. Only a few weeks earlier, we were preparing to flee the country with the rest of the expatriate community, fearing an outbreak of civil war.

As the interim government wound down and turned over authority to the newly elected government, Yunus told people around him that he was glad he had agreed to serve for this brief period. Clearly, he had a more positive experience in government during this brief stint than when he had returned from the United States in 1972 and was given a job and a salary but no work. On many days during this period, he would return to Grameen Bank after working in his ministerial office and brief his colleagues on what it was like to be inside the Bangladesh government that they had negotiated with, collaborated with, and criticized over the preceding decades.

Ten years later, another political crisis would prompt Yunus to consider becoming a political figure. During the weeks immediately after he was honored at the Nobel Peace Prize ceremony in Oslo, Bangladesh was teetering on the edge of anarchy or perhaps even civil war. Once again, the two mainstream parties could not agree on a formula for a national election for Parliament. Yet in 2007, it was not clear whether a compromise could be reached as it had been in 1996. In articles published in several daily newspapers, Yunus proposed a practical way to solve the impasse. However, despite his Nobel Prize halo, his proposal was not taken seriously by either party. An interim, military-backed government took power in January and began to take some long-overdue positive steps, such as launching investigation of politicians widely believed to be corrupt.

Still, the pathway to peaceful elections and the full restoration of democracy was not clear. The military-led government offered Yunus the chance to serve as prime minister. He declined on princple, as he did not believe the military should be deciding who ran the country. But the offer got him thinking.

Sensing an opportunity to serve his country in a new way, Yunus announced in early 2007 that he was going to form a political party that he named Nagorik Shakti (Citizen Power). It bore a striking resemblance to the hypothetical Amar Dol party that he had described in his speech at the Gano Forum more than a decade earlier. His plan was to turn over Grameen Bank leadership to his chosen successor once the election campaign began. Yunus's announcement stirred interest and debate both inside and outside Bangladesh.

Within a few months, however, he abandoned the idea of forming a new party and running as its leader for prime minister. A major factor was that the few politicians from the major parties whom he respected declined to jump ship and join his nascent effort. Many Grameen staff and friends around the world were relieved, because they'd feared for Yunus's personal safety if he entered politics, as many Bangladeshi government leaders have been assassinated since the country's founding in 1971.

Nonetheless, the political influence of the Grameen Bank had been growing since the mid-1990s in ways that did not grab headlines but were profound in their long-term implications. After the compromise that led to the 1996 national elections, Yunus (both before and after he was appointed an interim minister) told the clients of Grameen that, in a democratic

Bangladesh, the strength of the poor was in their numbers, and that every last borrower had a sacred obligation to vote. Furthermore, he urged all Grameen centers (composed of 40 to 50 borrowers) to parade to the polling booths together with banners announcing that they were all voting as an expression of their commitment to realize the Grameen ideal of poverty-free lives. When Bangladesh's small but influential Islamic fundamentalist party was virtually wiped out in the aftermath of the election, having their parliamentary delegation reduced from 18 to 2, Grameen Bank's efforts to ensure 100 percent voting by borrowers was cited as a major reason for their downfall, despite Yunus's strict orders to staff that they not speak out in favor of or against any party or candidate.

When local elections for union *porishod* (council) seats were held the next year, borrowers were again urged to vote. When some decried the lack of honest and competent candidates, Grameen staff members were instructed to encourage borrowers and their family members to run for office themselves. An impressive 1,753 Grameen clients and 1,572 Grameen family members (mostly clients' husbands) were elected, which represented 6.5 percent of all the union council seats in the country. Fifty-nine were elected as council chairmen, a powerful post. In 2003, the percentage of council seats going to borrowers or to their families rose to 9 percent, and 81 were elected chairmen.

Seeing these results in a single country, people began to ponder whether the 100 million families served by hundreds of microfinance institutions— many inspired by Yunus and modeled on Grameen Bank—could come together as a political force at the global level. At the very least, Yunus, as the undisputed leader of the movement, especially after winning the Nobel Prize, had the ability to influence those who shaped the global economy. In an interview published in the *Nepal Times* in mid-2007, he said, "The prize has made it easier for me to advocate for changes in relevant policies and regulations. Earlier, I used to scream and shout, and not many listened to me. Now I am seen as a wise man, and even my mere whisper carries a lot more weight."

Yunus's ouster from his role as managing director of Grameen Bank in 2011 by a government led by Sheikh Hasina is often linked to his brief flirtation in 2007 with forming a new political party and running for office himself. I am not sure it is quite that simple. But regardless, in a democracy people should be at liberty to establish parties and run for office without any fear of retribution from people in positions of public trust. Unfortunately, with every passing year, Bangladesh looks less and less like a country where its citizens freely choose their leaders. As a result, gifted people who might otherwise be willing to serve in public office go into exile or keep their mouths shut, and the number of people who don't bother to cast votes in elections grows with every cycle.

One can only hope that this state of affairs is a temporary aberration, especially considering the disciplined and peaceful manner in which Bangladesh's citizenry participated in the elections of 1991 and 1996.

6. Omiyale DuPart

IT WAS STILL WELL BEFORE DAWN when Omiyale DuPart was dropped off at Newberry Street by her daughter, but Les Papillons's chairlady felt that she was late. Then again, Omiyale often ran a bit late. Another 10 minutes and that spot on the sidewalk would have vanished, she thought to herself as she set up her table. Omiyale never liked to miss Sundays at Maxwell Street. Loud, dirty, and smelly it might be, but she felt at home there. Only at Maxwell Street could she unload merchandise that wouldn't sell anywhere else, provided it was at the right price.

On this day, Omiyale was being helped out by Janet, her younger sister and a fellow Full Circle Fund borrower, who had dreams of buying a first car with her profits. Together, they transferred all the stuff she wanted to sell from black garbage bags to a pair of fold-up picnic tables and a blanket spread out on the ground. They set out a used winter jacket, a winter hat, children's shoes, jewelry, oils, and spices. Some of the clothes were things that her children had outgrown and that had been lying around the house. Why not sell them? What's junk to me might be a treasure to someone else, Omiyale figured, hoping that she might take in $100 between 6 a.m. and 2 p.m., perhaps $150 if it got a little warmer. Such thinking is the essence of Maxwell Street.

Omiyale is a mother of eight who was born as Veronica Wilma Ramsey and raised in a Chicago housing project. Since childhood she'd suffered from a stutter, and for years she spoke as little as possible when she wasn't around family and friends. In the mid-1960s she met Paul DuPart, an aspiring artist, and they began dating. At the time, Veronica wore her hair "relaxed" (straightened), and often bleached it blond. Her wardrobe was full of name-brand miniskirts, and she talked of becoming a model. Paul was involved in the Black consciousness movement and was associated with the Nation of Islam. To him, Veronica was a prime example of a Black person who needed her awareness raised.

Paul explained to Veronica that she lacked understanding of who she was and who Black people were. He told her that her hair and dress—her entire concept of beauty—was adopted from Europeans, that her values and ambitions had been shaped by an "alien" culture.

Even the stutter, he suggested, was the result of conscious and subconscious doubts she had about herself and her heritage. If you can simply learn to take pride in yourself and your people, he said, the stutter will melt away like a stick of butter in a hot frying pan.

Veronica listened closely to her suitor's arguments, and occasionally attended educational events with him. Among the speakers they heard together were Malcolm X and Elijah Muhammad. In time, they participated in marches and volunteered their time with some Black nationalist organizations. Omiyale changed her name, dress, hairstyle, and diet to conform to Muslim requirements, and to the surprise of everyone except Paul, her stutter actually vanished. Black consciousness, she concluded, had solved what half a dozen speech therapists had failed to do.

The two were married in 1965, and within a year Omiyale was pregnant. They agreed that all of their offspring would be given African names and wear traditional dress. They would be brought up aware of their culture and heritage. If possible, they would go to the Institute of Positive Education, an all-Black private school on the South Side.

During the late 1960s and early 1970s, Paul worked in a succession of low-paying jobs while he took courses in the visual arts at Chicago State University, ultimately earning a bachelor's degree. He often studied during the day and worked at night. Although that meant hardship in the short term, they dreamed of a future in which Paul would find satisfaction and adequate remuneration as an artist.

Meanwhile, to try to develop a new source of income, Omiyale began taking jewelry classes that were being offered by the Chicago Park District. Always the star of her classes, within a few years she was able to make a wide variety of earrings, necklaces, and pins out of silver, gold, and other materials. She sold her handiwork to friends, often at house shows. (These are events where producers or traders who cannot afford a storefront can invite friends, family, and neighbors to buy their products. They are quite common on the South Side of Chicago.) Later she began selling her work at arts and crafts festivals. When Paul encouraged his wife to get a bachelor's degree at Chicago State University in the 1970s, she went part-time for a few years, but later dropped out. Instead, she learned to sew in another Park District class. Child-rearing was time consuming, and she enjoyed making and selling jewelry and dresses more than sitting in college classes with middle-class students half her age. For a time, she sold Tupperware after a successful Chicago-area saleslady recruited her to do so. That saleslady's name was Thelma Dean Ali.

By the mid-1980s, Paul was working as a mental-health aide at a psychiatric clinic, earning less than $20,000 a year to support a household that included five teenage children and two grandchildren. The family lived in Englewood. Omiyale had taken up selling at flea markets and rented a thrift shop in Hyde Park, the most affluent neighborhood on the South Side. On weekends, she often closed her store and brought merchandise that wasn't selling to Maxwell Street, where she frequently saw Thelma. The two women exchanged ideas and information, one suggesting a street festival that the other hadn't heard of and the other leaking word of a going-out-of-business sale where they could pick up merchandise for next to nothing. They came to respect each other's business savvy and began to share booths at summer festivals and other events.

When the landlord from whom Omiyale rented her thrift store (and with whom she had good relations) died, the new landlord doubled her rent from $250 to $500. She tried to continue running the store for a few months, but the higher rent cut too far into her profits. In late 1988, she closed the store for good.

Omiyale worked the flea market/Maxwell Street/arts and crafts festival circuit during the spring and early summer of 1989, but when a lamp company advertised a position for an industrial polisher, she applied for and got the job. It paid $18,000 a year, and she was struck by the fact that she was the only Black woman, and the only woman polisher, working there. Several colleagues remarked that she was chosen because of a new affirmative action policy, but that didn't bother Omiyale. By that time, she was taking care of one grandchild and another was on the way. She supplemented her income by digging up worms in the parks after work and selling them to coworkers who liked to fish. She also sold them merchandise left over from the thrift store.

During the last six weeks of 1990, two events occurred that were to change the course of Omiyale's life. The first was being laid off from her job; apparently, the lamp company didn't limit affirmative action with minorities to hiring—it spilled over to firings as well. The second event occurred several weeks later—she heard about WSEP and its largest program, the Full Circle Fund.

Omiyale heard about the Full Circle Fund by chance from a balloon seller outside the 75th Street subway station. Omiyale had never heard of anything like the fund before, but it seemed like a good idea to her. After attending an orientation meeting, she told Gwen Burns she would have a group of five ready to meet with her in two days' time. Gwen was pleased and surprised by Omiyale's eagerness. After all, most women were somewhere between skeptical and fearful after they listened to her spiel, and many took months of coaxing before they were ready to commit. But Omiyale was just weeks removed from being laid off, and the ability to get a loan without regard to her credit history was an opportunity she couldn't resist.

Omiyale called Thelma late at night after she returned from the orientation meeting to tell her about the fund. Thelma agreed to help her friend pull together three other women by Wednesday night. After Thelma hung up, she said a prayer to Almighty Allah that this might be a genuine program. If it was, Thelma knew, it could only have come from the Creator himself.

Thelma, Omiyale, and three other women met that Wednesday at the home of Omiyale's mother on Garfield Avenue in Englewood.

To Thelma and Omiyale, joining the fund meant more than simply access to a loan. In a pinch, both had usually been able to call in favors and borrow money from family members or other, more prosperous vendors. But the Full Circle Fund meant guaranteed access to increasing amounts of working capital as long as they repaid on schedule. There'd be no more begging, no more imposing on friends or fellow vendors for cash. Now they could concentrate on building up dignified businesses.

When Thelma took her first loan for $300, it nearly doubled the capitalization of her business. Omiyale was a bit more adventurous and took $1,500. In addition to credit, the program brought them in contact with other vendors, as well as with small, home-based manufacturers from whom they could buy on a wholesale basis. In the past, Omiyale and Thelma would often hear of lucrative events only after they'd occurred, because many vendors were unwilling to share useful information. Now, in a group with other women whose success was linked to theirs, they were more likely to get timely tips, and receive support and encouragement.

Back at Maxwell Street Market after many hours on her feet, it was a few minutes past 3:00 in the afternoon. Omiyale and Janet packed their merchandise into a taxi as they prepared to return home. They had grossed nearly $150 and heard about some upcoming events from other vendors. When everything was packed away, Omiyale jogged over to Thelma's table on Thirteenth Street to see how her friend was faring and to discuss the agenda for the center meeting to be held the following evening. A few minutes later, Omiyale was off on her way back to Chicago's South Side.

FOR THE MOST PART, the Full Circle Fund operates in overwhelmingly poor, Black neighborhoods. To understand the poverty of these areas, one has to consider Chicago's history.[32]

Chicago is arguably the nation's greatest blue-collar city, a product of the Midwest that lacks the sophistication of New York or the pretensions of Los Angeles. Chicago has been shaped by three distinct migrations—the first from Europe, the second from the Mississippi delta, and the third from Mexico. The result is a relatively young, very Catholic city, with neighborhoods that retain strong ethnic affiliations and a machine-dominated political system with plenty of graft to go around. It is also a city that suffers from more than its fair share of racial tensions, though there have been periods in its history when the races coexisted relatively peacefully.

At the end of the eighteenth century, the land on which present-day Chicago sits was forest and prairie, uninhabited except for the occasional Pottawatomie Indian who passed through it. Somewhere around 1790, a French-speaking Haitian named Jean Baptiste Point du Sable established the first permanent settlement in an area the Indians had named Chickagou, their word for the wild garlic that grew along the shores of Lake Michigan and caused a strong stench.

Six years later, du Sable, together with his Pottawattomie wife, Catherine, and their two children, moved on to Peoria. But in a short time he had left a lasting impression, for as late as 1835, Indians who by that time had been forcibly driven from the area were known to say, "The first white man to settle Chickagou was a Negro."

Between du Sable's departure and the 1840s, small numbers of Blacks fleeing the depredations of the antebellum South settled in Chicago. By 1850, Chicago had become an important terminal in the Underground Railroad, and while many Blacks escaping slavery continued their journey east or north to Canada, others stayed in the Windy City. By the time of the Civil War, a thousand Blacks were living there, mostly on the banks of the Chicago River. On the whole, they were accepted by white society, and on occasion they were held up as model citizens whom recently arrived immigrants from eastern and southern Europe would do well to emulate.

Still, Black people were welcome only in small doses. When emancipation was declared in 1863, there was considerable fear of a large influx of freed slaves from the South. But no such migration occurred, and by 1870 only a scant 1 percent of the city's population was Black.

Despite the Blacks' small numbers, resentment began to build among the white working class against those who did arrive. Blacks were accused of depressing the general wage level and taking white-held blue-collar jobs. Riots broke out periodically, often involving the Irish, whose antagonism toward Blacks was already the stuff of legend. But while Blacks' treatment in the stockyards was often harsh, the freedmen were able to make their influence felt at City Hall. Within 20 years of the abolition of slavery, most legal segregation outside the school system, including obstacles to voting, was expunged from city and state statutes. The slow process of achieving equality under the law had begun.

Between the Civil War and the First World War, Chicago's population exploded from 100,000 to more than 2 million. After the Great Fire of 1871 (which destroyed some 17,000 buildings) and a smaller conflagration three years later, neighborhoods realigned, and the Black Belt south of the Loop was born, initially covering a stretch of land 3 blocks wide and 15 blocks long.

As the Black population continued to grow, it began establishing its own institutions, including newspapers, social clubs, and churches. A small but influential upper class and a growing middle class emerged and tried to exercise some control over those immigrants from the South who failed to live by norms set by the church and "respectable" Black community.

On the eve of the First World War, Chicago's Black population had expanded to 40,000. The city, however, was more concerned about absorbing a flood of poor immigrants from Europe than about relations with the African-American community. Blacks themselves were afraid that this massive influx of whites would threaten their foothold in the stockyards. New arrivals, who were often discriminated against in their native countries, were eager to avoid starting at the bottom in the United States; having a class of people below them from the outset, as Blacks seemed to be, was doubtless reassuring. Despite this, ethnic communities of European origin and Blacks lived peacefully side by side in many neighborhoods. Racially mixed marriages were uncommon but not unheard of.

During the First World War, the European migration was reversed, with thousands of men returning home to take up arms. At the same time, the United States became the chief supplier for the Allied cause. This created a sudden need to boost industrial production in northern cities like Chicago, even as the workforce shrank. The stage was set for a historic migration of some 60,000 Blacks to Chicago between 1910 and 1920, a process facilitated in part by white recruiting agents (much hated by white Southerners who needed their cotton picked) who crisscrossed Dixie in search of laborers, and later by the stories of riches that filtered back after the first waves of migrants secured good-paying blue-collar jobs that had been previously reserved for whites.

Recalling the extraordinary nature of that migration, Nicholas Lemann has written, "It was undeniable that the economic opportunity [in Chicago] was greater; that moment in the black rural South was one of the few in American history when virtually every member of a large class of people was guaranteed an immediate quadrupling of income, at least, simply by relocating to a place that was only a long day's journey away."[33]

While the factory owners and politicians viewed the migration as a necessity, there was trouble in the streets. Newspaper headlines like "Negroes Incited by German Spies" and "2,000 Negroes Arrive in Last Two Days" did nothing to relieve the growing anxiety. One of the principal sources of animosity revolved around the question of where to house the new arrivals. The Black Belt, already overcrowded in 1910, needed to expand, and expand it did, at the expense of previously lily-white neighborhoods to the southeast. Real estate speculators of both races, eager to induce panic selling at rock-bottom prices by whites and then to make substantial profits by selling and renting those units to Blacks, made out handsomely and came to be widely detested by whites and Blacks alike. Homes of newly settled Blacks, as well as those of the real estate men who brought them there, were being firebombed by angry whites by this time. There were 58 bombings in the so-called transition neighborhoods in southeast Chicago between July 1917 and March 1921, one every 20 days.

In July 1919, the conflict boiled over in an event that would forever change race relations in Chicago.[34] A six-day riot was ignited when a Black boy swam into an area at the 29th Street Beach that was reserved for whites—by custom, not by law. The boy was stoned by whites when he tried to swim ashore, and after swimming back out into the lake, he drowned. Enraged Blacks retaliated, and pitched battles were being fought in the streets within hours. During the next six days, the Irish, who lived on the western edge of the Black Belt, made repeated incursions into the Black neighborhoods and burned buildings to the ground. Black youths responded in kind.

When the ashes had settled and the dead—38 of them—had been buried, the Black and white establishments tried to make sense of the madness that had engulfed the city. A blue-ribbon commission was formed, and it laid blame for the riot largely on the housing shortage and the resulting real estate speculation. The commission also found fault with the police, the courts, and white society at large for failing to deal justly with the Negroes (as they were called at the time) before the riot and failing to protect them once it began. For Black people, who had lived relatively peacefully in Chicago for decades, the riot marked the end of a relatively positive period in race relations.

A CUSTOMER WAS PUSHING AT THE DOOR of West Side Books, to no effect. "It sticks—push hard," Queenesta Harris shouted from behind her counter. Her voice barely carried through the thick glass, but the man got the idea and let himself in. It was perhaps the twentieth time that morning that someone had entered Victor's store that way.

As the customer walked toward the back of the store, he made eye contact with Queenesta but said nothing. "Hey, Ms. Johnson, where's Vic?" the man inquired. Dorothy Johnson, a seamstress who rented space from Victor, pointed toward a door leading to the conference room in the back.

In the front of the store, Queenesta strode up to the door and tried to fix it. She failed; the door had only two positions, open and stuck. Her attention drifted to a store across the street, on the corner of Mason Street and North Avenue, and fixated on a red neon signboard that had been placed in the window of a video rental shop three days earlier. It read, "JD's Records and CDs."

The establishment of JD's meant the end of Queenesta's reign as the only music retailer on her block. JD had most of the same titles she had, except that he carried a better selection of compact discs and charged about 50 cents more for each than she did. Though she didn't share with Victor her worries about being driven out of business, for the past several days, she had been a nervous wreck. More than anything else, she hated that neon sign. Queenesta guessed it cost $300, and she feared that a flashy gimmick like that might lure her customers away.

This development came at an inauspicious time for Queenesta. She had been hoping to devote at least half of her time that fall to selling Afrocentric children's books to Chicago public schools. She knew of only one other woman who was doing this in the city, and figured that this was the year to make a killing. Teachers' consciousness about these books had been raised, and by the following school year she was convinced another half dozen distributors would be competing against her. If she could get in good with a few teachers during the 1993–1994 school year, she might receive a regular income for years with little additional effort. But the politicians didn't allow her plan to go forward. In September, the Chicago public schools had no budget and could not legally open. A bankrupt public school system meant no business for the foreseeable future. She was thus forced to concentrate her energies and investment capital on her music business.

As she returned to her counter and began nervously rearranging her cassettes, Queenesta's mind raced. Should I carry more compact discs? Do I have to drop my prices? How in the hell can I get a damned neon sign myself? Is this place too "Black" for the 16-to-24 age group? Will they feel more comfortable buying from a music retailer who is housed in a video shop? Just then, two teenagers appeared outside the door. "Push hard, it's stuck!" an exasperated Queenesta shouted out. After making eye contact with them, she made a pushing motion with her right arm. Seeing that, the boys got the message and let themselves in.

"Hey, Queen," the taller of the two boys called out.

"Hey, guys, what can I do for you?" They came directly over to her case and crouched down as they looked at the tapes. Queenesta followed their eyes, feeling a little embarrassed that she didn't have more in stock.

"Queen, you got that Digital Underground tape yet?" the taller boy said without looking up from the case.

"No, I'll try to pick it up tomorrow. That's the new one, right?" She pulled out a little pad of paper and made a note—"Digital Underground, NEW!"—and underlined it twice.

"Yeah. Queen, your competition across the street is fading you," the shorter teenager said, drawing out the word *fading* (meaning, "besting") for effect. "He got the Digital Underground since last week."

Queenesta stared blankly, searching for a response. Seconds later, her customers completed their search of the tape case, fingered absentmindedly through the rack of budget CDs, and made for the door. As they disappeared into the mass of cars and people on North Avenue, Queenesta put her elbows on the glass case and buried her face into her waiting hands.

WHEN WHITE SOLDIERS RETURNED TO CHICAGO after the First World War, they wanted their old jobs back, and by and large, they got them. Black workers were either fired or demoted. Between this displacement and a brief recession in the early 1920s, most of Black Chicago's economic gains during the war years were wiped out, and communal harmony continued to deteriorate as the Black Belt nudged into new territory and unemployed Blacks were frequently employed as strikebreakers.

By 1925, however, a resurgent economy brought many unemployed Blacks back into the workforce, and racial tensions temporarily subsided. The five years before the Depression were by some accounts the most prosperous ones the Black community in Chicago ever enjoyed.

By the late 1920s, the Black Belt covered eight square miles. To anyone who was paying attention, it was apparent that Black Chicago was evolving into a different pattern from other ethnic groups, which tended to band together in "colonies" or ghettos for one generation and then disperse throughout the city once their children had become Americanized. This option was not open to Blacks, who, by virtue of their skin color and the legacy of slavery, could not move freely throughout the city without fear of attack by whites. There were certainly movements *inside* the Black Belt, but they were contained within the same contiguous geographical unit. It would be a half century before even upper-class Blacks could buy a house or apartment in any area of the city they could afford.

Not all Blacks disliked this apartheid-like arrangement. Many sensed that it held out the potential for unprecedented racial solidarity and uplift. Jesse Binga, a successful Black banker of the pre-Depression era, reminded Black Chicagoans that they had $40 million deposited in the city's banks and had property with a yearly tax assessment of $2 million. Binga's vision was of a growing class of Black businessmen who would serve and employ members of their own race. He pointed to seven Black-owned insurance companies that each collected $100,000 in annual premiums and the impressive growth of the city's two Black-owned banks (one of which was his).

This brief interlude of prosperity and optimism was rudely interrupted by the Depression, which by the mid-1930s had led to the dismissal of thousands of Black employees, the bankruptcy of Jesse Binga's bank, and much more. In response, the call for Black solidarity found new expression in a campaign known as "Spend Money Where You Can Work." The idea was that Black consumers should boycott white businesses that refused to hire them. When the campaign met with some success, it gained nationwide attention.

These victories were only a few drops in a sea of Black unemployment and despair, but they were enough to entice more Black migration from the Mississippi delta. Another 43,000 arrivals from the South poured in during the 1930s, including Thelma Ali's parents from Indianola, Mississippi.

After the United States's entry into the Second World War, the economy picked up, and for the second time in 30 years, there were severe labor shortages in Chicago. Not surprisingly, between 1940 and 1944 yet another 60,000 Black migrants arrived, aggravating the chronic problems of substandard housing, overcrowded schools, and inadequate medical, sanitation, and recreation facilities in the Black Belt. The population density there reached 90,000 per square mile—as opposed to 20,000 in neighboring white communities—and tuberculosis death rates for Blacks in the early 1940s were more than five times those for whites.

By the 1960s, Chicago mayor Richard J. Daley had perfected his political machine. As far as he was concerned, incoming waves of Black migrants meant more loyal Democratic voters. During his first several electoral triumphs in the late 1950s, support for Daley in Black wards on the South and West sides was strong and, in at least one case, decisive. The housing crisis continued to grow, however, with as many as 2,200 Black migrants arriving every week during the late 1950s. Daley and his inner circle had to decide how to respond. Inevitably, they threw their lot in with those wishing to maintain the color line rather than break it down. Their strategy for solving the housing shortage was to build vertically inside the Black Belt rather than promoting the kind of scattered housing patterns that had achieved the integration of other ethnic groups in the Second City. The Robert Taylor Homes—"the largest public housing project in the world, twenty-eight identical . . . sixteen-story buildings," according to one writer—was opened in 1962, and Blacks were herded into a place that would in time attain a notoriety virtually unparalleled in the industrialized world.[35]

Social movements led by Saul Alinsky, Martin Luther King Jr., the Black Panthers, the Nation of Islam, and others attempted to redress the growing poverty, anger, and isolation of the Black ghettos as well as the often violent racism that characterized the neighboring white communities. But progress was halting, where it was made at all. Soon after coming north for a campaign, King was prompted to say, after a particularly harrowing day of protests, "The people of Mississippi ought to come to Chicago to learn how to hate." Among the most controversial issues was that of overcrowded Black schools. So-called Truth Squads of Black mothers were arrested when they attempted to document that nearby white schools were operating well under full capacity. Yet, for many years, Daley was able to contain such protests while retaining an acceptable level of Black support in elections.

This equilibrium broke down after the riots following King's assassination in 1968, during which large tracts of Black neighborhoods on the West Side were burned to the ground. (Sadly, even a quarter century later, many had yet to be rebuilt.) Daley, incensed that things had been allowed to get so out of control, made his famous order for the police to "shoot to kill or maim" looters. From then on, many white politicians began to simply write off the Black community, their strategy being to win elections without their support and, consequently, without having any debts to pay to Black Chicago after being elected. With the dramatic exception of Mayor Harold Washington's historic election in 1983, the Black community became increasingly politically marginalized after 1968. At the same time, the social fabric of the Black community began to break down.

MEMBERS OF DISADVANTAGED GROUPS as diverse as Native Americans in the United States and Canada, Muslims in the southern Philippines, and low-caste Hindus in India can benefit from small loans delivered through organizations modeled after the Grameen Bank. Credit provided through peer groups allows poor people in these areas to capitalize on their survival skills and gives them a a chance to break the vicious cycle of discrimination in the labor market, low income, low savings, low self-esteem, and negative portrayals in the media. Needless to say, socioeconomic disadvantage often results from historical processes played out over hundreds of years and cannot, in most cases, be overcome quickly or easily. But the Grameen approach has some advantages over strategies that rely purely on the free market, private charity, government handouts, or hiring quotas. Low-income African-Americans and Latinos living in distressed inner-city neighborhoods have been showing since at least the 1980s that they can benefit from small loans provided in a supportive manner. This is particularly impressive and important when one considers the deteriorating socioeconomic conditions of many inner-cities over recent decades.

In 1965, Daniel Patrick Moynihan published his influential and controversial report *The Negro Family: The Case for National Action*. The report had many facets and subtleties, but critics focused on its treatment of the weaknesses of poor Black families. The attacks were sufficiently vicious to virtually bring to a halt most serious sociological research on the Black family for quite a while. According to sociologist William Julius Wilson, "After 1970, for a period of several years, the deteriorating social and economic conditions of the ghetto underclass were not addressed by the liberal community as scholars backed away from research on the topic, policymakers were silent, and civil rights leaders were preoccupied with the affirmative action agenda of the Black middle class."[36] For close to two decades, the ghetto virtually fell off the radar screen of the United States's consciousness.

Ignoring a problem does not, of course, ensure that it goes away. Much to the contrary, this one snowballed. While a quarter of all Black births were out of wedlock the year Moynihan released his report, by 1980 that figure had ballooned to 57 percent. The percentage of female-headed households rose from 25 percent to 43 percent over the same period. Although there were similar trends among other races, they were starting from much lower base figures and were well below the alarming levels in the African-American community. Nowhere were these trends being manifested more dramatically than in Black Chicago, and in few places in Black Chicago quite like Englewood.

The prevalence of single motherhood, caused in large part by widespread unemployment in the inner cities in the wake of jobs being moved overseas or to the suburbs, contributed to an unraveling of the social fabric of neighborhoods like Englewood, as did greater abuse of drugs and alcohol and the growing influence of street gangs on young men.

With gangs inevitably comes violence. In the 1990s, sociologists reported that the leading cause of death for Black men aged 15 to 34 was homicide. A typical entry on the police register page of the *Chicago Defender* on November 18, 1993, reads:

> Wednesday found criminal activity on an upswing in the city. . . . A male in his 20s was reported dead on the scene by police in the 110 block of South May Street. The victim had apparently expired from multiple gunshot wounds to the body. . . . An African-American male, age unknown, was in critical condition in Mount Sinai Hospital while watching a street fight in a parking lot on South Pulaski Avenue. The victim was allegedly stabbed for no reason. . . . A 16-year-old male was in good condition Wednesday after being shot in the right jaw. Police reports indicated that the teen was shot during an exchange of gunfire between rival gangs. . . . A citizen discovered the badly burned body of [a] man in an open garage in the 8100 block of South Racine Avenue Wednesday. The subject's age and identity could not be immediately determined.[37]

Nearly 5 percent of all Black males in that era ended their lives as a victim of homicide. Every four hours, a Black child received a gunshot wound. Yet those deaths often passed with barely a mention in the news media, and police rarely expended much energy trying to get to the bottom of Black-on-Black violence. Rather, excessive police violence against Blacks—rather than their efforts to protect them—has been a recurring theme that only in recent times has received the attention it deserves as a public policy and racial justice issue.

So, it is ironic that at just the moment when young Black males were achieving predominance over American youth culture through rap music and hip-hop fashion, as a group they were suffering from massive, sometimes self-inflicted, wounds. Princeton scholar Cornel West, searching for the reason behind the carnage, has written, "[There is a] sense of worthlessness and self-loathing in black America. This angst resembles a kind of clinical depression in significant pockets of black America."[38] Marian Wright Edelman, founder of the Children's Defense Fund, wrote in a 1993 newspaper article that a Black girl had a 1-in-21,000 chance of receiving a Ph.D. in mathematics, engineering, or the physical sciences but a 1-in-21 chance of being a victim of violent crime during her teen years and a 1-in-6 chance of having a child before she was 20. Edelman noted that children who "should be dreaming of what they want to be when they grow up, what they'll wear at their wedding, how many children they want to have and what they'll name them" were instead "planning their own funerals."[39]

The causes of these trends have for years been the subject of intense debate between and among liberals and conservatives. Some point to the isolation of the inner-city poor and their resulting lack of connection with job networks and positive role models. Others, especially conservatives, blame generous welfare programs and a lenient criminal justice system. Still others argue that in many respects, today's underclass exhibits behavior that is a predictable urban mutation of the social norms prevalent in the Southern sharecropper society following the Civil War.

The Los Angeles riots of 1992 were a frightening reminder of the widespread anger within these tracts of our major cities where crime is rampant, economic activity moribund, gang warfare a daily fact of life, and single motherhood the rule rather than the exception. As members of the media occasionally noted, a young man living in Harlem as recently as the 1990s was less likely to reach 65 years of age than a man living in Bangladesh.

The lack of any sustained program to revitalize the inner cities reflects the widely held belief among the public and lawmakers that there are no affordable solutions to these problems. So, with each passing month, the remnants of civil society vanish—corporations leave, schools become battlegrounds, parks become drug bazaars, and buildings that once housed working people and local businesses fall into disrepair. Along the once majestic Garfield Boulevard in Englewood, boards replaced windows by day and gunfire resounded through the night. All of this created fertile ground for conspiracy theories related to systematic and orchestrated Black oppression. Why else, an increasing number of African-Americans argued, were drugs, liquor, and guns (not to mention AIDS) made more accessible to them than basic amenities like supermarkets, police protection, regular garbage collection, and competent teachers? Nowhere were those feelings more strongly felt than in Chicago, arguably one of the most segregated and racist cities in the industrialized world.

These social ills are, ultimately, the reflection of an economic reality. Black urban poverty is more concentrated and visible than the rural deprivation of the Adirondacks or the Deep South. The Full Circle Fund set to work to demonstrate that the Grameen approach can work with those on the edges of the worst U.S. economic disaster areas, while other programs were making headway in Arkansas and South Dakota, which, along with Englewood, made up a fair cross-section of economic disadvantage in the United States.

THELMA WAS PERHAPS THE TENTH WOMAN to enter the room on October 3, 1993. Ever since Gwen had left, the Lindblom Park center meetings had been starting later and later, and they were not as well organized as they had been. On most occasions, no one took the time to arrange the chairs in a circle. The women sat theater style, a format that made the gatherings considerably less intimate.

Thelma greeted several women and took a chair next to Omiyale. The two began exchanging gossip and laughing as they watched a few more women straggle in. Thelma's head was covered in a scarf, and she wore ragged blue jeans. Omiyale also came to the meeting dressed informally. Other women had come in their Sunday best, some with small children in tow. Colete Grant, Gwen's replacement and an entrepreneur herself, sat at a table in a corner of the room, busying herself with paperwork as the room slowly filled.

When Geri came into the room, Thelma stood up and walked over to her as she was signing in. The two women hugged, but in less than a minute the conversation turned serious. Thelma urged a reluctant Geri to announce that she was going to hold some house shows to sell her aprons and gift baskets later in the year. Thelma then hugged Geri again and the two walked over to Omiyale, who looked up at the women as they seated themselves, peering over her bifocals. She was thumbing through a gigantic, overstuffed three-ring file that contained all her Full Circle Fund papers.

Glenda Harris arrived and ambled over to near the window, joining Thelma, Omiyale, and Queenesta. The women exchanged greetings, and as was her wont, Glenda touched each of them, plus Shayna, within a few minutes of arriving. But there was something restrained about her, and everybody sensed it. Finally Glenda blurted it out.

"Girl," she began as she looked at Omiyale, "I've made a decision."

Omiyale put her hand on Thelma's thigh and turned toward Glenda. "What's that?"

"You aren't going to be happy with this. I'm going to be dropping out of the circle."

"Oh, girl!" Omiyale couldn't contain her disappointment. "Why?"

"You have all given me so much inspiration and energy. You inspired me to get out there and sell my jewelry, but you know, my physical condition just doesn't allow me to run around to events like I've been doing, taking public transportation and all. It's hard just coming to this meeting." As Glenda spoke, her eyes moved from Omiyale to Thelma to Queenesta, and back again. "I'm gonna try to get into some kind of thing, where I sell through a catalog; that's the vision I'm into now. I can't keep up with you. But how much I've learned from you . . . oh!"

Tears welled up in Omiyale's eyes, and Glenda began to cry as well. "Thank you, for crying, for being emotional about this," she said to Omiyale.

"There ain't no reason for you all to get wet over this," Omiyale said even as she began to cry. "Glenda, you have done fine, and if someone is going to leave, this is the way to do it. You have paid off your loan and settled up with us. We're happy for you, really. We'll just miss seein' you every two weeks, that's all. So don't go gettin' like that, ya hear!"

Omiyale grabbed hold of Glenda's hand and squeezed it hard. The two looked at each other, speechlessly, as tears gently rolled down their cheeks. "I'm going to be in touch with you all, that's for sure," Glenda said.

Glenda Harris lived, along with roughly a dozen other people, with the McFerrens, a husband-and-wife activist team that took in people who had lost or abandoned their families and needed a place to stay. The McFerrens called their home a "mission house where whoever loved God and desired to live there could." Hardly any action was taken there without being preceded by a prayer. Among the people who shared the house with Glenda and the McFerrens was Gwen Burns. Both she and Glenda were from broken homes and regarded their landlords as the closest thing they had to parents.

Years earlier, while she was in the midst of her religious conversion and recovering from a drug habit that had turned her into a petty thief, Glenda had read an article about WSEP in a newspaper. But instead of following up her interest, she simply cut out the article and put it in her purse. It became a conversation piece, something she would unfold and show a friend. When she did so, she often expressed skepticism about whether such an organization would lend to low-income people without reference to their credit histories. In fact, she was convinced it must be a scam and told people as much.

When Gwen told Glenda in 1989 that she had interviewed for a job at WSEP, and then started working there, she discovered to her surprise WSEP actually *did* make loans to low-income women. Once she understood that, Glenda wasted little time in joining. Gwen was pleased to be able to suggest Glenda to Omiyale as a replacement for an earlier borrower in Les Papillons who had left the circle. At their urging, Glenda began selling her jewelry at street festivals and indoor bazaars. On occasion, when she went to Springfield to lobby for more funding for Chicago public schools with Mrs. McFerren, she brought her jewelry case with her and sold while she protested, often earning several hundred dollars in the process. By the time she decided to resign from the group, Glenda had gained enough regular customers to keep her business afloat and had high hopes of persuading an upscale catalog like Spiegel to carry her jewelry.

As the others arrived, Thelma continued to reassure Glenda. Finally, Colete called the meeting to order and the women settled down. Colete asked one of the women to say a prayer to begin the meeting. Most of the women liked the ritual, but Thelma believed that it had no place in a business meeting attended by people of different religions.

After the prayer, Colete made some opening comments and then asked for announcements. One woman talked about a forthcoming event called Dance Africa, while another asked about having a senior WSEP staff member come to a future meeting to give a talk about accounting. By the third announcement, Thelma began whispering, "Geri, it's your turn," in a soft voice. Yet Geri's hand remained by her side.

Finally, Thelma held up her hand and said, "Colete, Geri's got something to say."

"Geri," Colete said with a smile as she stood in the front of the room, "do you have an announcement?"

Geri bolted up from her chair and turned sideways so that she faced most of the other women in the room. Her mouth opened for a brief instant, but nothing came out. Finally, she said in a hurried voice, "You all know I'm making my gift baskets for Thanksgiving and Christmas, and I'm making . . . aprons, yeah, aprons; you've seen my aprons. I'm going to be having three shows in my home around the holidays, and I want all of you to . . . to bring your friends to my shows. I'll have the dates for you next week." As Geri sat down, she had a look of terror in her eyes. When Thelma patted her on the back, she looked around and smiled nervously.

Many budding entrepreneurs in the inner city can't afford a storefront to display and sell their merchandise. Instead, they hold shows in their own homes and in the homes of friends, where they can network and sell with little or no overhead or interference from government inspectors. For Geri, holding these events would be a milestone in her effort to expand her business. At Thelma's urging, she was going to invite several owners of retail establishments in Englewood to come to her home shows and consider carrying her merchandise on a consignment basis.

After the announcements, groups of five women gathered in different corners of the room for "circle business." In the middle of the room, members of Lindblom's newest circle held hands and bowed their heads in prayer. Months before the 1993 Middle East peace agreement, five Black women had joined together to ask God to bless their businesses and their circle, despite the fact that two of them were from the Nation of Islam and the rest of them considered themselves "Hebrew Israelites," essentially a Jewish sect. After their prayer, they began discussing the first two loan proposals they would put before the center's loan committee. They had named their circle "Let Us Make Woman."

Les Papillons gathered in a corner of the room, and Omiyale began collecting loan payments from each of the five women. There was discussion of Glenda's impending resignation, and what steps the others would take to replace her. Towards the end of the meeting, Omiyale noticed that Queenesta was being quieter than usual, and moved her chair closer to her youngest circle sister. "Queenesta, how is your business going?"

"Well, okay; a little slow, you know. It's just that this guy has opened up another record shop across the street from me, on North Avenue. And he has this red neon sign in his window. That sign, I don't have anything like it. I'm afraid people are attracted to stuff like that."

Omiyale closed her notebook and studied Queenesta, trying to gauge how discouraged she was. "You're gonna be all right."

Thelma, listening to the conversation, jumped in. "Are your prices competitive?" she began.

"Yeah, most tapes I sell for fifty cents less than he does."

"Well, I'll tell you what, business is business and people don't gonna be paying any extra fifty cent to look at a neon sign. Are your customers staying with you?"

"You know, they tease me, sometimes going back and forth, but most of them are still buying with me. I missed a couple of recent releases, so I lost some sales, but I won't let that happen again. I'm going to a different distributor."

"I think Thelma's right—you'll do fine if you keep your prices low," Omiyale added.

As the group moved on to other subjects, a low murmur of voices from other circles poring over similar problems echoed in the background. Queenesta appeared to have had a weight lifted from her. She would admit later that while she didn't feel she could be vulnerable around Victor, having the opportunity to let her guard down around the women in Les Papillons was a relief.

When the meeting ended at 9:30, Thelma walked over to Omiyale and said quietly, "I'm glad Queenesta has some competition. It will make her a better businesswoman. She'll have to work harder." Omiyale, listening to her old friend, pursed her lips and nodded. Several minutes later, the two women packed up their bags and began their journeys home.

THE DAY BEFORE THE NEXT MEETING, Queenesta looked in her cash box and realized she had just enough to pay her installment. Weeks before she would have been too frightened by the prospect of missing a payment to invest that money and try to turn it over in a day, but in the latter stages of 1993, she was feeling increasingly confident. That night, she went to the music distributor on the South Side, picked up a few popular titles she had run out of, and promptly sold all but one of them the next day. As she headed to the meeting, she congratulated herself for having taken a risk and then made $30 more than she needed for her payment.

During the meeting, Wanda X and Gheeliyah Rojas of Let Us Make Woman appeared before the loan committee of Omiyale, Thelma, and Leverta

Pack to present their loan proposals. Both were requesting $1,500. Gheeliyah made a concise presentation about how she would use her loan money to buy supplies for her greeting-card business. She was an artist, and a fairly talented one at that; her cards were distinguishable by their attractive designs and messages written in shiny gold ink on black paper. When Thelma asked her how many retail outlets sold her cards, she conservatively estimated 40. Although she didn't mention it, and perhaps didn't even know it, they were sold in stores as far away as New York and Washington, D.C. After some brief discussion, the committee approved her loan for the full amount requested.

Wanda asked for $1,500 for a new business making decorative gift boxes out of used cigar boxes. Thelma and Omiyale asked how many she had sold to date. Wanda said she hadn't sold any. When they asked about which events she was planning to sell them at, she said she wasn't sure. The discussion lasted for more than half an hour, roughly double the time it had taken for Gheeliyah's proposal, and at the end of it, the loan committee sanctioned only $800. Wanda was disappointed, but her circle members who had watched the process unfold were relieved. They had asked her the same questions about her intentions in a special meeting they had convened a week earlier. Once again, Grameen's policies that encourage peers to carefully assess loan proposals were paying dividends in terms of limiting credit risk and nudging budding entrepreneurs to make better decisions.

By the time the two women received their loans, JD's Records and CDs had closed up shop on North Avenue. The neon sign remained for several more weeks, but it was rarely turned on. By November, it was taken out of the shop's window for good.

Update: Since the 1990s

THE STATE OF MICROFINANCE, and more broadly, microenterprise development, in the United States and elsewhere in the industrialized world has continued to evolve and occupy an important niche in efforts to reduce poverty and barriers to entrepreneurship among low-income people. Many microloan clients in the United States are poorly educated in a formal sense, and especially for this reason are not attractive to many employers except perhaps for entry-level positions paying poverty-level wages. Some of these people have the capacity to start microbusinesses, but to pursue this path to economic self-empowerment, they immediately confront their lack of financial assets and connections useful for starting a business.

Grameen Foundation's principal mandate was to help those who were applying the Grameen strategy in other poor countries outside the borders of Bangladesh, but it has also been involved in the United States. GF actively supported three American MFIs—Project Enterprise (PE) in New York City, the Peer Lending Action Network (PLAN) Fund in Dallas, and the New Opportunities program of Volunteers of America–Los Angeles. It was a special honor for me to chair the Board of Directors of Project Enterprise on a volunteer basis, because I am a native New Yorker and because Yunus always urged me, and the Grameen Foundation, to remember the needs of those close to home and the potential of microfinance in addressing those needs. Its second executive director, Arva Rice, is the daughter of a self-employed African-American who worked long hours to put his children through college. She took over in 2003 from Vanessa Rudin and worked closely for years with its visionary co-founders Nick and Debra Schatzki.

In 2004, Arva inaugurated an annual awards dinner in Harlem that recognizes high-achieving borrowers and bestows a special honor on one of them—the Entrepreneur of the Year award. A jury of financial supporters and staff of PE selects the recipient from among 10 finalists, and it is always incredibly hard to choose among the street vendors, retailers, home-based daycare providers, caterers, and others who have overcome significant odds and sometimes tremendous hardship to start or expand microbusinesses with the support of PE. The PLAN Fund had its own growing portfolio of success stories. New Opportunities was hamstrung by regulatory barriers unique to California, but made some impact, however limited, before winding down operations.

The story of Project Enterprise borrower Ralph Neal points to the life-changing potential of microfinance in the United States. A Vietnam veteran and recovering drug addict, he began borrowing from PE in 1999 to finance a street-vending business in lower Manhattan. Loans starting at $1,500 helped him capitalize his business, and advice from PE staff and other borrowers enabled him to realize that his best product was watches. Business improved, but the attacks of September 11 forced him to close his microenterprise for a time. Even after that, he helped raise money to pay off a delinquent loan in his center. In 2003, he restarted his business, Ralph's Watches, with financing from PE. Since then, he supported himself through what he earned as a street vendor. He remained a constructive force in his center and lived drug-free.

Like Grameen, PE focused well more than half of its loans on women microentrepreneurs. One of the earliest was Annette Michael, a single mother with three children who had been laid off and was facing foreclosure on her home. In the spring of 2000, she sought and received a $1,500 loan to start a small-scale insurance business as a way to get back on her feet. She operated out of her basement at first, signified on her business card (in what represented a private joke she would share with others years later) by ACM Agency's being in "Suite B." Annette had the last laugh; over time her business grew from two clients to more than 800.

Within a few years, she had done well enough that she no longer needed loans from PE. She felt so grateful to the organization, however, that she continued mentoring PE clients. In recognition of her achievements in business and of the leadership she has provided to other borrowers, and in keeping with Grameen's emphasis on clients being involved in the governance of microlending organizations, Annette was ultimately elected to the organization's Board of Directors. She served there for several years, and continued to be one of the leading evangelists for microfinance in New York City. She annually contributes a higher percentage of her income to Project Enterprise than all but one of her fellow board members.

I recall a day in early 2008 when I was standing on 125th Street in Harlem, trying without noticeable success to catch a cab to the airport after having chaired a PE board meeting. Annette spotted me as she drove by in her car, pulled over, rolled down the window, and said playfully, "You need a ride to the airport? I can give you one, *but it will cost you.*" Without hesitation, I jumped in. She asked me how much cab fare would have cost. I told her about $20. She said that as long as I gave nearly that much as an extra contribution to PE, she was happy to go a bit out of her way and drop me off in time for my flight. Laughing, I quickly agreed, and we were off.

A FEW MONTHS AFTER ANNETTE gave me that lift, Shah Newaz began knocking on doors in Queens to see what interest he could arouse in an even purer replication of Grameen Bank than Project Enterprise represented. As mentioned earlier, what he would go on to launch would become by far the most successful effort at microfinance in any industrialized country.

One of Grameen America's early decisions was to focus initially on Latina clients who came from countries where self-employment among low-income people was common. While immigrants to the United States from Mexico, Central and South America, and Puerto Rico experience many challenges including discrimination, they did not experience the full array of disadvantages that African-Americans did. Grameen America got its footing serving a group that was a bit easier to engage once the language barrier was surmounted. Once it did, it began building up the ranks of its African-American and Native American clients. That would be one of the many adroit moves that helped the organization achieve what few thought possible when it was launched.

REREADING PARTS OF THIS CHAPTER in the spring of 2020 reminded me of the importance of looking at discouraging trends among any population, such as African-Americans, through multiple lenses or perspectives. At the time I wrote the first edition of this book, my vantage point and language were too slanted towards statistics of collective disadvantage and dysfunction; the words and phrases I used were both too antiseptic and too alarmist. They lacked a sufficiently strong rooting in the history of racial injustice in this country, perspectives that my own maturity and, in particular, the Black Lives Matter movement, have now helped me to more fully appreciate. In this edition, I changed some of that language, but kept most of it intact to retain my voice from that era of my life.

As someone who has enjoyed many obvious and subtle privileges during my five and a half decades on Earth, my education on these issues remains something of a work in progress.

7. The Haldar Para

FROM THE DAYS OF THE VERY FIRST group training conducted by Ruhul Amin, the epicenter of the Grameen Bank's work in Kholshi has been the Haldar (fisherman) *para* (a neighborhood or subsection of a rural Bangladeshi village). Of the 60 Haldar families in Kholshi, most live in a narrow patch of land bordered on the south by a raised dirt road and a tiny marketplace, and on the north by a canal that remains filled with water from the early days of the monsoon until well into the dry season. During the months of rain, each homestead plot, on which up to five families might live, are islands separated from the others by water that is six or seven feet deep. People ferry back and forth by boat, if they have one, or by walking across wobbly bamboo bridges. Others, particularly the children, simply swim from place to place.

To one walking among the huts during the rainy season, the number and variety of fishing nets is striking. Some, fresh from being used, are tangled with water lilies, still dripping, as they hang on a bamboo clothesline; others are in the process of being woven or repaired. The whole family joins in the work of net weaving, but it is usually the woman of the house who directs the process. Nets are strung out, then rolled up along a post on the hut's veranda, where each new knot is carefully tied.

Over the last quarter century, the men of the Haldar *para* have had to travel ever farther to ply their trade as an increasing number of the small rivers and canals flowing through Kholshi have dried up as a consequence of shifts in the nearby Jamuna River. Some of the fishermen have turned to farming and other professions, particularly during the dry season. The situation of Kholshi's Haldar women has, however, changed very much for the better.

Before Grameen Bank arrived in the Haldar *para*, net weavers like Devi, Shandha, and Amodini were in great demand for their services, but since they couldn't afford the working capital to buy the expensive thread they used, they were forced to work on a contract basis. A client would supply all the materials and pay the women 25 taka (60 cents) to weave them a net, a job that took as long as three days of full-time work. When they wove nets for their husbands, the women were often forced to borrow from the village moneylender. The loan was paid off by selling half or more of the family's catch over the first several weeks after the net was completed.

Access to capital from Grameen Bank changed all that. Now Amodini and Devi earn 100 taka or more from net weaving over a two-to-three-day period; during the months just before and after the beginning of the monsoon, business is brisk, and their nets can be sold in a market just a short distance from their homes. Grameen Bank loans meant that on a given net, these women's profits quadrupled. In a world where a few pennies can mean the difference between eating and going hungry, this was a big step up.

During the 1993 monsoon, Devi made a bold investment of 30,000 taka to lease a large pond in a nearby village for seven years. She made a 10,000-taka down payment, half of it coming from her seventh Grameen loan and the rest from her savings. The final 20,000 would be due at the end of the coming dry season. If she couldn't bring her husband closer to the fishing, she would bring the fishing closer to her husband.

From the beginning, the superstitious Devi had invested her money wisely, diversifying from net weaving into raising livestock and pigeons (which are commonly eaten in Bangladesh—and yes, they do taste like chicken). Now she was trying to solidify her economic position. Devi enjoyed the honor of having the center house located on her small house plot, and felt that she wanted her home to be a demonstration to the newer borrowers of what was possible through Grameen Bank.

In a house plot next door, Shandha and her family were, like Devi's household, in a constant state of motion: feeding cows, weaving nets, fishing, cooking, and stocking the birdhouse, which keeps a dozen or so pigeons. Sometimes the activity is frenetic, yet Shandha is firmly in control of all that goes on in and around her home. In a similar way, she is the matriarch of her center. No matter who is the elected center chief, Shandha retains a considerable amount of power. She counts the money and does most of the talking with the bank worker during the meeting; when there is a conflict, most of the women rely on her to speak up and resolve it. She has a motherly quality about her, and the women, a few of them 10 or more years older than she, seem to like being mothered by her. She's the kind of person who, if born into different circumstances, could easily have become a national political or business leader.

Yet there was a sadness about Shandha during 1993. Her five sisters, and many of her aunts and uncles, had emigrated to India. Sometimes she thought she would like to go there as well, but her husband was against it and Shandha was reluctant to give up her membership in Grameen Bank for the uncharted waters of India. Still, she was tempted. Many of her friends seemed to be planning to flee Kholshi in an era of growing Hindu-Muslim tensions. Though Hindus like Shandha rarely, if ever, spoke about it in public, there were fears that after the next anti-Muslim incident in India, the Muslims in Kholshi would bypass the Hindu temples and come directly after the Hindu people. Harassment from Muslims who were eager to buy up land from Hindus leaving for India had become a fact of life. Yet her general anger at Muslims was softened by her weekly contact with nearly 30 Muslim women at her center meetings.

As the 1993 monsoon wore on, Shandha became worried about Amodini, who lived nearby, perhaps three minutes away by boat. Amodini had performed well in her year as the center chief, yet just as she'd turned over the reins, things began going wrong for her. Her husband, Ramesh, got sick and couldn't go fishing more than once a month. Apparently, he suffered from a bleeding ulcer, caused perhaps by the same combination of tension and contaminated water that had afflicted Muhammad Yunus. To make up for his lost earnings, Manzu, their oldest unmarried daughter, took up fishing in the local canals with nets woven by her mother. Early in her father's illness, Manzu, along with her younger sister, snuck off one day in the family's boat without her mother's knowledge—believing, correctly, that Amodini wouldn't approve of their fishing alone—and made the case for allowing her to go when she came back with nearly 150 taka worth of fish. Amodini reluctantly agreed that they could continue fishing until their father recovered. At the same time, Ramesh and his wife were being pressured by Amodini's older brothers to move to India. Only her youngest brother offered quiet encouragement for her to stay.

When she joined the bank, Amodini was the poorest woman in the entire Haldar *para*, living with her husband and children in a flimsy shack. Once she had run from her ramshackle hut during a heavy rainstorm to take refuge in a tin house where her mother and brothers lived, and was horrified to see her mother standing in the doorway with a club, refusing to let her in—an experience that reminded her of a fundamental truth about her life.

Thirteen years earlier, Amodini had been forced to return to Kholshi from another village. The Dancing River had left her husband and his relatives with no choice but to scatter in a half dozen directions. Though she preferred to keep it a secret, there was no denying it—Amodini Rani Haldar was a *nodi bhanga lok*, a frequent migrant whose existence was on some level at the mercy of one of Bangladesh's massive and shifting rivers. To her mother and all but her youngest brother, that made Amodini less than welcome; at times, it made her feel something less than human.

BENDING OVER, AMENA SWEPT her small courtyard with a *jharu*, a short broom made of twigs. She swept expansively, leaving the dried dirt in neat circles. She put the organic debris in her garden and dumped the rest behind her house. In Bangladesh, sweeping is as much for appearance as for waste removal, as there is hardly anything one actually throws away. An entire class of people make their living by going from house to house buying up *bhanga jinish* (broken things) from people in exchange for homemade sweets. These throwaways are sold to wholesalers and taken to Dhaka for recycling. Other things are reused locally; for instance, used paper is made into packaging that is sold to local grocery stores. Apart from the omnipresent animal droppings, Bangladeshi villages are remarkably clean—not because the Bengalis are compulsive about such things, but because there is almost always another use for something after it has served its primary purpose. Long before recycling was popular in the United States, I saw the practice in its purest and arguably its most efficient form while living in Bangladesh and especially in rural areas like Zianpur and Kholshi.

After completing her sweeping, Amena began gathering the grass that her daughter had collected the day before and putting it in a feeding bowl for the newest member of her family—her cow. In December, Amena had applied for a seasonal loan from Grameen Bank. She told her husband, Absar Ali, that the 4,000 taka she received was for buying a cow, and he promptly went to the weekly Ghior market, which was famous for cow-trading. Within several weeks, the cow started producing a liter and a half of milk every day. Amena would give a little to her children and sell the rest to a milk wholesaler who came to her house. Amena would typically tell her husband that she earned less than she actually did.

Another addition to Amena's house plot was a tube well for pumping up groundwater by hand. She took out a Grameen loan in November to buy that, too. With access to a supply of fresh water, she was able to maintain and expand her vegetable garden during the dry season. By February, it covered nearly one-sixth of an acre and included pumpkins, eggplant, beans, chilies, and spinach. She fed some of her harvest to her family and had her daughter sell the rest in the Zianpur bazaar, from which she often received 100 taka ($2.50) per week or more.

The year before, Grameen had embarked on a large-scale program to give loans to borrowers for purchasing and installing these hand-pumped tube wells. They give their owners sufficient water for drinking and irrigating half an acre of land. For several years, UNICEF had provided subsidies to Grameen borrowers interested in buying tube wells, and the success of the initiative persuaded Grameen's management to adopt it commercially on a wide scale. Loans ranged from 1,500 to 5,000 taka, depending on the depth the pipes needed to be sunk to reach the water table.

As Amena finished feeding the cow, she took a short break, sitting down on a *piri* (low stool) and preparing *paan* for herself. It was 11 a.m. and the temperature was nearly 90 degrees. As she chewed on the *paan*, Amena looked around for her ducks and chickens. She now had 25 chicks and had given out another 10 on a sharecrop basis to her neighbors, lest her husband realize how big her business had grown. Yet none were in sight at the moment. Her eyes drifted to her garden, to her cow, and finally to the manicured courtyard in front of her. Inside the hut, the infant Shahjahan was sleeping, and she peeked inside to see him before beginning to pump up 20 buckets of water, one after the other, to irrigate her vegetable garden. The tube well had been sunk 30 feet from the garden, and she always felt a little sore after doing this chore. Yet when it was done, she looked on proudly as the earth lapped up the water. Amena took one last stroll through the garden, deciding which vegetables to send her daughter to sell in the Zianpur *haat* (twice-weekly market) in the afternoon.

As she returned to the courtyard, Amena heard her infant begin to cry. He had woken up, and wanted to be fed. Amena cradled him in her arms and began breast-feeding him. When he had had enough, Amena laid him back down on the blanket and began weaving a bamboo mat that she would either use or sell in the market. She had bought the bamboo with a few hundred taka she'd saved. Every few minutes, she would take a break, pick up a fan, and begin waving it above her son. After a short time, he fell asleep.

AS AMENA SAT THERE, WEAVING A BAMBOO MAT in her hut, her thoughts were turning to her brother. He had caused a lot of trouble for her, and she resented it. But what could she do?

Several months earlier, 22-year-old Mozafer Hossain had begun spending time with a married woman in her forties who lived in the village. Gradually, he started to call her his *dhormio ma*, which roughly translates as "adopted mother" or "godmother." There were a few raised eyebrows, but nobody made much of a fuss about it. One day, Mozafer and the woman—a mother of three—eloped to Dhaka and were married. He pulled a rickshaw to support them, and they were living in a slum near the Gabtoli bus station. On several occasions over the ensuing weeks, the woman's husband went to Dhaka to try to find his wife. Periodically, people who were close to the woman's husband came to Amena's house asking for information about her brother's whereabouts. When Amena told them she didn't know, they often insulted her brother and her family in coarse language. Amena was forced to spend many humiliating hours listening to such abuse.

The newlyweds had broken many taboos and crossed over a fine line separating two contradictory parts of the Bengali psyche—a modesty and conservatism dictated by Islam and an emotional, romantic, and even impulsive side. Since the bank's founding, stories have periodically circulated about borrowers who visited centers in other villages only to fall in love with someone else's husband. Occasionally, there are rumors of affairs between Grameen staff members, and there have been cases of harassment of female workers by male employees eager to arrange their own marriages. Yet despite Bengal's reputation on the Indian subcontinent as "the land of poets and lovers," Bangladesh is hardly a permissive society. When things like the elopement of Amena's brother happen, villagers are both horrified and titillated; they condemn and at the same time seem just a little jealous.

AMENA ENJOYED HAVING A COW OF HER OWN. A cow (or better yet, several cows) is a tool for achieving both economic progress and status in rural Bangladesh. It provides milk for consumption or to be sold in the market, pulls a traditional *langal* (plow) in the rice fields, and produces dung that is used as fertilizer or packed into cakes and used as cooking fuel after it hardens. With luck, a cow will yield a stream of calves that can be raised or sold. It can also be fattened and then sold for large sums of money at the time of the Eid festival. A cow's sudden death, on the other hand, can represent a major setback, especially for a poor family.

For most of Bangladesh's poorest households, the best that can be hoped for is to rent one from a wealthy family. But any increase in the value of a cow, and of any offspring, are shared with the owner, even though costs as feeding, inoculation, and veterinary expenses are borne by the sharecropper. Grameen has allowed tens of thousands of sharecroppers to become owners; indeed, while walking around Grameen villages one often hears borrowers excitedly talking about how they have become a *teen gorur maleek* (owner of three cows).

One borrower who made good through cow-raising is Oloka Ghosh, Amena's neighbor who was so instrumental in getting her into the center. As Amena was repaying her first loan, Oloka was caring for eight cows. Five years earlier, before she'd entered Grameen, she'd had no livestock at all. In hard times, her family had mortgaged their land and were forced to rely entirely on their caste profession—making sweets—for their meager income. But because they did not have milk of their own, they were forced to buy it in the marketplace. Sometimes, the prices were so high that they would have no alternative but to take a loss to fill their orders. Today, they have enough milk for both family consumption and their confectionery business, and they sell the rest. Oloka's husband has even learned enough about the milk business that he now makes extra money by trading milk, buying cheaply in one market and selling dear in another. The working capital he needs to do this comes by way of seasonal loans from Grameen Bank.

When Amena visited her friend's large, tin-roofed hut, she often marveled at the idea of a poor person coming to own eight cows. Normally, a *nod bhanga lok* squatting on a relative's land with virtually nothing to her name would feel ashamed walking into the home of someone who had comparatively so much. But Oloka had reached out to Amena and had welcomed her into her home and center. Sometimes, when they were alone, Amena shared with Oloka her dream of owning eight cows herself one day.

NO DESCRIPTION OF BANGLADESH IS COMPLETE without discussing the foreign aid it receives.[40] Development assistance is the international equivalent of welfare, only it is provided to nations instead of people. Virtually no village in the country is untouched by it, and thousands of people, foreign and Bangladeshi, rich and poor, have benefited from it. In a few cases, wealthy countries with progressive agendas, such as Sweden, Norway, Germany, and Canada, have made serious efforts to ensure that a significant portion of their development assistance has been used to reduce poverty. Even donor countries and international organizations with more complex objectives for their aid can usually point to at least one Bangladeshi project they have supported that has improved the lives of the poor. Yet, despite all the good intentions, success stories remain the exceptions.

One of the ways that Sheikh Mujib distinguished his administration from those that followed was his hostility to foreign donors. Charities faced major hurdles in establishing themselves in newly independent Bangladesh. On several occasions, even the mighty World Bank was put in the uncomfortable position of having meetings that it had traditionally run chaired by government officials. The hostility was in most cases more style than substance, as the country was in dire need of food, medical supplies, and other essentials after the war of independence. But Mujib and his political allies craved the appearance that they, not the aid agencies, were the senior partners in the effort to rebuild Bangladesh. This stance resonated with many Bengalis, who had long perceived themselves as second-class citizens in their own country.

After Mujib's assassination, the foreign community in Dhaka grew quickly, their expertise supposedly needed to manage a burgeoning portfolio of foreign-funded projects. By the late 1980s, the annual commitment of donations from the United Nations, the World Bank, and donor nations had ballooned to $2 billion—or $5.5 million every day. The primary beneficiaries of many projects, however, often appeared to be foreign and Bangladeshi bureaucrats. The community of contractors making their living off the aid business was doing quite well, but the people in whose name the aid was given often did not benefit much, if at all. Bangladesh became a desirable posting for professionals from wealthy countries eager to earn tax-free salaries while being cared for by a coterie of servants. (The attractiveness of Bangladesh was enhanced by the fact that it was virtually free of violence against foreigners— a pattern that came to an end on July 1, 2016, when terrorists attacked a bakery in a part of town populated by foreigners and wealthy Bangladeshis. Of the 29 people killed before the standoff was resolved, 20 were hostages, including 17 foreigners.) During that idyllic era for foreign aid workers, few among those who came to help dispense aid attempted to learn the language, to mingle with many Bangladeshis, or to find out much about life in the rural areas.

In the late 1980s, a study conducted on the aid industry in Bangladesh published some remarkable findings.[41] Among them was the fact that some three-quarters of all foreign assistance funds were being spent in the donor countries themselves, and that most of the rest paid for the services of a small cadre of Bangladeshi consultants, contractors, and firms. To a considerable degree, aid had become a means for wealthy nations to employ their own people to dump outmoded goods and ideas on the poorer ones. One foreigner who took a real interest in the country wrote:

> In the world of aid, almost no work is done by officials. Aid agencies contract with consulting firms to identify, cost out, and implement projects. . . . And consultants, who work for daily wages, albeit quite high ones, are not about to lose their friendliness with the aid agencies that hire them. One cannot imagine a Swedish aid agency, for example, recommending a project that did not use Swedish products. . . .
>
> And that, of course, is the problem. For the project often begins with the product, and the aid agency, responding to its political masters, [looks] for projects that sell the product. If Holland has excess capacity in its machine-tool industry or Britain wants to dispose of used telephone exchanges from Birmingham (two real examples), the aid agency will offer to give these items as aid.[42]

Meanwhile, many pressing needs in Bangladesh remain unmet because they do not require products with which donors are eager to part.

Among those who share the blame for this are citizens in industrialized countries. While they often respond generously with donations to relief and development organizations working in Bangladesh or other poor countries, they do little to ensure that these millions of dollars are used to make the developing world's poor self-reliant. As a result, the money ends up supporting some surprising ventures.

Some years ago, I was told a story by a U.S. government employee that illustrates the effects of private-sector lobbying on foreign aid. An American company that specialized in packaging lobbied for the passage of a piece of legislation to require that food aid sent to Bangladesh be bagged before it was shipped. The bill passed, and funds were spent to bag the goods, but when the shipments started arriving it was necessary to spend additional aid money to unbag them before the food could be distributed. In this way, resources are spent without much impact being made.

Even within the current system, a few talented Bangladeshis have resisted the temptation to enrich themselves by becoming highly paid consultants for Western aid agencies. They have instead accepted funds, used them with integrity, and paid themselves local wages, even though they could have commanded hundreds of times more elsewhere. These people include Akhtar Hameed Khan and his Comilla Cooperatives in the 1960s, Dr. Zafrullah Chowdhury's Gonoshasthaya Kendra ("People's Health Center"), Khushi Kabir's Nijera Kori ("We Do It Ourselves"), and the late Fazle Abed's BRAC. Yet, these initiatives have faced enormous obstacles. When the government tried to replicate the Comilla Cooperatives nationwide, it succeeded only in partly destroying their good name. When Zafrullah Chowdhury took on the multinational drug companies and accepted help in doing so from the Ershad regime, he was ostracized from the political and medical establishments. Some years ago, BRAC's nationwide network of highly acclaimed nonformal primary schools came under attack by Islamic fundamentalists, and dozens of the huts in which classes were being conducted were burned to the ground. Yet for the people these organizations served, they were often the difference between hope and despair, between life and death.

The misuse of most foreign aid is a double tragedy for Bangladesh. First, if used properly, it could do much more to improve living conditions in the rural areas and urban slums. If, for instance, $2 billion was simply transferred directly to the poorest ten million Bangladeshi families (representing half of the population in the mid-1990s) each family would each receive an annual grant of $200. This would represent a figure more than twice the size of a typical Grameen Bank loan in the 1990s. Even if they did not invest all the money, the recipients would use most of it to buy goods produced by other poor people, thereby energizing the rural economy. (Consultants and bureaucrats often deposit their money in foreign savings accounts or buy imported goods.)*

The reliance on external resources has a second pitfall. After occupying a proud place among the peoples of the world for hundreds of years, in the last half of the twentieth century Bangladesh was reduced to being a beggar among nations. The cumulative effect on the Bengali psyche has been profound. Many of the best and the brightest have left the country, and most of those who remain do so with one foot in London, New York, or Washington. Even those of humble origins flock to embassies of Western and Middle Eastern countries and wait in line for hours, only to have their visa requests refused by ill-mannered officials. Middle-class families spend precious taka on imported goods despite the existence of less expensive, locally produced merchandise of comparable quality. Their assumption is that if it is Bengali, it is of low quality.

Perhaps the state of the nation's self-esteem, stung in 1974 by Kissinger's remark about Bangladesh's being "the world's basket case," was best expressed in a 1992 televised debate between two groups of Bengali university students from rival campuses. The subject was "the Bengali character." One young man approached the lectern and said that Bangladeshis were scoundrels, cheats, and liars, unwilling to work hard and too willing to take bribes. Foreigners, on the other hand, were hardworking, honest, and law-abiding; in short, the antithesis of Bangladeshis.

---

* This thought experiment, which appeared in the first edition of this book, anticipated the "give direct" movement in international private philanthropy. While I admire this approach's intentions and efficiency, I still prefer efforts that involve starting, investing in, improving, and/or growing local institutions and institutional capacity. At their best, local development organizations like Grameen and BRAC can do something far more important than efficiently processing payments from rich people to poor people. Beyond the immediate good their work does when it is effective, they can build resilience and capture learnings that can help communities prepare for problems that don't yet exist and crises that can't be predicted. The difference is comparable to one between a school that occasionally receives bequests to support an arts program and a school whose board includes a permanent subcommittee dedicated to building, sustaining, improving, and growing a robust arts program.

A member of the opposing debate team asked his opponent, "If everyone is so honest in other countries, why do they need jails? Why do they need police?"

The first debater had a ready reply. The reason other countries needed to build jails and hire police was to deal with Bangladeshis who had left home and broken the law abroad.

Yunus hated the fact that so much aid was misused and that it often further enriched the wealthy while demoralizing the nation. Even as Grameen itself accepted large amounts of foreign assistance between 1983 and 1993, Yunus rarely missed an opportunity to publicly criticize the donor community in Dhaka. Even the agencies that provided Grameen with grants and low-interest loans were not immune. Despite Yunus's frankness—or, some said, because of it—the financial support continued to pour in. But, much to Yunus's dismay, organizations in other developing countries that were adapting the Grameen model were not so lucky; it took years of intense efforts by groups like the Microcredit Summit Campaign before could they attract significant funding needed to expand their work.

Most donor organizations would only fund research, not the credit-providing bodies themselves. In one case, a U.N. agency created to assist the rural poor sent five missions to investigate the possibility of funding a promising program in Negros, a poverty-stricken island in the southern Philippines. The project had been started after the precipitous fall in the world price of sugar, the crop upon which the entire island's economy was dependent. Within several months of sugar's plunge, more than half of the children there were victims of third-degree malnutrition. Each mission—which was composed mainly of European and American consultants—cost the agency several hundred thousand dollars in airline tickets, per diems, and professional fees. Yet, even after all that expense, more than a million dollars in all, they had been unable to make a decision about whether to fund the program. By mid-1993, the project was nearing collapse because of a lack of money. Had it simply received an amount equal to the cost of a single mission, it would have been able to reach several thousand more poor families and meet its monthly payroll. But that, unfortunately, is not how the aid business typically works.

In early 1993, Yunus decided that he would try to raise $100 million himself and then distribute the money to promising microfinance programs through the less-rigid Grameen bureaucracy. In talking up this proposal, he cited the successes of a pilot project that he had initiated which provided small grants and loans to these organizations. The initial response from international organizations was muted. But in the summer of 1993, Brian Atwood, the administrator of the U.S. Agency for International Development, newly appointed by President Clinton and eager to make his mark, provided a grant of $2 million to the replication fund.

By the fall, the World Bank was interested in making a contribution. The bank and Yunus had had a long and sometimes difficult relationship. The World Bank was the preeminent development organization, created immediately after the Second World War and charged with rebuilding Europe. When that was accomplished, it turned to the underdeveloped countries, a task that ended up being considerably more difficult. But the complexity of the problem didn't prevent the Bank from extending around $22 billion in development loans each year for projects designed by its staff. Every so often, a World Bank–funded project that failed received unfavorable media attention, and that particular boondoggle, or the World Bank itself, would be compared unfavorably with Grameen. To many people at the World Bank, Grameen represented an increasingly well-known success story in which the Bank had no role. That led to some tense moments between the two institutions over the years.

When the World Bank offered $200 million to Grameen in 1986, Yunus turned it down. His reasons—that he didn't need the money and wasn't eager to have arrogant World Bank consultants telling him how to do his job—were widely reported in the national and international press. What he didn't say was how much pressure Bank officials had put on the Bangladeshi government to accept the loan—pressure that the usually pliable bureaucracy admirably resisted. On another occasion, Yunus and World Bank President Barber Conable appeared on a forum that was being televised by satellite to dozens of countries. Out of the blue, Conable said that the World Bank was providing significant financial support to Grameen. Yunus replied that it was doing no such thing. Conable went on to repeat his assertion twice more, and both times Yunus denied it. Later in the program, Conable bragged that his economists were among the most talented and brightest people in the world. Yunus responded by saying that hiring smart economists doesn't automatically translate into policies and programs that benefit the poor.

At one point, the World Bank abandoned hope of direct involvement with Grameen and decided to make its own, super-Grameen Bank in Bangladesh, one which would combine features of Grameen with those of other well-known mission-driven organizations in Bangladesh. When the government asked for Yunus's opinion, he wrote a humorous memo mocking the idea, saying that if you took the head of a horse and the legs of a cow and the body of a goat, in theory you might have a good animal but in reality it would be of little practical use. When the World Bank abandoned that proposal, it expressed interest in providing substantial funding to the Bangladesh Rural Advancement Committee, the largest nonprofit organization in Bangladesh (and today one of the largest in the world). When those negotiations broke down, the Bank said it wanted to provide $75 million to a new, quasi-governmental foundation that Yunus had been instrumental in establishing that would provide low-interest loans to organizations willing to make credit available to the poor. After a lot of battles and some behind-the-scenes lobbying in Washington, the Bangladeshi government decided to take Yunus's advice and provide the equivalent of $13 million from its own resources to the foundation and refuse the World Bank funding. Finally, the World Bank took the project document for creating a super-Grameen and gave it to the Sri Lankan government, where it was dutifully accepted.

As these conflicts receded, a sympathetic official in the World Bank's headquarters talked to Yunus in 1990 about commissioning an evaluation of Grameen. After conducting such a study, the official pointed out, the World Bank could no longer argue with Yunus's work and might even come to respect it. It would also give the World Bank the role it wanted in Grameen's success, without giving it any operational power. Yunus discussed the proposal with his colleagues, and most of them recommended that he refuse it. They argued that such an evaluation would be hopelessly biased against Grameen, considering the tensions that had plagued the two institutions' relationship. Yunus was confident that the evaluation would be positive and decided to invite the Bank to do the research. His only condition was that it would have to include his response to the study in the final publication should he wish to do so.

In the spring of 1993, Yunus received a draft copy of the part of the evaluation dealing with the financial viability of Grameen. By taking data primarily from 1991 and 1992, years in which Grameen suffered its first large losses due to increases in staff salaries necessitated by a decision by the government, the World Bank researchers concluded that unless Grameen Bank raised its interest rate it would either be chronically dependent on donated funds or would have to fold up operations. Yunus protested, saying those two years were atypical of a general trend toward profitability, and asked the researchers to redo their calculations using data from the first six months of 1993. When they began using those numbers, the researchers were surprised to discover that they yielded results that were the opposite of the ones in their draft report. As the year wore on, Yunus began hoping that the processes of recalibrating the findings would allow him to include the data from the second half of 1993, as they were even better than those from the first half. He knew the World Bank researchers would resist having to throw out their initial findings, but he believed there was a strong case for them to acknowledge Grameen's financial strength. In any case, if they refused, he could rake them over the coals in his written response.

By 1993, the World Bank was eager to turn its relationship with Grameen around with a dramatic gesture, one that would conveniently be announced at a World Bank conference on world hunger that was scheduled for late November. The conference had been called in response to a 26-day fast by U.S. Congressman Tony Hall to draw attention to world hunger, and the media was sure to give it ample coverage.

Yunus left for a trip to the United States in which he was due to meet President Clinton on November 8. The meeting had been arranged by George Stephanopoulos, who had met Yunus in 1987 when, as a 24-year-old aide to Representative Ed Feighan, he had championed a bill that supported Grameen's approach to poverty alleviation. The initial meeting was postponed when a young White House aide wrote down the wrong date in the president's calendar. While his friends in Washington tried to reschedule the meeting, Yunus took a trip to Arkansas to attend a workshop on lending to the poor in North America.

Meanwhile, Yunus talked by phone with a senior official at the World Bank. After some lengthy discussions, the two arrived at an agreement under which the World Bank would make an initial grant of $2 million to support international replication of the Grameen Bank model. (The World Bank had been interested in making a larger contribution as a loan.) In exchange, the professor agreed to allow the Bank to announce the grant with all the fanfare it wanted at the hunger conference, at which Yunus was to be a keynote speaker. Word of the agreement was leaked to nonprofit groups that were trying to pressure the World Bank into making its lending policies more sensitive to the needs of the poor and the environment. Yunus was portrayed by some of the activist groups as having sold out. They feared that his speech at the hunger conference would be an endorsement of the bank's approach to poverty alleviation, one that activists felt was just a public relations ploy bought with a tiny sliver of the Bank's substantial resources. (The $2 million contribution to Grameen Trust was equivalent to less than the amount the Bank lends in an average hour.)

After returning from Arkansas, Yunus finally got an audience with President Clinton. Yunus presented Clinton with a letter that had been signed by officials of nearly a hundred prominent charities, such as CARE and Save the Children, urging that impending cuts in humanitarian foreign assistance be restored. The president promised to try to restore the cuts. The two men proceeded to talk about the developments that had taken place in Grameen and about the progress of the Good Faith Fund, an Arkansas-based organization Yunus had just visited that had started a Grameen-type program at about the same time the Full Circle Fund had gotten rolling. Yunus also acknowledged the positive changes that Clinton had brought to the U.S. Agency for International Development. He told of coming from a meeting there, and how after years of feeling as if he were in enemy territory while at AID, he now felt that he was among friends when he visited. The conversation shifted to the World Bank, which Yunus wanted to see changed as well. Clinton invited Yunus to prepare a paper on how the World Bank should be changed.

By the time Yunus addressed the hunger conference, the $2 million grant for replication to Grameen had been announced, and the Bank's public relations machine was playing up the organization's leadership in taking this "unprecedented and historic" step toward alleviating poverty and hunger. Yunus, meanwhile, had shown the Bank a draft of his speech and was asked to tone down his criticism of it. Finally, it was Yunus's turn to speak, and the activists and Bank officials nervously awaited his remarks.

Had the officials known Yunus better, they would have realized that there was no point in asking him to moderate his remarks. On many occasions, he has forsaken diplomacy and formality for brutal candor. At a 1998 conference convened by the Society for International Development, a professional organization for people working in Third World development, Yunus gave both the opening and closing speeches. His first address was an inspiring vision of a world free of poverty and the steps to achieve it. His second one was rather different. Standing before hundreds of attendees, he said, "I am very disappointed in this conference. I came here thinking it was going to be about ending poverty in the world. Walking around the conference the last few days I have discovered that what it is about for most people is negotiating their contracts for the next year." After a brief pause, his candid observation was met with a standing ovation.

Yunus titled his speech at the World Bank conference "Hunger, Poverty, and the World Bank."[43] After saying a few words linking the fight against poverty to the cause of human rights, Yunus went on the offensive. "The World Bank was not created to end hunger in the world" was his blunt assessment. "It was created to help development. To the World Bank, development means [economic] growth. Single-mindedly, it pursues growth to the best of its ability until it is distracted by other issues like hunger, women, health, environment, and so on. . . . . [The] people who work at the World Bank were not hired to eliminate poverty from the world. They were chosen for qualities which may not have immediate relevance for poverty reduction.

"In order for the World Bank to take poverty reduction seriously, these issues have to be resolved in favor of poverty reduction. This may require us to go back to the drawing board, to design the Bank from scratch." The latter sentence was widely quoted in the international press.

Toward the end of his speech, Yunus described how he thought the Grameen Bank and the World Bank were different. "Stories we hear about the enormous debt burden accumulated by a large number of countries around the world and the miseries caused by the structural adjustment programs imposed on them by the World Bank make us feel that our two banks work very differently.

"When we hear about how countries are made to pay these debts through their noses, surrendering the bulk of their export earning, leasing out valuable resources at throwaway prices to make extra income, sacrificing social and environmental considerations to earn enough to repay their huge debts, we find it difficult to accept that as banking. Causing misery to people, and to nations, cannot be banking." Not once in his remarks did he mention the World Bank's grant to support adoption of the Grameen Bank approach in other countries.

A CHILLY WIND BLEW THROUGH THE OFFICE, lifting up the edges of a few papers left over from the day before. Jobbar Ali sat at his table and studied the report that told him about the loans he would disburse in the afternoon. All of his staff had left for their center meetings earlier that morning, and it would be another 90 minutes before any of them returned.

It was Monday, and the entire staff had headed to Bagutia together. Since it was the dry season, the workers had all taken their bikes with them. Meetings were scheduled so as to allow the staff to travel in groups for most of their journeys. This was a holdover from the branch's early days, when there were concerns about bank workers being assaulted and robbed on their way to and from meetings.

One of the names on Jobbar's list of women to receive loans that day was Lutfa. He had met her several times during his 20 months as manager, and to him she was the kind of person that Grameen was created to serve. Yet he knew she faced hurdles that no other borrower in his branch had to confront.

Lutfa Ali lived in Munshikandi, a village about a mile south of the Zianpur bazaar that was notable for a large cigarette factory owned by the hamlet's wealthiest man. It was also the village where the first Grameen Bank center under the Shaymganj branch had been founded, its first two groups having been recognized a few hours before Shandha's and Nonibala's quintets were in December 1987.

Soon after Lutfa was born, her father died and her mother married a wealthy man in the village, even though he already had several wives and could not adequately care for Lutfa or her brothers and sisters. Lutfa, by her own admission, was a mischievous young girl, always getting into trouble with her guardians and peers. One day, while she was studying in the second grade, her entire body swelled up and she was incapacitated. After she was confined to bed and lived in constant pain for more than four months, the swelling finally went down, only to reappear several months later. Her mother called on several traditional healers to try to help, but nothing worked. By the time she was 12 years old, Lutfa was paralyzed from the waist down; her skinny legs would hang limply below her undersized body as she passed her days sitting in bed.

Developing countries, Bangladesh in particular, are not kind to people with disabilities. (And for that matter, before the passage of the Americans with Disabilities Act in 1990, neither was the United States.) Lutfa never had a chance to go to a hospital, or even to sit in a wheelchair, a device she had heard about but had never seen. She sat on tables and mats and beds, and over time taught herself how to spin rope from raw jute, make bamboo mats and fans, sew blankets, and even raise ducks. But she and her mother had no money for raw materials—whatever she had went to buy food, as they mortgaged all their land after Lutfa's father had died. Lutfa busied herself with her crafts, but she made negligible amounts of money because all the work she did was done on a contract basis. The owner supplied the raw materials, she supplied the labor, and as a result, she would get as little as 4 or 5 taka (10 to 13 cents) per day for her efforts. Still, at least it offered a distraction.

When Mannan Talukdar started working with the first Grameen Bank borrowers in Munshikandi as the branch's founding manager, Lutfa always asked to be carried over to where the training was taking place. She was not alone among the villagers in being curious and watching the process, but all the jokes she cracked about the Grameen rituals—the saluting, the slogans, the Sixteen Decisions—made her stand out. As she later admitted, she was mocking the bank while at the same time being secretly interested in joining. One day when she didn't come to watch the training, Mannan asked what had happened to her, only to hear that her body had swollen up again. He canceled the session, hurried to Lutfa's house, and immediately cut off her blouse with a pair of rusty scissors. Her body had become so swollen that some of her clothes were constricting the flow of blood to her extremities.

A year after the disbursement of loans to the first groups in Munshikandi, Lutfa sent word to Mannan that she wanted to join Grameen Bank. He visited her hut and they talked about what she could do with a loan. Lutfa explained about how she could make an impressive variety of handicrafts and, with the help of her sisters, raise ducks and pigeons as well. Mannan was encouraged but not convinced. He went to Tepra to have a meeting with his area manager, the well-respected but sometimes bureaucratic Abdul Wahab. After hearing the pros and cons of letting Lutfa in, Wahab simply said, "Why not try it?" That was all Mannan needed to hear.

When Lutfa's group began to prepare for the recognition test, Mannan conducted the training himself, fearing that she would have difficulty learning the material. To his surprise, she learned faster than anyone else in her group. In spite of all the teasing, she had managed to memorize most of the information when she had observed the first center being formed, and could still recite it a year later. After receiving her loan, Lutfa became one of the most prosperous members of her center. Through raising pigeons and ducks, selling duck eggs, and marketing her handicrafts, she was able to pay a weekly installment of almost 300 taka ($7.50). She even used some of her profits to lease a small farm so that her younger brother could farm it and they could "eat rice from their own land." Now it was time for another loan, and Lutfa was putting on her finest clothes as she prepared to leave for the branch office.

The bank workers slowly arrived back from the Bagutia center meetings. Most were drenched with sweat when they arrived. They began counting the money and entering the installments into the loan ledgers. (Until Grameen fully computerized its operations, every installment of every loan was noted three times—in the borrower's passbook, on the collection sheet, and finally on the loan ledger. Each month, Jobbar spent hours reconciling all of them to make sure there was no funny business going on.)

Once everyone had returned from the villages, there was some spirited discussion about who among the bank workers would do the marketing for their communal kitchen later that afternoon. Rohim mentioned that he thought it was time they should break down and have chicken with their evening meal—the monotony of vegetable gruel and tiny fish was getting to him—but the others argued against it. They wanted to keep the daily per person food cost at or below 24 taka, in part because several of the staff needed to send part of their salaries home to their parents and to siblings who were unemployed or still in school.

At 12:15 Lutfa arrived on a rickshaw from Munshikandi. When she'd come for her first loan, she arrived in a broken-down wooden cart pushed by her sister. Today, she could afford the one-way rickshaw fare of 6 taka. Lutfa's group chairman and another borrower helped lift her off the rickshaw and onto a bench in the office. A bank worker came over after a short while and gave her the forms she needed to sign. Other borrowers had to go up to the bank worker's table to complete their paperwork and then to the manager's table to receive their loan, but in Lutfa's case, the staff all came to her.

She enjoyed coming to the bank and all the attention she received; when Lutfa collected her initial loan, it was her first trip to Zianpur since she had become paralyzed. Women always asked her what she was able to do with her loan money, and she enjoyed telling others about each of her income-generating activities. She often brought things that she made so that she could show the other women how skilled she was in handicrafts.

At 2:30 p.m., Jobbar and Ahlim went over to Lutfa and presented her with 7,000 taka and a brown passbook. It was her sixth general loan, and one of the largest the branch had on its books. As she received the money, Lutfa smiled and said to her branch manager, "Sir, you should provide such good service to *all* your borrowers!" She drew out the word *all* for emphasis. When Jobbar laughed, the other borrowers—none of whom would have the courage to tease the *boro saar* ("big sir")—felt that it had been taken in jest, and began giggling among themselves.

Update: Since the 1990s

YUNUS'S COMMITMENT TO BUILDING a global microfinance movement based on his experiences in Bangladesh has remained a hallmark of his work since the original publication of this book. He participated in all of the global and regional meetings of the Microcredit Summit Campaign, something few people besides the founder of the campaign, Sam Daley-Harris, can say. He provided encouragement, training, and seed capital to anyone who seemed to have a chance at implementing his self-help strategy successfully in their country, while occasionally criticizing those who seemed more intent on using microfinance to become wealthy or famous.

A times, he felt pulled between being a spokesperson for microfinance in Bangladesh and globally. It annoyed him when foreigners took inordinate credit for some aspect of Grameen's success or the cause of microfinance. Inexplicably, aid agencies around the world that deploy more than $50 billion each year to fight poverty could not muster even $10 million towards the $100 million fund that Yunus proposed in 1993.

One person who did respond to that appeal was Ismael Serageldin, a senior World Bank official originally from Egypt. Providing significant direct funding to a Bangladeshi organization Yunus controlled was ultimately ruled out. But discussions between Yunus and Serageldin led instead to the creation of the Consultative Group to Assist the Poorest (CGAP), which was housed at the World Bank in Washington, D.C. However, within a few years, CGAP's leadership and Professor Yunus developed a rather adversarial relationship that has not markedly shifted since. Notwithstanding some real disagreements on substance, their inability to partner creatively seems to be based partly on style. The unplanned but somehow inevitable attempt by CGAP to seize the role of the *de facto* "global secretariat for microfinance" has irked many experienced practitioners and obscured some of the positive results they have been produced over the years. I suppose it is simply one more example of how successes in international development are often recolonized by experts from wealthy countries even if they originally emerged from the work of local social entrepreneurs.

In any case, Yunus was disappointed by the turn that CGAP took and began looking to other partners to advance the cause of poverty-focused microfinance.

Seeing how CGAP was veering from what he and Serageldin envisioned, Yunus gave his blessing in 1997 to the establishment of the Grameen Foundation (GF). A small circle of friends who believed in expanding microfinance in a way consistent with Yunus's values worked to make GF an effective enabler of organizations that aspired to be the Grameen Banks of other poor countries. I was one of those friends.

Over time, GF would become known for brokering landmark transactions between poverty-focused microfinance institutions and local banks, using loan guarantees, a small core staff team, and retired banking executives who volunteered their time. But long before we could think of loan guarantee schemes, Grameen Foundation needed to show that philanthropic resources mobilized in a privileged country like the United States could accelerate the growth and magnify the impact of microfinance in distant developing countries. The leaders of three microfinance institutions (MFIs) in India who were inspired and trained by Grameen Bank gave us that opportunity when they approached GF with an intriguing proposition in early 2000. Udaia Kumar, David Gibbons, and Sathia Devaraj told us that they were confident that they could collectively increase their outreach from 46,000 clients to 165,000 in 30 months if they could mobilize $8 million. Furthermore, they said that if Grameen Foundation could provide $1 million early in the expansion process, they could find the other $7 million from other sources, mostly within India.

Steve Rockefeller, the grandson of Nelson Rockefeller who would later join our board and chair our development committee, agreed to work with me during the spring and summer of 2000 to secure the $1 million. We received a big boost when Jim Greenberg (who also later became a board member) and his wife Lisa committed $500,000 as a matching grant. After several weeks of pounding the pavement, Steve and I had secured commitments totaling $1.3 million, but with a collapsing stock market we had our work cut out for us to actually realize $1 million in donations (one of many fundraising lessons I learned during this campaign). But we prevailed, and got the money to India by the end of the year. Our partners in India more than held up their end of the bargain; they reached 165,000 new clients six months early. In March 2007, I noticed that these three organizations and two other smaller MFIs (which later became GF partners and together had fewer than 4,000 clients in 2000) had just surpassed two million women borrowers.

In microfinance, small amounts of resources have a way of multiplying and having a major impact. Thanks to Udaia, David, and Devaraj's challenge, I learned the potential of small amounts of financial resources on a new level during this campaign. I will be forever grateful to our faithful contributors, our grassroots partners and to Steve, with whom I have developed a life-long friendship. This campaign was an important jump-start to the efforts of a handful of Indian microfinance visionaries and built credibility for Grameen Foundation as a reliable and effective partner.

The uniqueness and vitality of the microfinance movement emanated from the fact that it was made up of thousands of such initiatives, most led by private citizens who felt emboldened to work hard and sacrifice for what might otherwise be a lifeless abstraction: the massive scaling-up of a poverty alleviation strategy developed in Bangladesh. The brilliance of Sam Daley-Harris and his Microcredit Summit Campaign was that it stitched together all of that idealism and energy into one of the world's greatest bottom-up global initiatives, replacing atomized activity with loosely coordinated solidarity and teamwork. On a shoestring, he and his team helped empower thousands of people who would never meet and who had little to no expertise in actually providing microloans to build a global industry that has changed the world and that will endure far into the future.

MICROFINANCE AT ITS CORE REMAINS SIMILAR to the work that went on outside Yunus's classroom in the mid-1970s and in Kholshi in the mid-1990s. Like any maturing industry, however, this one has developed new leaders, competing schools of thought, and specialized niches that would have seemed implausible to those who got everything started decades ago. For example, in response to the potential of microfinance to serve borrowers like Lutfa described in this chapter, an organization called Mobility International has created and aggressively promoted a series of best practices related to including the disabled in microfinance programs. However, the essence of the microfinance strategy and its potential remain largely unchanged.

A global movement with a nimble campaign infrastructure and a charismatic leader like Yunus can attract some impressive allies. For example, in 2005, I had occasion to join a small luncheon where the rock star and international humanitarian Bono got to know Yunus. At the beginning of the discussion, Yunus uncharacteristically read aloud a letter to Bono that concluded with a request that he write a song about microfinance. Bono initially demurred, saying that everyone asked him to write songs about their causes and it was hard to do in practice.

For almost an hour Bono probed, trying to understand how this businesslike approach fit into the global movement to end extreme poverty. Yunus patiently answered questions while his daughter Monica—who, like millions, idolized Bono—beamed as she took it all in.

Finally, after the entrees were cleared, Bono listened to one more explanation from Yunus and in an instant got the essence of microfinance. He smiled broadly and raised a dramatic toast to Yunus, saying he now understood the power of microfinance and how it supported his antipoverty campaigning. He also surprised us by agreeing to try his hand at writing a song about microfinance, which hopefully he will do one day. Since then, the organizations that Bono helped start, including DATA and the ONE Campaign, have been strong allies of Grameen.

WHEN YUNUS RESIGNED AS MANAGING DIRECTOR of Grameen Bank in 2011, Shaymganj's founding branch manager Mannan Talukdar—whom the Nobel laureate had recruited in a tea stall in Tangail 31 years earlier—decided that he would also retire in an act of solidarity. His plan was to invest the lump-sum pension he would receive and to attend to family matters. He expressed interest in being my unsalaried traveling assistant to Grameen Foundation, but I was unable to make that happen for him.

But just a few years later, Mannan applied for a job at one of the other Grameen companies Yunus had set up. Sadly, he died suddenly of a heart attack in November 2017, shortly after completing a project. He hadn't even reached his 65th birthday, and left behind a bereft wife and two children entering adulthood whom my wife and I have come to know and consider part of our extended family.

To me, Mannan was a shining example all the talented Bangladeshis who found a sense of nation-building purpose while being employed by one of the organizations Yunus set up, and who worked diligently to advance those ideals while discovering their own potential as changemakers and as citizens.

8. The Maxwell Street Market

THE LOW MURMUR OF VOICES CHATTING at an elegant function could be heard from down the hall. Dapper security guards emerged from the mayor's chambers, and behind them walked Richard M. Daley. The son of Chicago's legendary mayor Richard J. Daley, who had become mayor himself in 1989, began shaking hands with members of the assembled crowd; his conversations were periodically interrupted by loud bursts of laughter and more handshakes. The man knew how to work a room.

The foyer on the fifth floor of City Hall is the venue for scores of receptions hosted by the mayor each year. On this evening in December 1993, the caterers had erected a long row of tables down the center of the marbled floor, on either side of which were offices and a large solarium. Elegantly dressed couples plucked hors d'oeuvres while men in full military regalia stood watch over the proceedings. In a few minutes, they would perform a changing of the guard. Above it all stood a cast-iron sculpture of George Washington.

As Geri Dinkins watched her city's mayor shaking hands and making the rounds, her own hands began shaking. What should I say to the mayor? Will I be tongue-tied up there on the podium? What if he doesn't like the apron? She held it out in front of her and frowned as she looked over the designs she had decorated it with—all having to do with the mayor's favorite sport, football.

Since 1990, Geri had been volunteering for the American Food Depository, a food bank for the families of veterans who had fallen on hard times. Mayor Daley, like his father before him, supported the group, perhaps in recognition of the abilities of veterans and those who assist them to cast votes in tight election races. Soon after the Depository's annual reception for volunteers and donors in December 1992, the mayor's office contacted Cynthia Simmons, the organization's director, asking whether he could host the following year's event at City Hall. She agreed.

When the mayor's office said that Daley planned to present Cynthia with a key to the city, Cynthia suggested that the Food Depository present him with one of Geri's aprons, as she owned several herself. When someone questioned whether the mayor would like the Afrocentric designs that normally appeared on her aprons, Geri replied that she could decorate it with any pattern the group thought appropriate. Cynthia suggested a football motif, since it was well known that Daley was a fan. That settled that.

At the reception, the mayor thanked the volunteers and presented Cynthia with the key to the city, and then a nervous Geri was called up to join him on the platform. As Geri pushed through the crowd, Cynthia explained that the mayor was being presented with a gift from the volunteers and veterans as an expression of their appreciation to him. The mayor shook Geri's hand and invited her up to stand behind the microphone. As Geri looked out into the crowd, her face went momentarily blank. She couldn't remember ever being in front of so many people before. But after a brief moment of quiet, she regained her composure. A wide smile broke out on her face as she said, "Mayor Daley, on behalf of the volunteers and the veterans at Hynes Hospital, I'd like to present you . . ." She paused as she fumbled with the apron, displaying it from several angles so that both the mayor and the crowd could see the design, ". . . with a gift, a handmade apron with a design I think you'll like."

She handed it to the mayor, and after looking at it for an instant, he held it out in front of him to see the entire design. Then, as he showed it to the group, he leaned over and whispered to Geri, "I *really* like it—thank you!" Geri felt his sentiments were sincere and she was relieved. The two stood and smiled as dozens of flashes went off in an orgy of photography. As Geri heard the applause from her fellow volunteers, her muscles relaxed and her knees buckled slightly. Her job was done.

The two stepped down onto the floor and posed for several more pictures, and as the mayor prepared to meet and greet some more voters, Geri leaned over to him and whispered, "I don't know if you remember him, but my brother Arnold Douglas went to school with you at De La Salle," a Catholic high school on the South Side.

"Oh, Doug—of course I remember him! Say hello to him for me!" And off he went, again—pumping hands, listening intently, laughing when the opportunity presented itself.

A short time after the mayor had left the event, a large, middle-aged Black man active in the Harold Washington Party—a rival to the Democratic Party, which Daley headed—tapped Geri on the shoulder. "Hey, I really liked that apron you gave the mayor," he said in a deep voice. "Can I buy a dozen from you?" Geri was surprised by the request, the largest she had ever received. As she fished through her purse for some paper to write down her newest customer's name and phone number, her mind raced. How many new customers would the exposure from this event lead to? she thought to herself. Could she handle the demand? In the months ahead, she would have to find answers to those questions. But right then, she was all smiles, trying to close the deal gracefully.

There were other important events for Geri over the holiday season. When she finally got around to holding the house shows Thelma had pushed her to announce at the fall meeting, they were well attended, and she sold nearly $1,000 worth of aprons and gift baskets. The $350 loan from the emergency loan fund—the FCF's name for Grameen's group fund—helped her buy some towels and utensils that she used, alongside soap, spices, and occasionally aprons, to fill the baskets. Some were generic, while others were custom-made for repeat customers. She also purchased fabric for making aprons. It was easily her busiest holiday season since being laid off, and the income was used to pay the utility bill and the mortgage, and to buy groceries. For the first time since she'd lost her job, Geri was spared the indignity of having to wonder whether her heat would be turned off at some point during the winter. Over the 1993–1994 winter, she made enough to pay all her utility bills on time.

During the planning of her final show, which was to be held shortly after the City Hall event, Geri called Fort Smith, a man she knew from her church, to do some networking. Fort had taken early retirement from the local phone company since his job was being phased out.

Fort was an entrepreneur who had started by selling jewelry at street fairs to make ends meet after losing his job. After learning the retail trade, Fort tried his hand at making jewelry from scratch, and was surprised at how easily it came to him. Sometimes, customers gently told him that he was selling his work for considerably less than its true value. They encouraged him to try marketing his work to North Side boutiques serving primarily upscale white clients. When he did, he succeeded. He also persuaded swanky mail-order catalogs like Spiegel to carry some of his pieces, and soon he was wholesaling his handmade earrings for $25 to $50 a pair. This was a major breakthrough, as it often takes WSEP borrowers like Glenda, many of whom are as talented as Fort, years before they are confident enough to charge that much.

But though his jewelry-manufacturing business thrived, Fort continued, from time to time, to feel the bite of racism. On one occasion, the perpetrator was not white, but Black. At a high-society function, he was making small talk with an African-American celebrity with national name recognition. The woman, noticing that Fort was admiring her earrings, said casually, "These are made by the famous jewelry designer Fort Smith—I bought them for one hundred and ten dollars."

"Madam," he replied after overcoming the shock of hearing that his earrings were selling at twice the suggested retail price, "I *am* Fort Smith."

"Oh, yes you are, dear," the woman said condescendingly. She could barely contemplate the idea that the "famous designer" the saleslady at the jewelry store had talked about was the Black man she was talking to. Only later that evening, when the master of ceremonies introduced Fort to the crowd, did she realize her error. Fort tells stories like this one with a self-deprecating wit that makes him a genuinely likable character.

In the fall, Geri had heard that Fort was opening a retail store in South Shore on Seventy-First Street. With her last show approaching, she telephoned him in early December to ask if he would be willing to give her some of his jewelry on consignment to sell at her home show; she figured it would go well with her aprons and gift baskets, and be sufficient reason to invite people who had already attended one of her earlier shows. Fort made a counteroffer: recounting to her some bad experiences he had giving out his merchandise, he invited Geri to have the event at his store.

Close to 20 people came to the show, and Fort liked what he saw of Geri's line of goods. Sales were decent. At the end of the event, Fort asked if she could leave some of her aprons and gift baskets at the store so that he could sell them for her. At first, he would give her the entire retail price, and if they sold enough of them, they would negotiate a wholesale price that she would get and a retail price he would charge. The arrangement worked well for both parties. In February, as Fort's retail business grew, he offered Geri part-time work at his store, which he called The Glitz. She would help keep accounts, clean up, assist him in making jewelry—"If I could learn to make earrings, so can you," he would tell her with a laugh—and deal with customers. In the spring, the job became full-time. By then, Fort had persuaded Geri to raise the retail price of her full aprons, which continued to sell well—from $15 to $30. They agreed that the wholesale price would be somewhere between $15 and $18. That was yet another business tip Geri would pick up from her employer.

After two years, Geri's period of unemployment, bankruptcy, and depression was over. The days of lying in bed, cursing her predicament, and wondering where the grocery money was coming from were past. Later that spring, after she had collected a month's worth of full-time wages (at $5 per hour), she would confide to a friend, "If it wasn't for the support of the women in the WSEP program, I would not have made it through these two years, financially or emotionally. The meetings gave me a reason to get out of bed and get on with my business. Left alone, I really think I might have died. Now, through working my business, through something I used to only do as a hobby, I have found employment again, stability again, certainty again."

Geri's experience points to an underappreciated strength of microfinance. Sometimes, a loan to start or restart a microbusiness can serve to stabilize someone's economic situation for a year or two after losing their job or having some other kind of setback. As a result of running their enterprise, they are able to stay active, make new contacts, and learn new skills. Sometimes that process results in a growing business, or a portfolio of seasonal businesses. But perhaps just as commonly in wealthy countries, it leads to the microentrepreneur finding a full-time job with decent pay and benefits. The advantages of this trajectory compared to being unemployed and relying on public benefits, private charity, or family support is one of many questions I hope that the research community delves into in the years ahead. In Geri's case, the option of having access to capital and encouragement to start a tiny business in between jobs seems to have paid real dividends. In fact, I am not sure she would have ever found the job with Fort Smith without having made the effort to sell her aprons and gift baskets.

THE MAXWELL STREET MARKET HAS OFTEN BEEN under threat of closure. In the 1960s, it was truncated to make room for the Dan Ryan

Expressway. Thirty years later, the University of Illinois at Chicago (UIC) was after the remaining city-owned land that the market stood on.

Opposition to UIC's efforts to close the bazaar came from two separate pressure groups that feuded with each other as much as with the university. The Maxwell Street Market Coalition was organized under the direction of Art Vasquez, a Hispanic community leader. It proved to be more vibrant than a group called Friends of the Market. The Coalition helped place pro–Maxwell Street op-ed pieces in the *Chicago Sun-Times* and was influential in persuading the city and the university to look into moving, rather than closing, the market.[44]

One of the objectives of the Coalition was to overcome the resignation that most vendors felt and instead create a sense of possibility and urgency. Thelma Ali, for one, had responded to their entreaties, attending several meetings during the fall and winter to discuss strategy or to organize protests. Among the events she attended was a November 30 meeting held at the Harold Washington Library where activists appealed to the city's Commission on Community Development to block the sale of the city-owned land the university wanted to buy.[45] Lew Kreinberg, a longtime political activist who was well connected to prominent Chicago progressives, arranged for U.S. Representative Bobby Rush, Alderman Madeline Haithcock, and State Senator Jesus Garcia to attend the hearing. After the university made a polished presentation, Rush, a former Black Panther who once beat back a primary challenge from an ambitious state legislator named Barack Obama, took center stage to blast the city and the university for not consulting with the communities involved, and called the plan to move the market "unwise and foolhardy." The mostly promarket crowd broke into wild applause at the end of his remarks. But as the meeting closed, the commission voted—without any real debate—to go ahead and sell the 500,000 square feet of city-owned land that fell within the jurisdiction of the current market. Despite the official rebuff, many activists were heartened by the display of solidarity from three prominent politicians. As a result, Kreinberg—who had joined the effort to save the market at the urging of Art Vasquez—assumed increasing importance within the Coalition.

I'd given Thelma and the other women in her group a tape recorder to use to record a diary of events while I was in Bangladesh. After the November 30 meeting, Thelma confided in the diary, "They be saying so much about helping the poor help theyselves, creating enterprise and markets and so forth—and here they's destroying the best marketplace the city's got. This just doesn't make no *sense*. And it's not fair to the small people who come here to make a few bucks." Several days later, after attending another meeting, she added, "This is like a comedy. The city spends all its time crying about economics, about lost jobs—and they ain't doing nothing to let people make a few dollars in this market. And then you hear the city talk about how much it's trying to encourage all these communities to get along with each other—the Palestinians, the Koreans, the Chinese—yet they closing the only market where all these ethnic groups come together in a harmonious situation. And then they's complaining about welfare, but there's lots of people who have been laid off who are staying off welfare because they's able to work their business in Jewtown. People's just greedy—greedy university and a greedy city."

The city was certainly hoping to profit from its policy. Clearing the neighborhoods immediately circling the Loop of eyesores like the market and public housing projects, and replacing them with upscale housing for professionals, meant big money for developers and construction firms that were vital to the mayor's candidacy, fewer traffic jams on the expressways, and an expanding municipal tax base.

But the opponents of Maxwell Street often tried to frame the debate in different terms. They described the bazaar as dangerous and as a venue for criminals to sell stolen goods. Many of these accusations were based on myths, half-truths, and, perhaps, the unbridgeable cultural divide between the uptight establishment who would reap the windfalls of gentrification and the colorful, multilingual patchwork of minorities and Bohemians who bought and sold at the market.

While people in the redeveloped communities nearby were often afraid to go to the bazaar on a typical Sunday morning, when 20,000 or more customers crowded into the market, there were rarely any violent incidents, despite the fact that only two policemen were assigned to the area. (And when one did see those officers, in my experience it was more likely that they would be shopping than patrolling.) Indeed, in an article published around this time, a veteran police officer from the area told a reporter, "We do get people coming down, saying they've found their stolen property in the market, but it's not common, and the merchants are quick to give things back. They don't want trouble."[46] (The officer, not surprisingly, "asked not to be identified for fear of angering the mayor.") Yet perception often bests reality. The selling of X-rated videocassettes with explicit covers, often sharing space on a peddler's table with diapers and back-to-school supplies, gave the market a seedy reputation.

The Coalition decided to propose that the university share the area with the market, but this proposal was often sidetracked by Kreinberg's desire to broaden the Coalition's mandate, to discuss citywide issues beyond the predicament of the market. Kreinberg was joined in the Coalition spotlight by Steve Balkin, a modest, impressive professor from Roosevelt University who worked placing opinion pieces in influential newspapers, contacting journalists, networking with University of Illinois students and professors who opposed the market closing, engaging sympathetic city officials, and more.

For years, Balkin had worked in a small economics department that was overshadowed by the more influential and conservative faculty at the University of Chicago in Hyde Park. Balkin concentrated his efforts on the theoretical and practical implications of encouraging entrepreneurship as a strategy for assisting low-income people. His hands-on experience has included training prisoners in the fundamentals of entrepreneurship so that they could start businesses upon being released.

Balkin's most comprehensive book, *Self-Employment for Low-Income People*, made a strong case for programs like WSEP while acknowledging their limitations. It described successful initiatives in Britain and France to get the unemployed started in business and argues for the adaptation of programs like Grameen Bank in the United States. But he made the point that for such efforts to succeed, the "overregulated" U.S. economy would have to be tinkered with to be made more user-friendly to low-income entrepreneurs. Above all, places like Maxwell Street, he argued, should be defended, expanded, and improved.

To Balkin, adapting the Grameen Bank to poor urban areas of industrialized countries and maintaining markets like Maxwell Street are inextricably linked concepts. Welfare and health care reform, community reinvestment laws (meant to discourage the practice of redlining), and striking down municipal ordinances that make home-based businesses illegal also play a part. But increasing access to markets that have low overhead and high traffic is perhaps the most basic need. It struck Balkin as ironic that at a time when the president of the United States and leaders from both parties were talking about creating federally supported "enterprise zones," and while Chicago was competing fiercely for funds to set one or more of them up, that same city was moving to eliminate an indigenous cauldron of entrepreneurship with a history of success spanning more than a century. Giving large, white-owned firms tax breaks to set up in low-income areas was one thing, but continuing to allow the poor a place to set up their own tiny businesses was apparently quite another.

When it became clear in 1989 that the University of Illinois planned to expand into the area where the Maxwell Street Market was held, Balkin saw it as a threat to a rare success story in the type of microcapitalist economics he had spent his life studying. In a report written with Alfonso Morales and Joseph Persky, he calculated that $3.2 million would be lost to the local economy in the first year the market was closed. But financial losses, he added, would not be the only impact. The market, he wrote, is a source of entertainment and activity for low-income youth and young adults, a diversion from crime, and a place where young entrepreneurs outside the corporate culture can exchange information on new products, sources of supply, stores for rent, people to do business with, and wage employment. Balkin's paper quotes one young vendor saying, "It keep [sic] you away from the street. I used to go hang around with my friends. Now, when I come home from the market, I'm tired and I stay home."[47]

Perhaps the most persuasive argument for continuation of the market, though, comes from the university itself. A 1993 memo from its Great Cities Advisory Committee—created to define the role the university should play in the community—said:

> Since the university is not the sole repository of knowledge, the pursuit of knowledge requires increased interaction with the off-campus public.
>
> Specific types of programmatic activities are recommended to assist in economic development of the UIC neighborhoods without displacing current residents, engage in technology transfer activities to increase business success [and] assist minority and female-owned businesses and new ventures . . .[48]

Yet the only technology the university was willing to bring to bear on Maxwell Street was a bulldozer, and whenever the concept of shared space was brought up, the university rejected it, saying it was unwilling to become a landlord for a "flea market." The fact that the market operated on the day the university was closed, or that Stanford University coexisted peacefully with a Sunday market on its campus, failed to move the UIC bureaucrats.

In the spring, the Coalition, like the Friends of the Market group before it, disintegrated into warring factions. An elderly Italian woman came up to Thelma Ali's table on Maxwell Street and, seeing her reading a flyer about an upcoming protest in front of City Hall to save the market, felt compelled to share something. "You know," she told Thelma, "they did the same thing to us thirty years ago. They said they wanted to take over the land, they said they were going to do all sorts of things to help us relocate and readjust, and once they tore down our neighborhood, we got nothing. Now this is happening to you, too. I feel so bad for you."

Such is the price of progress in America's so-called "Windy City."

DURING THE THIRD WEEK OF JANUARY 1994, WSEP held a dinner for Full Circle Fund members in the Prince Mustafa cultural center on Eighty-Second Street and South Ashland Avenue, owned by Belvia Muhammad, a borrower in the Let Us Make Woman circle. The event was arranged by Colete Grant, who hoped it would smooth over some of the concerns created by the unexpected departures of Gwen and Jackie in the fall. Talk about circle business or WSEP would be forbidden; the invitation announced, "No loan payments, no circle business, no talking shop." This was a time to break bread together and create warmer relationships.

Queenesta had been unsure whether she would be able to go to the dinner until the last minute. She had been working her counter at Victor's store all day, and it wasn't until 5:30 that she found a free minute to call Omiyale and ask if one of her daughters could baby-sit for Shayna while they attended the function. Queenesta prepared to leave the store before closing—something she knew Victor would give her a hard time about. But what did Victor know about being a single mother? And anyway, Victor was feeling somewhat contrite since Queenesta had confronted him about all the money he'd made on the T-shirts they had bought at last year's Black Expo. (As a result, her $150 rent was being waived for the first three months of the year.)

As Queenesta walked eastbound on North Avenue towards her car, she looked across the street, trying to discern whether any stores might be going out of business—ones that she might be able to move into once the cold weather broke. The sidewalk on the north side of the avenue was covered with a foul combination of snow, ice, and uncollected garbage; the stores were primarily seedy-looking fast-food joints with bulletproof glass separating customers from employees, and liquor stores owned by Koreans. City Sports, a successful white-owned sporting goods and clothing store, had the most attractive window; several vacant stores, however, created a more depressing picture. So intent was Queenesta on looking for a future home for her business that she walked past her car and needed to double back to it. If Omiyale could only repay her short-term loan, Queenesta thought, I'll have a clear path to opening my own store this spring. Until Omiyale cleared her account, nobody in her circle could take out any new loans.

Once she arrived at the Prince Mustafa cultural center, Queenesta searched for a place to put her coat. As she did so, her eyes wandered around the place, taking in the decorations. Drapes with African designs covered the drab blue walls that Belvia had inherited when she took over the storefront. A picture of Elijah Muhammad, the onetime leader of the Nation of Islam, was hung below a Chinese flag. On an adjacent wall, a large map of Africa hung to the right of a newspaper article about Muhammad that included a picture. Next to that there was a sign that read, "To Lengthen Thy Life, Lessen Thy Meals."

Belvia Muhammad had wanted to create a vegetarian restaurant and cultural center with Islamic and African décor. It was to get moral and financial support for this vision that she had joined WSEP. At the time of the dinner, she was concentrating her efforts on getting the license to open a full-fledged restaurant. On several occasions she had been tempted to start without the licenses, but Thelma Ali had helped persuade her to "do it legal." By year's end, all the required coursework in things like food safety would be completed. Until then, renting her storefront out for events like the WSEP dinner would pay the bills.

On this night, the middle of the main dining room was filled with a half-dozen long tables covered with white cloth and colorful ethnic centerpieces. The assembled staff and borrowers of the Full Circle Fund, a few coming from as far away as Rogers Park on the North Side, engaged in animated dialogue as they waited for the buffet to open. Staff tended to congregate with staff, and members tended to gravitate to other borrowers they recognized. Queenesta, dressed in a stylish gray sports coat she wore over a red turtleneck, went straight to Omiyale and Thelma, who were already sitting at a table in the front, discussing circle business despite the official restrictions on doing so. Omiyale had dressed up for the occasion, wearing a gold and black jacket and a black scarf around her head, while Thelma was characteristically underdressed. As the three began talking, Leverta Pack and Thelma Perkins from their center settled into chairs at the table and joined in.

After the meal, Colete called for people's attention and gave some brief introductory remarks. Clad in an elegant two-piece traditional African dress with a matching kufi and earrings (all made by Full Circle Fund borrowers), she stood behind a menorah that held seven burning red candles as she spoke (Colete, like some borrowers in the Lindblom center, is a Hebrew Israelite). Colete had never appeared so relaxed while speaking in front of a group; on this night, she finally seemed to shake free of the shadow of her popular predecessor Gwen. She began calling circles up to the front of the room, where she handed them carnations and certificates of appreciation, drawing attention to their latest accomplishments as they stood beside her. Periodically, she invited other enterprise agents—two had recently been hired—to do the same.

Toward the end of the program, Colete said, "And now I'd like to call up Les Papillons, a group that embodies persistence. These sisters have hung together and been unified under very difficult conditions. They are some bonded sisters." She paused, and the room fell silent as she cleared her throat. Colete seemed to be momentarily overcome with emotion. Then she continued, "At a meeting just a few weeks ago, they . . . I don't want to go into it, but for me they define the idea of sisterhood that this program is about." Colete was referring to a meeting in mid-October when Omiyale, faced with the prospect of falling behind on her payments on her short-term loan, broke down sobbing when she learned that doing so would prevent Geri from borrowing from WSEP for the Christmas season. The four women responded by urging Omiyale not to be so hard on herself and agreeing to loan Geri $350 out of their emergency loan fund. For Colete, it was a defining moment for the circle and for herself as a WSEP employee. She saw a group of borrowers solve their own problem rather than giving up or depending on the organization for a solution.

"Now I'd like to call up all the women in Les Papillons!" Loud applause broke out. Omiyale and Queenesta took their certificates and flowers and got big hugs from Colete, but Thelma stayed in her seat. "Pick one up for me, Omiyatta," she called out, using one of the several ways she slightly mispronounced her friend's name. Colete asked Thelma to come up, but again she refused. Perhaps she didn't want the attention, or maybe she just felt underdressed. When Colete asked a second time, all eyes turned to Thelma, but she sat, smiling and defiant, unwilling to go through with the ritual. Finally, Colete said she'd give the certificate to her later.

Queenesta spotted a tall WSEP staff member sitting by the wall. As far as Queenesta could tell, she had a look of disgust on her face as she watched; her disdain seemed focused squarely on Thelma Ali. How dare she look that way, Queenesta thought. That woman doesn't know anything about Thelma Ali. Anger boiled inside her. They're just looking at how someone dresses, and how they act in public, not what's inside, not how successful their business is! If they actually knew Thelma, they would realize what a talented borrower she was, Queenesta thought to herself. She looked at Thelma, her head wrapped in a ski hat and a silk scarf, her face bereft of makeup, her legs covered only in black denim pants. That, she thought, is a real entrepreneur—down at Maxwell Street every day during the spring and summer, taking a sewing class this winter to learn how to make African children's clothing that her customers had been asking for.

In the background, Connie Evans was giving her speech to conclude the program. But for the rest of the evening, Queenesta reflected on the cultural divide separating different Black social classes, which occasionally played out even within WSEP. All the same, despite occasional flare-ups and misunderstandings, WSEP was quietly proving that the educated Black professional class *did* have something useful to say and do for their economically distressed brothers and sisters. Even if some of the staff might look down on Thelma's fractured grammar and humble dress, in WSEP Connie had created a mechanism that allowed Black women professionals to administer a program that gave their low-income sisters access to loan capital and a forum for giving, receiving, and exchanging valuable business advice. Indeed, it was such a rare service and so well provided that the clients accepted the organization's few white staff members, such as Susan Matteucci and Tiziana Dearing (the public relations director), with a remarkable degree of openness. Sometimes, in the hustle and bustle of putting out a product and working through the internal politics that all organizations wrestle with, the significance of that achievement was lost. It took a person like Thelma Ali, who was so clearly benefiting from the program and considered it a work of divine inspiration, to remind everyone of how special it was.

A WINTER CHARACTERIZED BY HEAVY SNOWFALL and below-normal temperatures had at least one desirable effect—it kept potential perpetrators and victims of violence off the street. But it also brought the economic life of the city to a standstill and caused hundreds of thousands of dollars' worth of damage to Chicago's infrastructure. In January, peddlers and small-scale manufacturers like Queenesta, Omiyale, Thelma, Glenda, and Geri assessed their profits from the Christmas-Kwanzaa season and prepared to cash in on Black History Month (BHM) in February. Those weeks before BHM were a time for hunkering down and trying to resist the temptation to use working capital to meet nonurgent family expenses. Queenesta was busy lining up bookselling events for the following month while Thelma was learning how to sew at a city-sponsored program. Thelma was also looking into taking advantage of volume discounts by buying fabric in bulk and then selling some on a retail basis and using the rest to make children's clothing. She was determined to learn how to make the kufis that Omiyale had required her children to wear in the 1970s, long before they had become fashionable.

Black Chicago had been through a rough few years, but there was at least some good news. It was revealed in January that violent crime was down 4 percent in 1993, and in districts such as Englewood and Morgan Park where community policing was being tried, it had been reduced by as much as 19 percent.[49] During the first two months of 1994, Englewood in particular continued the progress it had made the previous year. The neighborhood's first homicide of 1994 did not occur until March; during the previous three years, there had been a murder there, on average, every four days.

A senior police commander in Englewood credited his community policing initiative as well as work focusing on prevention carried out by nonprofit groups such as the Christ United Methodist Church and People Educated Against Crime in Englewood (PEACE). (Formed in 1991 when Englewood led the city in homicides during a bloody turf war among local gangs, PEACE created after-school drop-in centers for students and brought in motivational speakers such as businesspeople and reformed gang members to talk to students in neighborhood schools.) Others thought the gang summit in the fall, during which a tenuous truce had been declared among rival groups, was having an effect. Whatever the cause, for the time being, prayers that the carnage that had come to characterize life in Englewood would abate were being answered.

THE RED DIGITAL DISPLAY READ 8:10 when Queenesta's alarm went off, but it was actually earlier than that. Queenesta set her clock 35 minutes ahead to give her a little push to get moving in the morning.

It was January 28th, and snow had been falling gently in Englewood since the night before; the temperature hovered at around 15 degrees. It was turning out to be a bitter winter, even by Chicago standards.

Queenesta rubbed the sleep from her eyes as she sat up. It was scarcely three hours since she had gone back to bed after Shayna had woken her up, suffering from chicken pox. As Queenesta showered, she considered the day ahead. First there was the issue of getting books on consignment from her wholesaler. The management of the store had changed hands, so they might not let her take as many books as she needed. Then there was the business of tracking down her sister's friend, whom she would try to hire to work the month of February; going to West Side Books (more than likely to receive a tongue-lashing from Victor for not being in the store that morning); finding someone to take care of Shayna in the afternoon; getting some cassettes from the music distributor; and attending a WSEP meeting downtown at 5:30. Queenesta peered into her bathroom mirror to see if another night of interrupted sleep showed on her face.

Queenesta was an attractive woman in her early thirties. As a statement of principle, she wore her hair natural rather than relaxing it with chemicals. She had done that a couple of times in her youth, but now, as a self-aware Black person trying to turn her brothers and sisters on to their culture and heritage, she has no time—not to mention money—for such things.

As she brushed her teeth, she thought about what she should be doing to realize the most challenging of her New Year's resolutions—opening her own store. Queenesta's successes at the end of the year had given her the courage to begin planning to go out on her own. Kwanzaa, a postharvest celebration held in Africa during December that many African-Americans observe, had been profitable. Most of her income had come from selling books. The rest had been from renting African clothing for customers to wear at special events such as weddings and cultural gatherings. She had come up with this idea in November during a week when she wasn't sure how she was going to make her loan payment. Within a few weeks, she'd made more profit in renting the clothes than if she had sold them. Dorothy Johnson, a seamstress who also rented space from Victor, was impressed with the way Queenesta created a thriving rental business from nothing; months later, she would ask for Queenesta's advice on how to begin a different type of rental venture herself.

During December, selling at Kwanzaa events was a good way to keep away from Victor's store, which for nearly two weeks had no heat. The staff was forced to spend those days wearing overcoats and mittens as they helped a dwindling number of customers. Victor blamed this on his Korean landlord, and was in a foul mood the entire month.

January was a time to rest up between Kwanzaa and Black History Month in February and the Black Women's Expo, held in mid-March. Queenesta was behind in her preparations for Black History Month, and dealing with Shayna's chicken pox, which necessitated taking her out of school for a week, complicated things further. Queenesta had planned to spend some time during the month looking for a new storefront, but she had little time to do so. Still, she continued to think about the move and to discuss it with close confidantes. The main question in her mind was whether she would try to locate it near Victor's store (so she could keep her regular customers) or move to another section of Chicago's Austin neighborhood.

At 7:45, it was time to rustle Shayna up and get her moving for the long day ahead. As Queenesta passed by the front door, she inspected the plastic sheeting she had taped over the cracks in the door to keep the frigid air out and the heating bill down. Upon entering Shayna's room, she gently sat down on the edge of her daughter's bed. As soon as she woke up, Shayna began reaching for her scabs. "Pat it, don't scratch it, Shayna!" As she got up and began walking to the bathroom, Shayna slapped her arms and her head.

While she cooked a breakfast that Shayna could eat in the car, Queenesta phoned the home office of her book distributor in New York. She was concerned that the local wholesaler wouldn't have all the books she wanted. That would be catastrophic during February, when there were thousands of dollars to be made selling Black-oriented books. During Kwanzaa, she had been forced to go to events with titles she knew didn't sell very well because her wholesaler's selection had been so poor. She wanted the New York office to send her a shipment directly. That, of course, would mean paying for them up front at 60 percent of the cover price. But she had events lined up, and more important, she had working capital. She was able to persuade Luther, her main contact at the head office, to send her two boxes of books she knew were in demand. He also tried to reassure her that the new management of the Chicago distributorship was in place and that she could count on them supplying her in the future. (Months before, some employees stole thousands of dollars' worth of books and almost drove the operation out of business.)

After getting off the phone with Luther, she called her contact at the McDonald's Corporation to confirm an event in its cafeteria in mid-February. "Hi, this is Queenesta Harris of Kids Are People Too," she began. "May I speak to Ms. Carter? Hi, yes, ma'am, I'm calling about the event on February eighteenth. Yeah, okay, right, similar to that, uh, can you hold for a minute?. . . Hello, hi, hold on, Sheila. . . . Yes, Ms. Carter, I just need the address. Uh-huh, okay. Are there going to be other vendors? Ah. Can I bring African artifacts and oils to sell? Yes? Good. I'll see what happens. . . . You want a variety of books, fiction and nonfiction? Okay. How about *Waiting to Exhale?* Yes. What? Oh, yes, I'll be sure to bring the Black Heritage Bible! People been asking about that? Yes, definitely. Okay . . . Thank you, Ms. Carter. . . . " The relatively new Black Heritage Bible was quite popular. In addition to the King James text, it carried footnotes and supplementary essays explaining African and African-American contributions to the Bible and Christianity. It was a big seller in Black Chicago, and since it retailed for nearly $50, each sale meant a profit of about $18 for vendors.

Queenesta talked for a minute by phone with Sheila, Victor's 21-year-old daughter, who looked to her for womanly advice. Sheila wanted to come and live with Queenesta, but Victor didn't want her living anywhere but with him or her mother until she got a full-time job. Victor resented his tenant for not giving her the same advice, but Queenesta thought the best thing she could do was to help Sheila think it through for herself. That situation was just one more reason she wanted to leave West Side Books.

She made another call, to her Chicago distributor, to try to get a hold of some more Black Heritage Bibles. She was told that there were 40 in stock, and that they were going fast. Hearing that, Queenesta canceled her plans to pick up compact discs and cassettes. Getting as many Bibles as possible was the first priority. Perhaps she could persuade the new manager in Chicago to let her have 8 or 10 on consignment. After making a few more phone calls to confirm events for February, she packed up Shayna's breakfast and finished her ironing. In this frenzy of activity, she spotted Shayna scratching her scalp again. "Pat, don't scratch! Pat it, Shayna!" she said with a combination of humor and exasperation.

"But, Ma! It itches. And my stomach hurts."

Queenesta drove Shayna to the school where Queenesta's older sister Venita worked as an aide. Venita was a rock in Queenesta's life—stable and dependable, even when her own life was chaotic. It was Venita who was able to get Shayna into school a year early, it was Venita who would often sell Queenesta's T-shirts and other merchandise to her students, and it was Venita who looked after Shayna when her mother needed to be minding the business.

"Hey, Neeta," Queenesta called out as she walked in the door. "Hey, Pommy," Venita replied, using a nickname that her younger sister had been known by since childhood.

Shayna's classroom was dreary, its walls built with cinder blocks, furnished with tiny plastic chairs for tiny people, decorated with construction paper that had lost its luster sometime between September and January. As the two sisters talked, Shayna began playing with classmates she had not seen since she had gotten chicken pox. Queenesta disapproved of the youngsters' influence on her daughter; they were rowdy and making little progress on their ABCs. She had noticed some bad habits Shayna had picked up since she'd started school here in September. She hoped to one day transfer Shayna to an elite high school on the North Side, where Queenesta herself had once studied.

"Neeta, can Shayna come over today around two?" It was a question Queenesta had asked many times, and one to which she virtually always received a positive answer.

"Sure, Pommy."

"And that guy who works here as a janitor that I met, I want to call to see if he can help me sell books during Black History Month. But I lost his number. You got it, Neeta?" Queenesta had three events on a single day in February, and even if she could get Omiyale to cover for her at one of them, she would have to hire someone to look after the other. Finding reliable people willing to accept pay of only $5 an hour to help her on occasion was one of many challenges she was coming to face in her business.

Queenesta left the school with Shayna and drove to her book wholesaler. She had established her creditworthiness there and could usually take as many books as she wanted, though there were limits on titles that were in short supply. Within a week, she had to return all unsold books and pay 60 percent of the retail price for everything that she sold. The wholesaler bought the books for half the retail price, making his margin 10 percent of the final selling price.

Queenesta found a new clerk at the desk inside the warehouse. She reminded him that she had a good record of paying for and returning books, and asked if she could load up a cart of books to take for Black History Month. The employee looked Queenesta and Shayna over and reluctantly agreed. Queenesta began walking up and down the aisles, picking up copies of books that had sold well during Black History Month the previous year. She was relieved to see that the store was better stocked than it had been during December. She flipped through new titles, especially works of fiction with which she was less familiar and new titles claiming to explain to Black men how to understand Black women, and vice versa. Those had sold very well during Kwanzaa. She took some time choosing a selection of Toni Morrison books; Victor had told Queenesta that demand for her novels had grown since Morrison had been awarded the Nobel Prize in Literature in the fall.

The narrow aisles were arranged like those of a college bookstore, with several copies of popular titles stacked on wooden shelves. Shayna alternately followed her mother and went her own way. Occasionally, she would pick up books with attractive pictures on the covers and try to sneak them onto her mother's cart.

After spending nearly two hours in the adult section and piling more than two hundred books onto her cart, Queenesta headed over to pick up some children's books. As she passed some well-known stories, she recalled an encounter with an older African-American woman customer last February. The woman had been delighted to see a Black Cinderella. Even though all her children were grown, she couldn't resist buying that particular book for her bookshelf. The look of wonder in the woman's eyes as she made the purchase was one of the fondest memories Queenesta had from her short time as a book retailer.

The man behind the counter got on the phone and called his boss in New York. After a few minutes of talking in a hushed voice, he put down the phone and yelled, "Hey, Miss Harris, Luther from New York wants to talk to you." Queenesta picked up one extension as the clerk listened on the other. Within a few minutes, he was convinced that Queenesta was reliable enough to give a large consignment of books.

A short time later, after making her selections of children's books, Queenesta approached the counter and began unloading. The manager piled the books according to price to make it easier to calculate how much Queenesta would owe next week. After some animated discussion, she persuaded the man to let her take eight Black Heritage Bibles and give her 10 days to settle up with him. After calculating the retail value of the consignment at $2,600, they loaded the books into cardboard boxes and Queenesta began lugging them out to her car. By that point, the snow had begun falling harder, and Queenesta nearly slipped several times on the sidewalk.

That completed, Queenesta dropped Shayna off at school and headed toward Venita's house a few blocks away; she would have to leave the books there until she picked her daughter up later that night. Queenesta mounted the stairs with her first box of books, and as she searched for a place to store them, she looked at more than a half dozen of her sister's children and grandchildren, many sitting on a musty floor as a Black-and-white television droned on in the background. An infant was lying on a ratty couch. There was a commotion in a back room.

Venita, Queenesta knew, had a hard life, though she took it all in stride and tried to be both loving and firm with all her little ones. Since the previous year, she had been studying at a nearby junior college in hopes of earning a teaching certificate; that qualification would double the money she was earning as a teacher's aide. To do so, on many days she worked from 8:00 to 4:00, raced home to change her clothes, cook dinner, and set up her oldest daughter for baby-sitting duties, and then leave to get to class by 6:00. Her classes usually ended at 10:00, after which there was homework to do. It was draining, but Venita, like her sister, had ambitions of improving herself. In a family that had known more than its fair share of tragedies and setbacks, they had similar dreams and did what they could to support each other. Their mother, living a half mile away in the house they grew up in, pitched in as much as she could.

It took 12 trips to bring all the boxes up, and when she was done, Queenesta's body was covered in sweat. She had only enough time to grab a quick meal, her first food of the day, before the Full Circle Fund meeting. Queenesta arrived at 116 West Washington Street at 5:30. She walked through the narrow hallway toward the elevator, rode it up to the seventh floor, and went directly to the conference room. There were already a half dozen women there, among them Pam Bozeman, a newly hired WSEP staff member who would run the meeting. Queenesta sat down and greeted a woman sitting to her left. She was not a borrower from the Full Circle Fund, but was involved in another WSEP program for self-employed women. Her business was selling gifts—stuffed animals, flowers, and toys—that were packaged inside of inflated balloons. She had some samples scattered around her chair. "I can't tell you how I get them in there, but I sure can sell you one!" she said to a woman sitting next to Queenesta. There were a lot of smiles in the room, and more than a few business cards were being exchanged as they waited for the meeting about a new vending opportunity—the Black Women's Expo—to start.

Some 20 years earlier, Jesse Jackson's Operation PUSH had begun holding a Black Expo in Chicago to showcase the products and services of well-established Black-owned businesses. This would give Black consumers a chance to sample goods produced by their own people. Over time, Black Expos began being held in other cities across the country, even though for many years they were not held in Chicago due to lack of interest. But in 1990, the Chicago Black Expo had started up again.

They were usually held in July. In 1993, a spin-off event was inaugurated— the Expo for Today's Black Woman, popularly known as the Black Women's Expo. The purpose was to showcase products used by Black women, and the idea was that it would become less profit-oriented than the revitalized Black Expo had become. A collaboration with V-103, a Black radio station, was negotiated that resulted in discounted advertising for the event.

In 1992, WSEP leaders were able to persuade the organizers of the Black Expo to allow them to buy a block of booths at a reduced cost. Their argument was that the Black Expo should not only be for large, already successful Black-owned firms but also for small businesses run by low-income people. Twenty women involved in the Full Circle Fund were able to rent booths during the 1992 and 1993 Expos, though with mixed results. The Black Women's Expo offered another opportunity for Full Circle Fund borrowers to sell, and the meeting Pam had called was to let them know about the deal WSEP had struck with the organizers.

Pam called for order at 5:45, just as Thelma and Omiyale rushed in and sat down. Clearly there was more interest in the Black Women's Expo than had been expected. As Pam started to talk, Omiyale began piling plastic containers of her cookies on the table in front of her.

Over the next two and a half hours, Pam went into detail about the offer WSEP had gotten from the Expo organizers and led the women through the forms they needed to fill out to take advantage of the opportunity. "The Expo organizers expect there to be fifty thousand customers over the three days, and we can get you booths for $450 each. That's $400 for the booth and $50 for a sixty-second advertising spot on V-103." It was a bargain deal, so good that nearly a hundred people not involved in WSEP had already called Pam to try to get in on it. This was WSEP at its best, negotiating the same kind of cut-rate package deals for its low-income entrepreneurs that larger firms can get for themselves by virtue of their size. Pam radiated justified pride at her achievement, and stayed late into the evening to help the women sign up for it. Her presentation was sprinkled with humor; the women, many of whom had never met her in person before, appeared to be taking to her well. For her part, Pam thought that the process of minority women overcoming the challenges they faced by starting microbusinesses was nothing short of "magical." As a Black woman from Chicago's South Side who had made it into the middle class, she respected the skill and faith needed for a low-income single mother to find her market niche and exploit it sufficiently to guarantee a reasonable income.

As a further concession, the Expo organizers had given WSEP women the option of sharing booths. Pam asked for a show of hands to see who planned to buy individual booths. Along with 11 others, Omiyale raised her hand. Thelma, sitting to her right, was aghast. She thought there was a tacit understanding that they would go in on a booth together. Thelma had gone as far as to borrow the money from another vendor at Maxwell Street to put down the $150 deposit that night. As she stewed, Thelma considered her alternatives. Since Queenesta was also going in alone, that meant she would have to either forgo being a vendor at the Expo or go in with someone she trusted less than the members of her own circle.

As the meeting broke up at close to 9:00, women gathered in small groups to discuss what it all meant. People who had agreed to share a booth exchanged telephone numbers, their hopes and fears, and plain old gossip. Queenesta went over to the table where Thelma and Omiyale were sitting and, sensing the tension between the two women, said a few words before excusing herself and beginning her long trek home. As she walked toward the elevator, several women pushed by her, hoping to grab a package of Omiyale's cookies before she sold out.

Queenesta trudged from 116 West Washington to the subway stop at the corner of Washington and Dearborn, and then to the station where she had parked her car. Finally, she drove to Venita's, picked up a sleeping Shayna and her books, and began her journey back to the South Side. After finding a parking space, she put Shayna to bed and then lugged the books one final time, from her car into her living room. It was a few minutes past 11:00 by the time she finished.

She would begin a similar routine tomorrow. Queenesta had a lot to do; it was only a few days before her busiest month of the year would get underway.

Update: Since the 1990s

THE SECOND HALF OF THE 1990S reversed some long-term trends in inner-city areas around the country, including Chicago. A booming economy created jobs, and savvy microbusiness owners were able to cater to the newly employed and other consumers and get ahead. The decreasing level of violence in Chicago also gave people a greater sense of security. Bill Clinton's legendary ability to project empathy with Blacks (and just about everyone else) gave previously marginalized groups a sense that they had a friend in the White House. And yet, in most cases, the greater a community's or person's initial disadvantage, the less they were likely to be touched by these positive developments, and more likely they were to disappear once the economy contracted and the country's optimism was ground up in the aftermath of the terror attacks of September 11, 2001.

The reality of the last-hired–first-fired trap was driven home to a new generation of minorities after the dawn of the new millennium. The persistent unwillingness of the country's European-American majority to acknowledge the reality of racism and its economic impact continued to loom large in the collective psyches of disadvantaged groups. The achievements of individuals such as Oprah Winfrey, Colin Powell, and Los Angeles Angels owner Arte Moreno were held up as proof that anyone in America could rise to the top of society if she simply put her mind to it—one of the enduring and most damaging half-truths in our culture.

Through boom times and recession, microfinance continued to play an important role in allowing certain segments of the urban poor and moderate income groups to go much further and faster than they would as employees. That this was often invoked as further evidence of the claim that with hard work anyone in this country could get ahead occasionally made practitioners uncomfortable, but the growing number of success stories—like the women of Les Papillons—and an emerging body of effective lending practices gave many reason to hope that the best days for this antipoverty strategy lay ahead.

As it happened, the future success of Grameen America would show that those hopes had not been misplaced.

9. Krishna Das Bala

KHASHEM STUDIED THE BOARD, a clenched fist separating his chin from a bent knee as he sat on the bed, clothed only in a *longhi*.[50] A candle flickered, illuminating Rohim's face. He, too, was pensive and staring at the pieces on a chessboard. On a bed a few feet away, Krishna Das Bala, a new staff member, was playing the tabla, a percussion instrument popular on the Indian subcontinent. In a dark corner of the hut, Mustafiz gossiped with Shahjahan.

Khashem picked up his rook and held it aloft for a moment before taking Rohim's bishop. While he did so, Anis, the peon (or office helper), walked into the hut with Ahlim. "Anis, sweep it up," Khashem ordered without looking up from the game. Anis inspected the ground where hundreds of flies lay dead or dying. Throughout the Bengali summer, which begins at the end of February and continues until May, the men mixed insecticide and molasses twice each day and left the concoction on a leaf from a banana tree in the middle of their hut in order to distract and poison some of the flies. This brought the men temporary respite from their torment, but in several hours another swarm would replace the one that had perished.

Anis picked up the banana tree leaf, dragged it outside, and began sweeping up the flies with a *jharu*. By the time he was done, Rohim had conceded the game to Khashem, and they decided it was time for dinner. They rolled out the bamboo mats, squatted down, splashed some water on their plates, and uncovered the aluminum pots filled with rice, vegetable curry, and lentils that had been prepared earlier in the evening by their cook.

"Mustafiz, Shahjahan, come and eat," Khashem said. It was an awkward moment; all six men were in the hut, but there was room for only three to eat in the communal area. Ahlim was the most junior bank worker, so he would wait, as would Anis, who, as the peon, would eat after everyone else was done. Khashem liked the idea of eating while listening to Krishna playing the tabla, so he, too, would dine later.

Khashem was the senior assistant, a post usually given to the most experienced bank worker at a branch and one that entails considerable accounting responsibilities in addition to the servicing of three or four centers (half the number that other bank workers managed). It is a position halfway between bank worker and manager, and it confers upon its holder additional unwritten authority and responsibilities. The men consulted Khashem, whom they called *boro bhai* (big brother), before making all but the most mundane decisions concerning their communal living arrangements. Khashem, in turn, was responsible for resolving personality conflicts, arranging going-away parties for departing staff members, and giving pep talks to colleagues who were falling behind in their work.

Krishna Das Bala had been transferred to Shaymganj in January 1994, and upon arriving was assigned to 10 centers. Among them were Centers 2 and 42, the ones in Kholshi's Haldar *para*. The manager, Jobbar Ali, thought it was a good idea to assign a new Hindu staff member to run centers whose leadership shared his religious beliefs. Though he liked and trusted Rohim, he was supposed to rotate responsibilities for particular centers at least once a year in order to limit the opportunities for collusion among borrowers and staff to defraud the bank.

When Rohim turned over his responsibilities for Center Number 2 to Krishna, he felt satisfied by what he had accomplished. After four years of holding steady at six groups, he had shepherded the members of the seventh group through the processes of formation, training, recognition, and taking their first loans. As the women moved steadily toward completing repayment of those loans, and applying for new ones, he was pleased with Amena and Firoza's steady progress, as well as Fulzan's, though hers was more halting. Nobirun, the group chairman, was struggling, and Alow had dropped out in December. Rohim's greatest satisfaction had come from the fact that all five women, with the possible exception of Firoza, had been extremely poor when they joined, well below the cutoff point in Grameen's means test.

In the wake of 1991 salary raises for Bangladesh's civil servants, which Grameen had felt compelled to match, the bank had decided to increase worker productivity by expanding centers from six to eight groups. Since then, there had been cases where the leadership of established centers had been reluctant to admit five women from very poor families into the newly forming groups. Older borrowers, many of whom had been extremely poor themselves when they had joined years earlier, often preferred women who were *already* at the economic level that they themselves had progressed to since joining. There were cases of destitute women being actively discouraged from joining old centers. Rohim believed that one of the most challenging parts of his job was to maintain the focus on the most vulnerable, and he took pride in Amena's group having been established in the true Grameen spirit. But he was quick to credit Shandha—the most important leader in a center of a half dozen influential women—with encouraging the inclusion of four poor Muslim women in the seventh group.

AS KRISHNA BICYCLED TOWARD THE HALDAR *PARA* on a Tuesday morning several weeks later, he saw farmers cutting stalks of rice with iron sickles and tying them into bundles that their children then carried on their heads back to their compounds. The light greens and yellows of the matured paddy that remained to be cut shimmered amid the deep greens of the bamboo jungles that surrounded the homestead plots. Many landowners and sharecroppers wore the smiles of a successful harvest, one that allowed them to settle debts, barter for other goods, and enjoy home-cooked *pitha* (pastries made from rice flour and molasses). Not a few foreign visitors, expecting the barren landscapes and emaciated children of the Horn of Africa, have been surprised by the lushness of Bangladeshi villages.

Only two-thirds of the women were at the center when he arrived, and that annoyed Krishna. Yet, he realized that many of the women had rice to thresh before the monsoon came, and decided not to make a big fuss about it. Most of the remaining members arrived within 10 minutes.

"Listen, I'm not going to delay very long today," he barked out as he took his seat. "Two of our staff are on vacation and I have to collect installments from four centers today." The women took that as a cue to forgo the ritual opening and closing of the meeting. Shandha handed Krishna her passbooks, and he began marking them up in his distinctive handwriting, with all the flourishes one would expect from someone who had been dreaming since childhood of being a professional artist. When he finished, he put them aside and took another handful of passbooks from Nonibala as he worked his way backward toward Amena's group, which was sitting in the rear.

The women initially responded to Krishna's seriousness by talking in hushed voices, but within 15 minutes, the usual animated dialogues—punctuated by laughter, gossip, and an occasional flaring temper—resumed. At one point, Krishna, without looking up, asked, "How has your rice harvest turned out?"

"Very good, sir," several women blurted out. "Ask Shandha how she did, sir," another said excitedly.

"Shandha?" Krishna said, looking at her as she counted her group's installments.

Shandha flashed an embarrassed smile, but upon prompting by Amodini through a playful poke in the ribs, said, "Sir, I have received forty *maunds* (more than one and a half tons) of rice this time!" Shandha looked at Amodini as she said it, and both smiled.

"My goodness," Krishna exclaimed, his raised eyebrows and dropped jaw revealing his surprise.

"Sir," Aduree called out from the second row, "I have made a big leap forward, too. Just last week I got back a half acre of land that I had mortgaged twelve years ago." Since the time when she'd persuaded Nonibala to allow her to join the bank, Aduree had been saving so she could get her land back. Money from her vegetable gardening and from her husband's rickshaw-pulling, cow-fattening, and chicken-raising ventures had been put aside. Slowly it had grown to 5,000 taka, two-thirds of the sum needed to get the land back. They'd mobilized the final 2,500 taka by selling some goats. Finally, they had saved enough to reclaim the land they had mortgaged to avoid starvation more than a decade earlier.

In rural Bangladesh, agricultural land is much more than just a place where you farm. There is something almost spiritual about the relationship between a family and its land. It represents status and power and, above all, food security. Other assets can be lost; a cow can be stolen or die, a house can burn down, a handloom can be damaged in a flood. But land is always there; indeed, natural disasters are as likely to improve its long-term fertility as to harm it. Bangladesh, one of the earth's largest flood plains, is home to some of the world's deepest and most fertile topsoil, which receives annual replenishment during the monsoon. Furthermore, it sits atop readily accessible groundwater that can be inexpensively pumped up for irrigated agriculture in the dry season. Despite growing problems related to the overuse of chemical fertilizers and unwise irrigation methods, land remains at the center of most dreams, hopes, and fears among rural folk. It is hardly an exaggeration to say that people have killed their next of kin in disputes over one one-hundredth of an acre of land; in the nearby village of Ruha, such things were said to be commonplace.

Grameen's impact can be measured by the fact that many of its borrowers are slowly reclaiming land mortgaged to wealthy neighbors. Others lease in new parcels and, on rare occasions, buy a small tract on the open market. The overall trend in the countryside is just the opposite—indebted small farmers are forced to sell off or mortgage their land until they have nothing left and become day laborers in the rural areas or migrate to the big cities. Rarely does one meet a rickshaw driver in Dhaka who was not a victim of this process, and who doesn't dream of one day reclaiming his ancestors' land.

"How much did it cost?" Krishna asked Aduree.

"Seven thousand five hundred taka [$190], sir. We repaid the money before the village *matbars* [elders], and everything is final. We will be planting *aus* and *aman* rice crops on it this year." Aduree enjoyed bragging about her accomplishments, and none more so than this one. She still felt she had something to prove to the other women, even six years after elbowing her way into the center. Though she didn't realize it, gaining access to half an acre of land had increased her assets to the point where if she were trying to gain entry to Grameen, she would be denied because she was too wealthy.

There was a lot of other good news in the center. Nonibala, her five-year-old son Dalim Kumar nestled in her lap, told of her income from making cottage cheese, *ghee* (clarified butter), and sweets. The price of milk in the market was low, which meant big profits for her family—often as much as 1,000 taka ($25) per day. (By comparison, Krishna earned about 110 taka, or $2.75, in base pay per working day after having received two promotions.) With the coming monsoon, fishing nets were in high demand, keeping Devi, Shandha, and Bedana busy. Firoza, from the seventh group, told of her plans to reclaim one-third of an acre of mortgaged land.

But not every story was a happy one. Amodini's husband was still sick, and getting sicker; she asked Krishna to approve a group fund loan to pay for medical treatment. A relative of Shandha's in the third group had migrated to India two weeks earlier, and Alow's spot in the seventh group remained vacant. Over the past three months, an unlucky member of the second group had been abandoned by her husband, felt despair when three of her cows died, and had suffered when her eldest daughter ran away from home.

Krishna finished with the passbooks and his collection sheet and began taking wads of bills from the group chairmen. The first two groups gave him around 1,300 taka ($33) each, while the next four owed about 200 taka less. Amena's group had the smallest installments, totaling slightly more than 600 taka.

Toward the end of the meeting, a woman from Devi's group snuck into the center. She handed her chairman some bills, reimbursing her for having laid out her installment money a few minutes earlier. Aduree upbraided the woman for being late, but she ignored the admonishment. Unsatisfied, Aduree stood up and began speaking angrily. "What excuse do you have for being late? I live farther away than any of you. We all have work to do with the harvest, but this is only one hour a week. What excuse could you have for being late, tell me. I'm never late to these meetings, ever!" The women listened as Aduree went on. Some laughed, others guffawed, and a few cheered. The offending borrower took it in stride, staring straight ahead with a blank expression during the outburst. Finally, Krishna told Aduree that her point was well taken. Aduree returned to her squatting position, and the meeting closed.

Before Krishna headed off to his other centers, he walked with Amodini to her hut and visited her husband. He greeted her family with the traditional Hindu greeting of *nomoskar* and inquired about what was probably a bleeding ulcer that needed prompt medical attention. Krishna didn't have time for the visit, but since he was new to the center, he felt he had to prove his willingness to do the little extra things that endear bank workers to their members. Amodini raised the issue of the group fund loan. Her fellow group members agreed to sanction it, but Krishna's approval was also necessary. He said he would raise it with the manager, and told Amodini to come with her group on the following Saturday. The loan would be for 2,000 taka ($50), but it would be given on the condition that she use it for modern medical treatment rather than the traditional healing that was the norm in remote villages, where many people had never seen as much as a bus or a paved road, much less a qualified doctor. Amodini agreed, and received the money in due course.

"HELLO, MANNAN! I HAD *HEARD* that you had returned. Come here," Muhammad Samsuddin called out. The Kholshi union chairman was taking part in an annual post-harvest festival held in the village of Baze Taluk. He had run into his old adversary Mannan Talukdar there, the founder of the Grameen branch in Shaymganj. Scores of vendors filled a half acre of land, selling clay pottery, bangles, necklaces, sweets, fruit, toys, and other merchandise, most of it for less than 5 taka. While many of the vendors and customers were men, a surprisingly large number of women had come. They were decked out in their best saris, holding their children's hands and pushing from stall to stall, bargaining over items lying on vendors' blankets. Thelma Ali would have fit right in here, and Omiyale would have done a brisk business selling her butter cookies.

Mannan, by that time working in Grameen's head office, had returned to the branch he had established on a weeklong assignment. He recognized Samsuddin and greeted him with a warm handshake. As is customary in Bangladesh, the men continued holding hands for the first few minutes of their conversation.

"Where are you posted now, Mannan?" the chairman asked.

"In Dhaka. I was transferred there from Manikganj, and joined the monitoring and evaluation department."

"So, you are some big important official now, Mannan," he said with a laugh. "Why don't you come join me for some coconut juice out on the field here." The two men walked toward an open spot on the grass, removed their sandals, and sat on them. Samsuddin called a young man over and ordered him to bring two coconuts. He looked the part of a union *porishod* chairman— slightly overweight, wearing a *panjabi* that covered his *longhi* as far down as his knees, and speaking in a deep, self-assured voice that comes from years of being in charge.

As they began talking, the chairman studied Mannan. He was 20 pounds heavier than when they'd last met. The accumulated tensions of more than a half decade of managing Grameen branches showed on his face. He was 42.

Mannan had not particularly liked Samsuddin when he had been the local manager. The chairman had stirred up rumors about Grameen and discouraged people from joining. He knew that people feared Samsuddin, whereas they respected Munaf, the former chairman. Mannan understood the difference, and acted accordingly.

Samsuddin wasted no time in reviving their old argument. "I'll tell you, Mannan, I still don't like this Grameen Bank you work for," he declared. "And I'll tell you why. People are taking these loans and they cannot use the money well. Many people are creating debts for themselves and getting into more trouble than they were in before. Sometimes I am called upon to help these people out."

Mannan raised his eyebrows to register disbelief. He had spent the past several days visiting borrowers he had trained and given their first loans to six years earlier. While there were a few cases where he was disappointed by a member's lack of progress, in many more instances he was pleasantly surprised, even humbled by what he saw. In every center he visited, women grabbed him by the hand and begged him to come see their new house, their cows, their chickens, their vegetable gardens, or their rice harvest. Whenever he tried to leave, there was always another woman who became agitated, refusing to let him go until he saw the assets that *she* had accumulated. It made for long days, but ones that were among the most satisfying of Mannan's life.

"But I will admit," Samsuddin said after a long pause, "that *some* of your borrowers are doing pretty well. One widow who used to be a servant in my household is now living in the southern *para*. She owns five cows! I think she has taken out loans worth sixty thousand taka from you, and is a rich woman now. But how am I supposed to find servants now that everyone can buy cows for themselves?" Samsuddin laughed at that one, and Mannan chuckled too.

The conversation shifted to the business of running the union. Samsuddin mentioned that it had been a bad year for him, as he had only been able to skim 600 taka off the wheat that he had been given by the government to pay for rural maintenance projects. The year before, he had pocketed many times that amount. "Being a chairman is not so easy," he reminded Mannan at one point.

As the conversation drew to a close, Samsuddin couldn't resist one final jab at the man who had brought Grameen Bank to his union. "Mannan, Grameen is okay and all that, though it causes me headaches. But tell me one thing—why is Grameen acting like a new East India Company? Can you tell me that?" Mannan frowned when he heard that.

For the previous few months, Islamic fundamentalists who opposed Grameen and the BRAC had been circulating wild stories in the press, claiming that the two organizations were part of a Western conspiracy to recolonize Bangladesh as the British East India Company had done three centuries earlier. Other rumors claimed that Grameen and BRAC staff had admitted that they'd taken a secret pledge to convert the rural poor to Christianity. On occasion, one could hear politicians in the rural areas telling stories of people digging up the corpses of Grameen borrowers to prove that they had been branded with a cross after joining.

Mannan didn't take the bait, but simply reminded his companion that Grameen was a Bengali-run program founded by a Muslim economics professor who was being mentioned as a Nobel Prize candidate. When the conversation ended a few minutes later, Mannan clasped hands with the chairman one final time and promised to try to visit him before he returned to Dhaka. Then he mounted a bicycle and headed toward the Zianpur bazaar.

It had been an emotional week for Mannan, as he had been able to do what few founder branch managers have done—inspect their handiwork years after being reassigned. He spent several hours each evening talking with the bank workers, impressing them with his ability to recite the names of virtually all 1,500 borrowers who'd joined during his tenure. He, in turn, was impressed with the way several of the staff members, including Mustafiz and Rohim, had done their homework on the project area. He thought their blunt assessments of who in the community were troublemakers and corrupt—judgments that influence decisions upon which a branch's success can depend—were largely accurate. They were grade-A bank workers, in his opinion, while one was below average, and all the rest were mediocre.

One morning he found Mustafiz lying on his bed, moaning and writhing as if in agony. But Mustafiz's anguish was from mental rather than physical pain. Mustafiz recounted the story of a borrower in the village of Baze Taluk who was selling her house, which had been built with a Grameen housing loan. She could not be talked out of it. The house had been dismantled early that morning and was being moved to the buyer's plot.

The staff considered this a serious matter. Perhaps the ultimate slap in the face a bank worker can receive is to have one of his borrowers sell her Grameen-financed house. In most cases, it is a response to a woman's inability to meet her weekly installment, a sign that Grameen has not helped her very much and that she is preparing to give up her struggle to live a dignified, poverty-free life. For Ahlim, the bank worker responsible for this center, it was a disappointment; for his colleague Mustafiz, it was an outrage. Yet neither had made any progress.

Mannan went to the scene and convened a community meeting. He described to the prospective house buyer the difficulties the sale presented to Grameen. He played to the man's ego, calling him a gentleman who could afford to buy a house anywhere. Why, Mannan asked, did he want to buy it from a poor woman who didn't have anything else? After about an hour of this cajoling, the man agreed to return all the building materials and to reconstruct the house, but he was unwilling to accept Mannan's personal offer to pay for the cost of rebuilding it; he promised to bear the expense himself, because he respected what Mannan had done for the community years earlier.

Next, Mannan turned to the woman who had sold her house. Now that she could have it back, would she in fact take it back? The crowd fell silent as it waited for her answer. She explained that she had sold it to buy a used rickshaw for her son, the family's only prospect for a steady income in the months ahead. Mannan proposed that she take a loan from the group fund to buy the rickshaw. The woman began to complain that her group members had not wanted to approve the loan, but before she could get very far, Assia Begum, the center chief, waved her hand and said to Mannan, "I'll handle it." That ended that. Two hours after Mannan had arrived in Baze Taluk, the agreement that had eluded four bank employees and a center chief was completed, and the meeting broke up.

On his last night before returning to Dhaka, Mannan spent several hours telling stories to the staff. One was about the 1998 flood, which occurred at a time when he and his staff lived together in an abandoned school classroom. One morning, the staff awoke to find that a foot of water was flowing through their makeshift dormitory and that a live cobra had snuck into bed with a bank worker. After killing the snake and securing their belongings, the men rented boats and spent the next four days visiting Grameen members. They had received no instructions to do so from their superiors; it was simply understood that in times of disaster, Grameen staff were expected to maintain close contact with their borrowers in order to assess their needs and to help in any way possible. Mannan described how he demoted his senior assistant to a bank worker when he hesitated for several hours before deciding to join in the disaster-response effort.

At one point during the flood, Mannan discovered a Kholshi borrower who had taken refuge on her roof and was in the middle of giving birth. He assisted with the delivery, brought her to a village midwife who lived on higher ground, and named the newborn Bonna (Flood). Since arriving at the branch,

Rohim had heard stories of how the staff had responded to the flood, and the loyalty among the borrowers that their actions created, so Mannan's accounts resonated.

A second story reflected the presence of mind and character needed to be an outstanding manager—a post Rohim dreamed of occupying one day. Mannan told of being posted to Shaymganj along with Ruhul Amin and Rofiq ul Islam. One evening, after the three men had spent several days together, the bank workers admitted that they had been branded troublemakers at the branches from which they'd been transferred. Both assumed that they had been sent to such a remote location as punishment for their transgressions. Mannan gave them a long lecture about how he would not hold past actions against them, and told them that if they worked hard, he would ensure that they received promotions. At the end of the conversation, the two bank workers looked at each other, both apparently wanting to ask a question but too shy to do so. Mannan encouraged them to say what was on their minds.

"Sir," Ruhul Amin began sheepishly, "what transgression got *you* posted here?"

Without missing a beat, Mannan thought of the perfect white lie. "Well, you see, I have quite a temper. On several occasions, I assaulted bank workers working under me."

During the ensuing months, Ruhul Amin—the founder of Shandha's center—and Rofiq performed as well as any bank workers Mannan had ever known. They, and Mannan, received their promotions in record time.

ONE AFTERNOON, SHORTLY BEFORE THE MONSOON, Krishna cycled to Amena's house. "*As Salaam o Aleikum,*" Krishna called out as he dismounted his bicycle after entering her courtyard.

"*Salaam,* sir," Amena replied as she walked out of her vegetable garden to greet him.

"So this is your garden, Amena," Krishna said as he walked over and touched some of the maturing eggplants, pumpkins, and chilies. "You sell these to wholesalers who come here?"

"No, sir, my daughter Aaki sells our vegetables at the Zianpur *haat,* and in the Kholshi bazaar, after school. Sometimes she goes to the Ghior *haat.* We get a better price that way. Lately I've been making a hundred fifty taka per week."

Amena called her son to roll out a bamboo mat on her earthen veranda so that Krishna could sit down.

"Very impressive," Krishna said. "She's studying in the BRAC school, right?"

"Yes, sir."

"And your chickens and ducks?" he asked as he took a seat on the mat.

"They're in the jungle, sir. Jackals have eaten a couple of the chicks. I . . ." She looked around and said in a hushed voice, "I have given out a dozen on a sharecrop basis, sir, so that my husband, you know . . ." Krishna nodded. He had heard about the situation from Oloka, and approved of Amena's strategy of keeping some of her assets concealed. He had been told that it was several months since she had received her last beating, and that slowly the abuse of the children was declining as well.

He asked Amena if she thought Rukia Begum should be allowed to join her group. Rukia had been a part of the original group that had failed its recognition test 14 months before.

"I think it is a good thing, sir. She will pass the recognition test this time. She has seen how well we've done and is eager for a second chance."

"She's not getting any pressure from relatives to join, is she?"

"I don't think so, sir. She wants to raise a cow. I think she'll fit in very well." Amena heard a faint noise, and it reminded her of something. "Sir, I think there's been some tragedy in Fulzan's compound. Perhaps you should have a look. I don't get along with the people who live near her, the families who were squatters along the side of the pond. But maybe you should go."

"What's happened?"

"Somebody said a child had died. I'm not sure."

Krishna looked at his watch. He wanted to inspect the loan utilization of two members in Center 42, and the afternoon was slipping away. Yet duty called. "Can your son show me the way?" he asked.

Long before Amena's son and Krishna walked up the steep slope separating Fulzan's house plot from the footpath 10 feet below, they had heard the cries. Fulzan's niece Zorina, who lived in a tiny thatch hut next to hers, was rolling in the dirt, screaming gibberish. Next to her, lying on a blanket, was the lifeless, emaciated body of her son. Incense was burning a few inches away from his head. The tiny corpse's shriveled skin, sunken face, and brittle arms reminded Krishna of pictures of famine-stricken Somalia he had seen in the newspaper.

Krishna looked at the body and gasped. He had not seen anything quite like this since the famine of 1974. Fulzan, Shundari, and group chairman Nobirun paced around the small courtyard, their pallid faces reflecting the seriousness of the moment. Each had seen the boy spend the last six weeks coughing and wheezing his way closer and closer to death's door, losing a little more body weight each day. Traditional healers weren't able to do anything, though one took 200 taka for trying.

"Fulzan," Krishna called out as he walked toward her. "Is that your sister?"

"That's my niece. Her only son has died, just now." As Fulzan spoke those words, the wailing resumed again. By now, the boy's mother was covered in dirt and her sari was in tatters.

In the year since she'd joined the bank, Fulzan had made some progress. She now ate rice from land farmed by her husband more than 10 months of the year, and had bought two sheets of tin for her roof with money she made from selling jute and duck eggs. For the first time in years, she would not be exposed to the elements during the monsoon. But not all was well. Two months earlier, her cow had died, forcing her to replace it with a sharecropped calf from a wealthy family. When she received her second general loan, she decided to invest most of it in leasing some more land for her husband to farm instead of trying her luck with another cow. With the few hundred taka left over, she bought some chicks and ducklings to raise. She was also pregnant, though it hardly showed, despite the fact that she was ending her second trimester. Fulzan was praying that this time she would have a boy.

For someone as poor as Fulzan, the path out of poverty—or at least to stable subsistence—would most likely be slower than that of her peers. It might take five years, or even 10, for her to see meaningful improvement in her living conditions. In between, there would be setbacks—cows that died, crops damaged by pests, medical emergencies. It was possible that one of those crises could ruin her, but with the ditchdigging to fall back on, and the support of people like Amena and Shandha, it was more likely that she would continue on her unsteady but generally upward course. When asked, she said that Grameen was her savior, but it took a discerning eye to distinguish the changes that had occurred in her life over the 14 months since she'd joined the bank. One measure of that change, however, lay in what she was *not*—the mother of a child who had succumbed to slow starvation.

"Listen, listen—listen!" Krishna yelled, trying to gain the attention of Fulzan's niece. "There's nothing to be gained by crying. Allah has taken your son, and that is final. No amount of drama will bring him back. Here, here's fifty taka to arrange for a proper burial." He handed the pink bill to Fulzan, and, turning back to the niece, added, "Put your attention toward that, would you?" Like many Grameen field staff, in such situations he sometimes gave money from his own pocket to help out.

In a softer voice he said, "Fulzan, I'm sorry to hear about your cow dying. I've heard you've sharecropped another cow."

"Yes, sir."

"Okay, I'm going over to the Haldar *para*. I'm late. See that the burial is taken care of quickly—don't let her be like this for long. It'll make her sick."

"Yes, sir."

Krishna descended to the footpath, grimacing as the wailing started again. He knew that Fulzan's family had just lost its first son in two generations, and understood what a blow that was to their social, economic, and psychological well-being. Over the next few days, Krishna continued to be haunted by the image of that lifeless boy.

AT THE HEAD OF THE PARADE were Yunus and Shah Newaz, the Dhaka zonal manager, talking casually as they walked through the village. Yunus was asking questions about what he had just seen at the Shekherchar Narsingdi office, a window on the future of Grameen. For the first time, a branch had been fully computerized, an experiment that had cut the bank workers' time spent doing paperwork by 70 percent. In an era of eight groups per center and three loans per borrower, it was the only realistic way to go. This personal visit had reinforced Yunus's commitment to computerize at least one branch in each zone by the first quarter of 1995. Bank workers had told him of the extra time they were able to spend with borrowers in the field, something that Yunus knew was necessary for Grameen to thrive.

Yunus and his entourage moved to an open air hut, where the center chief greeted him. "Sir," she asked Yunus after he sat down on a bench, "may I have permission to start this special meeting?"

"Yes, go ahead." The center chief shouted out orders, and the other women responded—arms forward, arms crossed, arms forward, arms crossed, arms forward, and then standing and crouching three times before resuming a relaxed crouching position. Yunus gave the center chief permission to sit down and then turned the meeting over to Shah Nawaz, who introduced the managing director. As he did so, Yunus surveyed the women and the men standing outside the hut. He liked going to the field, even though he did it less frequently now than he used to. It always seemed to teach him something that he could bring back and integrate into his work, and this day would be no exception.

"As Salaam o Aleikum," Yunus began after he was introduced. The women returned the greeting. "I have come here as a guest of your staff, and I would like to know a little bit about the progress you are making in your businesses. Many of you, I know, are involved with weaving. Is this a profitable profession? Have the loans helped you? Is it getting better every year or worse?"

The center chief stood up and saluted Yunus. "Sir, most of us are involved with handlooms, though some are raising cows and doing other things. I have three handlooms myself. When I first thought of joining the bank, the idea terrified me. Learning the rules and the decisions, signing my name, defying the things people said against the bank, taking money—it all seemed impossible. But I built up my courage, joined with some friends, and tried. After recognition, I received a loan of one thousand taka, and it felt like so much. I had never seen so much money before. I was frightened that I would not be able to invest it well and make the twenty-one taka I needed to meet my weekly installment." As she spoke, the woman stared at Yunus, swinging her arms to emphasize particular words and phrases. The constant state of motion of her hands partly disguised the fact that they were trembling.

"But now, I have made a lot of progress. Today, my weekly installment is more than one *thousand* taka—more than the amount of my first loan." She drew out *hazar*, the Bengali word for thousand, to make sure Yunus didn't miss the point. "And I have no problem paying it. So from being unable to dream of taking one thousand taka for an entire year I am now paying that to the bank every seven days!" She smiled broadly as she said that, and then opened her right hand, which had been clenched into a fist, as if to say, "I could give you one thousand taka right now, if you wanted it."

"Is this really true?" Yunus asked. He had never heard of a borrower having such a high weekly installment. It was not clear if he was asking Shah Nawaz or the center chief, but the borrower answered herself.

"Yes, sir, my installment is one thousand and sixty-one taka." Another woman, sitting two rows behind the center chief, stood up.

"Sir, I am the deputy center chief, and while my installment is not one thousand, but it is more than eight hundred."

A woman from the fourth row rose to her feet and added, "My installment is seven hundred fifty-one, and I have lots of money now. Here, look—I always have money just to carry around with me." She untied the end of her sari, revealing a handful of crumpled bills. She carefully unfolded and handed each of them to Yunus, one by one. There were three 100-taka notes, then a 50, then two more 100s, then a 20, then three more 100s. When she had taken them out of her sari, it hadn't looked like there were more than three or four notes of small denominations. (In Bangladesh at that time, the larger the note, the more it was worth, with two-taka notes being bigger than one-taka notes, and so on.)

Yunus inspected the bills, counted them, and returned the wad to its proud owner. He asked the women to sit down and said, "Is this just a few of you, or are there many with such large installments?"

"Oh, many, sir," one woman called out.

"Let me ask this. How many of you have installments of more than one thousand taka?" Three women raised their hands. Yunus looked at Shah Newaz, and then back at the women. "What about between eight hundred and one thousand taka as an installment?" Five more women raised their hands. He continued asking until he got down to 500 taka, and by then nearly 20 arms were erect.

"Well, when I started with Grameen Bank," Yunus explained, "I was giving out loans that were sometimes smaller than the one thousand taka that your center chief started with. I gave out loans for five hundred taka, for three hundred taka, for one hundred taka, even for thirty taka. These loans were no joke—they were serious business, and repaying was not always easy. So I am used to talking about small sums. But not until today had I ever heard of Grameen Bank members paying more in a weekly installment than they had borrowed when they joined. That is no minor accomplishment, and it is something I could never have never imagined. Until today."

The meeting drew to a close, and Yunus began his visits to the borrowers' homes to see their handlooms, their employees, their livestock, and their houses. As striking as the scale of their operations was the docility of many of the women's husbands. A few just stood beside their wives, tending a cow or a goat while their spouse explained the family business to the professor.

When he returned to the branch in the late afternoon, Yunus wanted to look at the books. He asked whether other centers had so many borrowers whose installment was more than 500 taka. The staff claimed that it was typical of more than half of the centers in the branch, and produced ledgers and collection sheets to prove it.

On his drive back to Dhaka with Shah Newaz, who would later go on to establish Grameen America, Yunus spent a long time in silent contemplation, and finally said:

> It really had never occurred to me that a woman's installment could be more than one thousand taka. I have seen the aggregate numbers coming into the head office, but I couldn't quite grasp what they meant at the level of a single borrower. So many critics say we are just lending to people and they are struggling along with small-scale operations, not growing, not breaking through to higher levels of productivity, not leaving poverty. But it is impossible to say that about a woman who is paying one thousand taka every single week. These are not struggling poor people—these are authentic rural entrepreneurs. I had never imagined.

Yunus drifted back into thought, and all Shah Nawaz could think to say was, "Yes, sir."

The van sped toward Dhaka, where Yunus would resume his daily routine the following morning. For many weeks, his thoughts would return to the 1,000-taka installments and to the crumpled 100-taka notes of the Shekherchar Narsingdi branch. He thought it signified the dawning of a new era at Grameen, and he wondered what the achievements, challenges, and risks of that era would be.

On May 24th, Rukia Begum traveled to a center in the village of Bilpara with Amena and Shandha and took the group recognition test for the second time. The program officer asked Rukia three questions, one about the group fund, another about the responsibilities of membership, and a third about the Sixteen Decisions. She answered them all without so much as a pause to collect her thoughts, and in so doing gained recognition and entry into the seventh group, more than a year after her failure. Five days later, she walked to the bazaar and took out a loan of 2,000 taka.

Update: Since the 1990s

I WAS CONCERNED TO DISCOVER, when I returned to Kholshi in 1995 and 2004, that Fulzan, the poorest member of the seventh group, had been unable to repay her loans on the schedule she had agreed to. Yet she had benefited from her participation in Grameen in some modest ways. Grameen was profitable enough to write off her loan even as she continued to make small payments on an irregular basis. Indeed, a repayment rate of 98 percent, which is consistent with Grameen's continued financial health, means approximately one loan in every center each year is not paid back.

Yunus and his colleagues were not perfectionists. Based on academic research and their own observations, they understood that many destitute people had overcome poverty through microloans or at least risen to the level of stable subsistence or moderate poverty. But they longed for microfinance to be an even more powerful strategy for those at the bottom of the heap, partly because a growing chorus of critics claimed, despite considerable evidence to the contrary, that microfinance was only effective with the moderate poor and the so-called vulnerable nonpoor. They also wanted to guard against the possibility of defaulting clients being harassed by peers or staff, especially when they had made a serious effort to succeed in their business and repay their loan. While they wouldn't advertise it, occasional defaults were an inevitable cost of doing business, and insulating the bank from accusations of harsh loan recovery practices that were being leveled against some microlenders was a smart and ethical approach. In fact, several of the new policies under Grameen II were aimed at reducing the pressure to repay according to the original schedule when that brought hardship.

Another aspect of Grameen II was its built-in accountability for tracking every borrower's progress toward a poverty-free life. The data from that tracking system and his own intuition convinced Yunus that some clients were simply too poor to thrive in his system, especially those who were utterly destitute. In response, Yunus developed a program designed for rural families that subsisted by begging. After many cycles of piloting, Grameen settled on a basic approach for lending to these people, whom they named *struggling borrowers*. All the normal rules of Grameen did not apply. Loans were very small (as little as $5), there was no interest, and repayment was optional and on whatever schedule the beggar desired. Repayment couldn't be made from money secured through begging; it must be from a Grameen-financed business venture. Each struggling borrower was given a badge identifying her with the Grameen Bank so as to lift her social status. No urban beggars, who are often organized in syndicates controlled by wealthy mafia, were accepted.

Each loan officer would identify one local beggar and encourage him or her to take a loan that would normally be for no more than $20. The beggar would be paired with a regular borrowing group in his or her village that would look out for him. The basic idea was that, as the struggling borrower went from village to village begging, he could also sell food, trinkets, or anything else to those from whom he begged. Local merchants were identified who would sell items to the beggars at a modest discount, which could then be sold from house to house with a slight markup. A few beggars were set up with cell phones to start pay-phone businesses, particularly if they tended to beg from a fixed location rather than wandering throughout the local villages.

To provide some relief from the elements, an umbrella and a mosquito net were given to the beggar for an optional, token payment. The beggars are covered by Grameen's loan insurance program that ensures forgiveness of the loan in case of death, and an additional cash payment of $9 to assist with burial expenses.

The excitement this generated among Grameen's field-based workforce was immediate and beyond Dr. Yunus's expectations. Within a few months, there were 20,000 beggars in the program, one per loan officer. They soon lobbied him to have more than one each. By late 2007, there were more than 100,000 participating, and several thousand of the earliest participants had given up begging entirely and joined Grameen Bank as regular members. Many more had reduced their reliance on begging as a source of income. With Grameen's profits nearing $10 million in 2005 and $20 million in 2006, it could afford this subsidized program that picked up where its mainstream loan program left off.

Inspired by this extension of the microloan model, organizations that felt an affinity for Grameen began to adapt this approach to local conditions. Fonkoze, the leading microfinance institution in Haiti and a Grameen Foundation partner organization for many years, developed a two-tiered program to serve those who were not ready to join a regular solidarity group. One provided six months of additional training and support, and another for the ultrapoor included enhanced services, including an asset transfer (grant), and estimated that within two years, beneficiaries would be ready for mainstream microfinance. Shah Newaz, mentioned earlier in this chapter, who later became the most experienced zonal manager in the history of the Grameen Bank, helped Fonkoze design its program at a summit on extreme poverty organized in 2005 in Haiti.

Fonkoze's summit ended up putting the organization at the center of what became an exciting global initiative to scale up BRAC's version of Grameen's struggling borrowers program, which turned out to be easier to adapt in different country contexts. With support from the Ford Foundation and CGAP, what became known to many as the "graduation model" and to others as the "ultrapoor program" was lauded as a practical model that researchers later confirmed was effective. Once again, Bangladeshi social entrepreneurs provided leadership and a replicable model to the global effort to eliminate extreme poverty by 2030.

Elsewhere, however, microfinance was becoming more commercially focused. Some microlenders made attractive profits in markets where transaction costs were low (due, for example, to high population density) or because the poor, so long exploited by moneylenders, were prepared by pay rates exceeding 30 percent and in some cases even 50 percent or more. Yunus sought to play the role of the conscience of the movement, choosing to innovate more by serving those who had been largely excluded from microfinance than by dreaming up ways to increase profits or to entice venture capitalists from rich countries to invest.

When I discovered back in the late 2000s ago that Latin American MFIs were more profitable, on average, than traditional Latin American banks, I was concerned even as many of my peers in the industry celebrated. I felt, as many did, that Yunus's voice and values were more needed than ever.

10. The Hip Hop Shop

OMIYALE DUPART STOOD ON HER PORCH on South Dante Street, waiting for her son Hkeem at 5:15 on a cool morning in early April 1994. She was surrounded by black plastic garbage bags containing 100 packets of warm butter cookies and another 100 plastic bags of fruit and some extra packaging. Omiyale had been feeling light-headed since 3:30, but she had no choice but to finish up and get ready for the morning rush hour.

February and March had been bitter months for Omiyale. Her troubles stemmed from having been unable to repay her short-term loan of $3,300 (taken to buy inventory for the Black Expo in July 1993) by the due date of Friday, October 1. Though she made a $105 payment on that day, nearly $2,300 remained overdue.

At the time, her circle members were supportive despite the large amount that was outstanding. Even Geri, who had been forced to take a smaller loan as a consequence of her chairlady's difficulty, told Omiyale to take whatever time she needed to repay. Queenesta asked if she could help sell some of Omiyale's merchandise from her counter at Victor's store. Thelma, though she gently questioned Omiyale about all the time she'd been putting into solving the problems of *other* circles (instead of getting herself back on track), let her friend know she was available for support. On several occasions, Thelma tried to arrange transportation for Omiyale so that she would not be late to events at which she was selling.

November and December 1993 were not good for her business, and some of Omiyale's modest profits had to be diverted into dealing with family issues. She made only two payments, totaling $120, on her short-term loan in

December, though she managed to keep current on her payments on her long-term loan. The final month of 1993 was hard on other borrowers, too; Thelma, perhaps the long-term FCF member with the fewest missed payments, bounced two checks to WSEP (but then made a triple payment during the first week of January to get up to date). In January and February 1994, Omiyale's business—trading African imports, selling handmade jewelry and home-baked butter cookies—continued to struggle, her profits too small to do anything more than make twice-monthly payments of $112 on her long-term loan, buy some merchandise for Black History Month, and put down a deposit for the Black Women's Expo, scheduled for the second week of March.

By February, Thelma and Queenesta were headed into the final stages of repaying their loans and were hoping to take larger ones to buy inventory for the spring and summer. Both began to wonder when, or even whether, their chairlady was planning on repaying her short-term loan. Peer support was being slowly transformed into a combination of peer support and peer pressure.* While Queenesta tried to help Omiyale by, for example, coordinating a series of vending events they went in on together during during Black History Month at Chicago State University, she was not above gossiping on the phone with Thelma about how many times Omiyale had missed deadlines for clearing the debt. With each passing week, the tension grew.

The following dialogue from a meeting in early March, just before the Black Women's Expo, gives a flavor of the prevailing mood in the group.

> Thelma: The first thing we need to talk about is the short-term loan. Why isn't it paid off? This is March seventh.
>
> Geri [to Thelma, embarrassed and trying to change the subject]: I saw you at Maxwell Street yesterday, and I wanted to show this to you. You can get fabrics, pieces, at Crate and Barrel, like scraps.
>
> Thelma: The question is, why is the short-term loan at two thousand, two hundred and fifty-two dollars as of February eleventh?
>
> Omiyale: It is still at that amount because I have not been making that money. I've been making payments on my long-term loan.

---

*It is important to note that the policies followed under Grameen II would have reduced if not eliminated the pressure element, since Omiyale could have rescheduled her loan. But Grameen II was still nearly a decade away from being rolled out by Grameen Bank in Bangladesh.

Thelma: We thought you were also making payments on this one. It's the eleventh month of this loan. We are hoping it will be paid off before April.

Omiyale: I'll be generating money from the Black [Women's] Expo.

Thelma: Say you don't do well at the Black Expo. What is the backup?

Omiyale [Irritation in her voice]: I've made arrangements to get money. If I don't make all the money, I've made arrangements to come up with it.

Thelma: What?

Omiyale: I'll take a loan from someone, okay.

Thelma: What date will it be paid off?

Omiyale: Tuesday, March fifteenth or sixteenth, which is it?

Thelma: Geri, please make a notation that Omiyale has made a commitment to pay it off by Tuesday. The season is beginning, and we need to figure out how to get some money [for our businesses].

Omiyale believed that Thelma's pressure was too harsh—retribution, perhaps, for Omiyale's decision not to share a booth with her at the Black Women's Expo. But however much she disliked the pressure, she recognized that the Full Circle Fund (and Grameen Bank before it) was set up to encourage such interactions, however uncomfortable, when borrowers fall behind (especially prior to the advent of Grameen II). The combination of reliable and well-designed products and services and their high expectations of clients is what differentiates Grameen and the Fund from nonprofit organizations and government initiatives that are unable to get—or even expect—their beneficiaries to put anything back into the program. That may have seemed fine to Omiyale in theory, but it was sometimes painful in practice. After all, she had *created* her group, and her center. Many women, including Thelma, owed their participation to her.

Queenesta, Thelma, and Omiyale all did reasonably well at the Expo. Even Geri, who took Thelma up on an offer to sell her aprons at her booth, made out fine, selling more than a half dozen aprons and taking orders for more. In fact, for the first time since WSEP had started putting together packages for its clients to participate in Expos, not a single woman failed to make at least enough profit to pay off her booth space. Several made substantial sums of money. This was a triumph for Pam, who was rewarded with a promotion. Thelma grossed $950, mainly selling clothing she had made at her sewing class, hair accessories, and dollar jewelry. For a woman who hadn't known how to sew six months earlier, it was encouraging.

Just before the Expo, Thelma celebrated the ending of the month of Ramadan, in which Muslims fast from dawn until dusk every day until the Eid festival. The day before the Expo began, she got dressed up in an Indian sari and went to her mosque. Thelma enjoyed praying with Muslims of different nationalities, and was always amused by the Pakistani women, who told her that they had never been able to go to the mosque before they came to America. Ending the fast gave her the strength she needed to endure the rigors of running her booth over the three long days.

Omiyale made $1,300 at the Expo, though after paying for her booth space and inventory she had only $405 profit left to make a payment on her short-term loan. When she explained that at the next meeting, the women did not press her to borrow the money to repay the rest of the loan, but instead encouraged her to keep paying a little at a time. Thelma recommended that Omiyale concentrate her efforts on baking and selling her butter cookies. She believed it was the best product her friend had. (Thelma once remarked, "Some people have a million-dollar idea and some don't. I don't. But Omiyale's cookies, if she markets them right, could make her a millionaire. They's so good—mmmm—you just eat one and you can't stop, you want to eat five or ten.") As far as Thelma could tell, butter cookies were Omiyale's ticket out of debt. Omiyale, as much as she resented the harassment, knew that the advice was sound, and after the Expo she began devoting her energies to her cookie business. With only a single oven, it took her close to eight hours and $33 worth of ingredients to make $100 worth of butter cookies. She knew it would only be by paying off her short-term loan that she'd be able to borrow enough to buy an industrial oven that would cut her production time by 70 percent.

Back in front of Omiyale's house, it was 5:25am. Hkeem jumped out of the car, apologized for being late, and started helping his mother load her bags into the backseat. Twenty-five-year-old Hkeem DuPart was a dashing ex-Marine who had served in Asia and Central America. While he sometimes cringed a bit at his mother's being a street vendor, he, more than anyone else in the family, consistently helped her out.

Once, when she was selling 1,000 T-shirts outside Chicago Stadium during the Bulls' push toward their first championship, he offered to be his mother's bodyguard because the stadium was located in a rough neighborhood. When his mother asked him to help sell, Hkeem feared the embarrassment of having one of his friends see him hawking T-shirts. Yet, after watching his mother make steady progress, he decided to swallow his pride, and in a short span of time sold more than 100 shirts. Even after that, it still shocked him when he saw Omiyale selling at Maxwell Street during the winter months, warming her hands over a burning garbage can alongside fellow vendors who looked like hoboes. If other ethnic groups accuse Blacks of being overly status-conscious and not industrious enough, Hkeem sometimes thought, they certainly hadn't met my mom.

Hkeem dropped his mother off by the corner of State and Eighty-seventh. Omiyale grabbed a packet of cookies in her right hand and a bag of fruit—a banana, an apple, a pear, and a few grapes—in her left and waited for cars headed for the expressway. One, a beat-up white Cadillac, refused to even slow down as Omiyale waved the cookies and fruit at the driver. A woman in a gray Honda decelerated, took a look, and smiled at Omiyale as she shook her head. Probably didn't have exact change, or access to her wallet, Omiyale thought. It's nice that she slowed down to make eye contact, though. Finally, she got the attention of a middle-aged Black man in an Oldsmobile. He stopped, rolled down his window, and said, "Are those one dollar?"

"Yes, sir, one dollar for the cookies and one dollar for the fruit!" Omiyale replied excitedly.

"Uh, give me some cookies." As he reached for his wallet be added, "And give me some fruit, too."

"Sure will." Omiyale smiled, handed him the two bags, and made change for a $5 bill. As the car pulled away, she felt that sense of relief a peddler always gets from making her first sale of the day. She headed back to her bags and grabbed some more.

At 7:45, she was down to ten bags of fruit; the cookies, as usual, were gone. She would have liked to stay, but there was a grandchild to send to school and appointments to keep. She stuffed the empty garbage bags into the one containing the leftover fruit and ran across the street ahead of an eastbound Number 87 bus. As Omiyale boarded and parted with her fare, she greeted the driver with a smile and headed to the back.

By 8:05, Omiyale was home, preparing Atukwe, the five-year-old son of Bayyinah, her second-eldest daughter, to go to kindergarten. Atukwe's mother had already left for her part-time job, so it was up to Omiyale to get him on his way.

At 8:23, Omiyale splashed some water on her face, laid her money out on the table, and counted it. It was mostly ones, a few fives, one ten, and one twenty—$189 in all. Since she had a little left over from last week to buy the sugar, butter, and flour, she crammed it all in her pocket as she hustled out the door—she was late! Alternately jogging and walking along Ninetieth Street, she progressed steadily toward Stoney Island Avenue. At 8:45, she arrived, sweaty and racked by a headache. Five minutes later, Colete pulled up in her car at the corner of Ninety-fifth and Stoney Island, from where they would drive to the WSEP office. They had agreed the night before to meet there.

"Hey, girl," Colete said. "You been up all night, huh?"

"Yeah," Omiyale replied with a sigh. "Just like last week. But I gotta get this paid off, ya know."

"You got the money?"

"Yeah, here's a hundred and eighty-nine. I might have more next week, but I wanted to give you this right now, before I have time to spend it on anything."

"All right. Let me write you a receipt." With her car still running, Colete filled in and signed the receipt, took the money, and counted it. "Great job, girl, I'll see you Monday night."

"Yeah, I guess you will. I'll try to have another payment then, a big one." As she began walking back to her house, Omiyale pondered the day ahead: catching a little nap, picking up Atukwe in the early afternoon, cooking him lunch, picking up her granddaughter from day care, buying fruit, flour, sugar, and butter from wholesalers, and getting the entire production process going again. There were rides to arrange and telephone calls to make.

At the Lindblom center meeting the following Monday, Omiyale informed her circle members that along with her payment on her long-term loan, she was making a payment on her short-term loan and had given Colete $185 the previous week. Most of that money had been earned from selling cookies and fruit on the Eighty-seventh Street on-ramp.

Those payments brought the balance on her short-term loan down to $857. Within a fortnight, it would drop to $586. Three weeks later, she went downtown to present Colete with a $400 money order. With that, the loans' principal and interest were finally fully repaid. As she clutched the receipt, Omiyale DuPart burst into tears. With the rest of the FCF staff looking on, Colete embraced her center chief until the last tear was spent.

By then, Queenesta and Thelma were in the final stages of preparing their loan applications, for $5,000 and $4,400 respectively. It was not a moment too soon, as both were on the verge of seeing investment opportunities for the summer slip away.

IN 1992, OMIYALE'S SECOND YEAR in the FCF program, she began having some success selling African imports. She initially became interested in African products from a cultural standpoint. Though her activist days were over, she still thought it was good for African-Americans to be in touch with their rich native culture. If she hadn't made much of a profit, it wouldn't have particularly bothered her. But to her surprise, she grossed more than $2,000 selling African imports at each of several events during the summer of 1992, and in the fall investigated the possibility of buying directly from Africa. Incautiously, she invested $2,000 in a joint venture with two Africans she had met at a festival—all of which she lost without ever seeing any merchandise. Yet, it is testimony to how far her business had come since she'd joined the program that she was able to withstand the loss without missing a payment on her loan.

In the spring of 1992, two of Omiyale's relatives passed away. She and her sisters stood to inherit a meaningful amount from the estate, but a protracted legal battle ended up consuming the bulk of the wealth. The entire episode made Omiyale bitter—couldn't she just have ended up with a small amount of money, something like $5,000 that would give her a little cushion in her checking account, ensuring that she didn't always have to be at risk of bouncing checks?

Repaying her short-term loan through cookie sales was a defining experience for her. Until then, baking butter cookies had been something of a diversion, something she enjoyed pursuing less than her African import and jewelry ventures. Indeed, she had been looking to phase it out. But the marketplace was becoming flooded with African goods, and she had a growing number of regular customers for her cookies. As she completed repaying her short-term loan and contemplated her next loan from the Full Circle Fund, Omiyale thought seriously about buying an industrial oven and getting a baker's license.

Her vision was to open a bakery from which she could sell on a wholesale basis what would be called Mama Omiyale's Lunchroom Butter Cookies. As far as Omiyale could tell, since time immemorial, kids had been eating butter cookies in Chicago's public school cafeterias. Her idea was to re-create a taste that the students had grown up with; only her cookies would be larger and sold in packets of four. The wholesale price would be $1 per package, the retail price double that. Even if she didn't match Mrs. Fields' success, it might at least get her to the point of having some spare cash in her bank account. Others suspected it could do more than that; as Thelma often reminded Omiyale, she rarely, if ever, failed to sell out, whether she was selling to poor folks or rich, white, Black, or Hispanic. Now it was time to test it on a larger scale, to see if this was indeed a "million-dollar idea."

IN THE MIDDLE OF APRIL, while Omiyale was in the throes of paying off her short-term loan and Queenesta was enjoying her first few weeks in a new store, the curtain opened on the final act of the Maxwell Street saga. Several weeks earlier, Isabel Wilkerson of the *New York Times* had run a tribute to the bazaar, writing, "For 120 years, the Maxwell Street Market has been the mall of the dispossessed. . . . Now Maxwell Street faces extinction."[51]

And face extinction it did on Wednesday, April 13, when the Chicago City Council voted on whether to sell the city-owned land that fell within the jurisdiction of the bazaar to the University of Illinois. Up in the observers' gallery, some 800 promarket activists watched, cheering those who supported their cause and booing those who didn't. Thelma Ali was there, as were Steve Balkin and Lew Kreinberg. They had all come to see the end, or, perhaps, they faintly hoped, to bear witness to a miracle.

What they saw was two aldermen nearly coming to blows over the issue; only police intervention prevented a fight. When the vote was taken, the motion to sell the land to the university passed 33 to 10. The *Chicago Tribune* reported the deliberations in the following day's paper in an article titled, "Ready to Rumble? Step into Council Chambers." While the *Tribune* had hardly adopted a pro–Maxwell Street stand, columnist John Kass did not sugarcoat his description of how the city had shafted the vendors by selling a market in which an estimated $20 million in sales are made each year for a measly $4.25 million. "The agreement," the article noted, "will evict more than 800 vendors by Labor Day, and only about half of them will be relocated in a truncated version of the market to be established on Canal Street between Roosevelt and 15th Streets."[52] Kass added that the planned Canal Street market area was itself already threatened, targeted by the city as a parking-lot-to-be for a proposed riverboat gambling complex. If there was one thing Mayor Daley had his heart set on more than the growth of UIC and gentrification of the area around the Loop, it was gaining approval for Chicago-based riverboat gambling. The market was to be moved out of the way of one speeding train only to be put in the path of another, larger one.

The Council, unfortunately, was not satisfied with dealing just one blow to Chicago's low-income entrepreneurs. On the same day it sealed Maxwell Street's fate, it passed another motion that significantly curtailed the right of peddlers to operate in the downtown area and around the stadium, where World Cup soccer games would be held in June and July. Street vendors, the City Council declared, would be shut out of the bonanza in the name of presenting a sanitized Chicago to the world. Low-income sellers would also be shut out of other events the city had scheduled at taxpayer expense, including the 1996 Democratic convention. Alderman Ted Mazola, the chief opponent of Maxwell Street (and one of the pair who almost came to blows over the issue), led the way on the peddler ban as well.

In the weeks after the vote, periodicals ranging from the *Washington Post* to the *Economist* commented on the passing of the market.[53] Reporters tended to wax nostalgic about the bazaar, but many were sympathetic to the desires of the city and the university. Most had more in common with the UIC and City Hall public relations people than with Black hubcap vendors and Mexican tamale makers. And, to be fair, there were some strong arguments for the university's expansion. But they weren't so strong as to preclude it from finding some kind of accommodation with the market. The compromise that many wanted was to let the university expand but to require UIC to share the space with the market on Sundays, keep the number and cost of vendor slots the same, and work with the vendors to clean the place up and improve it.

Chicago Tribune columnist John McCarron wrote about the failure to compromise:

> Nobody ever went to jail for a lack of imagination, so there's no sense calling it criminal that the University of Illinois at Chicago is about to snuff out the Maxwell Street Market.

The school is acting a bit paranoid. Arrogant, to be sure. Even a touch racist, though one hesitates to drag out that overused brickbat. But it's not criminal . . .[54]

McCarron went on to describe a compromise the city had proposed some years earlier. Although it was a pro-UIC plan that reduced the size of (but stopped short of eliminating or moving) the market, the university responded by fiercely lobbying against the proposal, which, by the time the City Council took its vote in April 1994, was long since forgotten.

McCarron closed his piece by reprimanding UIC for its refusal to assist the area's ethnic entrepreneurs and criticizing the university's lack of foresight, purpose, and imagination.

For lack of that imagination, Thelma and Omiyale were forced to begin considering how they would adapt their businesses to the loss of what some called the greatest poor people's market in North America.

PEOPLE VISITING THE FULL CIRCLE FUND occasionally ask about the borrowers who have left the program. Through 1993, all who had done so had settled their accounts, leaving the program with an enviable 100 percent repayment rate, even if many payments had been late. If Glenda Harris is typical of those who have stopped participating in the program, the impact of the FCF has been substantial.

Soon after Glenda left Omiyale's circle in the fall, she began working full-time for Westcorp, a community development organization located in one of the most depressed areas on Chicago's West Side. Westcorp was founded and directed by Correta McFerren, a fiery and charismatic woman mentioned in chapter six who had effectively become the godparent to dozens of people like Glenda who had taken refuge in her South Side home. Westcorp was involved in a campaign to reform the Chicago public school system, and also ran classes for young Black men and mothers. In all its programs, the philosophy was to be straight with the kids while giving them the tools to improve themselves.

Getting a full-time job did not, however, mean that Glenda's Ethnic Treasures went out of business. Far from it. To supplement her modest paycheck, she continued to manufacture jewelry. She sold it during protest marches, at picnics in the park, from her home, and, mostly from Westcorp's office in the basement of Malcolm X College. Janitors were among her best customers; they, like many others, discerned that Glenda's small velvet board was filled with quality jewelry at reasonable prices. Young people who hung around the office or the McFerrens' home often became part of the production team.

Glenda earned $300 to $500 per month from her business. She often had no choice but to stay up late twice each month to replenish her stock after her regular customers had received their paychecks and cleaned her out. That, combined with her salary, enabled her to buy more exotic materials with which to make more expensive jewelry, while having a surplus to save or to pay for communal expenses at the McFerrens' place. Her business income also made it possible for her to buy the medicine her doctors prescribed for her arthritis.

By the spring, Glenda was teaching jewelry design at several public schools; her favorite was one in which all the students were teenage mothers. She enjoyed the times when she was able to take an interest in a disruptive young mother and focus her energy on a project. Teachers often marveled at how she could transform chronic disciplinary cases into purposeful jewelers. With Glenda's encouragement, teachers at two schools where she taught set up tables to sell student-made jewelry on days when parents were required to come in and pick up report cards.

The quality of the students' work gave Glenda an idea. In Chicago, Black teenagers and Korean shopkeepers are often at each other's throats. Glenda would ask the shopkeepers, who were often accused of not putting anything back into the community, to agree to display and sell student-manufactured jewelry. In exchange for doing so, they would get a percentage of the retail prices—which Glenda figured would be sold for $6 to $10 per piece—and could post signs announcing that they were in a joint venture with a local school. That might be good for business, as the students were likely to urge their friends and relatives to go to the stores selling their jewelry. Small-scale creative acts of bridge-building and solidarity in low-income neighborhoods like this one often escape the media's attention but are still important.

Because of a funding crisis at Westcorp, Glenda and her colleagues received paychecks on March 15 and were not paid again until the MacArthur Foundation gave the organization a grant in the fall. For the intervening months, Glenda continued to work full-time at Westcorp but turned increasing energy toward her business. Modest living and steady sales kept her from financial hardship; indeed, she was often able to lend her colleagues and housemates small sums of money.

As she pursued Coretta McFerren's dream of educational reform and her own vision of linking wayward Black teens with ostracized Korean merchants, Glenda's Ethnic Treasures continued to grow. The business advice and encouragement of her peers, as much as the infusion of $1,500 in loan capital from the Full Circle Fund, had gotten her going. She stayed in close contact with Omiyale and Thelma, often inviting them to events at Malcolm X College where they could sell their wares. Sometimes, she would have customers sent her way by women from the Lindblom center. As a result, Glenda felt a strong sense of loyalty to her circle sisters and the Full Circle Fund, and continued to reap the benefits of her participation long after she had left.

DURING THE FIRST WEEK OF JUNE, Thelma and Queenesta received their new loans, which were among the largest ever given out by the Full Circle Fund. Before getting final approval, their applications had been pored over by their circle members, the center's loan committee, Colete, and, finally, a panel of senior WSEP staff.

Thelma presented a detailed analysis of her cash flow during the previous year and her plans for the coming one. She listed a series of events at which she would participate—the Black Expo, the Ghana Fest, the Haile Selassie Fest, Rock Around the Block, the Summer Kwanzaa Fest, the Evanston Garage Sale, the Afro-World Festival in Milwaukee, and the Taste of Oak Park. She also planned to be at Maxwell Street every Sunday and occasionally during the week for as long as the market survived. Her daughter Shashona would help out when there were two events scheduled on the same day.

Thelma listed the wares she planned to purchase with the $4,400 she would receive. Prominent among them were dollar earrings, toys, Tunisian body oils (on which the markup was more than 300 percent), hair accessories, plastic rings, sunglasses, T-shirts, and snappers—tiny, legal explosives that children play with, so much less powerful than a firecracker that you are able to actually set them off in your hand. She also wrote down some of the items in her fall back-to-school line, such as tube socks and sweatshirts. In all, it was an impressive presentation with which nobody argued.

On April 1, Queenesta had opened a store one block away from Victor's on Austin Boulevard. Now she was applying for $5,000. In the last three weeks of March, following the Black Women's Expo, Queenesta had turned her energies away from Victor's store and toward her own place. She bought glass display cases from stores going out of business, hooked up a phone and an alarm system, and decorated. She brought her cassettes and other goods over from Victor's at the end of March, but it was not enough to make her store look full. She asked Duwondes Nixon, her on-again, off-again boyfriend who had encouraged her to leave Victor's store, to become her partner. Nixon, as everyone called him, was a plumber who had some money stashed away. He agreed and invested close to $2,000. Queenesta put every last cent of her own into the store, ignoring her bills and living on a bare minimum.

Before the opening, Queenesta was nervous. Victor was planning to sell tapes and CDs himself and she had no idea how much business she might do. She didn't have to wait long to find out. On the first day she sold more than in her best *week* ever at Victor's store. Omiyale and Colete came, and saw for themselves the brisk business Queenesta was doing. During the last week of April, she made more than she had during her best *month* at Victor's. When she announced these results at a center meeting on April 18, Queenesta received a rousing ovation. Several borrowers expressed their interest in putting their merchandise in her store, which she had named the Hip Hop Shop and that was geared toward young people aged 16 to 24.

In May, sales remained strong, often exceeding $200 per day. She also continued to sell at outdoor festivals, and planned to do so more in the summer. When a man who had agreed to sell beepers out of the store decided not to follow through, Queenesta learned the basics of the beeper business in a week. By mid-June, she had 25 beeper customers (who brought her $150 in profit per month) and a toehold in a lucrative side business. (Until only a few years earlier, beepers had been used primarily by doctors. They became widely used by the general public, especially young people, during the half-decade just before cell phones became staples of modern life.)

At the end of May, she hired Nixon's teenage nephew Anton to work at the shop so she could be free to pick up merchandise and attend events. Anton related well to her customers. On one occasion, he filled the store with people to hear a series of rap artists perform. Sales approached $500 that day. For his part, Nixon—whom she described to her circle members as a "silent partner"— was performing plumbing work for some people to whom the Hip Hop Shop owed money and, in so doing, was getting the store's bills reduced. In late April, Queenesta and Shayna left their West Englewood apartment and moved in with Nixon, who lived in Austin, not far from the store.

Yet Queenesta still felt that her business was undercapitalized. Upon receiving the $5,000 from the Full Circle Fund, she immediately bought multiple copies of the most popular cassettes and compact discs, and other merchandise as well. She also put deposits down to reserve booths at several summer events.

The loan money hit her account in the second week of June. By that time, she had an increasing number of regular customers buying at the store, and the future looked bright for Queenesta Harris and her daughter Shayna.

IN JUNE 1994, PRESIDENT CLINTON OUTLINED HIS PLAN to reform the nation's welfare system. The debate about public assistance had rumbled on for years, with little effect. Opponents attacked the basic idea of welfare, dredged up examples of so-called welfare queens, and contended there was no incentive for many recipients to even try to find work.

Of course, there is a substantial American underclass, most noticeable among minorities in the inner cities, which depends on government assistance. A job is often seen as the answer to their problems. Clinton himself had instituted programs in Arkansas to encourage people to get "from welfare to work" and claimed in his 1992 campaign that 18,000 people had come off welfare in his state because they had found work. Now he wanted to institute a national *workfare* program to force people off welfare, and to limit benefits to two years for younger recipients in an attempt to force them to find a job.

But an individual, especially a single mother, is often worse off in a job than on welfare.

The kind of low-paying jobs that welfare recipients find often do not provide the health care they would receive under a government plan like Aid to Families with Dependent Children (AFDC), especially before Obamacare was passed in 2010. (In 1996, AFDC was replaced by Temporary Assistance to Needy Families, popularly known by its acronym TANF. According to a government website, the TANF program "is time limited, assists families with children when the parents or other responsible relatives cannot provide for the family's basic needs.") Out of a paycheck hardly larger than a welfare check, workfare participants have to find money for childcare and transport costs, in addition to being subject to any doctor or hospital bills. In a thoughtful article, Jason DeParle described the predicament of welfare mothers in the *New York Times*.[55] While many found work, they often had to return to welfare because they couldn't afford to stay off it. Up to 40 percent of all welfare mothers were "cyclers," he wrote, trapped in a series of low-paying jobs punctuated by stints on welfare.

While the addition of incentives like subsidized health insurance and childcare for those who return to the workforce might improve their situation, there is another avenue that can be explored. This is where organizations like WSEP and Grameen America can come in.

In *The Grameen Reader*, Muhammad Yunus wrote, "[The] removal or reduction of poverty must be a continuous process of creation of assets . . . by the poor person, enabling him to earn more and more. Self-employment, supported by credit, has much more potential for improving the asset-base of the poor than wage employment has."[56] Yet the obstacles to self-employment for the poor in the United States are substantial. Despite attempts to strengthen the Community Reinvestment Act, a law that encourages banks to lend in deprived neighborhoods where they traditionally accept deposits but do not make loans, it is difficult for even well-established enterprises to get credit. An article in the *Chicago Sun-Times* in July 1993 noted that 41 percent of small-business owners nationwide used personal credit cards to finance investments because they couldn't get bank loans.[57]

Welfare recipients are in a worse predicament. Asset limitations discourage them from legally accumulating money to start up a business. If they do manage to get going, any income, whether it is profit or not, may disqualify them from receiving benefits. Zoning regulations make many home-based business—one of the most practical options for a poor, single mother—illegal. (Such regulations generally don't apply to white-collar professionals working from home.) And many cities—New York, Chicago, and Los Angeles among them—have enacted legislation restricting the kind of street vending that is often the first step for a budding self-employed entrepreneur.

Despite these hurdles, a surprising number of the unemployed do try to escape from poverty and welfare by starting a business. One study found that 9 percent of unemployed male workers started up some kind of enterprise in 1980, and were three times as likely as someone with a job to do so.[58] "This research," concluded Steve Balkin, "refutes the conventional wisdom that low-income people are unlikely to become small-business owners because they lack skills," an argument that Muhammad Yunus was making 11,000 miles away. Slowly, a few policy makers and activists are beginning to recognize the untapped potential of the unemployed as entrepreneurs. Donna Wertenbach, the director of programs for Women Interested in Self-Employment, an organization in Hartford, Connecticut, has said, "Show me a welfare mother alone with two kids who manages a family on $600 a month, and I'll show you a financial wizard. The women who come to us are highly motivated, brilliant scramblers and they all know they have no other place to go."[59]

Self-employment holds a number of advantages over a traditional workplace for many of the unemployed. The hours are flexible—they can adapt a work schedule to fit any family situation. It allows people with street smarts and traditional skills, rather than book smarts and technical skills, to exploit their strengths rather than be held back by their weaknesses. As we have seen, many WSEP members have turned hobbies into jobs. Self-employment also allows individuals who do not work well at the bottom of a rigid hierarchy a chance to run the show.

In some countries, programs have paid unemployment benefits in a lump sum for those who want to start a business. In the United Kingdom, for example, the Enterprise Allowance Scheme was extended to 88,000 unemployed people in its first three years, and 86 percent of them were still operating their businesses three years later.[60] The cost of each job created was £650, or about $1,000. (By way of comparison, the average cost of creating employment through the Job Corps program in the United States, which focuses on wage employment for unemployed youths, is more than $15,000.) In France in 1984, one-third of all businesses started in the country were the result of a similar initiative. And all of these programs set the stage for the paradigm-breaking success of Grameen America starting in 2008.

Whether publicly or privately funded, programs that encourage self-employment offer both a way out of welfare dependency for enterprising individuals and a way to help the working poor who are stuck in dead-end jobs. WSEP offers an impressive example of the profound effect such ventures can have on people's lives. In some cases, WSEP enables a welfare mother to take out a loan and open a store or start a manufacturing or service enterprise. In others, the impact is more subtle, but no less important. Geri, Omiyale, and Queenesta, for example, joined the Full Circle Fund soon after becoming unemployed. Had they not been able to get loans and moral support to start a business—or in Omiyale's case, to recapitalize an old venture—any or all of them might have fallen into a cycle leading to welfare dependency, social isolation, and depression. Omiyale is a firm believer in that approach. "Everyone should, at least once in their life, be self-employed," she often says. "It builds character. I have said to my own children, you have to try it once. After you have created your own job, you can decide whether you want to work for someone else again."

WSEP demonstrated that access to credit, networking, and appropriate training for self-employment can play complementary roles to creating incentives for the unemployed and people on public aid to get jobs. Indeed, instead of merely pushing people to cycle between welfare and dead-end jobs, an additional set of policies and programs that open doors for self-employment can allow people to cycle in between running a business full-time, operating it part-time and working part-time, operating it part-time and working full-time, and working full-time with their business on hold. It creates more options for low-income people and allows them to explore their potential more fully; the current paradigm, in contrast, narrows options and limits potential.

Low-income African-Americans face an additional obstacle to starting a business—racism. One of WSEP's most important accomplishments has been to show that poor Black women from distressed neighborhoods can benefit from its approach. One of the reasons it has succeeded where so many initiatives have failed is that Black women have, not surprisingly, proven more willing to take a chance and join an organization run by other Black women rather than one run by people from other backgrounds. In addition, several foundations have, to their credit, been eager to fund a Black-run organization doing effective work in the inner city. Being trusted by beneficiaries, philanthropic organizations, and some government agencies has created a fertile ground for social change.

Yet, despite its success, WSEP employees, no less than the women they serve, feel the effects of racism all the same. Black professional women who work there often have difficulty hailing cabs in downtown Chicago. Connie Evans, who can remember the Ku Klux Klan marching in Franklin, Tennessee, when she was a child, is occasionally mistaken for a housekeeper by other guests when she stays at expensive hotels. When low-income white women come to WSEP orientations and find out that the organization's senior positions are all filled by Blacks, most never attend another meeting. White foundation representatives or journalists who are shown products manufactured by Black women who borrow from the Full Circle Fund often express an impolite degree of astonishment at their high quality.

A Caucasian WSEP staff member remembers having lunch with a white foundation official some years ago. Both agreed that helping Black women pull themselves up by their bootstraps was a noble objective. When the employee mentioned how appropriate it was that such work was being done by an organization headed by a Black woman, the foundation official became dismayed. Clearly embarrassed, she explained that it had never occurred to her that Connie Evans was Black. Before long she was saying, "Oh, and I had heard such *good* things about WSEP. I had no idea. . . ." After the meal was over, the employee burst into Connie's office, told her the story, and began cursing white people in a manner that would have sounded militant coming from a Black person.

Despite the reality of racism, there is a largely unknown legacy of Black entrepreneurship in the United States—a legacy that WSEP and organizations like it are trying to help revive. Even in the days of slavery, some Blacks were not only free but also prosperous farmers and merchants. Several thousand of them actually owned slaves themselves.[61] As early as 1853, northern Blacks began holding conventions on the subject of Black economic development. Their objective was to spur entrepreneurship while at the same time persuading Black consumers to buy goods produced by Black companies and sold by Black retail outlets. Leaders such as Booker T. Washington, Marcus Garvey, and Elijah Muhammad urged African-Americans to secure their economic base even as more traditional figures were arguing the nascent civil rights agenda. Yet the shadow of slavery loomed large.

"Free Blacks in antebellum America," writes one scholar, "exhibited many of the same characteristics as European immigrants: self-selection, an enterprising orientation, small [business] size, self-help institutions, and occupational niches. . . . If slavery had not existed, there would have been no large number of Blacks entering the U.S. economy, ignorant and penniless [after the Civil War]. If that [had been] the case, Blacks would have started in America on a firmer economic foundation and . . . there might be no underclass today. . . ."[62]

In a poorly conceived attempt to empower former slaves, the federal government created the Freedman's Bureau and the Freedman's Bank during

Reconstruction.[63] Neither made much headway, and the latter institution was forced to close in 1874, at which time the federal government refused to fully reimburse depositors. Only after several years did they receive 61 cents back on every dollar they had saved at the bank. This fiasco prompted W.E.B. DuBois to write, "Not even ten additional years of slavery could have done so much to throttle the thrift of the freedmen."

In recent years, however, Black establishment figures, including influential political leaders, have begun to place increasing emphasis on entrepreneurship. In many cases, they have adopted the ideas of Booker T. Washington and his focus on vocational education, self-improvement, and accommodation with whites. Present-day African-American leaders are attempting to find a more sensible balance between entitlements and responsibilities, and between economic and political empowerment. And despite its caustic rhetoric and checkered past, some attention is finally being paid to the constructive efforts of the Nation of Islam to inculcate self-respect, self-reliance, discipline, thrift, and entrepreneurship among its adherents.

Yet, at the close of the twentieth century, the rate of Black entrepreneurship remained relatively low. According to the Census Bureau, in 1990 there were only 425,000 Black-owned firms in America, an amount that accounted for 2.4 percent of all corporations, partnerships, and sole proprietorships.[64] The bureau also estimated that 3 percent of Black men were self-employed while the rate was 7.4 percent for whites, 9 percent for Chinese-Americans, and 16.5 percent for Koreans. Perhaps more important, the percentage of the nation's *assets* that African-Americans own is miniscule. Sixty percent of all Black households have a net worth of less than $10,000, and the median net worth of Black households is less than 10 percent of that of white households.[65] Lack of assets means lack of access to investment capital for potential entrepreneurs, which is compounded by the practice of redlining. Most Blacks see their future as employees and consumers, rather than as business owners and investors.

Yet it is precisely the steady progress Blacks have made as employees and consumers that may hold out promise for Black entrepreneurship, even among the poor. In 1991, African-American consumers spent an estimated $216 billion—or close to $600 million every 24 hours. In Chicago alone, Blacks spent $9.6 billion annually—a figure greater than the gross national product of all but three sub-Saharan African countries. Certain products that Blacks spend proportionately more on than on whites depend on African-American patronage for their survival. According to a 1991 article in the *Chicago Tribune*, "African-American consumers purchase 18 percent of the [nation's] orange juice, 20 percent of the rice and Scotch whisky, 26 percent of the Cadillacs, 31 percent of the cosmetics, 35 percent of soft drinks, 38 percent of the cigarettes . . . and 40 percent of the records and movie tickets."[66] (Note, however, that according to the U.S. Department of Labor, Blacks spent 20 percent *less* per household on all forms of alcohol compared to whites.) African-American males aged 13 to 24, who make up 3 percent of the U.S. population, bought one in five pairs of Nike athletic shoes.

If Black manufacturers and retailers can tap into this market, it will help them thrive. By one estimate, only 7 percent of Black spending ($15 billion) now goes toward Black manufacturers and retailers. To raise this percentage, African-American business owners can continue to educate Black consumers about the advantages of "buying Black" while at the same time doing their homework and investing wisely. Studies indicate that more than one-quarter of Black consumers take into account whether a product is being produced and sold by someone of their race, and anecdotal evidence suggests that this consciousness is growing. Thelma, Queenesta, Geri, Glenda, and Omiyale are all examples of women who have done their research, invested accordingly, appealed to racial solidarity (to varying degrees), and experienced some success. With assistance from programs like the Full Circle Fund, thousands of African-Americans (and other low-income groups) will be able to turn their undercapitalized hustles and hobbies into legitimate businesses capable of lifting them out of poverty.

Of course, this approach to poverty reduction in the United States has many skeptics, even after the previously unimaginable growth of Grameen America in the 2010s. It is true that some of the initial euphoria in the 1980s about applying the Grameen Bank model in the United States created some unrealistic expectations initially—expectations that would not be met for many years. But Omiyale, Thelma, Geri, Queenesta, and Glenda didn't really care about such matters. For them, the objectives were to borrow, invest, earn, meet family expenses, borrow again, invest again, and earn more. That they often enjoy what they do, or that they have met close friends through the program, or that they are periodically interviewed by journalists curious about their progress, is secondary. The main thing is money—how to invest it and how to make it.

Update: Since the 1990s

AFTER THE FIELD RESEARCH FOR THIS BOOK was completed in the mid-1990s, the progress of the women of WSEP was slow but steady, despite the phasing out of the Full Circle Fund and later, WSEP itself. Some of those stories are told briefly in the epilogue.

Unfortunately, the conditions in which they and thousands of other low-income entrepreneurs operate have not improved significantly, and in some ways have deteriorated. Street vending in major cities has remained under attack, most notably in New York City. Markets like Maxwell Street have been closed, moved, or scaled back. Superstores have proliferated and drawn customers with low prices that are possible only because of the large volume discounts they get from buying overseas, mostly from China. Regulations discouraging true home-based businesses (as opposed to telecommuting) have, if anything, become more restrictive. State-level banking regulations that discourage or prevent nonprofits from making business loans to low-income people forced a program in Los Angeles shut down.

Despite the reality that home-based microbusiness ownership has manifest advantages for some low-income people, particularly single mothers with more street smarts than academic credentials, it has not been recognized as a path to self-sufficiency and community uplift despite the efforts of many in the federal government and the occasional enlightened policy maker at the state or local level.

Maxwell Street Market remains a powerful case study of the neglect of microentreneurship as an important part of the economy, particularly for low-income people. After its forced relocation in 1994, the market continued to function but had lost much of its vitality and space. In September 2005, the city announced that it planned to relocate the market yet again. After several delays, this latest uprooting took place in the fall of 2008.

I am happy to report, however, that the market is still in operation 14 years later, though from the pictures on the City of Chicago's website, it seems to have lost some of its earlier character. In a conversation with Omiyale in June 2022, I learned that licensing requirements and higher fees have made it unattractive to many vendors, though Omiyale herself still sells there on occasion.

Nonetheless, the determined efforts of the now mostly forgotten activists and vendors like Thelma and Omiyale may have been decisive in ensuring that

Maxwell Street Market survived in some form. Pay it a visit on Desplaines Street the next time you pass through Chicago.

11. Dry Money in a Monsoon

BY EARLY JULY, THE 1994 MONSOON was in full swing in Bangladesh.[67] Meltwater from the Himalayas carried by swollen rivers to the Bay of Bengal was augmented by torrents of rain. Footpaths became canals, and farmland was transformed into swamps in which traditional strains of rice, jute, water lilies, and fish flourished. Dips in the dirt road leading from Zianpur to Kholshi filled with as much as four feet of water, making it impassable by bicycle or rickshaw. This tripled the length of the time it took for Grameen staff to travel to the Haldar *para*.

On July 12, Krishna traveled there the hard way. Avoiding the waist-deep canals along the main road, he weaved his way through rice fields in which the water often came up to his ankles. Still new to the area, he had to stop several times and ask farmers the most direct path to his destination. By the time he arrived at the Kholshi bazaar, he was 15 minutes late. The only way to the center hut from there was by boat, and it took him a few minutes to find someone to row him over.

As he sat down and began marking up the passbooks, women continued to arrive and fill out the groups. Many of those who were coming from other *paras* were soaked, having swum part of the way. Doing so required dexterity, as borrowers were obliged to present dry bills and passbooks to their group chairmen. Each Tuesday morning, one could sit in Amodini's veranda and watch the women swimming with one hand and holding their installments aloft with the other. Periodically, there was grumbling by Muslims who wanted the center hut moved, but it never amounted to anything. Shandha was well-liked and respected, and had lent virtually everyone money for their

282

installments on one occasion or another. So nobody was willing to push the issue.

During the previous month, Amodini had frittered her group fund loan away on traditional healers while her husband's bleeding ulcer continued to deteriorate. She had applied for an 8,000-taka general purpose loan, but Shandha and Krishna had agreed only to 5,000. It was on her return from collecting that loan that she found her husband dead. She ran to Shandha's house and cried for hours. Shandha promised to take up a collection after the next meeting to defray the funeral expenses, thereby keeping most of Amodini's loan money intact.

The demise of Amodini's husband was a reminder of the difficulty Grameen has faced in trying to break down rural superstition and reliance on faith healers. (Decades later, the COVID-19 pandemic would show that unscientific approaches to health care were hardly limited to Bangladesh or even to developing countries.) This is particularly true in isolated villages like Kholshi. On numerous occasions during the 1994 rainy season, Krishna was confronted with practices that ranged from comic to tragic. At one meeting, he noticed that most of the women had taken off their bracelets. A woman in a village some miles away was said to have dreamt that her son would die if she did not remove her bracelets. According to the story, she kept them on and then woke one morning to find that her child had died. Afterward, Krishna was dismayed by how many unadorned arms he saw. Still, he was pleased that at least one dissenter had said, "Allah gave me my son, and Allah will take him when the time is right. I'm not removing anything."

If that had been the end of it, Krishna wouldn't have been concerned. He felt that Amodini's husband's death, and the prolonged illnesses of two women in the center, would likely have been avoided with modern medical attention. Despite Krishna's warnings, precious taka had been spent on traditional healers instead. While a few borrowers did seek out qualified medical help, at times he felt dejected about how many of them continued to rely on quacks. When he heard that Supi, the current center chief, was considering spending several thousand taka on a "doctor" with no formal training to help overcome infertility so she could save her marriage, Krishna was enraged (though he could take solace in the fact that even in the case of divorce she would not be ruined, since she had registered a sizable amount of her family's land in her name since joining the bank, as required by Grameen's enlightened policies). He didn't even get involved in actively trying to discourage the practice of giving dowry, which was widespread in Kholshi and most villages in Bangladesh, Grameen or no Grameen.

Of course, there were reasons for the reliance on healers. Sometimes their treatment appeared to work, particularly when the only thing afflicting a patient was fear. More important, government hospitals were located considerable distances from many villages, were often left unstaffed, and usually offered low-quality care. Though free in theory, treatment by government doctors often came with a hefty price tag. A terrified patient would be wheeled into an operating room only to have the doctor inform him that he had no confidence in the abilities of the nursing staff or the cleanliness of the surgical instruments he had been given. The doctor would propose that the surgery be performed in his nearby private clinic, at a cost that would likely send the patient's family deep into debt. As if that wasn't enough, poor people, unable to afford hotel fees, often had no place to stay when their loved ones went into the hospital. (A bribe, however, would sometimes get them permission to sleep on the floor, alongside their relative's bed.) With the alternatives so uncertain, it was little wonder that promises from quacks to come to one's home and provide a cure for a few hundred taka were often accepted at face value. Several days after her husband died, Amodini told Shandha about her fear that her brothers would start pressuring her to move to India—which was exactly what occurred. Shandha, already reeling from the loss of four of her five sisters, strongly encouraged her to stay.

Three weeks later, Amodini was still in mourning and did not make it to her Grameen meeting (though she had given Shandha her installment). Krishna looked up from his paperwork, made sure that all the group chairmen were present, and said, "Listen. You know that it is time to elect a new center chief, don't you?"

"Yes, sir," a few women offered as they passed money back and forth.

"Well, you can begin deciding who you want to support." For the next 20 minutes, while Krishna and Shandha counted and recounted the taka, there were more animated discussions than usual. A few conversations were clearly confidential, while others were audible from Devi's hut 15 yards away. Women reached across rows and touched their group chairmen, urging them to declare themselves candidates and pledging their support. Some of the chairmen shook their heads, while others were coy.

Over a four-week period during the early part of the monsoon, tens of thousands of Grameen centers in Bangladesh rotated their leadership. While it is often a smooth process, it can occasionally be wrought with intrigue, deception, and double crosses at critical moments. The center chiefs hold the purse strings, having the power to reduce or deny loan proposals. They are the chief liaison between the bank and borrowers.

"Okay," Krishna said as he put a rubber band around the thick wad of bills he had collected. "It's time. Who do you think should be the next center chief?"

"Let it be Supi," one woman in the sixth row shouted out.

"Yes, yes," two more added.

"But you know," Krishna said with a touch of exasperation, "that Supi cannot be center chief, because she is not a group chairman this year. You know the rules, don't you?" Supi had been the fifth group's chairman for the past two years, and Grameen's bylaws had forced her to stand down a few weeks earlier.

"Sir, I don't want to stand for election," Nobirun said from the back row.

"Me neither," Zomella added from the second row, winnowing the list of candidates to five. "I think we should choose Shandha," she added, reaching forward and touching her nominee as she said the words. Before that could get very far, group one's chairman took herself out of contention. Shandha talked about how she was still depressed about her relatives' moving to India, and hinted that her husband was planning an August trip there to see if they might follow. The eligible candidates now stood at four.

Krishna had refereed dozens of elections over the years, and each was different. Some went by consensus, while in others actual votes were taken. The decision was often made before he brought it up, though occasionally the process played out in front of him. "What I think would be a good idea is if the four chairmen who are left speak up for themselves, saying why they would make a good center chief," he advised.

His proposal was greeted in silence. Finally, Zomella said, "Let it be Shandha. She can change her mind." Shandha declined again. As she did so, Krishna noticed that the normally talkative Zorina, the chairman of the third group, had hardly said a word all morning. Failing to take herself out of the running, Krishna thought to himself, was probably Zorina's way of declaring her candidacy.

Perhaps recognizing this herself, Shandha said, "I think Zorina would make a good center chief. Why don't we consider her?" Shandha's nominee smiled broadly, and within five minutes the decision was made. Zorina, after all, was a safe choice. She had been center chief once before, the first Muslim to hold the position. She had recently purchased a one-quarter share in a shallow tube well, and was receiving more than 2,000 taka in profit each winter from her investment. In short order, the chairman of the fourth group was chosen to be deputy center chief.

From the beginning of the Grameen experiment, Yunus had wanted to empower his borrowers politically as well as economically, though his early attempt to federate the centers at the village level had ended in frustration. But that hardly dampened his determination to make democracy real for his membership. Starting in 1983, when Grameen became an independent bank, borrowers were given the right to elect, from among themselves, members to Grameen's board of directors, reflecting the percentage of the bank's shares that they owned. By 1994, borrowers had bought more than 90 percent of the shares of Grameen, leaving the government's ownership at less than 10 percent and its representation on the board of directors limited. Though some accused Yunus of creating a governing body that would rubber-stamp his decisions, he felt it was an integral part of his democratic ideal. He later made rotation of center chiefs mandatory, after he had heard that some centers were being run by the same person since their inception and that elections had become a formality or, in some cases, had even been discontinued.

Yunus's belief that even people of very modest means could effectively manage their own affairs and those of the local institutions they depended on was unshakeable, provided, of course, that commonsense policies were in place to bring out the best in people.

THE AUDITORIUM ON THE THIRD FLOOR of the main building in the Grameen complex was alive with warm greetings among old friends. They were the bank's zonal managers, 12 men who were each responsible for hundreds of bank workers, tens of thousands of borrowers, and millions of taka in outstanding loans. They had gathered for the 1994 zonal managers' conference, an important forum for debate at Grameen in which participants are encouraged to criticize the head office and each other, in the belief that if peer pressure is good enough for the borrowers, it is also good enough for the zonal managers.

After a ceremony identical to the one that opens Grameen center meetings, Yunus addressed the conference. "Welcome to another family reunion. Together, we can look at where we are and where we are going." He paused and smiled, trying to put everyone at ease. "The most significant thing I can say as we look at the last year is how much more powerful Grameen has become because of our increased self-reliance and economic viability. We have been virtually free of foreign aid funds since the middle of the last year. Now, as you know, we are getting our funds from the money market and from Bangladesh Bank. Bangladesh Bank is a very clever bank run by clever people, and they have loaned us one billion taka [$25 million] during the last year—more than they have ever given to a single venture. Other banks are eager to lend to us on even more attractive terms.

"Our borrowers have increased their capability to absorb larger loans, and we have been able to meet their demand and become more financially secure in the process. Through the end of 1992, we had lent a total of $311 million. Through May 1994, our cumulative disbursement has risen to $1 billion." Yunus paused to let the figures sink in, and the zonal managers, noting the gap, looked up from their writing tablets and tried to make eye contact with the managing director. Yunus continued:

> Another way to measure our progress is that it took us seventeen years to lend our first billion dollars and yet we are on course to lend another billion between January 1994 and December 1995. We can now disburse half a billion dollars every year. One can also look at branch profitability. In 1993, one-third of all branches were profitable, and even fewer the year before that. In the first two quarters of 1994, half of the branches and half of the zones made a profit. Conservative projections indicate that 65 percent of the branches will make a profit in calendar year 1994. Now, Bangladesh Bank has promised to make a decision within twenty-four hours on any request for funds we submit to them, which befits our being the largest bank in Bangladesh. So please, tell your staff that what we dreamed about three years ago during our darkest hours has come true—even better than we dreamed.

Many of the men smiled knowingly, recalling the time when a trade union that was affiliated with the ruling Bangladesh Nationalist Party and run by disgruntled employees had brought banking operations to a virtual standstill for several weeks in 1991.

It had, indeed, been a successful year for the bank. But there were indications that as the scale of lending increased, there had been some drop-off in the quality of staff-borrower relations. Fewer staff members, some said, had time to visit sick children, inspect loan utilization, and stick up for their members in village disputes. While virtually no one doubted that many of the borrowers could, after eight or more years of borrowing, handle the large sums they were receiving, there were fears that bank workers, under pressure to increase their loan portfolios, were failing to distinguish between formerly destitute entrepreneurs who could easily invest 60,000 taka ($1,500) and women for whom a loan of 4,000 taka ($100) was plenty. In the head office, there were two schools of thought—one arguing that the increase in lending had been long overdue, the other charging that it was foolhardy. Yunus tended to fall somewhere in between the two extremes.

His opening address continued:

> There are also things in the last year that have not been positive, some of which we know about, and some of which we may not yet know about. How often, for instance, are borrowers simply taking their seasonal loans and using the money to repay their general loans? A borrower may do this occasionally, but if it is too widespread it signals future repayment problems for us.
>
> Some people have asked me about expanding the number of branches, the number of borrowers, and the number of zones. What we need to concentrate on right now is taking full responsibility for the two million poor families who have *already* joined Grameen Bank. We need to renew our sacred pledge to work with them to eliminate all signs of poverty from their lives. When the last family of those two million crosses the poverty line, our job will be complete—not before. So, one of the things I would like to do at this conference is inaugurate the concept of the poverty-free center. I am going to ask that you return to your zones and give me proposals for how we are going to measure this and make it an integral part of our planning, monitoring, evaluation, and auditing. I will also want estimates from all of you about where your zone stands now with respect to poverty-free centers and branches.

Faces were lighting up around the table, despite the growing heat and humidity in the room. (It would be years before Yunus would approve air-conditioning for the auditorium.) He went on to say:

> I will also be interested in tracking how many centers there are where every family has, and is using, a sanitary latrine. In how many centers is every school-age child in school? There are other matters we will take up in these three days—the drought in Dinajpur and Rajshahi districts, proposals to change how the group fund is operated, attacks on us by Islamic fundamentalists, and corruption with Grameen. We will hear about charges that the nonpoor are joining our old centers, and about the fundamentalists in Sylhet and Bogra, but also about the rebirth of Rangpur zone, which we considered closing down three years ago.
>
> But the main thing we need to consider is whether we are getting away from our main objectives. Are we still showing respect to all of our members, or do we treat them poorly in the rush to get all these loans out? Are we putting too much pressure on them to repay when they are in hardship, thereby creating more hardship? We need to recognize that there will be losses in this business, there will be loans that will have to be written off.
>
> Some of you have asked about our interest rates. As you know, the government continues to reduce its rates and to forgive loans, even though the beneficiaries of these loans are the wealthy people, the clever people. Yet to keep our institution strong we have not been able to do this. First, we should remind ourselves that when we raised our interest rate [on general and seasonal loans] from 16 to 20 percent in 1991, we promised ourselves that it was a temporary measure, not a permanent one.* Now,

---

* The manner in which this was done left the amount borrowers paid at the end of their loan cycle virtually unchanged. Before July 1992, borrowers paid 16 percent simple interest charged on a declining balance (thus amounting to about 8 percent of the principal) *and* a contribution into a life insurance fund that equaled one-quarter of the interest payment. When the interest rate was raised to 20 percent, the contribution into the life insurance fund was reduced to virtually zero, even though the amount paid out to deceased borrowers' families remained unchanged.

since we have made solid progress toward financial viability, we should think about reducing it. But the way I'm thinking about it, rather than actually reduce the rate we will keep it the same but divert one-fifth of the interest payments to other uses. For instance, we could create a scholarship fund that would ensure that no student in a Grameen family would be prevented from becoming a doctor or an engineer because of financial reasons. Or a health insurance fund for all of our members. The goal of this would be to ensure one hundred percent guaranteed health and education for all Grameen families. This is another thing we can talk about.

You may know about the spread of the Grameen approach internationally. We have had three thousand five hundred visitors from eighty-five countries visit Grameen in recent years, and now there are Grameen replications in more than thirty countries. And here in Bangladesh, there are 4.5 million families involved in poverty-focused lending programs. That means there are some twenty million poor Bangladeshis benefiting from Grameen or a similar program.

After Yunus completed his opening address, the 12 zonal managers each detailed the state of their zones. A few were frank about their failures and frustrations, while others painted unabashedly rosy pictures of the branches and areas they were supervising. Other officials also spoke. One was running a project to gain a foothold in the national and international textile market for Bangladeshi weavers, including some 50,000 Grameen borrowers who had taken loans for spinning and weaving. He said that in October 1993, the cumulative production by weavers who were cooperating with Grameen (many of whom were not Grameen borrowers) was 250,000 yards. By August 1994, that was their *monthly* production, and it was hardly keeping up with the demand. Others described experimental projects to develop fisheries, agriculture, health care, and biogas. One of the two women in the room talked about her UNICEF-funded program of training Grameen borrowers to be village midwives, and how it had appeared to cut maternal death rates in half.

The conference continued for three days. At times it was deadly boring, while at others, it alternated among invigorating, tense, and comic. Yunus was present virtually the entire time, and approved nearly every zonal manager's request to innovate and experiment. He appeared engaged but permissive. When one zonal manager gave a speech about the need to combat the fundamentalist threat by "going to the mosque more often to prove that we are good Muslims," Yunus nodded without noticeable emotion. On a few matters, though, he put his foot down. Someone suggested expanding the number of job classifications for which shoes were provided as work aids, and Yunus immediately dismissed the proposal. Keeping costs under control was clearly a priority for him.

With the conference nearing its end on the third day, Yunus made his closing address. He tried to capture all the elements of the conference, and the state of Grameen, through use of the English phrase *critical mass*. He proposed to his colleagues that over the past 12 months, the bank had made a quantum leap in its capacity to cause socioeconomic change and respond to institutional challenges.

His closing address ended with these words:

> We have met the fundamentalists, who have raised protests, burned our documents, incited people, and so forth, by organizing at the local level. Rather than overreact, we told the borrowers to stick up for what is theirs, and in the process many people who had never supported us before have now come to our side. This is not a threat anymore, but an annoyance. Certain zones have invented new slogans in which borrowers chant how they will support people who support them and organize against people who organize against them. We will copy and distribute these slogans, and the lessons learned from all this local organizing. I would almost say that the disturbances of the last year have been a blessing for us, not a curse. This is critical mass.
>
> Furthermore, we have unprecedented political strength. If we can ensure one hundred percent voting among the two million Grameen families in the next elections by ensuring one hundred percent registration now, the impact will be enormous. This is critical mass. We have fifty million dollars in group fund savings, and millions more in other savings accounts. There is not a single company in Bangladesh that we could not buy with our borrowers' collective savings. That is critical mass. We are now the biggest bank in the country, and we loan more money in rural Bangladesh than all the other banks combined. Our

borrowers have achieved this, and we have simply played the role of facilitator. Things that used to take us years, like the time for a branch to be profitable, are being cut in half. Now we must take advantage of this critical mass and accelerate the process of eliminating poverty from the lives of each and every member of Grameen Bank.

THE COURTYARD WAS BUSTLING WITH ACTIVITY. On a veranda, Nonibala Ghosh was cutting a tin pan full of *sandesh* (white sweets that look like small Christmas cookies) into bite-size pieces to be sold at a village festival later that afternoon. Inside the hut in which Nonibala and her husband slept, her 12-year-old son cranked the handle of a rusty machine that skimmed the cream off the milk he had poured into it. The cream would be used to make ghee. (Ghee is clarified butter, which is butter that has been simmered and strained to remove all water.) Another son stoked the flames underneath an industrial-size pan in which the milk would be cooked until it was ready to be transformed into cottage cheese.

Flies hovered over the tins of milk outside the hut that had yet to go through the creamer. A few feet from the oven, four cows were tied up, their heads buried in bowls of feed. Later, they would receive the special treatment that comes as a result of being owned by a Ghosh household—they would be fed whey, a by-product of cottage cheese production. People in the village said that that was what kept Noni's cows healthier than anyone else's.

Nonibala's eldest son walked his bike into the compound, having traversed a two-foot-deep canal that divided the household from Kholshi's main road during the rainy season. Strapped on the bicycle were two plastic containers that each contained about 10 gallons of milk he had procured from Bagutia. Earlier, Noni's youngest son had brought 10 gallons from the Zianpur bazaar, and Gopal, her husband, 30 from the Kholshi market.

"How much?" Noni called out to her son.

"Twelve, got it for twelve today." Buying milk for 12 taka per kilogram meant big profits for the household. (In Bangladesh, milk and other liquids are measured by weight, not volume. One kilogram is roughly equal to one quart or one liter. Thus, the price of milk in this example is 48 taka, or $1.20, per gallon.) The day before, Noni's eldest son had traveled to Dhaka to deliver a large order of cottage cheese, and he'd be making another delivery today. The family had a contract with a confectionery shop in the Kalabagan neighborhood to deliver whatever quantity of *chhana* (cottage cheese) it requested the evening before. That meant that each day, two of the men in the family packed up the *chhana*, laid it across the bicycles' crossbars, and began a 12-mile trip to Aricha, where one of the two would board a bus going to Dhaka to make the delivery and take the following day's order. When there were transportation strikes, the men would suck it up and bicycle the entire 60 miles from Aricha to Dhaka, returning the next morning.

Because of the low price of milk that day, Noni's family would likely see a profit of 400 taka ($10) from the cottage cheese and be able to make another 300 taka worth of ghee. But when the price of milk exceeds 15 taka per kilogram, as it does several times each year for a month or two, they are forced to absorb short-term losses to fulfill their contract.

For Gopal and Nonibala Ghosh and their five sons and three daughters, such risk-taking and profits are fairly recent phenomena. In 1987, the family was landless and owned very few assets. They earned money making ghee and *doi* (yogurt), but didn't have enough working capital to buy even one *maund* (10 gallons) of milk and had no cows of their own. All their dairy products had to be bought in the market. They often had to take loans from village moneylenders at 10 percent interest per month, and when they did, at least half of their profits went to loan sharks. There was rarely enough food to go around, especially when the price of milk was high.

Nonibala was born in 1950 in the village of Munshikandi, in a Ghosh *para* a short distance from the home of Lutfa, the paralyzed borrower described in chapter seven. Despite the size of her family, she doesn't remember considering her family poor—at least not the kind of poverty she came to know after her marriage. Her parents made ghee, *doi*, *chhana*, and sweets and sold them locally and in Dhaka. The family was not free from tragedy, however; her youngest brother died in childhood from typhoid fever, and her youngest sister succumbed to diarrhea as an infant.

Nonibala, who never attended a day of school, remembered spending her childhood bringing food to her male siblings and relatives when they worked in the fields. She recalls that when she turned 13, the marriage proposals began coming in. The first four were turned down when someone in Noni's extended family found something objectionable about the boy or his family. The fifth came from a well-known Ghosh family in Kholshi, and a union was arranged. A traditional Hindu wedding was held, but Noni thought it strange that the role usually played by her mother-in-law was taken by her husband's aunt instead.

After moving in with Gopal Ghosh's family, she learned that her mother-in-law was actually her stepmother-in-law. She was also told that Gopal's mother had died soon after giving birth to her only son, and that Noni's husband stood to gain as many as 10 acres in inheritance from his deceased mother. Arguments over who had the right to the land broke out soon after the wedding, and Gopal promptly filed a lawsuit against his father. Over the years, legal bills accumulated, and both father and son were forced to sell off land to pay them off. The two rarely talked to each other, although—in a nod to their deepening poverty—to save money, they often traveled together by rickshaw to the Manikganj courthouse. By the time Noni's father came to Kholshi and resolved the dispute by calling a *salish* (village court), the family had been ruined.

When Noni heard about Grameen Bank in 1987, she attended an informal community meeting at which Mannan Talukdar spoke. What he said interested her enough to convince her to go to the Kholshi bazaar for a "projection meeting" described in chapter three that was attended by some 6,000 people. Within days, she started forming a group. Before long, two groups were set—Shandha would chair one, Noni the other. It took them more than a month to undergo group training, during which several women learned to sign their names. After recognition and the submission of loan proposals, the 10 women went to the Zianpur bazaar to get their first loans. Though Noni was eager to receive her 2,500 taka and expand her business, she respected the Grameen practice of giving the first two loans to the neediest women in the group. In her case, they were Aduree and Zomella. She received hers in due course.

The family suddenly went from being unable to afford one *maund* of milk to being able to purchase six. For the first time in years, there was no need to rely on the village moneylender. Production, and profits, grew noticeably. After joining the bank, she sent her son to work in another Ghosh household to learn how to make cottage cheese, as she had a dream of resurrecting her father's business. Her son spent 18 months there and learned the trade. But on one of his last trips to deliver *chhana* to Dhaka, he was in a bus accident. The medical treatment cost Noni 16,000 taka, causing her to temporarily disinvest from her business. The 1988 flood hurt, too. But they were always able to make their weekly installment, and each new loan meant a replenishment of—if not an increase in—their working capital.

By early 1993, with Noni in possession of four cows of her own, the family, through her son, was ready to try to get a *chhana* contract in Dhaka. When the family her son had worked for learned of his plans to secure a contract, they threatened to kill him. An agreement was ultimately reached with one store owner, but to avoid suspicion, Noni's husband signed it on behalf of the family, instead of having her son do it. They told the store owner they were from another district, which helped ensure that no one would discover that Nonibala's son was involved.

Chhana production was profitable for 9 or 10 months of the year, and with a line of credit from the Grameen Bank, the family could bear the losses when the price of milk went up. If the need arose, Noni could take a loan from her group's joint savings fund.

Occasionally, Noni would talk about her progress. The family had four cows and a *chhana* contract by mid-1993. They were able to eat better than ever, buy new clothes for everyone, and marry off the eldest daughter—no small feat, considering that wedding expenses and dowry totaled 45,000 taka ($1,125). She worked hard, but the tension that comes from living in poverty was gone.

Noni has been the center chief once, but if the women had their way, she would have been elected two or three times. She enjoyed the authority that came with the position, but it took up too much of her time. After she began *chhana* production in 1993, she had hardly an hour of spare time between dawn and 10 p.m. In any case, she somtimes thought, people came to her anyway for advice, whether she was center chief or not. Her center was unique in that its two most powerful women—Noni and Shandha—were rather shy and unassuming, rarely speaking up during meetings unless the situation called for it. Supi, the most influential Muslim, was also rather reserved. Other women were full of bluster, but never earned the full respect of their peers to the degree that these three women had.

Cutting *chhana* was no simple task. After heating the milk slowly toward the boiling point, all the while stirring it to prevent it from turning, Noni would have her sons quickly transfer the hot milk into a metal canister. After letting it cool a few degrees, they'd measure out the whey, mix it in, and then carry the canister to a small pond, where it would be submerged in order to cool. Finally, this yielded a mix of cottage cheese and whey that they later separated using thin towels that served as sieves. It was a process that looked easy enough, but errors of only a few degrees or seconds could ruin a batch. This day, with an order of 50 kilograms of cottage cheese, required them to repeat the process four times.

Later that afternoon, the *chhana* was loaded on to the two bicycles and the boys cycled off with their loads. It was 4:00, and with luck they would arrive at the shop in Dhaka by 7:30. They would collect 3,500 taka and head to Aricha, where they would stay overnight with relatives. While they all slept, the *chhana* was turned into a dozen or more varieties of sweets by the store owner.

Wiping her forehead with her sari, Nonibala further smudged the dot of vermillion on her forehead. She lifted up the first canister of whey and carried it over to the trough where the cows were feeding. As she poured it in, one of the cows let out a loud belch while the other dug in. When she was done, there was cow dung to be packed into fuel cakes, though she was likely to give that task to her eldest son's wife. Then came bathing, cooking the evening meal, and preparing the ghee.

On a brief break from work, Nonibala reflected on the difference in life since she'd joined Grameen. "We have made ourselves a proud Ghosh family again. Just like people used to come to my father's place to congregate, gossip, and buy ghee, *doi*, and sweets, they are coming to our house now. I can help out my neighbors when they fall into difficulty, like my father did when he was alive. We may have more flies than most households," she said with a smile, "but I'm not sure you could find one that is more hardworking or more happy." That was as close as Nonibala Ghosh was ever likely to come to bragging.

Update: Since the 1990s

DURING THE LAST COUPLE OF DECADES, the achievement of critical mass that Yunus was describing in 1994 gained steam within Grameen and the microfinance movement globally. One can argue, as I often do, that the 150 million families connected to MFIs around the world represent the most successful effort to organize the world's poor in human history. New possibilities emerge every time Grameen or the wider movement reaches a new milestone in its growth.

For example, in seeking to address the chronic health problems faced by its borrowers, a sister company called Grameen Kalyan launched dozens of health centers alongside Grameen Bank branches in the mid-1990s. The achievements of this initiative would have been impossible if not for the infrastructure and relationships that Grameen Bank already had in place. To take an even more dramatic example, Grameen launched a solar energy company that installed more rural, home-based photovoltaic systems than anyone ever had before (or since). More recently, so-called fintech companies with interest in social impact have often developed partnerships with microfinance institutions.

Grameen's strategy of ensuring that most of the shares of the bank are owned by its poor clients has been adopted by some other microfinance institutions, such as Activists for Social Alternatives (ASA), a leading organization heavily influenced by Yunus that is based in South India. The Filipino MFI CARD, like ASA a longtime Grameen Foundation partner, adopted a similar ownership structure that included clients.

Even people who had questioned the soundness of this strategy recognized its merits in 2007, when the Mexican MFI Compartamos went public and generated hundreds of millions of dollars for its owners, who were mostly international agencies, wealthy Mexican investors, and its employees. In fact, the offering was so popular with investors that it earned the existing shareholders annual returns of approximately 100 percent compounded annually over an eight-year period. The clients of this controversial organization, which charged more than 100 percent effective interest at the time of the public offering, did not benefit from the windfall because, unlike their counterparts in Bangladesh, they had no ownership stake in the institution from which they borrowed.

After analyzing the IPO, Janet McKinley, a retired finance executive and major donor to Grameen Foundation and Oxfam America, suggested a possible solution. In the future, any MFI that benefits from philanthropic grants or below-market loans (as Compartamos did) should agree to allow their clients to buy nonvoting shares at pre-IPO prices in the event that their microlender goes public, so they can share in the windfall. While people debated the right approach, it was clear that an often-overlooked aspect of Yunus's philosophy and how he applied it to Grameen Bank's ownership structure had new relevance to a fast-evolving movement that was beginning to take on some of the best, and some of the worst, features of traditional commercial banking.

For his part, Yunus was critical of the Compartamos IPO and the business model and mindset that it was based on. While quite a few people believed that it sent a positive signal to the capital markets that microfinance was now a mainstream asset class, he disagreed. "Some are saying that the IPO will give a significant boost to the 'credibility' of microcredit in global capital markets," he argued. "But that's my fear, because it is the wrong kind of 'credibility.' It is leading microcredit in the moneylenders' direction. The only justification for making tremendous profit would be to let the borrowers enjoy it, along with or instead of external profit-driven investors. The ideal model would be one that puts full or majority ownership of the MFI in the hands of its clients."

12. The Black on Black Love Festival

TWO YOUNG BLACK MEN in their early twenties entered the store.[68]

"Hey, Queen," one said as he approached the counter.

"Hey, how you doing?" Queenesta replied, talking loudly over "Level of a Gangster," a song by the rap group Top Authority, that was being pumped out of a pair of speakers on opposite ends of the Hip Hop Shop.

"Oh, all right. Listen, you got that MC Eiht cassette in yet?"

"Naw, that's not gonna be released until the first week in July. I'll have it here the day it's released." MC Eiht was the hottest new rap artist, and Queenesta had been getting requests for his new release for at least a week. Among the songs the tape would contain were "Niggaz That Kill," "Compton Cyco," and "Nuthin' But the Gangsta." That's how they do it, she often thought; they begin building up demand for a product and then delay putting it on the market until people can't bear it any longer. Young people, she and recording company executives knew, love to have what they can't get.

The second young man stood silently alongside his friend. His eyes wandered around the Hip Hop Shop, darting from an eclectic collection of posters hanging behind the main counter to a second, smaller case holding compact discs, sunglasses, and a few pieces of hematite jewelry, imported from Nigeria.

Shirts for sale were printed with Black Pride messages, abstract art, and pictures of rap artists. Most of the baseball caps she stocked were blank with adjustable leather straps in the back; that, as Queenesta was discovering, was the preferred style that summer. In the back of the store was a black wooden cabinet filled with jars of penny candy, incense, and Snickers bars that went for 50 cents. Next to that was a metal rack filled with potato chips made by a Black-owned company that put Afrocentric antiviolence messages on the backs of the bags.

"You sell beepers?" one of them asked Queenesta as his friend squatted down and looked through the cassettes at the bottom of the case. (The rap tapes were displayed there, while the *dusties* and gospel titles were kept on top to attract the older crowd. Her more mature customers might get offended when they saw the rap titles and leave the store in a huff. Queenesta knew that teenagers, on the other hand, would look until they found what they wanted.)

"Yeah, a Bravo Plus will run you eighty bucks. If you have a beeper, I can turn it on for twenty-five."

"What's the monthly charge?"

"Ten bucks, and another five if you want voice mail. Here, let me show you a Bravo Plus. And we sell cases, too." Initially, Queenesta's agreement with the beeper wholesaler, Chicago Pagers, earned her $5 in commission for each $10 she brought in. Later, she successfully negotiated a 20 percent increase in her commission.

The young man who had been looking at the music stood up. "Let me see that one," he said, pointing to a cassette titled "Straight Up Gangsta Shit: Volume 2." The case had an illustration of three menacing-looking Black men holding smoking handguns. It was one of several "mixed" tapes Queenesta carried that contained copies of popular rap and hip-hop tunes, and was one of her most consistent sellers. In the beginning, she bought the so-called hot mixes from the wholesaler, but over time she began meeting the mixers and buying directly from them.

On this hot summer afternoon, another man in his twenties stopped by and asked for one of the preferred mixes. Queenesta opened the case from the back and plucked out a copy of the cassette. Under it were two more. "Here," she said as she handed it to him, "do you want to see a playlist?"

"Yeah," he replied as he studied the cassette's cover. It glorified defiant Black men who made fortunes through illegal and violent means. Images like that were stirring up controversy around the country—in op-ed columns, town hall meetings, and living rooms of the poor and the wealthy; among people who were Black, brown, and white. They made Queenesta uncomfortable, but they sold. So they stayed, at least for now. The best she tried to do was push positive, nonviolent rap artists like Arrested Development to customers she thought might be open to them.

Queenesta grabbed a black, three-ring notebook from behind the counter, opened it, and fingered through various mimeographed papers held in plastic covers. When she found the list of songs on the cassette, she handed it to her customer. He read it over, his feet tapping to the beat of a new song that was playing in the store.

"How much is this?" he asked, showing Queenesta the cover of the tape.

"Nine forty-nine, plus tax."

He reached into the pocket of his baggy shorts, pulled out a $20 bill, and handed it to Queenesta. "Here."

She clutched it, and as she headed to the back where she kept her cash register, she said, "That's ten twenty-two. Do you want a bag?"

"Naw."

The young man who had come with his friend was looking at the beepers through the store's third glass display case had a look of wonder on his face. As Queenesta gave the customer his change, he said, "I'm gonna come back next week and pick up one of those. How many months do I need to pay in advance?"

"Just one."

"Thanks," he said as the two began moving to the door. "I'll see you next week." Queenesta did her best business right after payday.

As the two walked out the door, a person inside the store could hear the new customer saying, "That's cool."

Queenesta looked at her watch. It was almost time to pick up Shayna from day camp. This meant closing the store for a few minutes at just the time business usually picked up, but such were the realities of being an entrepreneur and a single mother. As she locked the door and pulled the gate shut, she taped a handwritten note on the glass door. It read, "Be back in five minutes."

After they returned, Queenesta talked to Shayna about her day in between helping customers. She was training her daughter to sell the candy, as she had visions of Shayna going into business for herself one day, perhaps running a Hip Hop Shop location after it became a franchise. It kept her occupied and purposeful, and out of trouble.

Queenesta sometimes worried when Shayna played out on the street with the kids who lived in the apartment above the Hip Hop Shop. Those children spent most of their time unsupervised and had already lost one of their siblings to social workers from the Department of Child and Family Services. She was afraid that Shayna would develop a hard, street-wise edge. When Queenesta saw her daughter carrying the youngest child on her hip one day, she rebuked her. Babies, she told Shayna later, do not take care of babies.

Some of the teenagers who visited the Hip Hop Shop on that sweltering afternoon in late June seemed to know Queenesta; they tended to linger for a while after they had made their purchases. A few were allowed to come back behind the counter and switch the tape that was playing on the stereo, while others who were less bold just asked Queenesta to change the music. The ones who didn't know her tended to come and go quicker, though they sometimes fell into conversation with her or other customers. Queenesta was eager to get to know the young people who came into her store.

Some of the guys who came in that night bought cassettes and candy, while two purchased baseball caps and another gave her a beeper to turn on. The store was loud, lively, and frequented almost exclusively by Blacks, most of them young, many arriving in groups of two or more. The phone rang frequently, though sometimes Queenesta let it go through to her answering machine. On one occasion, a call came for a young man looking through the cassette case. It was sticky and hot, the humidity relieved only by two fans that pointed toward the area where customers stood.

At 8:30, Nixon arrived. Shayna gave him a big hug when he walked through the door, and he was soon bantering with customers and telling Queenesta about his day. Whenever someone left the store, he invariably called out in a loud voice, saying, "I'll holler at you later, guy."

Though the hours written on the front door indicated that the Hip Hop shop closed at 8:00, on this day Queenesta kept it open until five past nine. When the three of them locked it up, pulling iron gates behind the glass windows and the door, chaining them to cement pillars, and activating the alarm system, Queenesta and Shayna got in her Honda while Nixon headed to his beat-up van and drove to his apartment. Shayna would be in bed by 10:00.

As Queenesta was pulling out of her parking space, she looked at a storefront around the corner. Painted on its blue awning were the words "Moonlight Records—Tapes and CDs." Work was going on inside; preparations, she imagined, for a July 1 opening. She frowned as she stared, but tried to put what she saw out of her mind for the moment. She thought she knew why this store had come to her block, but instead of simply ruing her bad luck, she was devising a plan to confront her new competition. It was a good plan—but would it be good enough?

THELMA ARRIVED FIRST. Then Leverta Pack knocked on the front door of Geri's house on West Fifty-Ninth Street, in the heart of Englewood. A few minutes later, Queenesta's car drove up. As they waited for Omiyale, the four women exchanged small talk and tried to entertain Shayna.

"How much you do today, Queenesta?" Thelma asked.

"Uh, about $250. And I got three new beeper customers. I think in a few months, I'll be able to pay my rent through income from beepers."

"That's good."

Queenesta was dressed in a plain white shirt with three-quarter sleeves, shorts, and sandals. Her hair was still closely shorn from when she had it cut at the end of the Black Expo in McCormick Place, in a booth a few stalls down from her own. She and Nixon had grossed nearly $1,000 at the event, in addition to $200 they made at the store on Saturday. They sold sunglasses, T-shirts they had printed from drawings made by local artists, and African artifacts they were selling for a former tenant of Victor's (on which Queenesta's commission was 30 percent of the retail price). Thelma, vending from a stall in the next room, made $1,100 on dollar earrings, rings ranging from 25 cents to a buck apiece, necklaces that ran as much as $3, toys, snappers, whoopee cushions, and oils. Her best customers were children and teens. Parents seemed happy to bring their youngsters to her table—they could get something for each of their kids and still spend less than $10. Her daughter Shashona helped out on Friday and ran her table at Maxwell Street on Sunday. When she made good money, as she did that weekend, Thelma paid her daughter $20 or $30.

As the women waited for Omiyale, Leverta Pack asked Geri about the gift baskets she had sold for Mother's Day. Thelma let Geri know that she had found a new wholesaler for fabric and proposed that they make a bulk purchase together. A knock on the door interrupted the discussion. It was Omiyale. She walked in, greeted everyone, and settled into an empty chair.

It was July 12, time for the Lindblom center's loan committee and Les Papillons to hold a joint meeting to discuss Omiyale's loan proposal. If they approved, the women would sign off on it that night and Omiyale could submit it to Colete for final approval. At the center meeting the night before, Thelma and Geri had studied the paperwork, but time had run out. They had scheduled this meeting to go over the proposal in depth.

"Well, here it is," Omiyale began. "How do you want to go over this?" She held up a document consisting of about fifteen pages—a filled-in Full Circle Fund loan application.

"Omiyatta, I didn't see your cash flow for nineteen ninety-three when I looked over your loan packet last night," Thelma said. Her voice, with a noticeable edge to it so early in the evening, suggested rough waters ahead.

"I have, you know, cash flow for the last twelve months and the next twelve months' projections." Thelma thought Omiyale should have information from January 1993 onward. After some back-and-forth, the two agreed, with the concurrence of Leverta Pack, that what she had was sufficient. Then they turned to other issues.

"What parts should I go over?" Omiyale asked.

"Omiyatta, you need to go over *all* of it," Thelma said, drawing out the world *all* for effect. After the trouble the group had gone through during the last year, Thelma wasn't going to leave any stone unturned as they scrutinized Omiyale's current proposal.

"Okay, Name, Veronica DuPart." She read her address, phone number, and Social Security number. "Gross income from business in June, twelve hundred fifty-seven dollars. Other members of the household earning money in June: Jahlillah, three hundred dollars; Paul DuPart, twenty-one hundred dollars; Oloo, two hundred dollars. My products: African imports and general merchandise. How long have you been operating your business? Since nineteen ninety-one." As Omiyale read off sections detailing other aspects of her business, Thelma wrote furiously on a piece of paper.

"Current savings, one hundred sixty dollars. Inventory from warehouse, four hundred dollars. Amount of loan requested, five thousand three hundred seventy-five dollars. Term, eighteen months. Payment, one hundred forty-four dollars . . . Now here's the section where I break down what I'm going to spend it on. A used commercial oven, twelve hundred fifty dollars. Ladies' dresses, fifty pieces at twenty-five dollars each. Novelty toys, eight hundred forty-two pieces at fifty cents each. Hats, one hundred seventeen at five dollars each. Glow lights, twelve tubes at thirty-nine dollars each. Twelve dozen bangles, and they cost one dollar each. Do you want to hear all of these?"

"Yes," Thelma and Queenesta said in unison. Leverta nodded, while Geri sat still, expressionless.

"Two hundred eighty-eight pieces of earrings, which will cost me two hundred eighty-eight dollars. Twelve dozen anklets at a dollar fifty each and twelve dozen necklaces at two dollars each. And then two hundred fifty dollars goes in the emergency loan fund."

"Are you going to use the oven in your home?" Thelma asked.

"Yes."

"Why aren't you including the flour and butter and sugar you need for your cookies in your proposal?"

"No, I already . . . I have them already, and I will finance any more I need out of my profit."

There was a brief silence in the room. Thelma was weighing whether or not to pry further. She suspected that some of the loan money would be diverted to buy the ingredients Omiyale needed to make the cookies, and thought the proposal should reflect that. Was her friend overextending herself again? Was she planning on using the money to buy a plane ticket for her planned trip to Africa? Upon reflection, Thelma decided to let it go, at least for the moment.

"And here are the places where I will be selling," Omiyale began, breaking the silence. "Out of my home, at the Georgia Fest, the Cocofest, the Ghana Fest. . . ."

"Do you have deposits put down on these events, or are these just projections? I want to know if you're locked in or just thinking about it, Omiyatta."

"I don't have deposits on all of them. Just some of them." Thelma scrunched up her face in a way that showed she clearly did not approve. "But *you* weren't locked into the festivals you were doing when you did your loan pa—"

"When I put together my loan packet," Thelma shot back, "I was locked into *every* festival except Windows to Africa in September. I had put deposits down on *all* of them."

The meeting was tense, but Omiyale had expected as much. The preceding months had reduced her from founder and leader of the Lindblom center to a borrower whose judgment was open to question. After all the strokes she had received from people associated with WSEP, her fall from grace had left her somewhat bitter.

The previous Saturday, Omiyale had found refuge from her pain in an unlikely place. She had been invited to make a presentation about WSEP at a conference held in Washington, D.C., to a grassroots, nonprofit antipoverty advocacy group called RESULTS (which stands for Responsibility for Ending

Starvation Using Legislation, Trimtabbing, and Support). Connie had been asked to recommend one of her borrowers to go and speak, and she'd suggested Omiyale. The conference organizers had agreed that she would be able to sell handmade jewelry to the 300 conference-goers from a table in the back of the room after she gave her speech.

RESULTS (which I served for three years as its legislative director) is a unique organization in modern American politics. Founded in 1980 by Sam Daley-Harris, a former high school music teacher, it combined New Age philosophy and Sixties idealism with an impressive capacity to play political hardball. Overwhelmingly white and middle class (especially in that era), it has made significant contributions to the fight against world hunger by arm-twisting legislators into rerouting foreign aid funds toward new, innovative antipoverty initiatives and refocusing existing programs for the poor. Muhammad Yunus is a board member and a fan. In fact, it was partly at his urging that the organization had begun focusing more on domestic poverty in the late 1980s. The invitation to Omiyale was a step in that direction.

Early in the conference, RESULTS staff reviewed the year's accomplishments. Among those mentioned were millions of dollars in foreign assistance funds being shifted to health and education projects and a successful campaign to have the U.S. government make a $2 million grant to Grameen Trust, which Yunus had set up to spread his microlending model internationally. Omiyale was impressed. Here were people coming from all over the world, at their own expense, who had developed close relationships with their legislators and who were using those contacts to improve the plight of poor people. That such things went on had never occurred to her. Years had passed since she had participated in marches with Paul, and she felt politically impotent. Only once had she called her congressman, when Hkeem was having some difficulty in the Marines. She never heard back. Yet, these middle-class white folks were volunteering hundreds of hours a year to ensure that legislation be passed to enable poor people around the world and in the United States to borrow money as she was doing from WSEP.

When Omiyale took part with two other speakers in a panel discussion on microlending at 6:00 that evening, she told the story, haltingly at first, of how she had been laid off, found out about the Full Circle Fund, joined, and began borrowing, investing, and earning. She talked about other circle members, how they hustled and peddled and earned enough to stay afloat. The audience was spellbound, and after a short time many eyes in the crowd were moist.

Though they had been provided reading material on efforts to replicate the Grameen Bank in the United States, most of them had never been able to visualize it working. Yet, in a presentation that less than 15 minutes, Omiyale DuPart broke down the unspoken fear that the inner city was too far gone for Grameen-style projects to help. When she finished, Les Papillons' chairlady was given a rousing ovation. Later that evening and the following day, she sold nearly $500 worth of her jewelry and engaged in scores of animated conversations. Never had Omiyale been around so many white people and felt so comfortable with them. To the conference participants, she was not just a vendor but an inspiration and a source of hope. After so many months of struggle, it was an energizing experience.

Back in Geri's house and confronting a more skeptical crowd, Omiyale ran off a list of events at which she planned to vend from July through January, carefully noting which she had put deposits on and which she had not. She went on to describe the profit margin on all of her goods. She planned to sell the imports she brought back from Africa for quadruple what she'd paid for them, whereas for merchandise bought in the United States the markup was typically half that. If she could pick up goods at a going-out-of-business sale or auction, her margin would be higher.

She told the group of her plan to build up her production capacity to 2,000 packages of cookies per month, on which, if she sold all of them, her profit would be more than $1,300. With the new oven, she reported, she could make 100 packages in three hours, rather than the eight or nine it had taken her in the spring. Thelma pressed Omiyale on her plans to market the cookies until she was satisfied, while Queenesta questioned her projections for selling merchandise at fall and winter events, when business is usually slower. After more than two hours, the four women agreed to sign off on the proposal. Relieved, Omiyale passed around a form on which all the women put their signature.

Over the next two weeks, Omiyale prepared for her trip to Africa to buy merchandise. On July 27, she departed Chicago for Senegal and Gambia, money in hand and hopes high. The worst was over for Omiyale DuPart; it was time to get her business back on track.

IN JULY, QUEENESTA'S STORE BEGAN its fourth month of operation. A few days before Moonlight Records opened, she dropped her cassette prices and commissioned a struggling Black artist to make up a sign that read "Sale—All Cassettes $8.99." She paid him $20 for his efforts. Sales increased, but her profit margin, already thin, grew even smaller. (Queenesta would get current cassettes for roughly $6.50. The wholesaler or distributor was able to buy them in bulk from the record companies for about $1 less than that.) By then, Queenesta had confirmed her theory about why Moonlight had chosen a location so close to hers. It was being run by the brother of the man who ran the distributorship from which she bought most of her compact discs and cassettes wholesale. When they had seen Queenesta's sales increase substantially during the spring, they realized that she had a good location— one that they now planned to run her out of. Belatedly, Queenesta started buying from another wholesaler so that neither of them could get a clear picture of how her sales were going. But by then, the wholesaler's brother had committed himself to the location on North Avenue.

The impact of her competition, however, was not as severe as she had feared. When her copies of MC Eiht arrived, she sold out. A few loyal customers told her they had put off buying it until she got it in, which encouraged her. Another popular title, Big Mike's "Something Serious," was also going fast. By the middle of July, she was holding her own against Moonlight. Many Hip Hop Shop customers stuck with her, and the beeper business continued to grow. Baseball caps, T-shirts, sunglasses, and candy were steady sources of profit.

One day, a Black teenager came into the Hip Hop Shop and told Queenesta that he didn't feel comfortable in Moonlight. It was a revealing comment. She had created one of the few places in the neighborhood where Black teenage boys could come in and not evoke fear and suspicion. Korean and white store owners were considered the worst, glaring at Black teens— increasingly through bulletproof glass—and often asking them to make a quick purchase or move on. Even stores owned by Black adults, such as Moonlight, often did little to make teenagers of their own race feel welcome. It was if every 17-year-old kid was a gang member scheming to rip them off, and it made the young men angry.

Queenesta tried to create a different environment. No bulletproof windows, no partitions, no glaring. She said hello to all her customers, even the few she had heard were involved with the two local gangs, the Four Corner

Hustlers and the Gangster Insanes. If someone wanted to hear a tape, she played it. If the kids wanted to stick around for a while and talk with their friends, she let them. Many of the teenagers, in turn, realized when they were getting in the way of other customers, and moved to the sidewalk when it got crowded. They brought their friends to her store, and avoided Moonlight. They felt comfortable enough to approach her on the street and ask her when she was getting a particular tape in. It was not that she was oblivious to the fact that there were some bad apples; on two occasions, she caught kids trying to steal CDs from her case. But she was unwilling to run yet another place that indiscriminately treated young Black men in an inhumane way. Her attitude was generous; but more important, it was good business.

Her approach was paying off handsomely. Sales often totaled more than $200 per day, and were growing. Queenesta talked hopefully about opening another store in late August that would concentrate on beepers. A Black Muslim friend who worked for Motorola had promised to help her to set up a system so that she could turn beepers on herself.

For reasons that escaped many people at the time, including me, Thelma Ali had nagging doubts about what Queenesta was doing. To her, it all seemed too much, too soon. She didn't care for Nixon, and had reservations about mixing romance and business. The idea of opening up a second store so soon was too much for her rather conservative tastes. Thelma wanted to talk to Queenesta about her business at center meetings, possibly to allay some of her fears, but Queenesta often arrived late. She explained that she hadn't been able to close her store early because Nixon was working a plumbing job. The other women accepted her excuses, but Thelma's misgivings persisted.

THELMA ARRIVED AT 9:45, 15 minutes before the event was supposed to start. Shashona and her friend Luanda were with her to help out, and it appeared that they were the first to arrive. Confused, they spent their first few minutes wandering around the grounds of 4300 South Federal Street, one of the high-rises of the Robert Taylor Homes, a public housing project. Thelma was looking for the organizer of the Black on Black Love Festival, but she was nowhere to be found.

As Thelma glanced around, she grimaced. The concrete and dirt patches were covered with broken glass, and the fencing was rusted and covered with grass and weeds. The buildings looked innocent enough at 10:00 in the morning, but she knew better. Many of the women living here were drug users. Kids had little or no adult supervision, and gangs were said to run the entire operation. As she watched a few young men walk lazily from one building to another, Thelma said, to no one in particular, "Role models need to be people, not just things you read about in books."

Around her were a few big black plastic bags full of merchandise she planned to sell. On this day, her inventory was limited to goods that retailed for $1 or less. She had sold at housing projects before, and knew that the people who lived there didn't have much money. The event probably wouldn't bring her more than $60 or $70, but she felt a responsibility to go. Most vendors were too scared to go to festivals held in places like this. Another woman in the Lindblom center had canceled at the last minute, forcing Thelma to go to it alone.

Just then, a car pulled up along South Federal, and a teenager and a dark-skinned woman in a clown outfit got out. Thelma recognized Carol Simms—known to everyone by her nickname "Impy"—and her son Ian. She went over to help them unload. They had heard that Impy was going to perform at the festival, but figured that she would be a no-show.

Impy was a survivor. She was one of the cleverest entrepreneurs in the Full Circle Fund, but a string of family crises had prevented her from making much progress since she'd joined the program. Because one of her circle members had fallen into default in 1993, she could not take any additional loans from the Fund until her center raised the money to retire the debt. Impy, who had paid off two loans without missing an installment, was leading the effort to clear the arrears.

"Hey, Impy, when did they tell you they's gonna start this thing?" Thelma asked.

"Oh, they told me eleven."

"Eleven? They told me ten. Let's go inside and see what's going on."

The two women walked to the front of one of the buildings, leaving their children to stand guard over the merchandise. They saw benches filled with people, mostly men in their twenties and thirties. Others stood in small groups, and nearly everyone looked disheveled. Many were smoking cigarettes. A few younger people cracked up when they saw Impy's clown suit, but most didn't seem to notice.

Thelma and Impy walked through a doorway and into a hallway that was being mopped. Everything had a hard edge to it—the steel grates over the windows, the cinder blocks that had become dislodged from the walls, the expressions on people's faces. "Hey, we're looking for Ms. Issachar," Impy said as she peeked into a room with an open door.

"She's right in here," a teenager replied.

Thelma and Impy met Esther Issachar, and soon learned of the disorganized state the event was in. The festival was to start at 11:00, they were told, but it was clear that an 11:30 launch was more likely. Though the two women had been promised tables when they had signed up to do the event— Thelma had paid $20 to vend, whereas Impy was to receive $60, plus her table, for doing her clown routine—there was only one table, and that was reserved for selling artwork by local kids. Thelma tried to convince the organizer that she was due a table. "I would've brought one from home if you hadn't put that on the form," she said. But her pleas fell on deaf ears.

Thelma and Impy returned to the basketball court. They would try to make do with milk crates and some bits of wood. A half dozen teens wearing blue hard hats were sweeping glass off the concrete without noticeable enthusiasm or effect. Looking at the desultory manner in which the work was being done, Thelma said to Impy, "There's just too many people here stacked up on top of each other. It's just *too much!*"

Impy knew the Robert Taylor Homes better than Thelma did. She had been raised in one of its buildings, located a few blocks north, with her mother, Dorothy Carter, another Full Circle Fund borrower. When they had arrived in the 1960s, it was a relatively attractive place to live. New residents were screened and routine maintenance was done. By the time they moved out in the mid-1970s, the entire complex was in an advanced state of decay. Nearly two decades later, it was an urban badlands with few redeeming qualities. Vincent Lane, chairman of the Chicago Housing Authority, had proposed tearing down the high-rises and moving the people who lived there into low-rises scattered around the city. Alderman Dorothy Tillmon, an acerbic critic of the Daley administration not eager to have the voters who'd elected her dispersed, objected vociferously to the plan and called for Lane to resign. A combination of her opposition and bureaucratic inertia continued to stall the plan.

When Impy left the projects, she wanted to explore the country. She had met too many young people who had never even seen Lake Michigan, which was just a few miles away, much less other cities or states. At 16, she ran away from home, settling for some time in Oklahoma City. It was there she gave birth to her son, Ian. Soon after, she moved again, this time to San Diego. Ian was an attractive baby with soft, light brown skin, and she was able to get him into television commercials for diapers. The income supplemented the money she made doing odd jobs; by then, she was becoming a consummate hustler.

When she and Ian moved back to Chicago, Ian was making the transition from cute infant to handsome preteen. She got him some work modeling children's clothing at fashion shows. Ian was not only attractive but also strong and athletic. By age 12, there was already talk of his becoming an Olympic boxer. Some promoters were so eager to get him fighting that they bribed Impy to let Ian enter amateur tournaments, a fairly common practice for promising young pugilists. She, meanwhile, earned money printing business cards and jewelry, performing as Dready the Clown at birthday parties and special events, singing in nightclubs, teaching jewelry design at classes sponsored by the Park District, and vending at festivals and at arts and crafts shows.

In 1991, Impy joined the Full Circle Fund with her mother and began borrowing to increase the capitalization of her businesses. Her financing needs exceeded what first-time borrowers were allowed to take, so she persuaded her mother to turn over most of the money she borrowed to her. Within a year, she was becoming known as one of the program's success stories. Then disaster struck.

During the riots following the Chicago Bulls' second NBA championship, Ian snuck out a back door of their ramshackle house in Englewood. All the commotion excited him, and he wanted to see what it was all about. Within minutes, he was knocked unconscious when a blunt object thrown from the roof of a low-rise building crushed the right side of his face. Ten months later, he was released from the hospital with a reconstructed face, a glass eye, and permanent neurological damage. His careers in modeling and boxing were over, and he was placed in a special school for slow learners.

With financial and moral support from WSEP staff and clients, Impy pulled through. But by the time Ian was released from the hospital, her asthma had worsened. Then, the Full Circle Staff discovered that she and Dorothy Carter were related and forced Impy to leave her circle and form a new one. (One of the many rules the FCF had adopted from Grameen restricted membership in groups to people who were not blood relatives.) Impy joined a new group, one of whose members was a woman who drifted in and out of homelessness and began missing payments on a $1,500 loan. Impy was then pressed into service to help repay that loan, and organized a twice-monthly vending event at a local community college for all the women in her center, from which 15 percent of everyone's gross sales was given to WSEP to help retire the debt. At the rate they were going, it would take more than a year to finish the job.

In May 1994, local gang members began to recruit Ian. He was confused by the process, but knew enough to resist their overtures. He became angry when the young men called his mother a "Black African bitch" when they saw her on the street, and there were scuffles and fistfights. One evening, gang members called Ian to the alley and tried to douse him with gasoline and set him on fire. He was lucky to receive only minor burns. But as they fled, the teens set Impy's garage on fire, destroying it, her neighbor's garage, a van Impy had bought for $700, and nearly $2,000 worth of merchandise. A few days later, a bullet passed through her upstairs window and lodged in her wall, shattering a mirror along the way. With her insurance money, she was able to replace her merchandise, but there was nothing left to rebuild the garage or buy another van.

Vending and performing were ways for Impy to get her mind off her troubles while making some money. As she and Ian unpacked her bags, Luanda and Shashona erected two makeshift tables. A short time later, children began to arrive. They gravitated to Impy, who asked for nickels and quarters from kids who wanted to play some of the games she had devised. Others came to Thelma's table, looking longingly at her merchandise.

"Is this free?" one seven-year-old asked.

"No, these here's a quarter," Thelma replied, pointing to several boxes of rings she had bought for $6 a gross. "You go wake your mommy up and ask her for twenty-five cent." It was 11:25 on a Thursday morning.

Others crowded around the table, sampling the toys and frequently buying the snappers. During the entire festival, the crackling of snappers going off resounded in the background. The children's clothes were dirty and their behavior was often unruly. More than anything, they seemed to long for attention. Thelma gave it to them while keeping a watchful eye over her merchandise. At one point, she said to Shashona, "Where is these kids' adult supervision?"

Twenty yards away, a cookout was under way and rap music was playing loudly. Ian, increasingly oblivious to his mother's efforts to keep the children entertained, swayed to the beat of the music. He smiled as he watched adults and teens at the barbecue pit drink their stashes of alcohol.

"Come over here," Impy shouted. She led the children to a coat rack she had found on the street and converted into a basketball hoop. "It's a quarter to play, and whoever gets the most shots in wins a stuffed animal." The kids crowded into a ragged line, pushing one another in the process. A fight nearly broke out, but Impy distracted the boys and began collecting quarters. Toward the end of the game, she saw one boy who had lost making a G with his fingers, a gesture Impy recognized as a gang sign. "I hope that G is for God, little man," she said tartly before turning her attention back to the game. She gave the eventual winner a small stuffed bear—one of a batch she'd bought mail order for $2.75 a dozen—and began another game, in which the kids competed to get a steel ball to the bottom of a plastic maze.

Thelma was doing a steady business. Sometimes she let Shashona and Luanda run the table while she fell into conversation with Impy's mother, who had arrived at 12:15. She asked about what the Robert Taylor Homes were like in the 1960s.

"Oh, lovely. And look what's happened!" She pointed to all the broken glass on the concrete.

"I was vending once at Cabrini-Green," Thelma explained to Mrs. Carter, referring to another of Chicago's notorious housing projects, "and those kids started lighting everything on fire. I'm never going back there. Can you imagine that? All day I was there, and I didn't see one adult the whole time."

Dorothy Carter nodded in agreement, her gaze wandering over to the table selling arts and crafts for $5 and up. They had yet to make a sale. Thelma looked over there too, and when her eyes met Mrs. Carter's she said, "Can't really sell anything for more than fifty cent here."

"Yeah," Dorothy responded with a sigh.

"Hey, Mrs. Carter, could you please give me a stuffed animal? We have a winner here!" Impy called out. Her enthusiasm was beginning to wane, but she pressed on.

By 2 p.m., many of the youngest children had scattered, though some kept coming to buy things from Thelma and to play with Dready the Clown. Impy continued with the games, even when some of the older boys began mocking her. The cookout was progressing slowly, as most of the cooks were drunk by then. The event's organizer was nowhere to be found.

Impy Simms walked away from the Second Annual Black on Black Love Festival with $65 in small change and her $60 appearance fee. Thelma grossed $80. It was a small amount of money earned under trying conditions, but both hoped they had made a small contribution to the children who passed their days in the Robert Taylor Homes.

THELMA ALI'S MOTHER, MARY JUNKIM DEAN, lives in a rent-subsidized apartment on the North Side and supplements her pension by cleaning house for white families several times a week. "I don't have nothing against white folks," she says. "They work, save money, buy whatever they want, even a building. If poor people or Black people could save money and build something for themselves, imagine!" Among her heroes is the legendary Mayor Richard J. Daley, though she has doubts about his son, Chicago's current chief executive.

Mary Junkim was born and raised on a cotton farm near Indianola, Mississippi. Her father was a fairly successful cultivator, though not so prosperous that his children didn't have to sew most of their own clothes and the blankets they slept under. Mary remembers baling cotton from a young age and going to school only four months out of the year.

Mary's paternal grandmother was a slave who was freed as a child and later married a Native American. All his children and grandchildren loved Mary's grandfather; they were crazy about his straight Black hair and exotic facial features. Even though the marriage didn't work out, he kept in touch with Mary's grandmother and all the children and grandchildren until his death. Sometimes, he would come with his new wife and spend the holidays with them. Both he and Mary's grandmother lived into their nineties.

In 1937, Mary was seventeen years old and recently married to Jesse Dean. He convinced her that their future was in Chicago. He went up first, secured a job, and sent for her a month later. For several decades, the couple moved around the city, often living in or near a housing project until just before it began going downhill. Both Mary and Jesse worked in factories, though after some years Mary concentrated primarily on domestic work.

Mary and Jesse Dean had eleven children, including three sets of twins, Thelma being one of the first pair. Four of her children have died; two passed away in their twenties, and the other two in their early forties. One of her sons had been killed by the police, who had mistaken him for a suspect in an investigation.

While the children were growing up, the couple separated because of Jesse's constant drinking. But husband or no husband, Mary Dean had high standards for parenting. She stayed up late at night hand-washing clothes and then woke up early the next morning to iron them. "Oh, no, my kids didn't go to school with rough-dried clothes," she says. "And I used to get up and fix them breakfast, though nowadays people just tell their kids to pour some cereal or they give 'em a quarter to buy a candy bar on the way to school."

Mary remembers Thelma as a teenager who partied hard and wore miniskirts. She gave Thelma and her other children the freedom to attend parties, but she always picked them up herself when it was time to come home. They appreciated the freedom but respected its limits.

When Thelma was eighteen, she was invited to a party where most of the guests were Muslims. There was no drinking, no flirting, and no groping. All of the alcohol-induced sexual tension she was accustomed to was replaced by polite conversation. Everyone stayed until 5:00 in the morning, when the Muslims began to pray. "I watched them praying," she remembered, "and I said, 'What kind of mess is this?' But then I began thinking about it, and I realized that this had been the first time I'd been to a party and been able to be myself."

Several days later, a friend called Thelma to tell her that one of the Muslim men wanted to see her again. She resisted at first, but finally agreed to get together for Friday prayer at his mosque. Religion had never appealed to her, and she was afraid she'd get bored. But she liked what she saw: women sitting on one side, men on the other, everyone engaged in serious talk about families and responsibility. After that, Thelma became a regular at the mosque and stopped wearing miniskirts. She had several encounters with a man named Edward Ali; soon, he proposed marriage. Thelma agreed, and the two were wed.

Mary Dean wasn't sure about her daughter's marrying a Muslim, but she didn't interfere. When she saw him hurrying home from work in the middle of the day to change his babies' diapers and bottle-feed them while Thelma was out selling merchandise, she accepted him as one of her own.

The most Thelma's husband, a self-employed builder, made in a single year was $21,000. With five children to clothe and feed, that pushed their finances to the limit. They were never able to buy a house, and as renters with children they faced discrimination. Landlords, whether Black, white, or Asian, either refuse to rent to families (especially if the children are Black teenage boys) or charge 25 to 50 percent more than they would otherwise. It's one of those iron (though unwritten) laws in South Chicago that everyone knows and hardly anyone questions.

To ease the strain on the family, Thelma got involved in selling Tupperware. Before long she was invited to a sales conference in Atlanta, recruited into a supervisory role, and given a company car. That forced her to learn how to drive. Among the people she recruited to work under her was Omiyale DuPart. But after six months, she gave it up because several of her sales agents were failing to pay for merchandise the company had sent them.

Thelma decided that she liked selling, and began vending at flea markets, Maxwell Street, and other events where the entry fee was under $20. The capitalization of her business was extremely low, perhaps a few hundred dollars, but she was able to make extra money for family expenses and to involve her daughters in the enterprise. It was not until she joined the FCF that she would have the working capital to enter more lucrative events like the Black Expo or the Afro-World Festival in Milwaukee, where vendors are charged as much as $500 to participate.

Once, at an auction where she was trying to obtain cheap merchandise, she met a Jewish man in his early seventies named Harry Zimmerman. Both wanted shoes, and rather than engage in a bidding war they decided that Thelma would let Harry get all the adult sizes while he would not contest the children's shoes. That deal began a long friendship between them, and later between Thelma and Harry's son Marshall. The Zimmermans owned a men's clothing store on the corner of Halsted and Maxwell, and Harry had been a vendor at the bazaar in his youth. The Zimmermans were among the few merchants in the area who sold to Blacks on credit.

Over the years, Harry and Marshall let Thelma purchase merchandise through contacts they had, at a lower cost than she could get on her own. She appreciated that, and in turn she sold their tube socks from her table on the south side of Maxwell, since many people would not do back-to-school shopping at Harry's shack, which specialized in videos. Overall, Thelma thought most Jewish people were tolerant, generous, and industrious, and when she called the bazaar "Jewtown," as many people did, it was meant as a tribute to Jewish ingenuity and industriousness rather than as an ethnic slur.

She was impatient with Muslims and other Blacks who thought all of their race's problems were caused by Jews.

When Thelma and her husband were married, they attended a mosque associated with the Nation of Islam. They tried to screen out the teachings they disliked, but over time they switched to an orthodox mosque. To Thelma, who came to take her faith more seriously than her husband did, it was not right to mix Islam and racial separatism. She enjoyed worshiping with different races. The imam in the orthodox mosque that they ultimately settled into seemed to her to emphasize the right things, such as regular prayer and fasting during the month of Ramadan.

By 1993, Thelma was 42 years old, had been married for 24 years, and had five children ages 14 to 23. Her two sons worked in her husband's business when they weren't in school, something that kept them busy and, for the most part, out of trouble. Only Akbar, the younger of her two sons, had been tempted by gangs, but his parents and older brother talked him out of joining. Thelma's oldest daughter, Colleta, married a young Pakistani in the fall of 1993, and by the summer of 2004 there was talk of the tall and slender Shashona marrying a boyfriend who had gotten a job with the postal service. He wasn't a Muslim, but Thelma was willing to bless the union if it made her daughter happy. Both Shashona and Hyiatt (Thelma's youngest daughter) worked in their mother's business.

On some social issues, Thelma is fairly conservative. She opposes giving out condoms and information about homosexuality to schoolchildren, and has little patience for people who have an entitlement mentality. She says, "America has gold in it; you just have to go out and work for it." She also has no tolerance for people who are unwilling to put the time into making their marriage and families work. She, like her mother, is a realistic disciplinarian. Her kids can swear and listen to loud music, but not in the house. She knows that they drink at parties, but they know never to come in late or with liquor on their breath. Thelma and Mary also share the view that the things that matter most in life are hard work, thrift, simple living, and keeping one's family together.

THE COMMOTION STARTED AT 8:30 SUNDAY MORNING. Queenesta and Nixon were setting up their booth at the annual Haile Selassie Festival in

Washington Park. Thirty yards away, Thelma and Victor were setting up their booths. They had arrived nearly an hour before in an effort to secure a space and get ready for the festival's second day. Thelma had already sent her daughter to Maxwell Street.

Business had been good for everybody on Saturday, and Sunday was traditionally better. A pair of West Africans who had driven in from Los Angeles to sell imported jewelry and wood carvings had taken over the space that Dorothy Johnson, Victor's seamstress tenant, had used the day before. When she arrived, she spent 20 minutes trying to get her spot back.

Seeing her predicament, Nixon and Victor got involved.

"Hey, man," Victor said to one of the Africans, "why you being so disrespectful to Ms. Johnson and taking over her spot?"

"Those the rules—first come, first served. You got to get here early," the newcomer replied.

His companion jumped from behind his table. "You don't say anything! We got this space fairly, man. I do all the talking."

"The rules is," Victor began, "that you get the space you had on Saturday. Anyway, this is a matter of respect." Nixon, standing next to him, nodded in agreement.

The event organizer called on two off-duty cops who were acting as security to mediate. Both were Black and wore T-shirts that read, "Homicide, Chicago Police Department: Our Day Starts Where Yours Ends." Thelma wandered over and asked what was going on. After getting the story, she said to Nixon, "I'm afraid those *are* the rules. I've been coming here for three years. You gotta get here early on Sunday or you lose your spot."

After nearly 30 minutes of negotiations, the Africans agreed to share the booth, but there wasn't enough room. Angered but resigned, Dorothy found another space. After she was set, Victor came over to Queenesta's table, where she had laid out her merchandise: sunglasses, T-shirts, and cassettes.

Queenesta asked him a question. "Why'd you do that? Any other time you would have just kicked Ms. Johnson to the curb." She said it in a humorous way, and Victor laughed.

"I said I was with her, didn't I?" he responded absentmindedly as he fell into conversation with Nixon. As they talked, the first customers were beginning to arrive, and other vendors were setting up on the lawn, behind the tables that lined the footpath. They were the less serious vendors—many were just combining a day in the park and a little business, or were trying to avoid paying the entrance fee.

It was another hot, cloudless day that held out the promise of good sales. Anticipation was high, and Black Chicago came out in force for the festival. Omiyale was vending, as was her older sister Taile. So was Janet Johnson, Omiyale's younger sister, who had saved enough of her business profits to purchase her first car in June. Her next goal was to buy a house.

Colete was also there. She had joined with other Hebrew Israelites to sell vegetarian tacos. Wanda X and Belvia Muhammad, the Nation of Islam believers in the Let Us Make Woman circle, came by to see what was going on, as did former enterprise agent Jackie Taffee. Glenda showed up in the early afternoon and talked with her former circle sisters. Shayna sold cold juice from a cooler for a quarter a cup, while Nixon and Queenesta concentrated on sunglasses. Both engaged passersby in conversation, helped them select the right glasses, and then closed the deals. They sold for $5, four times the price Queenesta had paid through mail order. Over the course of two days, she and Nixon would go through close to two hundred pairs, outselling all the other sunglass vendors at the festival. When Nixon persuaded Queenesta to drop the prices of T-shirts from $10 to $8, they began to move too.

Thelma did a steady business selling T-shirts—the most popular had a large picture of Nelson Mandela—toys, sunglasses, and dollar jewelry. She stood there with her trusty purse slung around her torso, ritualistically reshuffling her merchandise every few minutes to make her table appear orderly. Between her sales at the festival and Maxwell Street, she grossed $550 over the weekend. Yet she was more disturbed than ever by Nixon.

She was also bothered by the incident with the West Africans. Thelma knew that the Africans were technically right, and she thought that Nixon knew it as well. Yet being right didn't seem to mean anything to Nixon. To him, might meant right, and he had been intent on putting the Africans in their place. He and Victor made an imposing pair, and they had been confident that the cops would side with them. But what will happen, Thelma thought, when Nixon and Queenesta run into difficulties? Will he be any more willing to negotiate in good faith with her than he was with the Africans? Thelma doubted it.

Earlier that month, Queenesta told Thelma that Nixon had proposed to her and that she had said no, at least for a year. Hearing that made Thelma even more worried. She feared that the relationship was headed for disaster, but when she tried to bring it up, Queenesta didn't want to listen.

As the sun set behind the festival, huge speakers pumped out live and recorded reggae tunes. "We don't know our history," one song declared, "we're killing ourselves. Black people—we don't know ourselves."

Darkness meant selling glow lights, those green, glow-in-the-dark necklaces so popular at night festivals. They retailed for $2, and selling a tube of forty meant about $45 in profit. Omiyale, Thelma, Queenesta, and Victor were all selling them. Queenesta outsold the others, sneaking behind the stage where all the reggae performers were relaxing and quickly sold out. Victor, not so lucky, was forced to let his last 10 go for next to nothing. But he had done well selling kufis, and had made several contacts with potential retailers. His dream was to manufacture hundreds of kufis per month and wholesale them for $3 each. Among those who agreed to try selling them was Thelma Ali.

THE LINDBLOM CENTER MEETING was nearly an hour old, and Colete announced that Joanne Sandler and Karen Doyle, two women from Washington, D.C., who had been observing the meeting, would spend the second hour asking the borrowers about their businesses as part of an evaluation of seven programs supporting self-employment for the poor. Doyle worked for the Aspen Institute's Self-Employment Learning Project (SELP), which was being funded by a foundation that had been providing support to WSEP and other programs. Sandler was a consultant for the evaluation project. Colete and Mary Morten, WSEP's director of policy, said that they would leave the room so as to allow the women to speak more freely.

There were some uneasy moments in the beginning of the discussion. Joanne Sandler said they were trying to learn what worked and what didn't about peer lending programs (which is what many U.S. philanthropy experts came to call Grameen-style efforts). One circle member who had never gotten her business started said, "You mean, you're trying to figure out how to support us, the participants—you're not talking about the women downtown, are you?" Thelma and Omiyale cringed at that one. Thelma especially resented the way a few of the women occasionally bad-mouthed the downtown staff. Some WSEP employees, she realized, were better than others, but why couldn't her circle sisters just appreciate what this program gave them, without complaining about what it didn't?

"*And* the women downtown," one of the guests weakly answered.

Embarrassed laughter and guffaws filled the room, and above it all, Thelma could be heard saying, "We're all in this together. We're all in this together, everybody."

One borrower started talking about the difficulty she and a male partner were having in getting all the licenses they needed to set up a small store and a restaurant in Englewood. "There are people out there, who make the laws, who do not want to see Black people out there, who make the laws, who do not want to see Black people succeed. And you can write that in your report and tell everyone in Washington." Thelma sighed audibly and raised her hand.

"See, in order to operate a business . . ." She paused, looking directly at the woman who had just spoken. "No matter how this society is set up, whether you feel the rules are wrong or whatever. . . . They might have been set up by the wrong people, but that is the law. You have to learn how to work around it."

"Ladies," Omiyale broke in, "we're going to move right along—"

"If you're going to do something," Thelma said over a lot of chatter, "you got to do it right. You can't help someone if they want to do it, if they want to operate it wrong." Omiyale, with some effort, finally restored order. The two visitors asked why the women had become self-employed.

There was a brief silence, which Thelma broke by saying, "I got into business to give my children more choices in life. When I grew up, all there was was to go to school, be educated, and work for someone. I had only one choice in life. I wanted to give my children five choices in life. The choices are to go to school and become educated and to come into their father's business, to go to school and become educated and to come into your mother's business, to go to school and become educated and to work for someone else, to be educated and work your own business, or to go to school and be educated and decide not to do anything." Women began to laugh, but over them, Thelma added, "But those five choices, that's why I started my business." Some began to clap.

Queenesta, with a sleepy Shayna in her lap, went next. "My reason was similar to hers. Because there's a trend, with, um, Black people, that they teach their children that they *have* to get *a job*."

"Right," one borrower concurred.

"And in order to break the psychological chains, I thought that it was up to me. I thought it was better to show her than to tell her. Now, I've been self-employed since soon after my daughter was born, so that's the only thing that she knows. And that's the only thing I want her to see. So that this is what her goal would be, to be self-employed."

Doyle asked about whether the prospects for wage employment in their community had gotten better, worse, or stayed the same over the last few years. The unanimous opinion was that the situation was worse. The women discussed the reality that most of the stores in their communities were run by immigrants who were inclined to hire their own people as they expanded.

B. J. Slay, who sold beauty care products and employed four people, spoke up. "Every other ethnic group supports each other, except for us. And until we do that, we can sit and talk all day long and nothing will change. Yet for most people, ignorance is bliss. When I worked, I didn't feel all this, but when you're out here hustling for your bills, you think about it. 'Cause you gotta make ends meet."

The meeting broke up a short time later. Thelma went over to Omiyale and wished her well on her trip to Africa. Though neither woman would admit it, the frost that had settled over their relationship during the first part of the year was lifting. It was none too soon, as the circle was about to be thrown into an unexpected crisis.

A CUSTOMER CAME TO THE GATE, peered into the darkened store, and paused briefly before pushing on the steel gate. To his surprise, it was locked. "Hey, man, we're not open today," Nixon called out. "We're gonna be closed through about Tuesday." The customer looked to his left, at a large wooden board that had been taped over a gaping hole in a shattered window. It was Sunday, July 31, at 3:30 p.m., still a half hour before the normal closing time for the Hip Hop Shop. But this was no normal day.

Nixon looked down into the main display case. It was empty. The sunglasses and baseball caps in the other cases remained, but the compact discs were gone. He reached into the case and took out a black baseball cap. No, I've never taken stuff from the store, he thought. Even when I've taken candy, I've put money into the register later. But in the process of putting the cap back, he stopped. What the heck, he thought as he pulled it out a second time and put it on. Nixon activated the alarm system, chained the bars behind the windows, and walked out.

Several weeks earlier, Nixon's van had broken down, making it considerably more difficult for him to take on plumbing work. That allowed him to spend more time at the Hip Hop Shop, which was fine with him since he was trying to get out of the plumbing business anyway. At first, Queenesta liked it, too; she was having to spend more time managing the beeper business and was making plans for opening the new store. But before long, it became an irritation. Nixon had ideas about remodeling the store and dropping the prices of the merchandise—ideas that Queenesta didn't agree with. And he had no money to finance his ideas. When Queenesta, always worried about keeping as much money as possible in cassettes (since she still did not have the selection that Moonlight Records did), said she wanted to keep things the way they were, Nixon began subtly challenging his partner's accounting methods. Before long, he was suggesting that she was socking away money without his knowledge. By then, he had become much more than the silent partner Queenesta had told her circle sisters about in May. Looming over the growing dispute was Nixon's unsuccessful marriage proposal.

On Friday, July 29, they were awakened in the middle of the night by a call from the police. Someone had smashed a hole in one of the Hip Hop Shop's front windows and set off the alarm system that automatically notified the police. Nixon, Queenesta, and Shayna rushed to the store and arranged to have the window temporarily secured for $80. Queenesta and Nixon suspected that the attack might have been the work of a local wino that Nixon had cursed out the day before when he had tried to beg inside the store. Nixon didn't deny that that was conceivable, but he resented the way Queenesta tried to blame him for it. Pretty soon, tempers got short, and old issues, like dropping prices, got brought up. At one point Queenesta asked angrily, "Why don't you let me buy you out of the business?"

"You want to *what?*"

"I want to buy you out."

"No way; we got to talk this thing out, but no way I'm getting out." Hearing that, Queenesta stormed out of the store. Nixon discovered the next day that Queenesta was moving her things out of his apartment, and he took the advice of a friend and removed the cassettes and compact discs from the store as a bargaining chip. That way, Queenesta would have to negotiate with him. Yet when she saw the empty cases, she screamed, "Why are you tryin' to gangsta the store, Nixon? Why?" and left. Gary Williams, Queenesta's mentor from her Allstate days, who also knew Nixon, came by that same weekend to try to mediate the dispute, but when he saw the merchandise gone, he gave up. Victor tried his hand at resolving things, but also came up empty. By then, Queenesta was living with her sister June, and her belongings were being stored in three different locations. Nixon had changed the locks on the store and was sleeping there (lest Queenesta somehow sneak in during the night).

Successive plans to recover the store from Nixon failed, principally because both of their names (rather than Queenesta's alone) were on the business license.

During the weeks immediately after the dispute erupted, it became difficult for Queenesta to do anything without losing her composure. She contacted her beeper customers to tell them that she was temporarily relocating that part of her business to Victor's store. She went into the Hip Hop Shop one final time to pick up her cash register and several other things that were indisputably hers. But when she tried to take a display case she had bought with loan money from WSEP, Nixon said no.

When she called Thelma to tell her about what happened, she didn't hear "I told you so," but received a commitment to approve a loan from the emergency loan fund after Omiyale returned from Africa. Queenesta somehow managed to make a $144 payment on her loan on August 9, and another one two weeks later. But Thelma recognized that Queenesta was in a precarious and dangerous situation—living in a tiny apartment with her sister without access to her inventory. More than anything, Thelma told her not to go back to the store.

In late August, Victor left for his own trip to Africa, and Queenesta agreed to look after the store. The beeper business had recovered, but it was barely enough to pay grocery bills and buy gas, much less to make her monthly car payment and meet her obligations to the Full Circle Fund. On September 5, she missed her first installment. At about that time, two more holes were smashed in the Hip Hop Shop windows. Nixon continued to operate the store, although he often couldn't open until the evening, when his plumbing jobs were complete and he could get back to Austin on public transit. He dropped the prices as he had long advocated.

Queenesta had no store, virtually no merchandise, and an outstanding loan. She moved back in with her mother for the month of September, and began planning how to restart her business.

Update: Since the 1990s

SO MUCH HAS CHANGED ABOUT MICROFINANCE since the 1980s and even the mid-1990s, from cell phones in the hands of borrowers to the computerization of bookkeeping in most MFIs to efforts to mobilize capital using methods associated with high finance, such as IPOs and securitizations. In India, some microlenders have effectively become agents for large banks, and the loans never even go on to the MFI's balance sheet—a process that is invisible to the borrower but still profoundly different from the models used in previous decades.

Yet, in its essence, the dynamic at the borrower level remains much the same. Whether in south Chicago or rural Bangladesh, there is a constant struggle to invest microloans in tiny, profit-making enterprises and to leverage the network of fellow borrowers one is often required to join. Borrowers function in a hostile environment that often includes brutal competition from larger businesses, health crises that are exacerbated by poorly functioning health care systems, unsupportive family and friends, and well-intentioned laws that work against the interests of microentrepreneurs. Queenesta and Omiyale were testaments to the "two steps forward, one step back" reality of microfinance participation. The peer support that the early innovators in microfinance imagined can sometimes become peer pressure that may spin out of control and work against the interests of both borrower and lender. A key feature of Grameen II was to deemphasize peer pressure while continuing and expanding the incentives for peer support. Still, further innovation that keeps the long-term interests of the poor borrowers, and especially the poorest borrowers, at the center of thought and action will need to be further developed.

Fortunately, practitioners and policy makers are coming together to try to solve some of the systemic problems with microfinance to ensure more rapid progress by borrowers. In the United States, the Aspen Institute and the Association for Enterprise Opportunity (AEO) have been at the forefront of efforts to study the achievements and limitations of the most successful microlenders and to propose concrete solutions. One idea that has been debated is to allow microentrepreneurs to buy health insurance collectively, realizing the volume discounts that large corporations enjoy. Under the leadership of Connie Evans since 2009, AEO has helped increase awareness of and support for African-American micro- and small-business owners.

Best practices have been distilled to ensure that lessons do not need to be relearned. Combining microfinance with business training, networking, peer counseling, and assistance with properly registering one's business with the relevant government agencies are emerging as sound strategies that would not be relevant in Bangladesh but are often essential in the context of wealthy countries. Fundamentally, microfinance in the U.S. is about breaking down the isolation experienced by low-income people in general, and especially immigrants and African-Americans, which ends up being a major barrier to economic self-empowerment. The catchy tagline of a New York City microlender captures the strategy well: "Small Loans, *BIG CONNECTIONS*."

I SUPPOSE THIS IS OBVIOUS, but it is worth saying anyway: I came to admire and genuinely like the Chicago women featured in this book. While they all had flaws and (with the possible exception of Thelma) made mistakes, they were all determined and skilled microentrepreneurs who were open to being helped by their peers and by WSEP. They also trusted me with intimate details about their lives and let me spend time with friends and family in order to get to know them better. I gave each of them the option of having me use a fictitious name in this book rather than identifying them publicly, and each declined to go that route.

There were qualities I liked about each of them, but the one whose pragmatic and open-minded approach to her business and to life taught me lessons that I still rely on today is Thelma Ali. Her willingness to speak uncomfortable truths and to boldly and unapologetically cross the chasms of race, class, and religion to form alliances and friendships have always been needed. But in 2022, they feel more important than ever.

I tried to track down these women as the manuscript for this edition of the book was being developed. I did not reach any of them initially, but I did find a flyer for an online event held in March 2022. It was a winter concert titled "Black Is . . ." being put on by the Chicago Association of Black Story-Tellers. The Mistress of Ceremonies was one Omiyale DuPart, and the picture of her suggested that she hadn't visibly aged much since the mid-1990s. Mother hens like her and Shandha apparently can never quite escape their roles as community leaders. I hope they never do.

13. The Sixteen Decisions

KRISHNA WAS HOLDING A CENTER MEETING in the Haldar *para* at the end of the monsoon season. Sitting on a mat, he began silently marking up his collection sheet and the passbooks. Krishna wasn't a big talker. Unless there was some reason to speak up, he busied himself with his paperwork and let the women run the meeting the way they saw fit. Sometimes Shandha thought Krishna should take a more active role in maintaining discipline; for her, his lecture on timeliness the previous week had been long overdue. No matter how well respected Shandha was, she knew a bank worker could have a more immediate impact on the goings-on in her center than she was able to. Shandha was, after all, a realist—bank workers were educated (and most were men), and she was an illiterate woman. In few societies do a person's education and gender assume more importance in how much respect they are accorded than in Bangladesh.

Krishna called for the passbooks from each group and deducted the week's installment from the running balance. For general and seasonal loans, he subtracted 2 percent of the principal, for tube-well loans 1 percent, and for housing loans 40 taka. As he did so, he reflected on how much more difficult it was being a bank worker in 1994 than it had been five years before. Then, there was one passbook per borrower for general loans and perhaps two or three housing loans per center. Servicing a center meant filling in roughly 40 passbooks each week. On this day, Krishna would be handed more than 100 from Shandha's center alone. The volume of money that was collected each morning, and lent out each afternoon, had grown proportionately.

One striking thing about Grameen center meetings is the manner in which financial transactions are conducted. Before Krishna collected the money, he wrote in each borrower's passbook that she had paid her installment in full. Only later was the money collected, and even then, it was handed over by the group chairman, not the individual. When Krishna was ready for it, he collected 1,265 taka from Shandha's group. He compared the amount with what they gave him last week, and if there was any difference, he checked to make sure it was because they had received a new loan or paid one off. He would assume that there were no missed payments unless he was told otherwise. Collecting the money from the group chairman is meant to reinforce the idea that the primary problem-solving unit in the Grameen system is the group, not the staff. In Grameen branches where irregular payments are common, bank workers are often forced to collect the money first and to do so from each individual borrower directly.

Another striking thing about center meetings in Bangladesh is how cramped they are. Shandha's center house is no more than 20 feet long and 8 feet wide. Every Tuesday morning, 35 women, as many as 10 children, and one bank worker squeeze into it. The meetings in Chicago, by contrast, are attended by fewer people in spaces more than six times larger. Chairs are spread out there, reflecting a zone of privacy that Westerners respect and Asians have difficulty comprehending. In many respects, though, the actual content of the meetings is the same in Chicago as in Bangladesh: the money changing hands, the problem-solving, the gossiping, the exchanging of business tips. In both places, the pleasure the women take in being with other women in an environment where their economic (rather than domestic) responsibilities are the center of attention is palpable.

As the meeting wore on, currency notes began piling up in front of Shandha. Amodini, wearing the white sari of Hindu widowhood, sat next to her friend and tried to straighten the stacks out. It was a small gesture, but it signified that she was starting to feel like herself again; the period of mourning for her husband was winding down. On Shandha's advice, Amodini was husking rice to earn extra money, since the market for fishing nets was shrinking with the conclusion of the monsoon. It took Amodini some days before she found the wherewithal to follow Shandha's advice, but once she did, it gave her a sense of purpose. It also supplemented the income her daughter brought in from fishing, since Amodini had virtually no livestock in the months after her husband's death. (She had been forced to sell whatever she had to meet her weekly installments, arrange the funeral, and pay off the quacks.)

"Will you have five women for me next week?" Krishna asked Shandha as he looked up from counting some bills.

"Yes, you can give them their first training next Tuesday, if you want." Pressure had come from the area manager to increase the number of groups in each center to eight. Shandha had said in the spring that she didn't think there was anyone else who wanted to join, but now, in September, she was singing a different tune. Among those who were expressing interest in joining was Amodini's sister-in-law.

"Tell them to come here then," Krishna replied. "Are there any loan proposals today?"

Four women stood up. Krishna took down the first three proposals. They generated little controversy and were completed in a short time. Then came Rasheda from the fifth group, who had recovered from typhoid in July and wanted a loan for a tube well.

"Sir," Rasheda said, "I need a tube well. Please sanction a three thousand taka loan."

Krishna looked up from the form on which he had noted the three loan proposals that he had already agreed to. He studied Rasheda, and surveyed the women sitting in her row. "Rasheda, how can we trust you?" Two years earlier, Rasheda had sold the house she built with a Grameen Bank housing loan. Even though she had never missed a payment on the loan, the bank saw it as a major breach of discipline. Now she had to face the consequences.

"Sir, I need a tube well. We have to go a great distance to fetch water now."

"You said you needed a house three years ago, but then you sold it. Why will this be any different? Maybe it will be safest to give you no tube well loan, after what you've done."

"Sir, I will use it well."

"Sit down," Krishna said. He returned to the other three loan proposals and let Rasheda stew. She pulled her sari over her face and began to cry. Krishna said suddenly, "Group number five chairman, stand up."

A woman sitting on the far left of the group stood. "Do you support this loan proposal?" Krishna asked impatiently.

"Yes, sir."

"Will it be used correctly, or will she sell it?"

"She will use it correctly, sir," the woman replied firmly but respectfully.

"Supi, stand up." The former center chief rose. "What about you—do you support it? Will you take personal responsibility with your group chairman, to make sure the loan is used properly?"

"Yes, sir," she said, looking Krishna in the eye as she spoke the words.

"Zorina, stand up." The dark-skinned center chief joined the other two women. "What about you?"

"I support the proposal, sir. She needs a tube well for drinking water and to irrigate her vegetable garden. She will use it right. She came and spoke to me about it yesterday."

Krishna surveyed the three women. Finally, and inevitably, his gaze shifted to Shandha. "What about you?"

Though she was sitting no more than a foot apart from the others, Shandha stood up too. She looked back at Rasheda, made eye contact, and looked down at Krishna. "I am behind it too, sir," she said softly.

"Okay, sit down, all of you," he said. "Rasheda, stand up." He went through the formalities of asking her all the information he needed for the draft loan proposal—her husband's name, the amount, and the use. Then he called the four women applying for loans, and the center chief, to come up and sign the proposal. When that was complete, he asked the women to practice a ritual that they hadn't done for some time—chanting slogans at the end of their meeting. The manager was likely to come to the first group training session, and he liked to see things done by the book.

Shandha was the only one who remembered how to lead them in the slogans. With everyone standing, she called out, "Unity, hard work, and discipline."

"Unity, hard work, and discipline," the other women echoed.

"That is our creed," Shandha yelled.

"That is our creed," they repeated.

They went on to recite other slogans about their children's education, building dignified housing, and drinking clean water. They ended with a chant that has a distinctive sound to it in Bengali, though it loses something in translation. "The light of Grameen Bank," Shandha intoned. The women repeated the words. "May it burn in every household."

UNDERSTANDING GRAMEEN ULTIMATELY REQUIRES some familiarity with Muhammad Yunus's core beliefs. A careful reading of his lectures and correspondence in 1993 and 1994 highlights the four ideas that underpin his life and work—simplicity, sacrifice, gradualism, and faith. Since Yunus feels that his ideas are more important than his tangible accomplishments, let's unpack each of them briefly.

Pervading all of his work is the notion "Keep it simple." It is undeniable that the influence of Nicholas Georgescu-Roegen, his mentor from Vanderbilt, is still felt. Yunus believes that most technical jargon can be eliminated, which opens up specialized knowledge to common people. If it takes a little longer to explain an economic or scientific concept using layman's language, the inclusiveness is well worth the extra effort. To his thinking, the shallow intellectual stays mired in complexity, while the true intellectual strives for simplicity. Georgescu was a true intellectual, and Yunus tries to be another. His arena, however, is an organization rather than a classroom.

As Yunus created Grameen, he resisted all attempts to make the bank's policies more complex. He instructed his staff that business should be conducted openly, explained thoroughly, and expressed in simple mathematics that even a determined illiterate person could grasp. For example: Repayment is made in 50 equal installments of exactly 2 percent of the loan amount. The "tax" that was for years deposited in the group fund is precisely 5 percent of each loan amount. (Calculating 2 percent and 5 percent of a round number is something most anyone can do.) Savings is one taka. Interest is paid in the two weeks after the payment of the last installment, making the repayment period exactly one calendar year. One of the few downsides of Grameen II was that it brought a lot more complexity into Grameen's lending and savings programs.

But simplicity is more than an operational strategy. Yunus has tried, often with a touch of humor, to convince people that problems, and their solutions, are not inherently complex. Rather, it is people who make them appear that way. In a seminar on the malaise of the Bangladeshi economy, Yunus is likely to interrupt a jargon-riddled academic debate and say something like "I think the problem is that people aren't working hard enough" or "If people in government became sincere about serving the country, these problems should clear up." His tendency to reduce societal problems and their solutions to what he sees as straightforward and tangible elements has earned him admiration among laypeople and a certain degree of hostility among experts who spend years—indeed, entire careers—trying to master complexity that Yunus appears to wish away.

If simplicity is one pillar in the foundation of Yunus's philosophy, sacrifice is another. To him, putting in long hours, finishing a job properly, forgoing costly conveniences like air conditioning, encouraging fierce competition among colleagues (to bring out the best in all of them), and making do with a modest salary are all self-reinforcing and inextricably connected to any serious attempt to address poverty. If his staff is unwilling to make sacrifices for the good of the bank, he wonders, how can they ask the borrowers to do so for the good of their centers? When it is argued that Yunus should raise wages of his senior staff because their abilities and work ethic would be worth many times that on the open market, he shrugs. When a senior staff member with 10 years of outstanding service to Grameen leaves to take a cushy job abroad, Yunus says all the right things while privately fuming about how people use successful poverty-alleviation programs to land high-paying jobs. Part of sacrifice, he believes, is keeping one's word, whatever the cost. In 1993, on the evening that Yunus collapsed at a center meeting and spent the afternoon undergoing tests that revealed he had a severe ulcer, he snuck away to a function in his honor he had promised to attend at the Belgian embassy.

His third core belief is gradualism. Yunus has concluded that lasting social change most often—and perhaps always—comes slowly rather than in a burst of revolutionary fervor. While he is apt to lay out bold visions of, say, a future world without any poverty or even unemployment, his approach to reaching those goals is notably gradualist in nature. This principle has shaped his effort throughout his career. Partly as a result, his methods and achievements have occasionally been belittled. Journalists and researchers sometimes seem to take delight in pointing out how modest his achievements have been in certain areas, especially if measured over lengths of time that are unrealistically short given the nature of social change.

I recall one day sitting with Yunus in his living room and expressing my alarm about the fact that many Grameen clients in Tangail district were using their materials Grameen sold them for constructing sanitary latrines—what we in America would call outhouses—for other purposes. His wife Afrozi peered up from her newspaper and asked what the issue was. Yunus simply said with something between a laugh and a sigh, "They aren't yet accustomed to using latrines." He minimized the breakdown between Grameen's intent and its results in those villages, since he understood that behavior change often happens maddeningly slowly. He was playing the long game. Yet I expect that the day after our conversation, he quietly placed a phone call to Tangail to ask them to look into the matter.

His gradualist approach has not been universally appreciated. Leftist politicians and academics have blamed him for not going further in attempting to redistribute assets. Many who were drawn to radical politics have scoffed at the idea of giving credit while stopping short of advocating their preferred solution: land reform. The right, on the other hand, has called him a welfare advocate disguised in capitalist clothing. In both cases, his program does not match up to their ideals. In reality, of course, Grameen doesn't match up with all of his own ideals, either. But it passes the test that guides all the major decisions in his life: Is doing it an improvement over the status quo? Time and again, when people find fault with Grameen, Yunus admits its theoretical and programmatic deficiencies while defending it as a solid and practical step in the right direction. A man who was more of a perfectionist, or more impatient about bringing about sweeping social change, would have either abandoned the Grameen experiment or run it into the ground. Instead, he has let it evolve in a way that has allowed millions of people to benefit.

But the belief that stands above all the others, and sets Yunus apart from most of his peers, is his faith—not in religion, but in people, especially poor people. In late 1994, I was talking to an American who had returned to Bangladesh after an absence of several years. His understanding—and love—of the country was still obvious. When pushed, he spoke disparagingly of the aid agencies in Bangladesh and even about leaders of well-respected nonprofit organizations in the country, and he saw flaws in the Grameen Bank. Intrigued, I asked him about what he thought of Yunus as a person and as a thinker. His answer was revealing:

> Yunus is a mensch. All the other organizations, whether donor or nonprofit, share the belief that these poor Bangladeshis can't really do anything for themselves—they need handouts, subsidies, something. From the early 1970s, Yunus was the only one saying, "Hey, these people can do something for themselves; they have abilities. There is nothing inferior about Bangladeshis." That's what sets Yunus apart.

That faith in the ability of his fellow citizens is what makes Yunus, after all the dust has cleared, a capitalist, though a unique one. Many people who share his commitment to the poor reject capitalism. At very least, they want to soften capitalism's hard edges for the poor by instituting subsidies, welfare programs, and protectionism. But Yunus is unapologetic about his championing of capitalism and his belief that the poor will be able to compete effectively if the obstacles preventing them from doing so are removed. He yearns for a more humanistic, but no less competitive, economic system. In an expansive speech given in June 1994 to a Rotary convention in Taipei, he spelled out his views:[69]

> The essence of capitalism is expressed in two of its basic features: profit maximization and market competition. In their abstract formulations these were not supposed to be conspiratorial against the poor. But in real life, they turn out to be the killers of the poor. . . .
>
> The profit maximization principle is recognized as the best principle to ensure the optimal use of resources. Free market competition ensures that you are pushed out of any uncomfortable position when your competitor finds a better product or a better way of doing business. It is the driving force for all innovations, technology changes, and better management.

The bases of capitalism were sound, Yunus was saying, but when they are put into practice, they often create unacceptable outcomes.

> In the conceptualization of the capitalist world we have installed a greedy, almost bloodthirsty, person to play the role of profit maximizer. Not only have we deprived him of all human qualities, but we have empowered him by giving him all the institutional support he can use while depriving that support to everyone else (for example, banks will give him all the money he wants, but not recognize other people). On top of it, we conceptualize that the entrepreneurs are a very rare and special breed of people. We are lucky to have them with us. We must give them all the privileges they ask for.

Yunus believed that everyone has marketable skills, and he wanted the capitalist world to reflect that. We went on:

If we imagine a world where every human being is a potential entrepreneur, we'll build a system to give everybody a chance to materialize his or her potential. The heavy wall between the entrepreneur and labor will be meaningless. If labor had access to capital, this world would be very different from what we have now. We build what we imagine. In the past, we have imagined the wrong way, [and] as a result we got a wrong world. By formulating our axioms the right way, we can create the right world.

In the right world, we'll have to forget that people should wait around to be hired by somebody. We must instill in everybody's mind that each person *creates* his or her own job. We'll build institutions in such a way that each person is supported and empowered to create his or her own job: self-employment. Wage employment will come into the picture only as an alternative to self-employment. The more self-employment becomes attractive, wide-ranging, and self-fulfilling, the more difficult it will be to attract people for wage jobs. Women, minority groups, the physically handicapped, and the socially handicapped will benefit from self-employment becoming more rewarding and convenient.

Mass production of a product leads to economies of scale under any production system. But there is nothing that makes it obligatory to organize this mass production under one roof. Home-based production based on self-employment can be as mass-scale as in a single-roof, wage-based factory system. The more we can move toward home-based production by the self-employed masses, the more we can come close to avoiding the horrors of capitalism.

In this alternative vision of the capitalist world, instead of one motivating factor—greed—to keep it in motion, we can introduce social consciousness or social dreams as another motivating factor. Both types of people can be in same marketplace, using the same tools and concepts of capitalism, but pursuing completely different goals. In addition, there will be middle-of-the-roaders, who will mix both greed and social objectives, according to their tastes and abilities.

This alternative vision of the world will not be as black as it turned out under the greed-alone scenario. This capitalist world can accommodate all shades: white, gray, and black. I think this is the most realistic vision of the world under any framework, capitalist or noncapitalist.

I am inclined to believe that the role of social-consciousness-driven entrepreneurs will become more important than the role of greed-driven entrepreneurs in the newly configured capitalist world. The role I am assigning to social-consciousness-driven entrepreneurs in the new configuration of the capitalist world is assigned to the state in a socialist framework. The state did not do a good job in this role.

Can capitalist concepts, tools, and frameworks allow, support, and promote economic activities leading to achievements of social objectives in parallel with narrow personal objectives? My answer is an emphatic yes. Yes, it can be done, provided we can create, strengthen, and widen the role of social-consciousness-driven entrepreneurs through building supportive institutions, state policies, educational systems, and social rewards mechanisms and creating international support systems and solidarity networks. . . .

By joining the ranks of social-consciousness-driven entrepreneurs [he urged the Rotarians], you'll gain more in social respectability than you'll lose in dollars and cents of personal income. Above all, you'll be a happier person. If you become social-consciousness-driven entrepreneurs with your total commitment, I can assure you you'll build an entirely different world than what we have now. The world that we can build will be free from poverty and human indignity. . . .

This philosophy articulated by Yunus has some surprising dimensions. Yunus argues against the provision of free health care and education for the poor. He suggests that the important thing is that people be given the means to earn an income so they can pay for health care, education, and other essentials. Until such time as they can pay with money, these goods should be provided in exchange for a *social payment,* such as a poor person agreeing to organize a sanitation program in his or her village. He also argues against protectionism, arguing that the poor can compete in the international marketplace and that the beneficiaries of protectionism are most often the "rich and clever" people (even though tariffs and quotas are often erected in the name of workers and the poor). These arguments are heresy among many progressives, but they are consistent with Yunus's faith in people being able to find their niche in the marketplace if given access to the same tools as wealthy entrepreneurs. To Yunus, capitalism under conditions of equal access to investment capital is ultimately a progressive socioeconomic system. Above all, he dislikes the idea of special rights for certain classes of people. Entrepreneurs do not deserve special access to credit any more than the poor deserve special access to free health care. In Yunus's ideal world, the wealthy would not have privileged access to money for investment, and the poor would not have privileged access to money for consumption.

Yunus's brand of humanism leads to a dim view of formal religion. He occasionally comments that the unattainably high standards of conduct to which the leaders of the great religions hold people make them ashamed to participate actively in their places of worship. Religion, in his mind, should take into account the reality of people's lives; moreover, religious leaders should strive harder to improve people's lives here on earth. While he is a proud if not especially devout Muslim, he occasionally laments that Islamic leaders oppose Grameen while Christian priests in places like the Philippines are among its most enthusiastic supporters. Once, when asked about whether he worshiped any God, he responded by saying that he worshiped "the God in each human being."

AMENA WALKED GINGERLY NEXT TO A ROW of plants in her vegetable garden, picking off a few green chilies and eggplants to be sold later in the afternoon. She placed them in a basket she had woven some years before. Amena was agitated. Her husband had returned from Dhaka the night before, where he had been pulling a rickshaw to earn money. His absence had given Amena a chance to reshuffle her livestock, since he had found out about some of the chicks and ducklings she had sharecropped out before the monsoon. It was a constant game they played, and while she was unable to conceal all of her assets and earnings, she was able to hide some. She had even bought a small share of an irrigation pump for the coming winter rice crop without her husband's knowledge.

"Come here," Absar Ali shouted to his wife. "We're going to talk now." Amena's parents had already huddled with her husband under the shade of a tree. Amena pulled up a low stool to join the family meeting.

Four weeks earlier, word had reached Amena's compound that her younger brother, the one who had eloped to Dhaka with the older, married woman, had been killed by a truck one night while pulling a rickshaw. His body was delivered the following day and he was buried on Amena's father's homestead lot. Ever since, people had been coming to the house and sometimes saying insensitive things. For example, a few suggested that Allah had harshly judged Amena's brother's actions by taking his life. It was a dark time for the family.

"What do you think we should do?" Absar Ali asked his father-in-law. Amena's father had a haggard look about him. Amena and her parents had each lost at least five pounds since the death; none of them were eating regularly as they dealt with their grief.

"I think we should move to Munshikandi. This is a bad place for us, with bad memories. We have relatives there; we can stay with them. There are others there from our home village."

"I don't like this place anymore," Amena's mother said in a whisper.

Absar Ali looked at his wife. "What do you think?"

"It is your decision, of course, but I think that we should stay here," Amena began. "We should see if we can buy this land. Perhaps we could pay in installments, over several years. Then we could finally settle down somewhere."

"Amena," her father began, "we are people of the broken river. Wherever we go, the river will follow us. That is our destiny. We will never settle down."

Absar Ali interjected, "But I think Amena is right. At the moment, we are squatters. If we go to Munshikandi, we will be squatters. But here we have the possibility of purchasing some land. We may get a loan from this bank to help buy some land to live on. Then we can stop being people of the broken river. I think we should stay."

"Father," Amena began, "many people have accused us of many things, but have you noticed that no families from my borrowing group have said anything? They have remained supportive. If we move, we lose the ability to borrow, we lose this garden, we go back to living off the moneylender." Amena had a more purposeful look about her than she had had in several weeks.

"I think we have a good thing here," Absar Ali said as he took out a cigarette and began twirling it in his fingers. "Amena has gotten involved in a good thing. We can buy aluminum cookware, we can buy our own rickshaws, someday we can take a house loan. I think we should stay."

Amena's father looked at his son-in-law and began to cry softly. "He is gone, my son is gone, nothing will bring him back," he said haltingly. "But if it is Allah's will that we stay here, and if it is your will, then perhaps we will remain here."

Amena seemed to finally have the commitment she had sought for so long. Immediately after her brother died, Amena's husband and parents had begun talking about moving out of Kholshi. Amena wanted to find a way for them to stay. The first person she talked to was the uncle who had inherited her grandfather's land. Amena had convinced him to sell her family the quarter acre of land they now lived on for about 15,000 taka ($375). Then she sent her husband to talk to her uncle. She didn't tell him how far she had gotten in the negotiations, but suggested that the uncle would be willing to sell for a reasonable price. That would ensure that Absar Ali believed that the deal was his, not Amena's. After her husband returned from that meeting, Amena began to discuss the benefits of staying in Kholshi with him. She emphasized the BRAC school, the hand-pumped tube well they had bought and sunk, the vegetable garden, and, most important, the membership in Grameen. Amena painted a picture of a future in which her loans for investment would grow to 10,000 taka per year, they would receive a housing loan of 25,000 taka, and they would perhaps one day come to own an irrigation pump capable of irrigating 20 or more acres. She also talked of his owning a small fleet of rickshaws, of leasing several acres of land, of buying expensive fishing nets at a discount from her friends in the Haldar *para*. On one occasion, she suggested that they visit some of the older borrowers in her center to see what a Grameen-financed house looked like.

Absar Ali didn't commit himself to settling in Kholshi until the family meeting. Amena's parents were in no condition to move on their own, which virtually ensured that they would remain in place for the time being. If she could arrange for the family to put a down payment on the housing plot, their roots would be firmly planted in a village where they would be likely to spend the rest of their lives.

Despite the tragedy and uncertainty that characterized the fall, Amena and her husband's businesses were growing. During the second week of September, they sold a cow for 5,000 taka that they had bought a year earlier for 2,500. They used half of the money to buy a new calf and the rest to repair their house, invest in the cookware business, and buy some ducklings. The vegetable garden continued to be productive. That kept expenses on groceries down and yielded a steady stream of income from sales that their daughter Aaki made at village markets. Amena continued to do a good business raising chickens and ducks. By the fall, 20 months after she had received her first loan, Amena had 3,000 taka stashed away, money she hoped to use to put a down payment on her land and pay school fees for Aaki. Absar Ali was doing well in his cookware business and pulling a rickshaw in Dhaka when sales were slow. He was so busy, and so dependent on his wife for investment capital, that his beatings of her had virtually ceased for the first time since they were married.

After the meeting broke up, Absar Ali hoisted his inventory of aluminum cookware on his shoulder and headed off to work. Amena returned to her vegetable garden, and Aaki fed the chickens before going off to school. Amena spent more than an hour weeding and pruning the plants, and as she did so she tried to imagine what this small plot of land would look like in 10 years' time—what kind of house they would live in, how many cows they would have, how much rice they would receive after each harvest, what sort of job Aaki would have. They were dreams that people of the broken river rarely indulge in, and though they were new to Amena, they were not unpleasant.

IN 1994, THE SHAYMGANJ DAULATPUR BRANCH disbursed 35 million taka ($875,000), received 24 million taka ($600,000) in loan payments, and earned a profit of approximately 600,000 taka ($15,000).[70] As in previous years, not one payment was missed by any of its 2,400 female borrowers. In January 1995, the branch had 519 groups spread throughout 71 centers, and a cumulative disbursement of 73 million taka ($1.8 million). These milestones were achieved despite being situated in an area where the poverty and malnutrition are severe even by Bangladeshi standards and where entire villages periodically disappear into the advancing river.

Were the Shaymganj Daulatpur branch the only thing Muhammad Yunus had created, it would be an impressive accomplishment. But as 1994 closed, there were 1,045 Grameen Bank branches that reached into more than half of all the villages in the country. Many of those branches outperformed Shaymganj, either because they were older, were run by better staff, or were situated in a more prosperous region of the country. Sirajul Islam, the area manager responsible for Shaymganj and eight other branches, is often teased by colleagues who say that he runs a "half area." Because of the poverty and uncertainty created by the river, his disbursements and profits are 40 percent lower than those of his colleagues elsewhere in the Dhaka zone. He fears his promotion may be delayed as a result.

The genius of Muhammad Yunus's work is not that he figured out how to empower poor people with loans, but that he was able to develop a model that he could replicate more than a thousand times while maintaining a reasonable degree of control over the quality of the enterprise. The difference is critical to understanding the implications of what he has accomplished. One branch can serve 2,000 people, whereas a thousand branches can serve 2 million. It takes an entirely different set of skills to start a pilot project than it does to successfully scale it up. Pilot projects reach hundreds of people; institutions that boldly expand can touch millions and evolve to meet community needs on a large scale in increasingly better ways through a continuous learning process.

In circles where poverty and environmental issues are discussed, one often hears the slogan "Small is beautiful." Tiny programs tailored to local needs are romanticized, while anything big—governments, corporations, even large nonprofit organizations—is distrusted. Rarely is it considered that while small may often be beautiful, small is, after all, still small. A world in which thousands of successful pilot projects reach a tiny percentage of the world's poor, and leave the vast majority untouched, is a world where mass poverty is destined to persist and deepen.

It is hardly an exaggeration to say that nearly every major problem facing the world has several solutions that have been proven effective on a small scale. But only if the best of those projects can be replicated or franchised, and expanded while maintaining reasonably high quality, will there be hope for resolving the interconnected mesh of social, environmental, and economic injustices that are tearing at the insides of humanity.

Muhammad Yunus has demonstrated that large-scale replication of an effective antipoverty strategy can be both successful and profitable. He resisted the temptation to keep Grameen small (and easily controlled by him), and in the process reached two million borrowers (and later, nearly four times that number), created a decentralized management structure, and trained a workforce of thousands of people. Doing so has not always been easy. Striking the right balance between keeping all Grameen branches similar while allowing for innovation and experimentation came after years of trial and error. The conditions that gave rise to widespread employee discontent in 1991 were a result of bigness, and so was the gradual decline in the zealousness with which some employees carried out their duties.

Fueling the aggressive expansion program was the managing director's faith in the ability of people to use credit well even when they were not directly supervised by him. Many Grameen critics predicted disaster when Yunus was not there to monitor everything, but their fears have proven largely unfounded. Bangladeshis, long portrayed as lacking the skills for middle management and business ownership, have demonstrated those abilities as Grameen staff and borrowers. The continued success of Grameen Bank even after Yunus was forced to retire in 2011 is perhaps the ultimate testimony to his success as an institution-builder and the most forceful refutation of the claims by some that the bank's success was due to the force of his personality.

Other poverty-focused credit programs in Bangladesh, many of them Grameen imitators, reached 2.5 million *additional* families by the mid-1990s. Furthermore, institutions modelled on and trained by Grameen Bank reached millions more in other countries around the world. For years, people from dozens of countries came to Bangladesh to learn how Grameen works so that they can start similar projects after returning home. My colleagues Nurul Alam and Mike Getubig led a major initiative, in collaboration with the Dhaka-based Grameen Trust, to develop a manual for how to start and operate a microfinance program using Grameen's techniques. The result, something called "The Grameen Guidelines," is freely available for download on the Internet.

For many years, one of the most serious criticisms of Grameen was that credit was not the magic bullet that some accused Yunus as touting it to be. The problem of poverty, critics argued, was complex, and needed a solution that took into account not only its financial dimensions, but also things like ignorance, political powerlessness, and ill health. Other programs that provided credit, for example, required that borrowers undergo a six-month course on literacy and political organizing before they were allowed to take a loan. Experts scoffed at Grameen's requiring as little as seven hours of training before releasing loans to borrowers. The conventional wisdom questioned whether poor, uneducated people knew what to do with small loans without more guidance from above.

Yunus rejected these ideas. He admitted that poverty was a multifaceted problem, but he did not believe it necessarily needed a multifaceted solution. The poor, he argued, already had skills, were already politically conscious, and were already aware of the need for schooling and taking care of their health. It was first and foremost their lack of income that made using their skills and knowledge impossible. Providing investment capital for additional income generation, he asserted, would unlock the capacity of poor people to solve many, if not all, of the manifestations of poverty that affected their lives.

The success of the Sixteen Decisions tends to support Yunus's thesis. (See the Appendix for an English translation of the decisions.) Ten years after they were framed, research has confirmed that there had been significant progress in most areas. A high percentage of borrowers tended vegetable gardens and planted saplings, sent their children to school, and had improved the condition of their housing. While motivation and training from Grameen employees certainly played a role in some cases, many of the borrowers would have taken most of these steps regardless of the bank's urgings. They are simply the widely accepted actions one takes to escape poverty when there is additional family income. Most poor Bangladeshi families, for example, don't keep their children from school because they don't value education. Far from it—they accord it high importance. But lack of income—due to unemployment and indebtedness to village loan sharks—makes sending children to school unaffordable. Some Grameen borrowers in Kholshi were at one time squatters on government land that was effectively ruled by a wealthy family. Before joining the bank, they were not growing vegetables near their huts because the fruits of their labor had in the past been seized. When they received loans from Grameen to buy their own homestead land, they became avid cultivators. In many cases, the poor lack only the financial resources— not the motivation— to break through social backwardness.

For the bank workers on the ground like Krishna, the spirit of the Sixteen Decisions showed itself in the solidarity it engendered. In Center Number 2, generous group fund loans were sanctioned for sick members. Borrowers who were unable to pull together enough money to make their payment at a center meeting received interest-free loans. When the husband of a group member became ill during the summer of 1993, she was given a group fund loan and an additional 400 taka from a special onetime collection. After her husband died, borrowers contributed the food the woman needed to put on a modest funeral reception that allowed her to begin life as a widow with a modicum of social dignity.

The fourteenth decision states, "We shall always be ready to help one another. If anyone is in difficulty, we shall help him or her." Members of Grameen's 130,000 centers do help one another, even if stories about mutual support have occasionally been exaggerated for the benefit of journalists and other visitors. This support serves as an important shock absorber for the bank and its members, enabling them to weather tough times. If Shandha's center implemented this decision more faithfully than most, it was still a powerful stabilizing force in the lives of millions of poor and formerly poor families whose social support network had been virtually nonexistent before they joined the bank.

Yunus's approach, then, is simple, hands-off, and replicable. But that does not guarantee success for everyone who tries it. Hundreds of frank discussions with Grameen staff and borrowers have left me with the impression that roughly 60 percent of the members who take loans are able to make steady and sustained improvements in their life after joining. Another one-quarter or so may spend years making small, halting improvements in their standard of living. Much of their progress, however, can easily be erased by a natural disaster or major family illness. For the final 10 to 15 percent of borrowers, participating leads to no impact or even a negative one. While these figures may vary slightly across different regions of the country, there is a surprising degree of agreement among staff about their accuracy in describing a typical branch. While a new generation of researchers have emphasized the "modest" nature of the typical improvements microcredit clients in other countries make in the first year or two of borrowing, they have yet to try their randomized controlled trial methodology in Bangladesh. Rather, they have focused on discrediting studies using other approaches that found Grameen and BRAC to be having a major positive impact. I stand by my conclusions that were formed through months of fieldwork across the country.

While one could argue that a more intensive, hands-on approach would be helpful to those borrowers who are unable to achieve more progress, Yunus responds by saying that failure by borrowers can almost always be traced back to mistakes made by his staff in administering the credit program. His faith in poor people's ability to get out of the rut is virtually unshakable. But more to the point, if Grameen tried to solve every problem of every borrower, it would almost certainly lose money and be unable to operate on the scale it does now.

In 1980, all the programs in Bangladesh providing credit to the poor (including Grameen) reached fewer than 100,000 families. Fourteen years later, that figure had grown to 4.5 million, or an increase of more than 4,500 percent. By 1994, close to half of all families living in poverty in the country were borrowing from poverty-focused programs. Instead of paying 120 percent annual interest to moneylenders, these families were paying 15 to 30 percent interest to development organizations. The difference represented a massive transfer of capital from loan sharks to poor people. The impact on poverty, landlessness, the oppression of women, and political powerlessness at the village level has been profound. Since then, the impact has grown and accelerated.

TOWARD THE END OF THE MONSOON, Fulzan gave birth to a premature, underweight newborn. To her and her husband's despair, it was a girl. Had it been a boy, Fulzan's relationship with her husband would have improved dramatically. As it was, he became distant, and spent more time with his first wife. It seemed that whichever of his two wives bore him a son first would become the favorite.

The second half of 1994 was remarkably unkind to Fulzan. The pregnancy took its toll on her. Her cow died, and when the owner of her sharecropped calf asked for Fulzan to return it, she received only 300 taka, even though she was due at least 500. Fulzan took in a calf from another family. The fragile state of her health and that of her infant precluded the possibility of ditchdigging for many months. Raising cows, ducks, chickens, and vegetables was her only source of income besides the crops her husband cultivated on land she had rented.

In October, she took all the profits she'd accrued since she'd begun to borrow and invested them in improving her small hut. She bought two sheets of corrugated tin, and with them was able to secure her entire roof for the first time. She replaced the rotting thatch that had constituted her walls, thereby plugging the gaping holes that had denied her any real privacy during her adult life. She also bought some wood and had her husband build her a door with a latch that allowed her to lock it from the inside. All of this cost her 2,000 taka. While her renovated hut was barely 20 square feet and five feet high, far smaller than those of the older borrowers in her center, it provided the best living conditions she'd ever enjoyed. Shelter for her two children was a priority for her, as it was for her group chairman, Nobirun, who made similar improvements in her hut after the 1994 monsoon.

At about the time that Fulzan was working on her house, the eighth group completed its group training and attempted to gain recognition. But on the appointed day, the women were not equal to the challenge. The group chairman was unable to begin the meeting correctly, and, rather unexpectedly, one woman couldn't stop giggling. As the day for the retest neared, two members of the original quintet dropped out. When Shandha spread the word that the group was looking for two new women in a hurry, Fulzan sent her niece Zorina, who had returned to the area with her husband in August. She had only two days to learn all the rules, but Zorina knew some already from the time when Fulzan was training, and she did so well that Shandha decided that she would be group chairman.

The reconstituted group passed. When it came time to make loan proposals, Zorina asked for 2,500 taka while the other four, all Hindus, asked for 5,000. Zorina used the money to buy some chickens and goats. Amodini's sister-in-law, who was the group secretary, invested her money in a convenience store that she ran out of her hut. Within two weeks, she was grossing 300 taka per day, as it was easier for the women in the Haldar *para* to buy from her than from the shopkeepers in the male-dominated Kholshi bazaar. Soon her weekly profit soared to 400 taka, more than enough to make her weekly loan installment of 100 taka. Zorina didn't have such immediate success, but it was hard to tell from talking with her. She radiated optimism, and was proud of being group chairman.

In the end, Fulzan Begum seemed destined to struggle harder for her progress than most other women. If Amena falls into the category of borrowers who make rapid and permanent progress out of poverty, Fulzan and Zorina would fall into the second category of women who make halting progress that is constantly in danger of being reversed. After nearly two years as a borrower, she still had a hard life. But no one who had seen her hut both before she joined Grameen and after she made the repairs in October 1994 could deny that, despite all the setbacks, the ability to borrow had brought a few important improvements to her life in a relatively short period of time.

IN EARLY OCTOBER 1994, rumors swept through the Grameen head office that Yunus was going to win the Nobel Prize for Economics. A few days later, it was announced that three American economists were sharing the award for their work on game theory. Many concluded that Yunus's work was not theoretical enough to pass muster with his fellow economists. Nobody ever receives the Nobel Prize in Economics for something practical, they said. Tradition was not about to change, at least not in 1994.

On October 16, Yunus traveled to Des Moines to receive the World Food Prize, a lesser award but one that still carried a $200,000 cash prize. Grameen's managing director announced that the money would be used to endow prizes for bank workers and borrowers who performed exceptionally well. In a story about Yunus's receiving the award, *USA Today* columnist Mark Memmott wrote, "The three winners of the Nobel Prize in Economic Science got a lot of attention last week. Reporters called from around the world. Their pictures were in newspapers everywhere. Meanwhile, another economist who won a major award last week received his $200,000 in relative obscurity. But Muhammad Yunus," Memmott concluded, "didn't seem to care. . . ."

Update: Since the 1990s

DURING THE TIME WHEN YUNUS WAS WAITING for permission from his government to transfer the $200,000 he received as part of the World Food Prize to Bangladesh, he put it in an interest-bearing bank account where it earned $12,000. Half of that was given to Grameen Foundation as its initial seed capital. This $6,000 was multiplied many times, and in just the first 10 years after its establishment, it channeled more than $200 million in new resources to support practitioners of poverty-focused microfinance.

In my latter years as CEO of Grameen Foundation, and even more since I stepped down, the foundation followed Yunus's lead by developing programs complementary to microfinance that focused on helping subsistence farmers, improving health care systems, and, through a program called Taroworks, helping front-line workers in any type of mission-driven organization or social business gather and transmit data instantaneously to allow for better and more responsive decision-making.

Grameen Foundation was not expected to support Grameen initiatives in Bangladesh, since they were so advanced and were encouraged by Yunus to mobilize funds from within Bangladesh and, if needed, from several financing entities within the Grameen Family of Companies. For a number of years, however, we formed an alliance with Grameen Shikkha ("Rural Education") to allow friends of the Grameen Foundation to endow scholarships for the children of Grameen clients who were at risk of dropping out of high school because of various costs related to their education. For just $1,000, a permanent endowment could be set up that pays about $10 per month to a student until they are ready for higher education—a sum that might sound small, but one that in Bangladesh can go a long way towards purchasing books, uniforms, and tutoring. Once students make it to college, those costs are subsidized by the state in the case of public universities or financed by the student loan program of Grameen Bank if a student goes to one of the growing number of private universities in Bangladesh.

While Grameen Foundation's network of volunteers and donors has been focused outside the borders of Bangladesh, we also tried to be helpful to Yunus and his team whenever possible. Scott Leckman, a Utah-based general surgeon, arranged for health checkups for Yunus that determined that he suffered from sleep apnea, and then worked out a way for him to be treated for it. This increased his energy level and made him feel, as he once told me, "ten years younger" and "like a new-built man." Two cataracts were removed from Yunus's eyes in the late 1990s and he dispensed with glasses for the first time in years. Khalid Shams, Yunus's deputy for many years, underwent triple bypass surgery in Utah. All of the fees for these procedures were waived. In another case, an Indian-American doctor who read the first edition of this book contacted Yunus and told him about cutting-edge research he was doing on ulcers. He later successfully treated Yunus for his ulcer, which has not recurred.

Clearly, a constituency exists to nurture not just the institutions involved in microfinance, but also its leaders. Grameen Foundation has continued to channel people into the movement who want to help, leveraging whatever skills they may have and want to contribute. For more about the establishment, successes, failures, and lessons of Grameen Foundation, check out the revised edition of my book *Changing the World Without Losing Your Mind: Leadership Lessons from Three Decades of Social Entrepreneurship* (Rivertowns Books, 2021).

THE MOST SIGNIFICANT EVOLUTION of Yunus's philosophy in recent years was his articulation of the concept of a *social business enterprise*, which he now simply refers to as a *social business*. This hybrid institutional form is the culmination of ideas he had been talking about and developing for years. The basic proposition is to create for-profit businesses with shareholders who are interested in preserving their capital but not in earning financial dividends or profits for themselves, at least not in the normal sense of those terms. Rather, they seek *social profit* in the form of positive, measurable impacts on societal problems such as poverty, ill health, illiteracy, and environmental degradation. If financial profit is earned, it is plowed back into the enterprise to do more good for society. He outlined his vision and gave practical examples of it in action in his exceptional book (written with my publisher Karl Weber) *Creating a World Without Poverty: Social Business and the Future of Capitalism* (PublicAffairs, 2008). They followed that up with an even better book that drew on some of his early successes with this new organizational model: *Building Social Business: The New Type of Capitalism that Serves Humanity's Most Pressing Needs* (PublicAffairs, 2010).

Yunus created some terrific social enterprises, such as a joint venture with the Danone Group (the French company known in the United States for Dannon yogurt), and challenged business and nonprofit leaders to develop support institutions for social businesses, including ratings agencies, a stock market, business school tracks, and more. He used his Nobel lecture to promote the concept and to gently urge the Norwegian telecom that was his joint venture partner in creating GrameenPhone to stay true to the social business ideal. He had been assured by the former chairman of Telenor, upon the launch of the company, that Grameen Bank could become majority owners in time and that Grameen clients could buy up those shares before it went public. However, when GrameenPhone turned out to be a successful and lucrative company, the Norwegian founders were reluctant to give up control. The tensions gradually abated, and in recent years Grameen enjoyed receiving around $1 million per month in dividends which it could deploy to innovative social businesses.

Grameen Foundation responded to Yunus's effort to define a new paradigm by creating two social enterprises. One was Grameen Capital India, a joint venture with ICICI Bank (the largest private bank in India) and Citibank, which was a fierce rival to ICICI in the Indian market. After a long registration process, Grameen Capital India became operational in 2007 and has served as a Mumbai-based investment bank for MFIs and other social enterprises across India. More recently, the foundation launched an impact investing fund called Grameen Impact India that invests in ventures spanning financial services, subsistence agriculture, affordable education, clean energy, and health care.

Yunus remains a committed humanist, although I have never heard him use that word. When he said, during his quixotic effort to start a political party in early 2007, that the Bangladeshi government should remain fundamentally secular in nature, he was criticized by those who seek to use religion to divide people for their political benefit. Even some of those who agreed with Yunus on this point counseled him to keep quiet. Some say that his commitment to being philosophically consistent doomed his candidacy. If that's the case, I say, Good for him!

In the meantime, he has become a powerful spokesperson for the climate change movement. I recall when he addressed Grameen leaders in 2015 in Bangkok and unveiled the theme that would guide him from then until now: creating what he called "a world of three zeroes." By that he meant, a world with zero poverty, zero unemployment, and zero net carbon emissions. He teamed up again with Karl Weber and came out with a terrific book titled *A World of Three Zeroes* (PublicAffairs, 2018), which compellingly outlined his new, expanded vision and how he hoped to realize it.

GRAMEEN II BROUGHT CHANGES large and small to borrowing groups like those in Kholshi. Today, borrowers sit on benches arranged in a U-shape rather than on bamboo mats and in rows. Loan officers like Krishna receive computerized printouts that already have the expected payments and savings deposits recorded. Now, all loan officers need to do is to mark exceptions, which tend to be rare. This vastly simplifies the work that bank staff have to do in center meetings.

Some old-timers in Grameen bemoaned the complexity of Grameen II compared to the original approach, but change was inevitable if the methodology was to stay relevant to the hundreds of types and sizes of businesses that borrowers were operating, many of which had financial needs that did not conform to the simple, one-size-fits-all products that characterized the Grameen Classic system that was used before Grameen II.

DURING THE YEAR IMMEDIATELY AFTER I FINISHED writing the first edition of this book, I tracked developments in Kholshi and Englewood and with Grameen and WSEP. For the most part, the progress of the women themselves and of the two institutions they were associated with continued in the same halting but impressive manner that it had during 1993 and 1994. Despite ongoing (though nonviolent) struggles with her husband, Amena built up savings and assets by continuing to raise livestock and expanding her vegetable garden to virtually every inch of the land around her hut. Devi joined with other weavers in the Haldar *para* to sew a huge fishing net that was then sold for more than 10,000 taka during the beginning of the monsoon. Shandha and Nonibala further grew their businesses, while Fulzan settled into her newly purchased homestead plot with her husband and children. Sadly, in August 1995, her oldest daughter died from a snake bite.

A series of events unfolded during the monsoon that profoundly affected the Shaymganj branch. On the night of May 29, 1995, a meeting was held in Munshikandi, a village near the Zianpur bazaar. Local elders—mostly politicians, but also a few religious leaders and moneylenders—persuaded many husbands of Grameen borrowers in the village to stop payment on their loans. Among the arguments the elders used was that Grameen was un-Islamic and that protests would force the bank to lower its interest rates. In reality, the elders were acting primarily in their own self-interest. As a few would admit later, disrupting the relationship between Grameen and its borrowers would revive their moneylending businesses and increase the number of destitute women willing to be servants in their households.

The anti-Grameen campaign was successful, at least at first. On the day following the meeting, the branch experienced its first missed installments since it was founded in 1987. Instead of finding women borrowers in the Munshikandi centers that morning, the bank workers found husbands and village elders presenting grievances and demands. Grameen employees responded that the recent policy changes that they disliked had been made by the bank's board of directors, a body on which borrowers served. Changes to those policies were possible, but would take time. Later that same day, bank workers went directly to the houses of some of the women and spoke to them. The men, however, stood firm: No changes, no installments. The following day, the elders informed the bank that they would no longer allow any direct contact between staff and the women. When the bank workers attempted to go to center meetings anyway, they were stopped on the village paths by the elders and their henchmen, who forcibly sent the Grameen employees back to the office. Within a few weeks, this conflict had spread to virtually every village in which the branch had centers. The local member of Parliament, as well as an opposition leader who planned to challenge the M.P. in the coming election, spoke out in favor of withholding payments. The branch's repayment rate temporarily plummeted to 8 percent. Periodically, letters from borrowers arrived at the branch office; they would explain that the women wanted to repay but were afraid to. In Kholshi, Amena and Shandha were the last borrowers to back down and stop paying. (They were also among the first to start up again once the conflict was resolved.)

As the manager and bank workers searched for a solution, a severe flood hit the area. Soon after the waters receded and the monsoon rice was replanted, another flood struck. After that inundation abated and rice was planted for a third time, an unprecedented third flood occurred. In many ways, this disaster was more severe than the "flood of the century" that had hit the nation in 1988.

The local Grameen employees huddled with their supervisors in Tepra and Dhaka to devise a strategy to get the branch back on track. First, word was spread that Grameen would distribute money from the borrowers' disaster savings fund, which had been established after the flood of 1988. When the borrowers came to the bank office to collect nearly 200 taka each—this was a trip few husbands were willing to oppose—the link between the bank and its borrowers was reestablished. At the same time, Grameen took legal action against those who were preventing bank workers from traveling to the centers, an act that had its intended effect: intimidating the intimidators.

By October, virtually all center meetings were being held again, and repayment rose to nearly 50 percent, despite the floods' devastation; in Shandha's center, it was nearly 100 percent. By December, it was clear that the branch had weathered two simultaneous attacks—one from the enemies it had made in the community, and the other from nature.

14. "We're Here for You"

THELMA COULDN'T WAIT ANY LONGER. "Okay, let's go over my receipts," she said to the three other women of Les Papillons and a prospective new member named Margaret Roberts, a friend of Queenesta's who was going through the orientation process. It was just before 8 p.m. on October 17, 1994, and they were in the Lindblom Park field house for their twice-monthly center meeting. Fifteen minutes earlier, the women had divided into small groups according to which circle they belonged to, and there was a lot to do.

Thelma pulled a crumpled, weathered plastic bag from her purse, reached inside, and grabbed its contents—nearly one hundred receipts she had been given by wholesalers from whom she had bought merchandise in June and July. She believed in doing things by the book, even if Colete didn't always pressure her or the others to do so.

Over the next 20 minutes, Thelma went through her ratty pile of receipts, some for as little as five dollars. She read them out—"Hair accessories, twenty-seven dollars and fifty cents"—one by one and passed them around. The other women inspected each of them in turn and then handed them to Geri, who was keeping a running total to make sure it was roughly the same as Thelma's loan amount.

Borrowers are required to go over receipts before their circle sisters and show them to a senior WSEP staff member to ensure that merchandise they promised to buy with their loans was, in fact, bought. Thelma's demeanor during the process was solemn, her voice strictly monotone. She believed there was something sacred about receiving credit and handling it with integrity, and it showed. Les Papillons would not be treated to any of her usual humorous outbursts on this night.

"Geri, what's the total at now?" she said at one point.

"Uh, wait a minute . . . it's at four thousand five hundred and twenty-two dollars."

"Well, I really don't have to do any more, because that's more than my loan amount. The rest of these receipts are for things I bought after I started rolling my money over." After a brief pause, she said, "Queenesta, are you going to be able to go over your receipts?"

"Uh, you know, all of my merchandise was stolen, and so were my receipts," she said weakly.

Time was running short, as there was a guest speaker there that night. Omiyale, Thelma, and Geri began paying their installments. Omiyale wrote a check for $144, while Thelma counted out $100 in fives, tens, and ones, and Geri produced a check for $11. As the women gave Colete their payments, Thelma suggested that Omiyale present her receipts for the loan she received in July at the next meeting. Les Papillons' chairlady had returned from Africa in August with two suitcases full of merchandise on which she had spent $1,500, and by mid-October she was well on her way to selling it all for $6,000. Omiyale was considering another trip to Africa in February, to be financed out of her profits. She was eager to do business with a Gambian wholesaler she had met on the last day of her trip who was willing to offer her extremely good prices. In September, she had bought a used commercial oven and set it up in her house and was now producing a hundred cases of cookies in under three hours.

"SO, QUEENESTA, YOU AREN'T MAKING a payment tonight, right?" Thelma asked matter-of-factly as she began putting her receipts back in the plastic bag.

"No." It was her fourth straight missed payment, dating back to September 5. On October 1, Queenesta had opened a new store, called Q's, that was eight blocks east of her old location, and she was specializing in beepers. She hated the fact that she was behind, and felt angry with Thelma for bringing it out in the open. "Kathleen [Robbins, WSEP's loan fund manager] told me that she will be coming out to my store and working out a new payment plan for me. My installment will be based on what my actual revenue is from my store. Once we work that out, I will not technically be in default, as long as I continue paying my new installment."

Thelma and Omiyale were dismayed. Even though it meant that the circle's borrowing privileges would not be suspended, it was an unprecedented arrangement (though one that anticipated the policies of Grameen II). Thelma and Omiyale resented that Queenesta had gone over their heads, and were disturbed that Robbins had apparently gone along with her. Thelma had agreed to sanction a $1,000 loan from the group's emergency loan fund a month earlier, even though she had doubts about the way Queenesta was going to use it. She felt that she and the others deserved more than this fait accompli.

"Queenesta, are you *sure* that is what Kathleen is sayin'?" Thelma asked. "They ain't never done nothing like this before," she added, looking at Omiyale.

"Kathleen said this is what they are going to do to help us out."

"But you done already missed four payments," Thelma responded. Her voice was calm, but she was on the verge of losing her cool. "How are they going to get you out of default without you making those four payments up?"

"It doesn't sound right to me," Omiyale added. Queenesta bowed her head and covered her eyes with her hands. She began to weep softly, and for a moment the group sat without a word being spoken.

Then Margaret jumped in. "You know, when I heard what this group was about, about people coming together and supporting one another and being sisters, I was so inspired and I thought I just had to join. But how you're being with Queenesta, this isn't sisterhood. Queenesta didn't lose her merchandise through any fault of her own. It was stolen. She isn't responsible for this." As she spoke, Margaret looked at no one in particular, but it was obvious that her displeasure was focused on Thelma. She was hoping to get Omiyale on her, and Queenesta's, side.

"Look," Thelma said in response, her hand karate-chopping the table for emphasis, "it's not about who's responsible or *whatever*—it's about doing things right, by the rules. The rules this organization set up are good rules, and we agreed to go by them. I don't want to get into the issue of why Queenesta lost her merchandise, because ever since the Haile Selassie Fest, and even before, I've been saying that this man is *no good*. If Queenesta had asked my advice, I would have said, 'Don't move in with him, don't get involved with him, break off the partnership, whatever.'"

"I'll tell you why I did what I did," Queenesta said as she fought back more tears, "because Kathleen seemed like the only person who was able and willing to help me through this whole thing."

"You never asked—" Thelma began.

"Let me say something," Omiyale interrupted. "I want to say something." Thelma leaned back in her chair, and despite her frown, she was eager to turn over the floor to her chairlady. "I have not said very much about it, but I went through some hard times earlier this year with my short-term loan, and I still have scars and I have to say that you never really seemed to want any help or advice from me with all that's happened. And I just think that if you're going to do something with Kathleen, we should be involved."

Thelma, looking Queenesta directly in the eye, added, "Listen, if it takes you months to clear this loan, that's okay. We're here for you. If all you can pay is ten or fifteen dollars every two weeks until the end of the year, do that. We all want a solution; we all want you back on your feet. Just don't stop coming to the meetings, don't drop out of communications with us. As long as you're here, we can work out a solution."

Geri and Omiyale concurred. Then Colete was drawn into the conversation, and after hearing about Queenesta's discussion with Kathleen Robbins, she agreed that no decision could be made without involving her and everyone in the circle, if not the entire center. That compromise, and Colete's serene demeanor, seemed to put everyone at ease. The women completed the short orientation session, which consisted of reading some of the Fund's rules out loud and asking whether Margaret had questions, and began moving back to join the larger group. As they stood up, Thelma said, "Queenesta, just don't stop coming. We can work this out, whatever it takes. Just don't stop coming."

Q'S WAS LARGER AND AIRIER than the Hip Hop Shop. The carpeted shopping area was filled with two racks of T-shirts, a metal shelf containing household merchandise (such as baby oil, paper towels, and glass cleaner) that all sold for a dollar, and a small nook area along one of the walls. In the corner opposite the door were two glass display cases placed perpendicular to each other that, together with a wall and a partition, created an enclosed area for salespeople. In the cases were baseball hats, beepers, and jewelry. The partitions that separated the shopping area from Queenesta's office and the manufacturing station were six feet tall; the bottom half of the partitions was plastic, while the top half was made of glass. That allowed anybody working behind the partitions to observe the entire store.

During September, when she and Shayna were living with her mother, Queenesta had searched for a place to live and a location for a new store. She was able to arrange for an apartment and a shop in the same building. The prospect of living and working in the same place galvanized her to seek a $1,000 loan from Les Papillons' emergency loan fund, put down her deposit with the landlord, and get current on her payments to the Chicago Pagers, a beeper wholesaler. Several days before opening, she registered her new business and lease in her own name.

Restarting her venture was difficult. There was the issue of merchandise—she had virtually none left. The only way to get through the period when her income from beepers would not meet her store rent of $500 would be to take in subtenants. As fate would have it, Victor was facing a crisis of his own in September.

His landlord was raising his rent from $700 to $850, and he would have none of it. In fact, he was tiring of holding seminars and book signings, and saw his future in manufacturing kufis. His daughter Sheila had become a talented seamstress over the past year, and he soon had another woman working for him as well. Between the two young women and Victor, they could produce hundreds of kufis per month, and demand was growing.

Victor was also looking to get out of the book business. When he opened West Side Books in 1990, it had been the only store on the West Side selling Black-oriented books. By the fall of 1994, there were six. By then, much of his income came from other merchandise, such as clothing, household goods, and jewelry. In any case, he figured that he had made good money for a couple of years but that now, with the book market saturated, it was time to get out. When Queenesta told Victor about her new location, he proposed that he come in as a subtenant. He would be willing to contribute his display cases and shelves from his old store if Queenesta would let him liquidate some of his stock of books at her store. This suited her fine, and they made all the arrangements and raced to be ready for an October 1 opening.

Early in October, a man Victor knew became Queenesta's second subtenant. He wanted to sell dollar merchandise from one display cabinet and a metal shelf. Queenesta thought it might not appeal to the younger crowd she was targeting—baby lotion and sponges are more likely to be bought by adults—but it was rental income, and she jumped at the opportunity.

One chilly, windswept day in mid-October, Omiyale phoned Queenesta at the store and asked her how things were going. "Oh, slow, I guess. But it's coming along, you know," she said. The conversation was brief, but Queenesta appreciated the call. She and Omiyale had become closer in recent months. Omiyale kept telling her to focus on the positive side of what had happened— now she lived where she worked, Nixon was out of the picture, her business was hers and hers alone, and she had not lost any of what she had learned in the past two years. Omiyale had been impressed with the store when she came out to see it, and told her so. "You're better off than you ever were, Queenesta," Omiyale would often say that fall, "and someday you'll see that more clearly than you do today." The more she said it, the more Queenesta believed it.

Yet there was still a sadness about Queenesta as she sat in her store that day. Her dispute with Nixon had become a rather public one. She didn't like having to defend herself before friends, acquaintances, and even complete strangers about things dating back to her childhood and her relationship with Shayna's father. Moreover, all of the conflicting advice she was getting confused her. She decided to stay away from Nixon. There were moments when Queenesta blamed herself for the entire mess; had she made some better decisions, she might have been able to keep the Hip Hop Shop and its merchandise. Moving in with Nixon, she realized, had been riskier than she'd thought at the time. But she was a proud woman who didn't like to share her self-doubts with many people. Mostly, she wanted to lay low while she got herself back on her feet. Naming the store Q's was part of that—remaining somewhat anonymous to the public while showing people who know her that she, and not Victor or any other man, was in charge.

"Hey," Victor called out to a visitor sitting on a couch next to Queenesta's desk, "don't you think it's amazing?" Victor, smiling mischievously, was standing in his manufacturing area, which was littered with fabric, scraps, sewing machines, and flyers. "Don't you think it's amazing that Queenesta landed on her feet? After all that happened, here she is in a store, she's opened it, and she has two tenants. What do you think?" Victor McClain clearly admired and respected Queenesta. For all his rough edges, he was big enough to be able to joke about how their roles had been reversed.

Before the person to whom Victor had directed his question could answer, a customer walked in the door, and Queenesta rushed out to help him.

By the time she returned, Victor was sorting through fabric, his question long since forgotten.

DURING HIS CAMPAIGN FOR THE PRESIDENCY in 1992, Bill Clinton suggested that Muhammad Yunus should win the Nobel Prize. Furthermore, he said that, if elected, he planned to start a thousand Grameen-style microenterprise programs, organizations like WSEP, in the United States. This, combined with the prospect of an overhaul of the health care and welfare systems, and the possibility that changes would be accomplished in a manner that took into account the needs of the self-employed poor, gave many people familiar with the microenterprise field reason to hope. Furthermore, members of Congress ranging from liberal Democrat Tony Hall to conservative Republican Fred Grandy were talking about the need to encourage self-employment as a path out of poverty.

During Clinton's two terms in office, some of those hopes were realized, while others never saw the light of day. Yet, no one can deny that presidential attention opened doors for microenterprise programs. But exposure is a double-edged sword; it has also given critics of the approach new opportunities to articulate their doubts. How these critiques were answered, both in foundation-sponsored seminars and in places like Queenesta's store and the Lindblom Park Field House, went a long way toward determining that U.S.-based microenterprise programs in general, and Grameen-style peer lending projects in particular, were not short-lived fads but instead something more substantial and important. But it would take Grameen America's success to put those questions to rest. In the years before it got going, there were impassioned debates about its relevance to American poverty that still resonate today.

There are three areas where challenges were made in the mid-1990s to the viability of peer-based microenterprise programs, which by then had been in operation for a decade. They revolved around the issues of cost, impact, and scale.

By several measurements, the products that WSEP offered its clients, including the Full Circle Fund, were expensive. WSEP's Full Circle Fund spent more in salaries and other administrative costs than it made in loans during its early years. This is much more than it costs Grameen and other successful projects in the developing countries to lend, though the FCF provides additional services that are arguably required by its borrowers but not needed in developing country contexts. During its years in operation, interest earned on its loan portfolio covered only a small fraction of WSEP's (or the FCF's) institutional costs. Few programs in the United States could claim to be doing much better until Grameen America came on the scene.

Given the cost structures in the two regions, one would be surprised were it otherwise. In Bangladesh, a university graduate with a master's degree who begins work at Grameen Bank earns less than 3,000 taka ($75) per month, including benefits. This is roughly equal to the average loan size of first-time borrowers. In WSEP, an entry-level employee with a master's degree earned more than $3,000 in monthly pretax income, including benefits—roughly four times the average amount of a first-time loan. Moreover, were Grameen to drop its entry-level salary by 20 percent, it would still get thousands of qualified applicants; were WSEP to do the same, it would have difficulty filling staff positions.

The criticism that programs like WSEP are too expensive misses several other crucial points. First, it fails to recognize that when successful programs like Grameen were in their youth, and when the field of developing world microlending was new, most programs lost considerable sums of donor, government, and foundation funds. Only as the best programs matured did people even begin to talk about breaking even after all subsidies were withdrawn. (Before that, many simply marveled that a nonprofit organization could get most of its loan repaid and cover even a quarter of its operating costs through interest and fees paid by borrowers.) By using strict criteria for what constitutes income and expenditure, Grameen arguably experienced its first truly profitable year in 1994—17 years after the first loan was given out. Even when using these strict criteria, which exclude income Grameen has received from investing some of its idle funds, by the middle and late 1980s, it was operating near the breakeven point, and the losses were largely attributable to the establishment of significant numbers of new branches as part of an aggressive expansion program. (New bank branches, like many new businesses, tend to lose money for a few years while progressing toward profitability.)

Only through thousands of cycles of trial and error by field staff, continuous attention to cost-cutting, and the growing capacity of borrowers to absorb larger loans (while requiring less supervision) was it able to achieve this profit. Most other projects in developing countries that have made a profit in a shorter time have done so without focusing on extremely poor clients. Thus, to expect the programs in industrialized countries to break even when they and their field are relatively young is to expect more out of them than was expected of their forerunners in places like Bangladesh, which did not have to deal with rich country wages, regulations, and welfare disincentives. As it turns out, this initial period of experimentation did go on longer in the United States than in most other countries, but it did finally culminate in a crushing of the cost curve.

But even if Grameen America hadn't proven the potential to do microlending in a sustainable way, there would have been a case to continue these programs. Indeed, it would probably be fairer to compare programs like the Full Circle Fund with training programs, government transfer payment schemes, workfare programs, and enterprise zones based on their cost effectiveness. If, dollar for dollar, WSEP can increase the poor's income or get people off welfare rolls—and on to the tax rolls—more efficiently than other interventions, then it will have a legitimate claim on public and philanthropic resources. Data collected by the Aspen Institute indicated that when held to this more realistic standard, even back in the 1990s WSEP and similar programs met or exceeded efficiency benchmarks set by many other employment and poverty reduction strategies. For instance, the institute noted that the cost per job created in six microenterprise development organizations averaged roughly $4,000, about one-third as much as some traditional employment programs.[71]

If these agencies, like the projects in developing countries, can slowly reduce costs and increase revenue so they come closer to the breakeven point, all the better. But to call for discontinuing support for these programs, as some policy wonks and people in the philanthropic community did in the early years of U.S. microlending, by holding them to a higher standard than the projects with which they are competing for resources, seemed foolhardy. The subsequent success of Grameen America showed why this was the case, in quite dramatic fashion. Once again, it became clear that playing the long game—intensively but patiently—is the only way sustainable social change occurs.

Another criticism of peer lending programs is that they have not been able to attract significant numbers of poor entrepreneurs to participate in them. And some claim that the default rates experienced by these programs were unacceptably high. By the end of 1994, WSEP had made loans totaling nearly

$1 million to some 500 women. Of this amount, two-thirds had already been repaid and another $50,000 had been collected in interest payments. All but about two dozen loans had either been paid back or were outstanding and were being repaid more or less on schedule. These numbers are neither embarrassing nor overwhelming. Certainly, they are not comparable to the track record of Grameen's millions of borrowers. Many early North American programs, including some modeled after Grameen, were not able to achieve even the modest outreach and repayment figures reached by WSEP; a few have hardly been able to attract any clients and have experienced high delinquency rates. Critics take these findings to suggest that peer lending programs have little to offer them in their attempt to start or improve their business. Others question the wisdom of encouraging the poor to be self-employed in the first place, and advocate that the focus should be on getting them jobs. (Rarely, however, do those arguing this point consider that people without high school degrees often get stuck in dead-end employment with few benefits or growth opportunities, and that those with criminal records are often barred from many professions even after they pay their debt to society.)

These arguments, however, fail to recognize that during Grameen's first four years of operation, it barely reached 500 people. In fact, at the conclusion of 1979, many of the borrowers who had joined either were leaving the program or were in default. But Yunus and his students learned from their mistakes in Jobra as they set up operations in Tangail. That second phase progressed faster, although this was in part due to their taking some shortcuts, such as including large numbers of male borrowers—a decision that led to a repayment crisis that was subsequently solved in the mid-1980s. What Grameen's own experience demonstrates is that even in Bangladesh, a program's early years, particularly when the field is new in that country, are rarely characterized by large numbers of participants and perfect repayment. In reality, the early years serve primarily to educate the staff of an organization through a laborious process of experimentation. If, in the course of that process, people like Zorina (the beggar woman from Jobra) or Thelma Ali are able to benefit, all the better. And this is precisely the experience in North America, where the more successful programs are learning from their experiments and the best of the new programs are setting a new standard for repayment and participation in the pilot phase. As Yunus realized in Bangladesh, business at new branches begins slowly, and later grows as the first borrowers experience success and people hear about it. In Asia, no less than in Chicago, the vast majority of poor women approach credit programs with trepidation. It takes time to gain their trust.

To have microlending programs reach their full potential in the United States, there will need to be some larger policy changes. Breakthroughs will be unlikely to occur unless some headway is made in changing the zoning, social welfare, and health care policies that work against the self-employed poor. Indeed, it is a wonder that so many women have already tried to leave welfare by joining these programs despite the fact that they gave up, or risked giving up, a monthly check and health benefits when they did so. It is only slightly less remarkable that so many others have opted for self-employment over welfare after they lost their jobs. Unless the incentives are reversed, so that work is more rewarding than welfare and so that self-employment is a viable alternative to wage employment for people who want it, it would be naïve to think that these programs will have the societal impact they did in places like Bangladesh.

But grow they did. Even without much in the way of policy change, microfinance in the U.S. became larger than anyone could have imagined in the 1990s, largely due to Grameen America coming on the scene in 2008. Indeed, it would have been difficult to predict in 1980 that in a disaster-prone country with a moribund economy, a pilot project with a decidedly mixed record of success would, over the next 15 years, grow into a financial institution serving more than two million people, lending millions of dollars every working day, earning enough to make a modest profit, and training people from dozens of countries spanning five continents to reproduce its success. Now we have finally embarked on a similar period of growth in the developed world. The microenterprise movement in the United States came a long way in the first decade since its first pilot projects were launched in the mid-1980s. During the process of trial-and-error experimentation that followed, a great deal has been learned about how to adapt an antipoverty strategy that originated in places like Bangladesh to the realities of impoverished communities in developed countries.

In an effort to accelerate the process of refining the approach and lobbying for policy changes that would benefit poor entrepreneurs, organizations pioneering the microenterprise approach in North America formed a coalition called the Association for Enterprise Opportunity (AEO) that has held a series of successful conferences. On several occasions, Muhammad Yunus has participated in the group's deliberations, providing technical advice and moral support. As mentioned earlier, in 2009 AEO hired Connie Evans, the founder of WSEP, to be its CEO. She has done a terrific job leading the national microenterprise movement in exciting directions ever since.

THE SUN WAS SHINING NOW, though Thelma and Janet Johnson, Omiyale's sister, hardly noticed it. They had once again arrived before dawn to set up their tables at the new, relocated Maxwell Street Market. At 7:00 a.m., they were already helping customers who had walked to the Fourteenth Street viaduct, one of two that was part of the new bazaar. The vendors' tables were partly illuminated by fluorescent lights, whose casings were covered with several years of accumulated dirt. Wind whipped through the tunnel, often leaving tablecloths and merchandise fluttering in its wake. Thelma wondered what the wind conditions would be like in December and January.

Two teenage girls walked up to Thelma's black wooden coffee table and inspected the merchandise on her table. The hair wraps were still popular; she let them go at three for $1, having bought them for $2 a dozen from a Korean wholesaler on Clark Street. The Tunisian oils had been selling slowly since she moved to the new market; she had encouraged her regular customers to stock up in August, the last month of the old bazaar, and had sold only $600 in oils since then. Still, she brought the oils to the new market, hoping that the old customers would find her when they ran out. She had put her stall number on her business card and given it to them. She also hoped to be able to build up a new customer base here.

Two girls bought $4 worth of hair accessories, and as they walked away, Thelma called out, "Thanks a lot, and tell your friends about me, ya hear." It was 7:35 a.m., and she had already made $45. Her trusty leather purse was slung around her torso as usual, and she was filling it with quarters and small bills. She was suffering from a head cold, and was thinking about buying some chicken soup from a vendor on Canal Street, the new market's main drag that ran perpendicular to the two viaducts.

Thelma left her table with a friend and walked toward Canal Street, passing several vendors she knew and two she didn't. This market isn't so bad, Thelma thought as she came out from under the viaduct. The sunlight felt warm on her skin, but it forced her to shield her eyes, as she'd been in a shaded area since 5:50 a.m. It's a different type of traffic, she thought, more white and Hispanic, less Black. But different doesn't always mean bad, she knew. She looked to her left and saw Marshall Zimmerman. He was doing fairly well selling shoes, and during the week he was selling videos on a street corner near the site of the old Maxwell Street Market. Down a little farther, just out of sight, was Mamadu, the Senegalese purse vendor with whom she was friendly.

The old market had died a soggy death on August 28, 1994. A few activists tried to instigate a protest but had little success. "The vendors and their customers," the *Chicago Tribune* explained the next day, "had known for months that a squeeze play by Mayor Richard Daley and the University of Illinois at Chicago was going to wipe out the market. If there was any fight left in them, there was no sign of it." Within days, the few vendors' shacks that remained were torn down, a handful of protesters were removed, and most of the area that had constituted the bazaar was fenced in and bulldozed. Weeks later, broken asphalt wedges jutted into the air at the same sharp angles they had assumed in the early days of September. So urgent was the university's need for the land that they left it alone for several months after having hurriedly made it unusable to vendors and customers.

On September 4, the new market opened. As expected, it had manifest disadvantages compared with the original. There was room for only 400 vendors, less than half as many as used to crowd into the old bazaar. Vendors were forced to pay higher fees ($15 each week for small spots like Thelma had, and $35 for larger spots in which the vendor could park a car), were prohibited from selling certain goods (for example, food) without the appropriate licenses, and were not allowed to sell certain other merchandise (such as X-rated videos) under any circumstances. Business was down for most vendors. Parking was difficult for customers to find, and the location had no history and was unfamiliar. Fewer people came and they tended to spend less. And, perhaps most noticeably, the raucous and irreverent edges of Maxwell Street had been smoothed, its naked grassroots capitalism airbrushed away.

Yet the new market was not without its redeeming features, and as the weeks passed, business slowly improved. The original plan for the reconstituted bazaar, drawn up by a New York consulting firm that was paid $80,000 for its efforts, was to transform it into a New England–style yuppie market. Activists and vendors protested, and the city ordered that the plan be redone. Later versions were more in keeping with the spirit of the original Maxwell Street, and once the market was inaugurated, a few of the city employees who were charged with overseeing it relaxed some of the regulations, further enhancing the bazaar's charm and character. Welcome additions to the new market included portable toilets, trash cans, and Dumpsters. By October, even vendors who claimed their sales were off by 70 percent were saying, "It's not so bad. We'll give it a try. It'll need time to develop. Let's see."

The poor, as they have throughout history, adapted to the whims of the establishment and were doing the best they could—not because they are more magnanimous than wealthier folks, but because they have no other choice. The new market was inferior to the old one, but not so inferior as to make it useless to them. They continued to need money, and there was still money to be made—albeit less than there had been before.

Thelma stayed. It was her most consistent source of income after the summer festivals were over. Janet also stayed, her dream of owning property alive and well. Omiyale, who arrived at 7:55 a.m., kept coming, too. On this day, she was selling old inventory, her cookies, and a few of her African imports.

As Thelma returned to her stall, a customer came up and bought some dish towels from her. Another purchased a wood carving of a Thai temple for $20. Some teens came by and toyed with a lighter in the shape of a gun. When someone wanted to buy some tools but only had a $100 bill, Thelma brought it to Lewis, who sold used books and records, for change. He had it, but wasn't sure the bill was genuine. Another vendor inspected it closely and pronounced it okay. Lewis promptly pulled out a wad of tens and twenties and made change for Thelma.

Down at the other end of the viaduct, Omiyale was bringing out the last of her merchandise from her car and setting up alongside Janet. There were children's two-piece outfits for $4 that she had picked up for $1 at a going-out-of-business sale, an adjustable knee brace, a cardboard box full of butter cookies, a Halloween costume, and a few pairs of mittens.

Omiyale sold two children's outfits and several packages of cookies. A few people opened the knee brace and looked at it, but none would part with $15. She offered it for $12 to one woman, who then decided against it after hesitating for a moment. Omiyale felt sure it would go for $10, $5 more than she had paid for it. As three Mexican women crowded around Janet's table, a car parts vendor from the other side of the viaduct came and bought six packs of butter cookies.

Other vendors were among Omiyale's best cookie customers. Indeed, when she wanted to unload 100 packets in a hurry, she always went down to the stores near the site of the old Maxwell Street Market and sold them there, even on weekdays, even after the market had closed. Rarely did she return with anything except small bills and an empty cardboard box. During the fall, she would often bake in the morning, sell fresh-made cookies in the early afternoon, and hold a house party to sell her African imports in the late afternoon. Somewhere in there she would return calls to Colete and Leverta Pack, pick up butter, flour, and sugar, fix meals for her family, and pick up her grandchildren from school. It was a busy lifestyle, but she was keeping up with her payments and making good money. In October, she was planning a roller-skating party for December that would raise money to retire the debts of two defaulters in her center.

Thelma, Omiyale, and Janet would remain down at the new Maxwell Street Market until late on that mid-October afternoon. By then, they had made more than $300 between them. Janet saved most of her profits for the down payment on the house she hoped to buy one day, and Omiyale put hers aside for her plane fare to Africa. For Thelma, it meant another payment on a sewing machine she had put on layaway. She hoped to have it in her apartment by December, so that she could spend the winter months making children's kufis and other Afrocentric clothes to sell at a small number of winter events she attended in the South, at the Black Women's Expo in March, and throughout the following summer. She was also considering taking a loan of $24,000 from the Small Business Administration through WSEP. Doing so would mean spending most of the summer on the road doing events. The idea both intimidated and excited her, and as she returned home at 6:00 that Sunday evening, she was deep in thought, trying to decide whether to take the risk. Perhaps the Almighty Allah, she concluded for the time being, would give her a sign to guide her. Until then, she would keep her tried-and-true formula—borrowing, investing, earning, and reinvesting, with most of her merchandise retailing for $3 and under. It was not exactly glamorous, but she often enjoyed it. Most important, it helped pay the bills. And that, after all, was what mattered most.

Update: Since the 1990s

IN CHICAGO, THELMA'S BUSINESS continued to thrive during the summer months of 1995. She resisted the temptation to take a large Small Business Administration loan. Omiyale progressed toward completing the courses necessary to get her baker's license and sold a lot of cookies. Glenda continued working for Westcorp and making jewelry, while Geri found another full-time job after Fort Smith closed up his retail business to concentrate on manufacturing and wholesaling. Queenesta's business grew impressively, and do did those of her tenants. Shayna transferred to the elite North Side grammar school that her mother had attended.

Still, a cloud hung over the group's achievements in 1995. Queenesta was able to make only token payments on her loan, usually $50 per month but occasionally as much as $200. As a result, lending to members of Les Papillons was temporarily suspended. Relations among the women became strained again. It seemed at times as though the circle might dissolve, but it didn't, at least not that year. Instead, the women struggled together to make their businesses thrive without loans from WSEP and to raise the money needed to retire Queenesta's debt.

INSPIRED BY THE EARLY SUCCESS of groups like WSEP, hundreds of organizations sprung up in the 1990s whose purpose was to assist low- and moderate-income people to start and expand micro- and small businesses as ways to contribute to grassroots-level community development and create good, flexible jobs that were particularly relevant to single mothers who preferred to start their entrepreneurial ventures in their homes, where they could look after children while tending their business. Yunus addressed a conference of U.S. microlenders in 2007 as a way of showing support and providing encouragement. A few leading providers were recovering as much as 70 percent of their costs through interest charged on loans and fees, reducing the need for philanthropic support for this already cost-effective approach to creating jobs in low-income neighborhoods.

By then, Yunus was well on his way to launching Grameen America, which would shake up the field in ways no one—including me—could have imagined.

In the late 1990s, WSEP gave birth to a successful for-profit sister organization—WSEP Ventures. Connie Evans spearheaded this forward-thinking social business and turned over the day-to-day operations of the nonprofit organization to others. The Full Circle Fund was phased out as an active program of WSEP (the nonprofit) in the late 1990s even as organizations like Project Enterprise drew lessons and inspiration from that pioneering effort and built on WSEP's many accomplishments. Omiyale and Thelma in particular continued to take part in other WSEP programs over the years.

In February 2006, on its twentieth anniversary, WSEP and WSEP Ventures completed their life cycles as social change agents, passing the torch to a new generation of organizations that saw self-employment as a path to self-empowerment for low-income Americans. WSEP certainly had much to be proud of based on its two decades of work serving women and the microenterprise development sector.

Building on its early experiences with the promotion of individual savings and asset accumulation within the Full Circle Fund, WSEP pioneered Individual Development Accounts (IDAs)—an innovative approach that led to the development of hundreds of programs and tens of thousands of new low-income savers and asset-holders around the country. Scores of women involved in WSEP's programs have become homeowners and business owners. Overall, more than 6,000 Chicago-area women had started and developed businesses through WSEP and microfinancing, and their lives and communities were forever changed as a result.

The staff and clients of WSEP and organizations like it were able to keep the American microcredit flame lit until a new entrant was able to take it all to a new level in the 2010s. We owe them our gratitude and should study the evolution of the Grameen model in the United States to gain a fuller and more realistic understanding of how societal change actually occurs.

Epilogue

THROUGHOUT THIS EDITION, I have made an effort to include developments within Grameen Bank and WSEP and in the larger environments in which they operated—the microfinance movement, the international campaign to end extreme poverty, and a globalizing economy. Trying to fully integrate updates on the lives of the women profiled in this book would have been an impossible undertaking. I have, however, tracked their stories to some extent, and their uneven but steady progress has reaffirmed my belief in microfinance, and also my desire to ensure that the model continues to improve and serve the poor better through more responsive products and more efficient delivery models.

Perhaps ironically, it has been easier to keep up with the women in Bangladesh than with their counterparts in Chicago. The fact that the rural Bangladeshis tend to remain in a fixed location for most of their lives, and that the flight of Kholshi's Hindus to India never materialized, may explain this circumstance, at least in part.

In 2004, when on a sabbatical from Grameen Foundation, I went to Kholshi for a visit that was shortened to a few hours because transportation there had become more difficult due to the shifting of the Jamuna River. I visited and talked extensively with Nonibala, Amodini, and Shandha, who were all doing well. Noni was a village phone operator, and her husband walked around the village most days trying to drum up business. Calls would come in from far-flung locales, such as Saudi Arabia and Malaysia, and he would answer, tell the caller to try back in 20 minutes, and then run to the home of the neighbor with whom the caller wanted to talk. Noni owned more than 10 cows. Amodini's spirits had brightened as the painful memory of her husband's death receded. Shandha remained the mother hen of the center, and her son was one of the first recipients of Grameen's "higher education loan," which amounted to 70,000 taka. The value of her home, which she had constructed in stages, was about 200,000 taka, or $4,000 based on the exchange rate at that time. Before joining Grameen, her home was probably worth less than $200.

Towards the end of my visit I found Amena. We exchanged only a few words, but what remains imprinted on my mind to this day is her face. Previously gaunt, her visage had filled out. She almost looked slightly pudgy. Clearly, her nutritional status had improved significantly over the previous seven years. Overall, the branch was one of the laggards of Dhaka zone in terms of financial performance, due mainly to the fact that the shifting of the massive Jamuna River had semi-permanently submerged one entire village it served and parts of several others. This led dozens of borrowers to default and many others to relocate and join other Grameen branches nearby. Still, the branch was marginally profitable, and the tensions between the local elites and religious leaders that had emerged as a problem in 1995 had abated.

On a return visit three years later I learned of more progress. Shandha's son was in his final year of study for a master's degree in management from a respected university in the capital city of Dhaka. Shandha had three cows worth 60,000 taka and had leased an acre of land for 80,000 taka, which enabled her to eat rice from her own land throughout much of the year. Amodini had made a clean break with the funk that had enveloped her after her husband died. The daughter who began fishing after her father died, in order to keep the family afloat economically, had married a white-collar worker in the garment industry. Nonibala had amassed more than 100,000 taka in working capital in her business and retained the contract with a Dhaka confectionary. They'd bought a small motorized boat in order to more easily procure milk during the rainy season, and also to transport the cottage cheese to Aricha, from where it was loaded onto a bus each afternoon. One son had learned to be a silversmith. Noni told me matter-of-factly, "The one reason we are thriving is Grameen Bank."

IN THE WAKE OF HER HUSBAND'S DEATH in 2006, Oloka Ghosh opened her own small confectionary shop in the Kholshi bazaar, demonstrating the resilience that Grameen borrowers can exhibit when setbacks strike. Aduree was not doing as well. She had sold the house she had built with a Grameen housing loan. Her husband was working in Dhaka and returned home irregularly. Devi Rani Halder, on the other hand, had leased a fishing pond for 100,000 taka and was very proud of that achievement. She bought her husband a small boat and wove him a fishing net; together, they were worth about 25,000 taka. In addition, her family had opened its own sweet shop in a local market. Her home was also valued at about 200,000 taka.

I did not see Fulzan in 2004. I assumed that she had never paid back the loan she fell behind on in 1995. To my surprise, I learned that she had somehow paid that loan back, and had then taken out several others. But her husband's repeated illnesses, and her expenditures on treatment and medicine, had her falling behind on a subsequent loan she had taken out in 2005. However, she took advantage of the ability, under Grameen II, to reschedule loans that were in default and was making irregular payments on her overdue loan at the time of my visit.

When I returned in August 2007, the entire part of the village where she lived was underwater due to a major flood. However, Fulzan contends that she has improved her life since joining Grameen, even though by all measures she is still quite poor. She eats three meals on most days, whereas before Grameen it was one or two. Her three children are all in school, though it remains to be seen whether they will be able to pass the exams required to make it to higher education. Unlike Shandha and Noni, she cannot afford the private tutors that are usually needed to advance in the Bangladesh educational system. She continues to earn money from ditchdigging when work is available. She sleeps on a simple bed rather than on the ground. These are modest improvements, but they feel very real to her.

Microfinance will never make a significant positive impact on every client, but I believe that if Grameen II had been in force when Fulzan joined, she might have had a more positive experience. Ongoing innovation in the model, in Grameen and beyond, will hopefully make microfinance more responsive to the realities of the lives of people like Fulzan. When I consider the modest but real improvements she experienced, and those of others like Amena who were unquestionably among the "poorest of the poor" when they joined Grameen, I scoff at the sweeping statements made by many so-called experts that only the moderately poor and nonpoor can benefit from microfinance. Such simplistic pronouncements are not only wrong but have an unfortunate tendency to shape policy and practice among those to follow whatever "best practices" seem to be in vogue among the international development elites. I am not, however, making the equally unsupportable sweeping statement that microfinance can help or is appropriate for every desperately poor family in the world.

For her part, Amena participated in Grameen Bank for more than 10 years and made steady progress. But in 2005 her husband had a vision of moving to Savar, a major city that is a suburb of Dhaka, to be a full-time rickshaw puller. She wanted to remain in Grameen Bank somehow, but it proved impossible, so she got her savings back and formally withdrew as a member. She remains in sporadic contact with Grameen borrowers in Kholshi, and her husband apparently has stayed true to his pledge to refrain from spousal abuse. Her children were in school in Savar the last time I got an update. Perhaps she is destined to live out her life without putting down roots anywhere, but if her children continue with their schooling, the generational cycle of poverty and repeated migration may finally come to an end.

A few years back, after the flood transformed the entire area, the Kholshi centers were shifted to the Ghior branch of Grameen, something that all of the borrowers I knew disliked. They were campaigning to be reclassified as Shaymganj centers, and my sense is that they were such influential borrowers that their advocacy would ultimately win over Grameen's management.

In August 2007, the floodwaters were beginning to recede after a wetter than normal monsoon, but what was left were muddy roads that made movement a slow process. Traveling two miles to Zianpur was easier than five miles to Ghior, especially in these conditions. The Zianpur bazaar had finally been electrified, and new businesses, including 10 small restaurants, had sprung up.

Center number two, which Shandha led, had expanded to about 100 members and had taken an interest-free loan from Grameen to build a larger center house in the Grameen II style—one that had benches for all borrowers and the loan officer, and where people sat in a U-shape rather than in rows. Despite all of its setbacks, Shaymganj was a profitable branch, earning 200,000 taka in 2006. There were 32 beggars in the struggling members program.

Overall, progress was uneven, as is usual in rural Bangladesh. But it was also palpable, particularly when compared to what existed in 1987 and even in the mid-1990s. People were grateful for having the chance to receive capital and use it to chart their own destinies, and clearly valued the connections they now had to each other and to an institution that had, however imperfectly, continued innovating and trying to serve their financial and other development needs for more than two decades. Just the fact that loan officers showed up week after week to do the bank's business with the clients was a signal that they were not alone but had a strong organizational ally in their journeys to overcome the poverty that had been the curse of their ancestors since the beginning of time.

ONE OF MY FEW MAJOR REGRETS ABOUT the first edition of this book relates to Connie Evans. I wish that I had been more thoughtful in how I wrote about her. I sometimes damned Connie with faint praise despite her steady and at times bold leadership of WSEP and within the microfinance community. Only after I began leading a nonprofit organization myself could I fully appreciate her skills, determination, and accomplishments. I may never fully comprehend the obstacles that she faces as an African-American female leader, but I have more of an inkling now.

When I was in touch with Connie in July 2007, she was just emerging from an 18-month sabbatical. She was in good spirits and was looking for meaningful work. I was thrilled to learn that she was appointed the head of the Association for Enterprise Opportunity a short time later. She has been doing a great job in that critical role as a national spokesperson for microfinance and microbusinesses in the United States.

BUILDING ON CONNIE'S WORK AT WSEP and the efforts of hundreds of others around the country, Andrea Jung of Grameen America has done a remarkable job leading a growing team and indeed an entire national microfinance movement in the United States.

I first met Andrea over breakfast a few weeks into her tenure as CEO, and we met up again in Bangladesh and a few times in her office. She also came and spoke at the welcome dinner for one of my final board meetings at

Grameen Foundation. I have always been impressed with her professionalism, her collegiality, and the results she achieves.

We caught up once more around the time this edition went to press. Before diving into questions about how she not only survived but thrived during the COVID-19 pandemic, I asked her about why she took the job in the first place. She could have started her own organization or taken over others that were less demanding and, arguably, more prestigious. At the time she took it over, Grameen America had a lot of rough edges and some complicated stakeholder issues to resolve.

Her answer was telling. She said she didn't feel the need to invent a new success model to address a problem like poverty if one already existed, particularly one that helped women, had the potential for reaching a large number of people, and had needs that fit her talents and passions. Grameen America fit the bill precisely, so she jumped at the opportunity.

She turned her organizational skills and her dedication to empowering women to taking Grameen America to an entirely new level of performance. When she inherited it, the organization was just reaching $100 million in cumulative loans that averaged under $2,000 each; within a few months of our conversation, it would surpass the $3 billion mark. The average loan size had crept up to around $5,000 as a result of meeting the needs of its most successful and mature borrowers.

Andrea viewed microfinance practiced in the Grameen style to be a perfect structure for reaching large numbers of people, particularly since it had an "economic engine" that allowed for financial sustainability both at the client level and at the lender level. Her investments in technology allowed the organization to pivot to online center meetings in the early days of the pandemic without missing a beat. Amazingly, of the 140,000 loans given out since COVID forced this change in approach, precisely one was in arrears. All the rest had either been fully repaid or were current.

Bangladeshis on loan from Grameen Bank had originally played key roles at Grameen America. A few remained, including one who spoke excellent Spanish from a time when he served in Mexico, but Americans who spoke English and Spanish had taken over most of those roles. Shah Newaz has been on a long-term assignment helping to replicate the Grameen America success story in Australia. Andrea's year-old initiative to serve more African-American clients was going well; among the learnings was that developing partnerships with community organizations that had earned the trust of Black microentrepreneurs was critical.

Having wrestled the issues of technology, compliance, and institutional sustainability to the ground, Grameen America under Andrea's leadership is on course to earn substantial profits over the next decade through giving loans averaging less than $5,000 each to hundreds of thousands of people who wouldn't come close to qualifying for a commercial loan from any other lender. Nearly 50 years since Yunus gave out his first loans in Bangladesh, the adaptability of the Grameen model under the right leadership remains one of its most impressive hallmarks.

ON A SUMMER DAY IN 2007, I called the DuPart household and spoke first to Omiyale's husband, Paul, who was as pleasant as ever. Later that day I caught up with Omiyale herself.

I had not talked to her in years, yet we fell into easy conversation. She has continued to work as a street vendor, and has done reasonably well. Her love of Africa that developed from her early trips there to buy merchandise for reselling in south Chicago led to a new business—leading delegations of middle-class African-Americans to Ghana for a modest fee. She more or less gave up the cookie business when she moved into a smaller home some years back, one that could not accommodate the commercial oven she had bought in 1994. Her children were taking good care of her, and she felt secure enough to be contemplating semi-retirement in the next few years. Her youngest daughter had a major car accident in 2006 and Omiyale needed to put her business on hold for a couple of months to care for her child. She liked not having to wake up at the crack of dawn to secure a spot on the sidewalk or at a summer fair. The dashing Hkeem was working in real estate, and she was mentoring one of her daughters in how to run a boutique that she had opened. While she seemed saddened that none of her children had completed college, Omiyale was proud of each of them and felt a measure of contentment that I had not sensed a decade earlier. Her email address included the following words: "on the go DuPart." How appropriate!

Omiyale updated me on some of her microfinance friends. She said that Thelma Ali continues her business, delivering pithy bits of wisdom to anyone who will listen, and focusing on selling products that retail for under $5. For her, business remains based on volume, not margin. Thelma Perkins, another vendor who was in the Lindblom center, keeps at her business, week in and week out. Omiyale sees her at various events, especially during the summer months.

Queenesta, with whom Omiyale has remained in sporadic contact, kept Q's open for quite a number of years on the West Side. She apparently resolved her conflict with Nixon, settled the financial issues between them, and later got married (to someone else) and had a second child. Omiyale suspected that she closed down her business when she had the second child, but was not sure. Attempts to track down Queenesta on my part were not successful.

Geri moved and continued her business on the side, but was able to find her niche in the workforce. Microfinance had apparently given her confidence and contacts that she needed to find that niche. Glenda has been elusive, but through mutual friends Omiyale reported that she continues to work various jobs, produce beautiful jewelry, and engage in social action to improve the quality of education. Former WSEP loan officer Gwen Burns left Chicago for a time; when she returned, she had lost a lot of weight and seemed much happier.

Overall, Omiyale felt that her time in the Full Circle Fund was important for her and for many of the women who benefited, and she felt that the evolving microfinance field in the United States would continue to be relevant to low- and moderate-income microentrepreneurs. She had been tickled to learn of Yunus's Nobel Peace Prize and valued her connection, however lapsed it may be, to him and to the global microfinance movement. In that way, she felt a bond with millions of current and former microfinance clients. Indeed, she is proud to be a participant and a benefactor of a civil society-led campaign that resulted in the creation of hundreds of dynamic local microlending organizations and that had opened up new possibilities for so many people in need.

With the help of her son Hkeem, who is now a Facebook friend of mine, I caught up with Omiyale in the spring of 2022. (As far as I can tell, none of the other women featured in this book have any social media presence themselves.) Across two conversations, Omiyale exuded the same warmth, family values, entrepreneurial spirit, and hopeful energy that I have always associated with her. A few days after our second chat, she was set to travel to Ghana to negotiate a large purchase of shea butter that her daughters could import and sell as part of their own business. The importance she placed on passing down her commitment to entrepreneurship to the next generation was undiminished.

Omiyale told me that she had occasionally run into Queenesta, who had focused for some years on home-schooling her children, and Thelma, who was still vending. Colete, she shared with a sigh, had passed away. Omiyale remains active in the lives of all her children and grandchildren, and reported proudly that one of her grandkids had recently graduated from college.

She ended our first conversation with words that are in the classic Omiyale style and said with a sincerity that I found both refreshing and touching: "Have a blessed and magnificent day." I did as I was told.

AS THIS BOOK WENT TO PRESS, I found a notice online that indicated that Queenesta had died in January 2022 at the age of 61. I was sorry to realize that her life had been cut short at such a young age.

On a happier note, her daughter Shayna appears to be a thriving professional, a living manifestation of her mother's dreams for her, as expressed to me back in 1993-1994.

IT MAY BE TEMPTING TO DIMINISH or even ignore what microfinance has accomplished. I don't believe such pessimism is well-founded. Yunus had a deep insight about the untapped potential of the world's poor women and the role that affordable financial services could play in unleashing it. In the process, he inspired a generation of people—myself included—to do our part in applying that insight on a global scale. Today, women like Shandha and Omiyale and their children and grandchildren are bearing the fruit of both their own hard work *and* the mostly unrecognized efforts of millions of people to make the promise of microfinance real for as many people as possible.

Yunus—who turned 82 on June 28, 2022, and remains active—received recognition for his part in this evolution, though at great personal cost. Still, 11 years after Yunus resigned under pressure as Grameen Bank's managing director, that flagship institution is doing remarkably well. So are hundreds of other organizations Yunus helped launch or inspire, including a growing number of social businesses. Those institutions, and the powerful ideas that he forced two generations of experts and concerned citizens to consider, represent his most lasting legacy.

Acknowledgments

THE FIRST EDITION OF THIS BOOK was nearly five years in the making; it should not be surprising, therefore, that the debts incurred in writing it have been substantial. The women who are featured in the book, and in some cases, members of their families, their friends, and colleagues, devoted themselves to it for nearly two years. The women in Chicago, for instance, agreed to keep a diary during this time and to share its contents with me. Furthermore, there are women who went through the process of telling me their life stories but do not appear in this book.

The idea to structure the book along the lines that I did, and to include the women from Chicago so prominently, came from my gifted former agent, Joel Fishman. The people at John Wiley and Sons and Random House were pleasures to work with. Kelly O'Connor and Ian Jackman, who were my editors at various times, worked tirelessly on this book. Ian took the flab out of my early, and rather verbose, drafts while retaining what was right about them. Kelly had important insights into how to make this edition fresh and important in the aftermath of the Nobel Peace Prize announcement. Debra Englander and Ann Godoff provided sage advice and reassurance. And for greenlighting and supporting this new edition, I am indebted once again to Karl Weber of Rivertowns Books.

A number of my friends and colleagues agreed to read the working manuscript and give me their comments. They include Steve Balkin, Dipal Chandra Barua, Karen Doyle, David Gibbons, Alan Gold, Sam Harris, Nick Langton, H. I. Latifee, Sharon Mason, Susan Matteucci, Bob Philips, Jennifer Robey, Khalid Shams, Helen Todd, and Lynn Walker-McMullen. Muhammad Yunus read the chapters as they were being written and provided valuable feedback. But among this group Steve Dewhurst stands alone, for the amount of criticism he provided, the good humor it was wrapped in, and the speed with which he made it available—usually faxing it to me in Bangladesh within

24 hours of receiving a batch of new chapters. Jason Loughnane was generous in sending his detailed comments on the introduction to this edition on a tight timeline.

In researching this book, it was necessary to conduct scores of interviews. Among those who agreed to talk with me were Muhammad Shah Alam, Absar Ali, Muhammad Jobbar Ali, Lutfa Ali, Shashona Ali, Thelma Dean Ali, Venita Allen, S. M. Shamim Anwar, Assaduzzaman, Krishna Das Bala, Steve Balkin, Dipal Chandra Barua, Aduree Begum, Amena Begum, Firoza Khatoon, Fulzan Begum, Nurjahan Begum, Rasheda Begum, Rukia Begum, Supi Begum, Zomella Begum, Zorina Begum, Lynnette Boone, Pam Bozeman, Gwen Burns, Kazal Chowdhury, Peggy Clark, Stacy Craighead, Mary Dean, Tiziana Dearing, Fred DeLuca, Geraldine Dinkins, Hkeem DuPart, Omiyale DuPart, Connie Evans, Gopal Ghosh, Nonibala Ghosh, Oloka Ghosh, Colete Grant, Odette Gueringer, Amodini Rani Haldar, Devi Rani Haldar, Shandha Rani Haldar, Lynn Hardy, Della Harris, Glenda Harris, June Harris, Queenesta Harris, Mary Houghton, Muzammel Huq, Muhammad Jakaria, Janet Johnson, Sukor Kasim, Muhammad Abdul Khashem, Dulal Chandra Kor, Joanne Kyle, H. I. Latifee, Cawa Levi, Wanda Little, Victor McClain, Susan Matteucci, Muhammad Munaf Mia, Belvia Muhammad, Muhammad Abdul Mustafiz, Nixon, Jewell Pates, Debra Payne, Thelma Perkins, Jannat Quinine, Harun ur Rashid, Claudette Redic, Alma Jean Richardson, Muhammad Abdul Rohim, Gheeliyah Rojas, Rebecca Rosofsky, Muhammad Samsuddin, Shabnum Sanghvi, Khalid Shams, Carol Simms, B. J. Slay, Fort Smith, Muhammad Abdul Mannan Talukdar, Steve White, Gary Williams, Muhammad Yunus, and Marshall Zimmerman.

A number of other people and institutions contributed to this project. The staff at the Harold Washington Library and the Chicago Historical Society were extremely helpful during my frequent visits. The staff and volunteers of RESULTS, where I worked from 1989 to 1992, were (and are) a source of inspiration. The Wallace Genetic Foundation and the Fund for Innovation and Public Service provided funding that enabled this book's initial research to be conducted. Several books influenced my thinking on the issues addressed herein. Prominent among them were *The Promised Land*, by Nicholas Lemann; *There Are No Children Here*, by Alex Kotlowitz; *Black Metropolis: A Study of Negro Life in a Northern City*, by St. Clair Drake and Horace R. Clayton; *Bangladesh: Reflections on the Water*, by James Novak; and *Among Schoolchildren*, by Tracy Kidder. Barbara Charbonnet, Sam Harris, Nick Schatzki, and Lynn Walker-

McMullen led a fund-raising drive to buy me the computer on which this book was written. Randal Castleman and the late Robert McCardell, English teachers of mine at the Horace Mann School, taught me how to write. Duane and Mary Wainwright, my in-laws as of June 1994, were patient and supportive while their prospective son-in-law spent his engagement with thousands of people (most of whom were women) but rarely with their daughter. Salehuddin Azizee, one of Grameen's two in-house professional photographers, spent long hours taking pictures. Mir Akhtar Hossain contributed his time and effort to many of the logistical requirements of producing the book, as well as his warmth and friendship during some trying times. Masud Isa assisted by providing statistical analyses of Grameen, and the computer unit he oversees, headed up by Naznin Sultana, helped me out of many a jam. Carol Petersen, her son Dan, and Jim Dickert were gracious and generous hosts during all six of my visits to Chicago. Above all, there were Connie Evans and Muhammad Yunus, who not only contributed their time and expertise but also allowed me to have unlimited access to their organizations as I researched this book.

My parents, Robert Counts and Carolyn Fox, and my stepparents, Norma Hakusa Counts and John Fox, gave me the confidence and courage to attempt such an undertaking and considerable moral and material support once I began. And tying it all together, my wife, Emily, played the roles of editor, coach, friend, patient fiancée, wedding planner, and (finally) supportive spouse while I struggled through the research and writing processes.

In the preparation of the 2008 edition, I was assisted by many of the same people who were helpful with the original edition. These include Muhammad Abdul Mannan Talukdar, Omiyale DuPart, my wife, Emily (now of 28 joyous years), Muhammad Yunus, Dipal Chandra Barua, Abul Hossain, and Connie Evans, to name a few. Those who were helpful mainly on this edition were my agent Jim McCarthy, Debra Englander, Kelly O'Connor, and Stacey Small of John Wiley and Sons, Jessica Massie, Kay Hixson, Vidar Jorgensen, Lucy Billingsley, Bob Eichfeld, Phil Smith, Betty Sams, Mike Getubig, and Joe Mwangi-Kioi.

I am indebted to everyone who helped make Grameen Foundation first a reality, and over time a significant player in the global microfinance movement. The list of people who have contributed to GF over its first decade goes into the thousands, but among those who have been most helpful are (in alphabetical order) Harmohan Ahluwalia, Muhammad Nurul Alam, John

Anderson, Bob Annibale, Tania Ashraf, Akhtar Badshah, Eric and Trisha Bam, Catherine Barnett, Doug Barry, Dipal Barua, Randy and Nancy Best, Dustin Buehler, Nigel Biggar, Lucy Billingsley, Peter Bladin, Tricia Bridges, Deborah Burand, Sherita Coates, Nick Craig, Manon Cypher, James Dailey, Sam Daley-Harris, Geoff Davis, Susan Davis, John Doerr, Jennifer Drogula, Beth Dunphe, Bob and Lore Eichfeld, Dave Ellis, Leslie Enright, Vikram and Meera Gandhi, David Gardner and the entire Motley Fool network, Mike Getubig, David Gibbons, Jim and Lisa Greenberg, Dick and Lois Gunther, Ahasan Habib, Gary Hattem, Heather Henyon, Kay Hixson, Mohammad and Fadi Jameel, Jean Kaiser, Paul Kane, David Keogh, Vinod Khosla, Meredith Kimball, H. I. Latifee, Dina Levy, Jacki Lippman, Craig and Susan McCaw, Fiona McDowell, Janet McKinley, Lynn McMullen, Ann Margolin, Paul Maritz, Jennifer Meehan, Leslie Meek-Wohl, Patrick Meriweather, Erik Miller, Gwen Moore, Lamiya Morshed, Zaher Al Munajjed, Alberto Munoz, Yvette Neier, Camilla Nestor, Regina Nobles, Chandni Ohri, Pierre and Pam Omidyar, Bob Ottenhoff, Iqbal Paroo, Chris Pascucci, Julie Peachey, Vertraille Polo, Omar Qandeel, Bill Rentz, Steven C. Rockefeller Jr., Donna and Ed Rohling, Vanessa Rudin, the late Jim Sams and his wife Betty, Craig Sarsony, Marshall and Pam Saunders, Sameer Sheikh, Penny Shone, Wayne Silby, Sharmi Sobhan, Janet Thompson, Emily Tucker, Barb Weber, Henry and Holly Wendt, John C. Whitehead, Tim Wood, Liselle Yorke, Helen Yuen, and of course, Muhammad Yunus. Without personal encouragement from my wife, Emily, my late father Robert M. Counts, my mother Carolyn Counts, and my stepparents Norma Counts and the late John Fox, my brothers Michael and Doug (as well as my departed sister Pam), and my wonderful and growing list of in-laws, out-laws, and nephews, I would have long since taken up a less stressful (and no doubt less rewarding) line of work.

While these people and many others contributed to this book, I alone am responsible for its contents and any errors or omissions it may contain.

Alex Counts
Hyattsville, Maryland
June 2022

Appendix: The Sixteen Decisions

1. We shall follow and advance the four principles of Grameen Bank—Discipline, Unity, Courage, and Hard Work—in all walks of our lives.
2. We shall bring prosperity to our families.
3. We shall not live in dilapidated houses. We shall repair our houses and work toward constructing new houses as soon as possible.
4. We shall grow vegetables all year round. We shall eat plenty of them and sell the surplus.
5. We shall plant as many seedlings as possible during the plantation season.
6. We shall plan to keep our families small. We shall minimize our expenditures. We shall look after our health.
7. We shall educate our children and ensure that we can earn to pay for their education.
8. We shall always keep our children and their environment clean.
9. We shall build and use pit latrines.
10. We shall drink water from tube wells. If it is not available, we shall boil water or use alum.
11. We shall not take dowry at our sons' weddings, nor shall we give any dowry at our daughters' weddings. We shall keep our center free from the curse of dowry. We shall not practice child marriage.
12. We shall not inflict any injustice on anyone, nor shall we allow anyone else to do so.
13. We shall collectively undertake larger investments for higher incomes.

14. We shall always be ready to help each other. If anyone is in difficulty, we shall help him or her.
15. If we come to know of any breach of discipline in any center, we shall go there and help restore discipline.
16. We shall introduce physical exercises in all of our centers. We shall take part in all social activities collectively.

Formulated in a national workshop of 100 women center chiefs in Joydevpur (about 30 miles north of Dhaka) in March 1984, the Sixteen Decisions might be called the social development constitution of Grameen Bank. All Grameen Bank members are expected to memorize and implement these decisions.

Source Notes

[1] The report can be found at https://www.ifpri.org/publication/credit-alleviation-rural-poverty.

[2] A link to the speech can be found at https://grameenfoundation.org/stories/blog/reflections-on-the-latest-studies-on-microcredit.

[3] Belatedly but still helpfully, Jonathan Mordoch and Tim Ogden of New York University have been raising important questions about how research conducted in the 2010s was misunderstood. See Mordoch's paper in *World Development* 127, "Why RCTs failed to answer the biggest questions about microcredit impact," and Ogden's chapter titled "Understanding the Impact of Microcredit" in *The Future of Microfinance*, edited by Ira Lieberman and others (Brookings Institution Press, 2020).

[4] Find my review of his paper and a link to the paper itself at https://www.centerforfinancialinclusion.org/a-review-of-the-case-for-social-investment-in-microcredit-by-tim-ogden

[5] "Worm's Eye View: Interviews with Women of the Grameen Bank," Alexander M. Counts, ed. (Washington, D.C.: RESULTS Educational Fund, 1992), iii.

[6] Chittagong University Rural Development Program, *Annual Report 1978–1979* (Chittagong: Chittagong University, 1980), 9.

[7] Iftikhar Ul Anwar, "State of Indigenous Industries," a chapter in Sirajul Islam, ed., *History of Bangladesh: 1704–1971, vol. 2* (Dhaka: Asiatic Society of Bangladesh, 1992), 273.

[8] Haroun Er Rashid, *Geography of Bangladesh* (Dhaka: University Press Ltd., 1991), 141. The traveler was Sebastian Maurique.

[9] Iftikhar Ul Anwar, op. cit., 278.

[10] James J. Novak, *Bangladesh: Reflections on the Water* (Bloomington IN: Indiana University Press, 1993), 75.

[11] Iftikar Ul Anwar, op. cit., 275–277.

[12] Iftikar Ul Anwar, op. cit., 297–302.

[13] Mosharaff Hossain, *The Assault that Failed: A Profile of Poverty in Six Villages of Bangladesh* (Geneva: UNRISD, 1987), 11–13; and James J. Novak, op. cit., 55–58.

[14] Rehman Sobhan, *Bangladesh: Problems of Governance* (Dhaka: University Press Ltd., 1993), 79.

[15] Larry Collins and Dominique Lapierre, *Freedom at Midnight* (New York: Simon and Schuster, 1975), 114.

[16] Badruddin Umar, "Language Movement," from Sirajul Islam, op. cit., 427.

[17] Anthony Mascarenhas, *Bangladesh: Legacy of Blood* (London: Hodder and Stoughton, 1986), 10. Reference to Rakhi Bahini is from the same book, 37, and the information on the 1974 famine, including the quotation in the *Guardian*, 43–44.

[18] Background information on the mismanagement of deep tube wells can be found in Chapter 19 of Betsy Hartmann and James Boyce, *A Quiet Violence: View from a Bangladesh Village* (London: Zed Books, 1983). The information about Tehbhaga comes from interviews with Yunus, Dipal, and Latifee, from interviews with farmers and others conducted on a trip I took to Chittagong in July 1989, and from H. I. Latifee, "A Report on Nabajug Tehbhaga Khamar" (Chittagong: Chittagong University, Department of Economics, August 1980).

[19] Statistics on worsening Bangladesh poverty come from Mosharaff Hossain, op. cit., 28–33.

[20] Jowshan ara Rahman, "Jobra: The Grameen Bank Project," *Shishu Diganta*, April 1980.

[21] Muhith was appointed finance minister a second time many years later, and was forced to manage a conflict between his Prime Minister and Yunus over several difficult years. Yet, when he died in 2022, Yunus issued a magnanimous statement that focused on the positive work they had done together. The statement was covered in the *Daily Star*, Bangladesh's leading English-language daily newspaper: https://online.thedailystar.net/news/bangladesh/news/days-muhith-bhai-was-jubilant-full-pride-dr-yunus-3016381.

[22] This chapter relies exclusively on firsthand observations and interviews by the author.

[23] From a speech by Muhammad Yunus, "Anything Wrong?" (Dhaka: Grameen Bank, 1990).

[24] Isabel Wilkerson, "Graduations: Where 500 Began, 150 Remain," *New York Times*, June 13, 1994, A1, A9.

[25] Information on Englewood in the period 1850–1920: *Local Community Fact Book, Chicago Metropolitan Area, based on the 1970 and 1980 Censuses*, edited by the Chicago Fact Book Consortium (Chicago: Chicago Review Press, 1984), 172–75.

[26] "Englewood: Hot Gang War Spot," *Chicago Daily News*, April 26, 1968. Statistics on demographic change from *Local Community Fact Book*, op. cit., 172–75.

[27] William Reckenwald and Colin McMahon, "Deadly End to Deadly Year," *Chicago Tribune*, January 1, 1993, 1.

[28] Information on the rate of Black business ownership: Jawanza Kunjufu, *Black Economics: Solutions for Economic and Community Empowerment* (Chicago: African-American Images, 1991), iii. The information concerning how much Black consumers spend on Black business is on 53–55.

[29] For information concerning immigrants' economic success in the United States, see Ivan Light, *Ethnic Enterprise in America: Business and Welfare*

Among Chinese, Japanese and Blacks (Berkeley: University of California Press, 1972); Ivan Light, "Immigrant and Ethnic Enterprise in North America," *Journal of Ethnic and Racial Studies*, April 1984, 195–216; Ivan Light and E. Bonacich, *Immigrant Entrepreneurs: Koreans in Los Angeles, 1965–1982* (Berkeley: University of California Press, 1988); and Steve Balkin, *Self-Employment for Low-Income People* (New York: Praeger, 1989), 51–68.

[30] Historical information on Maxwell Street: Ira Berkow, *Maxwell Street: Survival in a Bazaar* (Garden City, N.Y.: Doubleday and Co., 1977), 10.

[31] This chapter relies exclusively on firsthand observations and interviews by the author.

[32] Chicago history through 1919: St. Clair Drake and Horace R. Clayton, *Black Metropolis: A Study of Negro Life in a Northern City* (Chicago: University of Chicago Press, 1993), 3–77.

[33] Nicholas Lemann, *The Promised Land: The Great Black Migration and How It Changed America* (New York: Knopf, 1991), 41.

[34] Chicago history from 1919 through the 1960s: Drake, op. cit., pp. 3–77; and Mike Royko, *Boss: Richard M. Daley of Chicago* (New York: Plume, 1971).

[35] Lemann, op. cit., 92.

[36] William Julius Wilson, *The Truly Disadvantaged* (Chicago: University of Chicago Press, 1987), 3. The statistics in the next paragraph are found in the same work, 21.

[37] "Overnight Violence Leaves 1 Dead, 8 Hurt," *Chicago Defender*, November 18, 1993, 4.

[38] Cornel West, *Race Matters* (New York: Vintage, 1993), 27.

[39] Marian Wright Edelman, "Violence Crushes Youths' Dreams," *Chicago Defender*, November 15, 1993, 12.

[40] Discussion of foreign aid under Mujib: Rehman Sobhan, *The Crisis of External Dependence* (Dhaka: University Press Limited, 1982), 166–201.

[41] Study on aid industry information: Rehman Sobhan and Syed Hashemi: "Beneficiaries of Foreign Aid," in Rehman Sobhan, ed., *From Aid Dependence to Self-Reliance: Development Options for Bangladesh* (Dhaka, University Press Limited, 1990).

[42] James Novak, op. cit., 5–6.

[43] Yunus speech to the World Bank: Muhammad Yunus, "Hunger, Poverty, and the World Bank" (Dhaka: Grameen Bank, 1993).

[44] The pro–Maxwell Street pieces in the *Sun-Times* were written by Raymond R. Coffey. They were "UIC Expansion Plan: Does It Make Sense?" July 16, 1993; "Maxwell St. Ready to Fight Local Bully," July 18, 1993; and "UIC, City Created Maxwell St. Mess," July 20, 1993.

[45] Harold Washington Library meeting: interviews with people in attendance, and Ethan Mitchell, "Opposition Mounts to Maxwell St. Shutdown," *Chicago Defender*, December 1, 1993, 1.

[46] Quoted in the *Economist*, April 23, 1994.

[47] Balkin report on financial losses: Steve Balkin, Alfonso Morales, and Joseph Persky, *The Value of Benefits of a Public Market: The Case of Maxwell Street* (Chicago: Roosevelt University, July 1993). The quote from a young vendor is from page 19 of this paper.

[48] Steve Balkin, Alfonso Morales, and Joseph Persky, "Why the University of Illinois Is Wrong," mimeograph, February 1994, 4.

[49] Drop in crime information: Fran Spielman, "Community Policing Area Leads City's Crime Drop," *Chicago Sun-Times*, January 21, 1994, 14. The information on the drop in crime in Englewood comes from Julie Irwin, "Murders Plummet in Englewood," *Chicago Tribune*, March 1, 1994, 1 (Chicagoland section).

[50] This chapter relies exclusively on firsthand observations and interviews by the author.

[51] Isabel Wilkerson, "Change Threatens a Legendary Street Bazaar," *New York Times*, March 23, 1994, A14.

[52] "Ready to Rumble? Step into Council Chambers," John Kass, *Chicago Tribune*, April 14, 1994, 1.

[53] *Washington Post* and *Economist* articles: Megan Garvey, "The Last Sale of a Faded Urban Market," *Washington Post*, April 12, 1994; "Goodbye, Maxwell Street," *Economist*, April 23, 1994, 31.

[54] John McCarron, "On Maxwell, No Need to Circle the Wagons," *Chicago Tribune*, August 22, 1993, section 7, 3.

[55] Jason DeParle, "Welfare Mothers Find Jobs Easy to Get But Hard to Hold," *New York Times*, October 24, 1994, A1.

[56] David Gibbons, ed. *The Grameen Reader*, 2nd ed., revised (Dhaka: Grameen Bank, 1994), 47.

[57] Discussion of business use of personal credit cards: "Some Cash-Poor Firms Just Charge It," *Chicago Sun-Times*, July 27, 1994, 54.

[58] Discussion of unemployed males turning to self-employment: D. S. Evans and L. S. Leighton, *Self-Employment Selection and Earnings over the Life Cycle* (Washington, D.C.: U.S. Small Business Administration, Office of Advocacy, 1987), quoted in Balkin, op. cit., 35.

[59] Donald R. Katz, "Where Credit Is Due," *Investment Vision* magazine, August/September 1991, 54.

[60] Discussion of U.K. and French programs: Balkin, op. cit., 105–108. Job Corps information: Amy Kazlow, "Corps for Troubled Youth Now Finds Itself in Trouble," *Christian Science Monitor*, February 2, 1995, 1, 8.

[61] Kunjufu, op. cit., 15.

[62] Balkin, op. cit., 71.

[63] Information on Freedman's Bank and DuBois quote: Balkin, op. cit., 71–74.

[64] Census Bureau statistics on Black firms and business ownership among different ethnic groups: Andrew Hacker, *Two Nations: Black and White, Separate, Hostile, Unequal* (New York: Ballantine, 1992), 108–109.

[65] Information on Black net worth: *State of Black America 1994* (New York: National Urban League, 1994), 20. According to the Census Bureau, the median net worth of Black households in 1988 was $4,169, while that of white households was $43,279. That tenfold gap didn't budge a bit over the next three decades. According to the Brookings Institution, the average net worth of white families in 2016 was $171,000, while that of Black families was $17,150.

[66] Information on Blacks' consumption: National Urban League, op. cit., 51–84; Nancy Ryan, "Marketing to Black Consumers," *Chicago Tribune*, June 9, 1991, section 7, page 6.

[67] This chapter relies exclusively on firsthand observations and interviews by the author.

[68] This chapter relies exclusively on firsthand observations and interviews by the author.

[69] Yunus speech: "Grameen Bank: Does Capitalist System Have to Be the Handmaiden of the Rich?" keynote address delivered at the Eighty-Fifth Rotary International Convention, held in Taipei, Taiwan, June 12–15, 1994 (Dhaka: Grameen Bank, 1994).

[70] Statistics on Shaymganj are from interviews and inspection of loan ledgers and forms at the branch. Muhammad Abdul Rohim was particularly helpful in tracking down these statistics.

[71] Cost-per-job-created estimates: Interviews with Peggy Clark, of the Aspen Institute, and Rona Feit, a consultant formerly with the Corporation for Enterprise Development, a Washington, D.C.–based think tank. WSEP statistics: *1993 Microenterprise Briefing Packet: Facts and Figures on Seven U.S. Microenterprise Development Programs* (Washington, D.C.: Self-Employment Learning Project, 1994), supplemented by updates contained in my correspondence with the Aspen Institute and WSEP.

Index

abandonment, by husband, 157
ACM Agency, 189
Activists for Social Alternatives (ASA), 297
Aduree (borrower), 107, 243, 373
AEO. *See* Association for Enterprise
        Opportunity
AFDC. *See* Aid to Families with Dependent
        Children
African-Americans, 145–46, 190
    business ownership by, 136
    as consumers, 278–79
    racism faced by, 238, 276–77
Afro-World Festival, 142, 144
Agency for International Development, United
        States (USAID), 206
Agriculture Bank. *See* Krishi Bank
Ahlim, Abdul, 97, 210
Aid to Families with Dependent Children
        (AFDC), 273
Aklima (cook), 87–88
Akula, Vikram, 25
Alam, Nurul, 343
Alam, Shah, 97–99
Ali, Aaki, 151, 340–41
Ali, Absar, 147–48, 150–51, 338–41
Ali, Amena, 147, 150–52, 196–98, 341, 372, 374
    cow bought by, 194–95
    death of brother of, 338–39
    giving birth to child, 148–49
    land bought by, 340
Ali, Edward, 316–17
Ali, Hazrat, 156
Ali, Jobbar, 92, 101–2, 109–10, 143–44, 207–8,
        240
    Ali, L., teasing, 210–11
Ali, Lutfa, 208–11
Ali, Muhammad Jobbar, 87
Ali, Thelma Dean, 128–29, 169–71, 182–83, 227–
        28, 314–15, 327
    at Black Expo, 303
    at Black on Black Love Festival, 309–10
    children of, 318

DuPart, O., pressured by, 261–62, 304–5
    emergency loan fund offered by, 325
    end of Ramadan celebrated by, 263
    Harris, Q., doubted by, 309, 356
    loan application of, 271
    Maxwell Street Market and, 140–42, 221–
        22, 365–67
    Nixon doubted by, 320
    receipts from wholesalers listed by, 354
    Small Business Administration loan
        considered by, 368
    as teenager, 316
    Tupperware sold by, 317
Alinsky, Saul, 178
Allstate (company), Harris, Q., at, 132–35
American Food Depository, 216–17
Amin, Ruhul, 191, 250
Anis (office helper), 240–41
Anisuzzaman, A. M., 64
anniversary, celebrations for Grameen Bank,
        12–13
Arrested Development (rap artist), 300
ASA. *See* Activists for Social Alternatives
Ashraf, Tania, 83
Aspen Institute, 326, 362
Assaduzzaman "Assad" (project coordinator),
        51, 70
Association for Enterprise Opportunity (AEO),
        326, 364–65, 375
Atwood, Brian, 203
Awami League (political organization), 153

Bahini, Mukti, 46
Bala, Krishna Das, 89–90, 240–45, 250–53,
        282–84, 328, 330
Balkin, Steve, 223–24, 275
Bangladesh, 24–25. *See also* Kholshi,
        Bangladesh; *specific topics*
    Britain controlling textile industry in, 43–
        44
    Dhaka in, 84–85, 113
    famine in, 31, 47, 53, 160

farmers in, 26–27, 49–50, 59, 242
floods in, 110, 249, 374
foreign aid received by, 199–201
hunger in, 90–91
jute mills separated from, 44–45
meetings in, 94–97, 102–3, 210–11, 329
people with disabilities in, 208
per capita income of, 53–54
poor people benefited by economic growth
    in, 113–14
recycling in, 184
trade in, 42
women in, 55
Zianpur in, 85–86, 98–99, 110, 374
Bangladesh Bank, 67, 69, 287
Bangladesh Economic Association (BEA), 58
Bangladesh Information Center, 37–38
Bangladesh Nationalist Party (BNP), 76
Bangladesh Rural Advancement Committee
    (BRAC), 151–52, 200, 204, 259
Barua, Dipal, 41-42, 49, 70, 112
BEA. See Bangladesh Economic Association
beggars, Grameen Bank lending to, 257–58
Begum, Amena, 104, 250–51
Begum, Fulzan, 105, 108–10, 257, 373
    as ditchdigger, 155–56
    Grameen Bank loaning to, 157–58
    hut improved by, 346
    poverty of, 252
Begum, Khulsum, 94
Begum, Korimun, 102
Begum, Nobirun, 95, 102–3
Begum, Nurjahan, 65–66, 82
Begum, Rasheda, 93, 330
Begum, Rukia, 100, 103–4, 251–53, 256
Begum, Zorina, 67, 103–4, 285–86, 347
BHM. See Black History Month
bidhimala. See constitution
Big Mike (rap artist), 308
Binga, Jesse, 177
Black Belt, in Chicago, 172–74
Black community. See also African-Americans;
        Black people
    in Chicago, 172–73
    marginalization of, 178
    McClain on, 135
Black consciousness movement, 167–68
Black Economics (Kunjufu), 135–36

Black Heritage Bibles, 232
Black History Month (BHM), 228
"Black Is . . ." (concert), 327
Black on Black Love Festival, 309–10, 315
Black Panthers, 178, 221
Black people. See also African-Americans
    in Englewood, 124–25
    as entrepreneurs, 277–78
    pursuing jobs at white-led companies, 131
Black Women's Expo (Black Expo), 127, 137, 143,
    260, 262, 303
BNP. See Bangladesh Nationalist Party
Bono (rock star), 214
borrowers, of loans, 16, 63, 286. See also circles,
    of borrowers; husbands, of
    borrowers; meetings, of
    borrowers; specific borrowers
    detailed case history of, 17
    disaster savings fund aiding, 353
    improvements in lives of, 345, 371–72, 378
    in international textile market, 290
    Rohim training, 101
    selling house built with housing loan by,
        248–49, 330
    traditional healers relied on by, 283–84
    turning over loans to husbands, 162
    Yunus, Muhammad, impressed by
        progress of, 254–55
Bozeman, Pam, 235–37
BRAC. See Bangladesh Rural Advancement
    Committee
bribes, Grameen Bank rejecting, 70–73
Britain, controlling textile industry in
    Bangladesh, 43–44
Building Social Business (Yunus, Muhammad),
    350
bureaucrats, benefiting from foreign aid, 198–
    99
Burns, Gwen, 121–22, 126–28, 144, 170, 378
Burrows, Frederick, 44–45
the Butterflies. See Les Papillons

CAN. See Community Agent Network
capitalism, Yunus, Muhammad, championing,
    335
CARD (microfinance institution), 297
CARE (relief organization), 119
Carter, Dorothy, 311, 314

celebrations, of Grameen Bank anniversaries, 12–13
center chief, at Grameen Bank, 284–86, 295
CGAP. *See* Consultative Group to Assist the Poorest
Chashee, Mahabub Alam, 56–58
check-cashing companies, 120
chhana. See cottage cheese
Chicago, Illinois. *See also* Englewood; Maxwell Street Market; University of Illinois at Chicago
    Black Belt in, 172–74, 176–78
    Black community in, 172–73
    homicide in, 126, 180, 229
    meetings in, 126–30, 144, 182–86
    poverty in, 171
    South Side of, 122, 169
    violence in, 126, 130, 145, 180, 229
Chicago Association of Black Story-Tellers, 327
Chicago Black Expo, 235
Chicago City Council, 267–68
Chicago Defender (newspaper), 180
Chicago Pagers (wholesaler), 300, 358
Chicago Police Department, 319
Chicago Tribune (newspaper), 267
Children's Defense Fund, 181
Children's Fund, United Nations, 67
Children's Horizons (*Shishu Diganta*), 67
Chowdhury, Zafrullah, 200
Christ United Methodist Church, 229
circles, of borrowers. *See also specific circles*
    Let Us Make Woman as, 185, 186–87, 225, 320
    Les Papillons as, 128, 130, 167, 184–85, 227
Citibank, 350
Citizen Power (*Nagorik Shakti*), 163
climate change movement, Yunus, Muhammad, championing, 351
Clinton, Bill, 117, 206, 238, 273, 360
Clinton, Hillary, 117
Comilla Cooperatives (development organization), 200
Community Agent Network (CAN), 22
Community Reinvestment Act, 274
Compartamos (microfinance institution), 297–98
computerization, of Grameen Bank, 253
Conable, Barber, 203

constitution (*bidhimala*), of Grameen Bank, 66
Consultative Group to Assist the Poorest (CGAP), 211–12
consumers, African-American, 278–79
cooperatives, Yunus, Muhammad, demonstrating successful, 286
cottage cheese (*chhana*), Ghosh, N., producing, 292–96
counsel (*porishod*), elections of, 165–66
COVID-19 pandemic, 21–22, 376
Creating a World Without Poverty (Yunus, Muhammad), 350
crowds, at bazaar in Zianpur, 98–99
curtain or veil (*purdah*), secluding women, 60

Daiyan, Abdud (Sheikh), 70
Daley, Richard J., 177–78, 216, 315
Daley, Richard M., 216–17, 268, 366
Daley-Harris, Sam, 11, 211, 213, 306
DATA (organization), 214
Dean, Jesse, 315–16
Dean, Mary Junkim, 315–16
Dearing, Tiziana, 228
DeLuca, Fred, 139
DeParle, Jason, 274
Devaraj, Sathia, 212, 213
Dhaka, Bangladesh, 84–85, 113
Dhaka University, REF at, 40
Dinkins, Geri, 129–30, 184–85, 216–20, 260, 378
disaster savings fund, 353
ditchdigger, Begum, F., as, 156
Divine Principles (circle of borrowers), 128
Doinik Janakantha (newspaper), 155
Dowla, Asif, 112
Doyle, Karen, 321, 323
Drayton, Bill, 16
DuBois, W. E. B., 277–78
DuPart, Hkeem, 263–64
DuPart, Omiyale, 126, 129–30, 167–71, 182–83, 260
    African imports sold by, 265, 377
    Ali, T., pressuring, 261–62, 304–5
    at Chicago Association of Black Story-Tellers, 327
    cookies sold by, 263–64, 266–67
    in FCF, 306–7, 378
    Harris, Q., and, 131, 137–38, 185–86, 261, 359, 378

loan fully repaid by, 265
proposal of loan by, 303–5
RESULTS presented at by, 305–6
vendors sold to by, 368
DuPart, Paul, 167–69

East India Company, 247–48
East Pakistan. *See* Bangladesh
Edelman, Marian Wright, 181
elders, against Grameen Bank, 352–53
elopement, by Hossain, Mozafer, 196
emergency loan fund, 218, 227, 325, 358
The End of Poverty (Sachs), 114
Englewood (Chicago neighborhood), 181
    Black people in, 124–25
    violence in, 126, 130, 229
    white flight in, 125
Enterprise Allowance Scheme, 275
entrepreneurs
    Black people as, 277–78
    as low income, 280
    poor people as, 161, 256
    single mothers as, 301
    social-consciousness-driven contrasted
        with greed-driven, 337
Ershad, Hossain Muhammad, 77
Ethnic Treasures (business), 269, 271
Evans, Connie, 38, 276–77, 326, 365, 370
    WSEP led by, 138–39, 374
Experimental Rural Branch (*Poreekkhamulok
    Grameen Shakha*), 65
Expo for Today's Black Woman, 236

faith in poor people, of Yunus, Muhammad,
    334–35, 342–43, 345
famine, in Bangladesh, 31, 47, 53, 160
farmers, in Bangladesh, 26–27, 49–53, 59, 242
Fazal, Abdul, 48
FCF. *See* Full Circle Fund
"Financing the Rural Poor" (seminar), 67, 68
A Fistful of Rice (Akula), 25
floods, in Bangladesh, 110, 249, 374
Fonkoze (microfinance institution), 258
Ford Foundation, 115–16
foreign aid, 198–202, 206
Forostenko, Vera, 37
The Fortune at the Bottom of the Pyramid
    (Prahalad), 16

Freedman's Bank, 277–78
Freedman's Bureau, 277–78
Friends of the Market, 221
Full Circle Fund (FCF), 122, 130–31, 167, 170–72,
        235, 279–80. *See also* circles, of
        borrowers
    DuPart, O., in, 306–7, 378
    Harris, G., impacted by, 269
    phasing out of, 370
    Simms in, 310, 312–13

Gandhi, Mahatma, 43
Gangopadaya, A. K. M., 69–70, 77
Gano (Democratic) Forum, 153, 155
Georgescu-Roegen, Nicholas, 36, 332
Getubig, Mike, 343
GF. *See* Grameen Foundation
Ghosh, Gopal, 292
Ghosh, Nonibala "Noni," 96, 99–100, 371
    cottage cheese produced by, 292–96
    Grameen Bank impacting, 196, 372
    income of, 244
    Mannan Talukdar convincing, 294
    price of milk impacting, 293
Ghosh, Oloka, 149, 151, 197, 373
Gibbons, David, 23, 212–13
"give direct" movement, local development
        organizations compared with, 201
GKF. *See* Grameen Krishi (Agriculture)
    Foundation
The Glitz (store), 219–20
GMF. *See* Grameen Motscho (Fisheries)
    Foundation
Goldberg, Arthur, 142
Goldberg, Joseph, 142
Goldberg, Nathanael, 23–24
Gonobahini. See People's Army
Good Faith Fund, 206
gradualism, of social change, 333–34
Grameen America, 20–21, 146, 239, 279, 362
    Jung impacting, 375–76
    repayment installments for loans to, 62
    Yunus, Muhammad, launching, 369–70
Grameen Bank, 10–11, 32–33, 65, 96–97, 105.
        See also Shaymganj Daulatpur
        Branch, of Grameen Bank; staff, of
        Grameen Bank; *specific topics*
    Ali, L., joining, 209–10

anniversary celebrations for, 12–13
attacks against, 110–11
beggars lent to by, 257–58
Begum, F., loaned to by, 157–58
bribes rejected at, 70–73
celebrations for anniversary of, 12–13
center chief at, 284–86, 295
computerization of, 253
conference of zonal managers for, 286–91
constitution of, 66
cycle of poverty broken by, 15
East India Company compared with, 247–48
elders against, 352
evaluation of financial viability of, 204–5
faith in poor people fueling, 342–43
Ghosh, N., impacted by, 196, 372
Grameen Telecom leveraging
        infrastructure of, 81
Hossain, Mahabub, studying impact of, 23
housing loan by, 248–49, 330
independence of, 78
interest rates of, 289
Latina clients focused on by, 190
loan insurance program, 258
loans for tube wells, 195, 330–31
men's centers not formed as policy of, 106
near universal applicability of, 119
net weavers lent to by, 192
oral exam demonstrating understanding
        of rules, 100
political influence of, 164–65, 291–92
poor people loaned to by, 15
profitability of, 287, 361
recruitment of staff by, 70–71
reliance of traditional healers challenging,
        283
Rohim working at, 89
Shaymganj Daulatpur Branch of, 341
slogans of, 331
World Bank contrasted with, 203, 207
Yunus, Muhammad, learning from first
        years of, 363–64
in Zianpur high school, 86, 98–99
Grameen Capital India, 350
Grameen Community Agents (relief program),
        22
Grameen Foundation (GF), 22, 80–81, 212, 348

"The Grameen Guidelines" (Grameen Trust),
        343
Grameen Impact India, 350
Grameen Kalyan (welfare), 81–82, 297
Grameen Krishi (Agriculture) Foundation
        (GKF), 79
Grameen model, 116, 119, 259, 341–42
Grameen Motscho (Fisheries) Foundation
        (GMF), 79
GrameenPhone, 79–80, 350
The Grameen Reader (training materials), 274
Grameen Shakti (Energy), 82
Grameen Shikkha (Education), 82, 348–49
Grameen Telecom, 79–81
Grameen Trust, 306, 343
Grameen II, 110, 257, 261, 373
        complexity increased by, 332, 351
        flexibility in, 18, 111
        peer pressure deemphasized by, 326
gram montri. See village ministers
gram sorkar. See village government
Grandy, Fred, 360
Grant, Colete, 182, 184, 225–26, 265, 320, 379
Great Depression, 176–77
Greenberg, Jim, 212
group fund loan, 244–45, 249, 283, 344
group tax, on loans, 63–64
Grzywinski, Ron, 115

Haile Selassie Festival, 318–19
Haldar, Amodini Rani, 91–92, 95–96, 106–7,
        193–94, 244–45, 347
        group fund loan frittered by, 283
        Haldar, S., advising, 329
Haldar, Devi Rani, 94, 192, 373
Haldar, Manzu, 193
Haldar, Ramesh, 193–94
Haldar, Shandha Rani, 93, 192–93, 243, 282–83,
        328, 372
        Begum, Z., nominated by, 285–86
        Haldar, A., advised by, 329
Hall, Tony, 205, 360
Hardy, Lynn, 127
Harris, Glenda, 127, 182–83, 378
        FCF impacting, 269
        Les Papillons joined by, 184
        solidarity built by, 270

Harris, Queenesta, 130, 224–26, 230–34, 237–
        38, 355–56
    Afro-World Festival discussed by, 144
    Ali, T., doubting, 309, 356
    at Allstate, 134–35
    competition of, 176, 302
    DuPart, O., and, 131, 137–38, 185–86, 261,
        359, 378
    at Haile Selassie Festival, 318–19
    Hip Hop Shop owned by, 272, 299–300,
        308–9
    killing of brother impacting, 133
    Nixon in conflict with, 324–25, 349
    as single mother, 132, 134
    at West Side Books, 132, 135, 174
Harris, Shayna, 134, 231–33, 301–2, 369
Hasina (Sheikh), 27, 163, 165–66
Hebrew Israelites, 185, 320
Heinemann, Tom, 27
Hindus, Muslims contrasted with, 44, 90, 159,
        160, 193
Hip Hop Shop (store), 301–2, 323–24, 325
    beepers sold at, 300
    Harris, Q., owning, 272, 299–300, 308–9
    Q's compared with, 357–58
homicide, in Chicago, 126, 180, 229
Hossain, Akhtar, 33–34
Hossain, Kamal, 78, 153
Hossain, Mahabub, 23
Hossain, Mozafer, 196
Houghton, Mary, 115–17, 123
housing loan, Grameen Bank, 248–49, 330
Howlader, R. A., 61
hunger
    in Bangladesh, 90–91
    in United States, 119
    World Bank conference on, 205, 207
"Hunger, Poverty, and the World Bank"
        (Yunus, Muhammad), 207
Huq, Mafazul, 69
Huq, Muzammel, 33, 89
husbands, of borrowers
    abandonment by, 157
    Begum, A., beaten by, 104
    borrowers turning over loans to, 162
    withholding installments, 352–53

ICICI Bank, 350

Individual Development Accounts (IDAs), 370
Industrial Development Bank, 35
installments, for loan repayment, 15, 128, 254–
        58, 285, 334–35, 360–61
    to Grameen America, 62
    husbands withholding, 352
"Institutional Framework for Swanirvar
        Bangladesh" (Yunus, Muhammad),
        58
insurgents, staff of Grameen Bank joined by,
        30, 73
interest rates
    of Grameen Bank, 289
    of loan sharks, 14–15
    recovery rates compared with, 68
investment, social services contrasted with, 116
Islam, Rofiq ul, 250
Islam, Sirajul, 341
Islamic fundamentalists, 54, 289
Issachar, Esther, 311

Jackson, Jesse, 235
Jai Jai Din (magazine), 155
Jamuna River, 85
Janata Bank, 61, 64
Jannat-i-Quanine, 65–66
Jatiyo Rakhi Bahini (paramilitary force), 46–47
JD's Records and CDs, 175
Jinnah, Muhammad Ali, 44–45
Job Corps (program), 275
jobs
    bribes and, 70–71
    self-employment contrasted with, 322–23,
        336
    welfare cycling with, 276
Johnson, Dorothy, 230, 319
Johnson, Janet, 365, 367
Joyce Foundation, 123
Jung, Andrea, 20, 375–76
jute mills, Bangladesh separated from, 44–45

Karim, Enayet, 37
Kass, John, 267
Khandker, Shahid, 24
Khashem (senior assistant), 240–41
Kholshi, Bangladesh
    Amin in, 191
    famine in, 160

floods in, 374
Hindus in, 159
Rohim at bazaar in, 91
Kids First (circle of borrowers), 128
King, Martin Luther, Jr., 178
Kissinger, Henry, 38
Kor, Dulal Chandra, 74–75
Kreinberg, Lew, 221, 223
Krishi (Agriculture) Bank, 64–65
Kumar, Udaia, 212, 213
Kunjufu, Jawanza, 135–36
Kwanzaa (celebration), 230

Lane, Vincent, 311
Latifee, H. I., 41
Latina clients, Grameen Bank focusing on, 190
Leckman, Scott, 349
Lemann, Nicholas, 173
Let Us Make Woman (circle of borrowers), 185,
    186–87, 225, 320
"Level of a Gangster" (song), 299
LIFE (circle of borrowers), 128
life insurance fund, 289
loans. See specific topics
loan sharks, 14–15, 293
local development organizations, "give direct"
    movement compared with, 201
Los Angeles riots (1992), 181

Magner, Marge, 82
Mannan Talukdar, Abdul, 10, 71, 99, 209, 214–
    15, 247–48
    Alam, S., choosing, 98
    on floods, 249
    Ghosh, N., convinced by, 294
    Shaymganj Daulatpur Branch founded by,
        246
marginalization, of Black community, 178
Martyrs' Day (Shaheed Dibosh), 48
Matteucci, Susan, 123, 228
Maxwell Street Market, 143, 167, 220, 280–81
    accusations of stolen goods at, 222
    Ali, T., and, 140–42, 221–22, 365–67
    closure threatening, 224–25, 267–69
    new and old, 366
    as source of self-employment, 142
    UIC buying land of, 221–24, 267–69
    vendors at, 140–41, 264, 365

Maxwell Street Market Coalition, 221, 223
Mazola, Ted, 268
McCarron, John, 268–69
McClain, Victor, 132, 137, 225, 272, 319, 358–60
    on Black community, 135
MC Eiht (rap artist), 299, 308
McFerren, Correta, 183, 269
McKinley, Janet, 297–98
meetings, of borrowers
    in Bangldesh, 94–97, 102–3, 210–11, 329
    in Chicago, 126–30, 144
    Yunus, Muhammad, requiring, 62–63
Memmott, Mark, 348
men's centers, not formed as policy of
        Grameen Bank, 106
MFIs. See microfinance institutions
Michael, Annette, 189
Microcredit Summit Campaign, 202, 211, 213
The Micro Debt (Heinemann), 27
microfinance, 10, 14, 23, 257, 379. See also specific
        topics
    farmer suicides blamed on, 26–27
    poverty in reduced by, 24–25, 28–29
    in United States, 19, 187–89, 364
    Yunus, Muhammad, on credibility of, 298
microfinance institutions (MFIs), 212–13, 325
microlenders, profits of, 259
minister of interim government, Yunus,
        Muhammad, as, 163
Mitchell, Marq, 19
Mobility International (organization), 213
monsoon, Shaymganj Daulatpur Branch
        impacted by, 352
Moonlight Records (store), 302, 308
Morales, Alfonso, 224
Mordoch, Jonathan, 25
Morrison, Toni, 234
mothers. See single mothers
Moynihan, Daniel Patrick, 179
Muhammad, Belvia, 225, 226
Muhammad, Elijah, 167–68, 226
Muhith, M. A., 77, 154
Mujib (Sheikh), 45–47, 56, 198
Mushtaq, Khondokar, 47, 56
Muslims, Hindus contrasted with, 44, 90, 160,
        193
Mustafiz, Abdul, 97, 248

Nabajub Tehbhaga Khamar. See New Era Three
        Share Cultivation Scheme
Nag, Rotun Kumar, 28
Nagorik Shakti. See Citizen Power
Nation of Islam, 128, 168, 318
Neal, Ralph, 188
The Negro Family (Moynihan), 179
Negros, Philippines, 202
Nepal Times (newspaper), 165
Newaz, Shah, 20, 189–90, 253, 255, 258–59, 376
New Era Three Share Cultivation Scheme
        (*Nabajub Tehbhaga Khamar*), 51–52
New Opportunities program, of Volunteers of
        America, 188
Nixon, Duwondes, 272, 318–20, 324–25, 349
Nobel Prize for Economics
        Yunus, Muhammad, winning, 10–11, 27,
            71, 83, 112, 163–65, 347–48

Obama, Barack, 221
Odell, Kathleen, 24
Ogden, Tim, 29, 112
ONE Campaign (organization), 214
Operation PUSH (organization), 236
oral exam, demonstrating understanding of
        Grameen Bank rules, 100
orthodox mosque, Nation of Islam contrasted
        with, 318
Oxfam America, 297

Package Inputs Program (PIP), 52
Pakistan, 35–38
pandemic, COVID-19. *See* COVID-19 pandemic
Les Papillons (circle of borrowers), 128, 130, 167,
        184–85, 227, 303–5, 369
passbooks, loans detailed in, 93
PE. *See* Project Enterprise
PEACE. *See* People Educated Against Crime in
        Englewood
Pearl, Danny, 111
Peer Lending Action Network (PLAN) Fund, 19,
        188
peer pressure, Grameen II deemphasizing, 326
People Educated Against Crime in Englewood
        (PEACE), 229
People's Army (*Gonobahini*), 73
Perkins, Thelma, 377–78
Persky, Joseph, 224

Philippines, 202
PIP. *See* Package Inputs Program
PLAN. *See* Peer Lending Action Network Fund
The Poor Always Pay Back (Dowla and Barua), 112
poor people, 14, 58
        constitution defining, 66
        economic growth in Bangladesh
            benefiting, 113–14
        as entrepreneurs, 161, 256
        faith of Yunus, Muhammad, in, 334–35
        farmers contrasted with, 59
        Grameen Bank loaning to, 15
        skills of, 74
        Yunus, Muhammad, against
            protectionism of, 337
Poreekkhamulok Grameen Shakha. See
        Experimental Rural Branch
porishod. See counsel, elections of
poverty, 13, 53, 111, 252, 293–94. *See also* poor
        people
        in Chicago, 171
        exploitation of, 60–61
        Grameen Bank breaking cycle of, 15
        microfinance reducing, 24–25, 28–29
        Yunus, Muhammad, on, 343
poverty-free center, Yunus, Muhammad
        inaugurating, 288
Prahalad, C. K., 16, 80
President's Award, Yunus, Muhammad,
        recieving, 52
Prince Mustafa cultural center, 226
Project Enterprise (PE), 19, 188–89
protectionism of poor people, Yunus,
        Muhammad against, 337
purdah. See curtain or veil

Q's (store), 355, 357–58, 378

racism, African-Americans facing, 238, 276–77
Rahman, Abur, 72–73
Ramadan (Islamic month), 263
Ramsey, Veronica Wilma, 126, 167–68. *See also*
        DuPart, Omiyale
randomized controlled trials, in social science,
        162–63
"Ready to Rumble? Step into Council
        Chambers" (article), 267
recognition (*shikriti*), 95

recovery rates, interest rates compared with, 68

recycling, in Bangladesh, 184

religion, Yunus, Muhammad, on, 338

REP. *See* Rural Economics Program

replicability, of Grameen model, 116, 119, 259, 341–42

Responsibility for Ending Starvation Using Legislation, Trimtabbing, and Support (RESULTS), 11, 305–6

Rice, Arva, 188

Robbins, Kathleen, 355–56

Roberts, Margaret, 354

Robert Taylor Homes (housing project), 309–11, 314–15

Rockefeller, Steve, 212

Rohim, Muhammad Abdul, 87–88, 90, 96, 108–9, 150, 241–42
    accounting by, 93–94
    at bazaar in Kholshi, 91
    borrowers trained by, 101
    Grameen Bank worked at by, 89

Rojas, Gheeliyah, 186–87

Roodman, David, 25

Rural Economics Program (REP), Dhaka University, 41, 59

Rush, Bobby, 221

Rutherford, Stuart, 18

du Sable, Jean Baptiste Point, 171–72

Sachs, Jeffrey, 114

sacrifice, demonstrated by Yunus, Muhammad, 333

Samsuddin, Muhammad, 246–48

Sandler, Joanne, 321–22

SBSK. *See* Sonali Bank—Krishi Shakha

self-employment, 274
    jobs contrasted with, 322–23, 336
    Maxwell Street Market as source of, 142
    welfare contrasted with, 275–76, 364

Self-Employment for Low-Income People (Balkin), 223

Self-Employment Learning Project (SELP), 321

Serageldin, Ismael, 211

Shaheed Dibosh. See Martyrs' Day

Shams, Khalid, 33, 349

Shaymganj Daulatpur Branch, of Grameen Bank, 341

Bala transferred to, 89–90, 241
Mannan Talukdar founding, 246
monsoon impacting, 352

Shekherchar Narsingdi office, 253

shikriti. See recognition

Shishu Diganta. See Children's Horizons

Siddika, Asma, 71

Simmons, Cynthia, 217

Simms, Carol "Impy," 312–15

single mothers
    as entrepreneurs, 301
    Harris, Q., as, 132, 134
    unemployment and, 180
    on welfare, 135

Sirajul Islam Bhuyian, 101–2

Sixteen Decisions (social constitution), 100–101, 344

skills, of poor people, Yunus, Muhammad, impressed by, 74

SKS Microfinance, 25

Slay, B. J., 323

Small Business Administration loan, through WSEP, 368

Smith, Fort, 218–19

social business, Yunus, Muhammad on, 349–50

social science, randomized controlled trials, 162–63

social services, investment contrasted with, 116

Society for International Development conference (1998), 206–7

solidarity, engendering Sixteen Decisions, 344

"Some Political Thoughts from a Nonpolitical Citizen" (speech), 154

"Something Serious" (album), 308

Sonali Bank—Krishi Shakha (SBSK), 75

South Shore Bank, 115–16

South Side, of Chicago, 122, 169

staff, of Grameen Bank. *See also specific staff*
    insurgents joining, 30, 73
    recruitment of, 70–71
    Yunus, Muhammad, saluted by, 32, 34

Stephanopoulos, George, 205

"Straight Up Gangsta Shit" (cassette), 300

Taroworks (program), 348

tehbhaga. See three share system

Tehbhaga tube project, 49–52, 58

Telenor (company), 350

textile industry, in Bangladesh controlled by Britain, 43–44
three share (*tehbhaga*) system, 50
Tillmon, Dorothy, 311
Todd, Helen, 30
Top Authority (rap group), 299
traditional healers, 283–84
tube wells, Grameen Bank loans for, 195, 330–31

UIC. *See* University of Illinois at Chicago
Umar, Bodruddin, 155
unemployment, 117–18, 180, 273–75
UNICEF, 67, 195
United Nations Children's Fund, 67
United States. *See also* Chicago, Illinois; Grameen America
    Agency for International Development of, 206
    hunger in, 119
    microfinance in, 19, 187–89, 364
University of Illinois at Chicago (UIC), Maxwell Street Market land bought by, 221–24, 267–69, 366
USAID. *See* Agency for International Development, United States

Vasquez, Art, 221
veil. *See* curtain or veil
vendors, at Maxwell Street Market, 140–41, 264, 267–68, 365, 368
village government (*gram sorkar*), 57
village ministers (*gram montri*), 58
violence, in Chicago, 126, 130, 145, 180, 229
Volunteers of America, New Opportunities program of, 188

Wahab, Abdul, 209
Wall Street Journal (newspaper), 17, 110–11
Washington, Booker T., 277–78
Washington, Harold, 178
Weber, Karl, 351
welfare, 117–18
    jobs cycling with, 276
    self-employment contrasted with, 364
    single mother on, 135
    workfare contrasted with, 273–74
    WSEP enabling mothers on, 275–76

Wertenbach, Donna, 275
West, Cornel, 180
Westcorp (organization), 269–71
West Pakistan. *See* Pakistan
West Side Books (store), 132, 135, 174, 358
White, Tami, 120–21
white flight, in Englewood, 125
wholesalers. *See also specific wholesalers*
    Ali, T., listing receipts from, 354
    of books, 231–34
    recycling and, 194
Wilkerson, Isabel, 267
Williams, Gary, 133–34, 325
Wilson, William Julius, 179
women. *See also* single mothers; *specific women*
    in Bangladesh, 55
    curtain or veil secluding, 60
    isolation of, 54
    underestimation of poor, 16
Women Interested in Self-Employment (organization), 275
Women's Self-Employment Project (WSEP), 122–23, 236–37, 280, 312–13, 321–22, 363. *See also* Full Circle Fund
    Burns resigning from, 144
    Evans leading, 138, 375
    as expensive, 360–61
    Houghton establishing, 117
    IDAs pioneered by, 370
    mothers on welfare enabled by, 275–76
    Small Business Administration loan through, 368
    support by, 220
    traditional employment programs compared with, 362
workfare, welfare contrasted with, 273–74
World Bank, 203–7
World Food Prize, 348
A World of Three Zeroes (Yunus, Muhammad), 28, 351
WSEP. *See* Women's Self-Employment Project
WSEP Ventures, 370

X, Wanda, 186–87

Yunus, Monica, 62, 83, 139, 214
Yunus, Muhammad, 29, 48, 51, 58–59, 152–54, 287. *See also specific topics*

with AEO, 364–65
Bono with, 214
capitalism championed by, 335
in Chicago, 116
climate change movement championed
by, 351
Conable contradicted by, 203
cooperatives and, 63–64
core beliefs of, 332
on credibility of microfinance, 298
critical mass referred to by, 290–91, 296
demonstrating successful cooperatives,
286
education of, 34–36
facing intransigence of bureaucrats, 72
faith in poor people of, 334–35
at "Financing the Rural Poor," 68
foreign aid criticized by, 202
Georgescu-Roegen influencing, 36
government mistrusted by, 39–40
Grameen America launched by, 369–70
as guarantor of loans, 61
learning from first years of Grameen
Bank, 363–64
meetings required by, 62–63
as minister of interim government, 163
Nobel Prize for Economics won by, 10–11,
27, 71, 83, 112, 163–65, 347–48
on poverty, 343
poverty-free center inaugurated by, 288
President's Award received by, 52
printing and packaging plant opened by,
35
progress of borrowers impressing, 254–55
against protectionism of poor people, 337
on religion, 338
replicability prioritized by, 116, 119, 259,
341–42
resignation forced onto, 28
sacrifice demonstrated by, 333
self-reliance spoken on by, 56–57
skills of poor people impressing, 74
on social business, 349–50
staff saluting, 32, 34
with welfare recipients and unemployed
people, 117–18
at World Bank conference on hunger,
205–7

World Food Prize received by, 348
with Zia Ur Rahman, 75–77
Yunus Social Business, 28

Zianpur, Bangladesh, 85–86, 98–99, 110, 374
Zianpur high school, Grameen Bank in, 86, 98–
99
Zia Ur Rahman, 37, 57, 75–77
Zimmerman, Harry, 317, 366
Zomella (borrower), 285
zonal managers, conference of Grameen Bank,
286–91

About the Author

ALEX COUNTS IS THE AUTHOR OF SEVERAL BOOKS, including *Changing the World Without Losing Your Mind: Leadership Lessons from Three Decades of Social Entrepreneurship (Revised Edition)* (Rivertowns Books, 2021), an independent consultant to nonprofit organizations (including the India Philanthropy Alliance), was an affiliated faculty of the Do Good Institute at the University of Maryland's School of Public Policy from 2017 to 2021, and is a senior adviser and ambassador at large for a)plan coaching.

He also wrote *When in Doubt, Ask for More: And 213 Other Life and Career Lessons for the Mission-Driven Leader* (Rivertowns Books, 2020), which prompted Ashoka founder Bill Drayton to say, "Alex Counts has been critical to creating and building the global microcredit movement from its start. He knows how to lead. And how to write! When in Doubt, Ask for More will help you be a more powerful leader—and have fun doing so."

In 1997 he established Grameen Foundation with the support of Nobel laureate Dr. Muhammad Yunus and became its President and CEO. He did so after having worked in microfinance and poverty reduction for 10 years, mostly spent living in rural Bangladesh. He ran the organization for its first 18 years, and remains a friend and volunteer of Grameen Foundation. He served as the President and CEO of American India Foundation in 2016-2017.

A Cornell University graduate, Counts's commitment to poverty eradication deepened as a Fulbright scholar in Bangladesh, where he witnessed innovative poverty solutions being developed by Grameen Bank. He trained under Professor Muhammad Yunus, the founder and managing director of Grameen Bank, and co-recipient of the 2006 Nobel Peace Prize. Since its modest beginnings, sparked by a $6,000 seed grant provided by Prof. Yunus (who was a founding board member and continues as a director emeritus), Grameen Foundation grew to become a leading international humanitarian organization.

In addition to his most recent books, Counts's writings include *Small Loans, Big Dreams: How Nobel Prize Winner Muhammad Yunus and Microfinance Are Changing the World* and *Voices from the Field*. Counts has also been published in *The Washington Post*, the *Stanford Social Innovation Review*, *The Miami Herald*, *The Christian Science Monitor*, *The Chronicle of Philanthropy*, and elsewhere. In 2007, he received the Distinguished Alumni Award from Horace Mann School. While at Cornell University, he received the John F. Kennedy Memorial Award, given annually by the Class of 1964 to the graduating senior who is the best example of the ideal of public service articulated by our 35th President.

Counts was a founding member of the Advisory Council of the Center for Financial Inclusion, and served for 12 years before becoming a member emeritus in May 2020. He has served as the chairman of Fonkoze USA and co-chair of the Fonkoze Family Coordinating Committee—two governance bodies of the largest microfinance institution in Haiti. He was a founding member of and served as co-chair of the Microfinance CEO Working Group (which today is the Partnership for Responsible Financial Inclusion). He is a Court Appointed Special Advocate for foster children in the state of Maryland. His blog covers topics related to excellence in nonprofit management and beyond.

Before establishing Grameen Foundation, Counts served as the legislative director of RESULTS and as a regional project manager for CARE-Bangladesh. He loves listening to and promoting live music in intimate venues, especially blues and bluegrass, as well as other genres. He speaks Bengali and lives in Hyattsville, MD with his wife, Emily and their cat, Meena.

CPSIA information can be obtained
at www.ICGtesting.com
Printed in the USA
JSHW022150130922
30471JS00001B/2